The Writings of
James Fenimore Cooper

Gleanings in Europe: Italy

Gleanings in Europe

Italy

James Fenimore Cooper

Historical Introduction and
Explanatory Notes
by John Conron and
Constance Ayers Denne
Text Established by Constance Ayers Denne

State University of New York Press   Albany

The preparation of this volume was made possible (in part) by a grant from the Program for Editions of the National Endowment for the Humanities, an independent Federal agency.

CENTER FOR
SCHOLARLY EDITIONS
AN APPROVED EDITION
MODERN LANGUAGE
ASSOCIATION OF AMERICA

The Center emblem means that one of a panel of textual experts serving the Center has reviewed the text and textual apparatus of the printer's copy by thorough and scrupulous sampling, and has approved them for sound and consistent editorial principles employed and maximum accuracy attained. The accuracy of the text has been guarded by careful and repeated proofreading according to standards set by the Center.

Published by
State University of New York Press, Albany
For information, address State University of New York Press, State University Plaza, Albany, N.Y. 12246

Library of Congress Cataloging in Publication Data

Cooper, James Fenimore, 1789-1851.
  Gleanings in Europe, Italy.

  (Cooper editions)
    1. Italy—Description and travel—1801–1860. 2. Cooper, James
Fenimore, 1789–1851—Journeys—Italy. I. Denne, Constance
Ayers. II. Title. III. Series: Cooper, James Fenimore, 1789–1851.
Selected works.   1979.
DG426.C77 1980   914.5'04'8   79-15177
ISBN 0-87395-365-7
ISBN 0-87395-460-2 (pbk.)

Contents

Acknowledgments

For institutional support in the preparation of this volume, the editors wish to thank Martin Stevens, Dean of the School of Liberal Arts and Sciences, Baruch College, The City University of New York; President Mortimer H. Appley of Clark University; and Marcus McCorison, Director and Librarian of the American Antiquarian Society. Timely assistance from the National Endowment for the Humanities ensured the completion of this and other volumes.

The editor of the text wishes to acknowledge the generosity of the Faculty Research Award Program of The City University of New York for assistance in the form of two grants in 1972–74 which enabled her to do research in England and Italy. She is also deeply indebted to a number of people at The New York Public Library. Her work there was greatly facilitated by Faye Simkin, Executive Director of The Research Libraries, The New York Public Library, Astor, Lenox and Tilden Foundations; Walter Zervas, Administrative Associate of The Research Libraries, who made the Frederick Lewis Allen Memorial Room and the Wertheim Study available to her during the preparation of *Italy*; Lewis M. Stark and Maud D. Cole, Keepers of Rare Books; Lola Szladits, Curator of the Henry W. and Albert A. Berg Collection of English and American Literature; Frank E. Bradley, Genealogical Specialist, Local History and Genealogy Division; L. Dawn Pohlman, Chief, Cooperative Services Division; Thomas Bourke, Beth Diefendorf, Rodney Phillips, and Natalie Seweryn, General Research and Humanities Division; and Alice C. Hudson, Map Division. She also wishes to acknowledge the courtesy of the British Museum, which granted access to the Reading Room and the Department of Manuscripts during the summers of 1973 and 1978. Her thanks go as well to the many librarians and curators who assisted generously by lending books and patiently answering queries and whose institutions are mentioned in the footnotes of the Textual Commentary.

Mr. Conron wishes to express his appreciation for the courtesies extended by Eve Anderson, Librarian, The Valentine Museum, Richmond, Virginia; Abbey Hodges, Photographic Services, Wadsworth Atheneum; Charles B. Ferguson, Director, and Lois L. Blomstrann, Assistant to the Director, The New Britain Museum of American Art; the Library Staff, Worcester Art Museum; and the staffs of the photographic reproductions services at the Museum of Fine Arts, Boston, The Metropolitan Museum of Art, The Denver Art Museum, and Harvard University Library for providing assistance with the illustrations.

The editor of the text is also grateful for the special efforts and scholarly assistance of C. J. Denne, Jr., Associate Professor of English, College of New Rochelle; Kay S. House, Professor of English, San Francisco State College; Clara M. Lovett, Professor of History, Baruch College, The City University of New York; Barbara F. McManus, Associate Professor of Classics, College of New Rochelle; Marie-Hélène Messager, O. S. U., Assistant Professor of French, College of New Rochelle; Kenneth W. Staggs, Associate Professor of English, Trinity University; Sandra Capararo Tetreault; and Frank A. Perone and Gale A. Spencer, student assistants at Baruch College, The City University of New York. Mr. Conron is grateful for the special assistance and editorial advice of Cheryl S. Conron and Maura L. Conron.

Thanks also go to Lea and Febiger, Philadelphia, Pennsylvania, successor to the publisher of *Italy*, for providing information otherwise unavailable; to David J. Nordloh, Indiana University; and to Vanchai Ariyabuddhiphongs, Ella Conger, and Frances M. Miceli, for their expert secretarial assistance.

The Index has been prepared by James Dempsey with the aid of work-study students at Clark University. Some of the illustrations were prepared by Herbert Walden.

Illustrations

Most of the illustrations for this volume picture spaces of particular importance to Cooper in his Italian sojourn. Some, however, are included less for their topographical value than for their relation to a tradition of landscape painting of which Cooper was aware even before he entered Italy, and which epitomized the picturesque perception and treatment of landscape. For Cooper and his contemporaries, two seventeenth-century painters stood out in this tradition. In his paintings of the Apennine Mountains and the Italian coast (see Plate III), Salvator Rosa (1615–1673) fused the picturesque with the sublime, picturing an Italy characterized by dramatic contrasts between light and shadow, by the powerful energies of wind or water, by abrupt and rugged natural forms, by the powerful figures of banditti, and by a brush stroke that emphasizes the roughness of these things. Cooper incorporated some of these effects into his verbal sketches of Italy. But like Thomas Cole (Plates II and IX) and George Inness (Plate X), he was drawn much more to the Italy of Claude Lorrain (1600–1682), which was characterized by the effect of *sfumato* (an atmospheric haze which warms and softens objects), by harmonies between natural forms and human artifacts, by figures in contemplative or processional postures, and by a brush stroke which, like the light, softens textures and makes outlines melt and flow into one another— all producing an effect of otherwordly repose (*il riposo di Claudio*). Like Cole, Cooper saw the Italian landscape as an embodiment of the Arcadian ideal, though the places which most powerfully evoked this ideal for Cooper were the "wasp-nest looking" villages perched, like Sorrento (Plate IV), on Italy's coastal cliffs.

and XII) had been for several centuries the most dramatic event in the Italian travels of pilgrims, tourists, and artists. Inness's view of Rome from the Campagna typically concentrates on the dome of St. Peter's and the massive bulk of the Vatican. Where Cooper entered Rome from the south, however (see text, pp. 189–190), Inness's view is from the north; the garden and wall in the foreground are those of the Villa Giulia.

PLATE XI   *St. Peter's at Rome*, drawn by Giovanni Battista Piranesi (1720–1778) and engraved by D. Roberts. In Costello, Volume II, facing p. 121. See text, pp. 190–191.

PLATE XII   *Cardinal Polignac Visiting St. Peter's, Rome*, by Giovanni Paolo Pannini (c. 1691–1765). Oil on canvas. 29⅛ × 39¼ inches. Courtesy of The Metropolitan Museum of Art. For Cooper's descriptions of the interior, see text, pp. 191–192 and 233–236.

Following page 256

PLATE XIII *The Capitol, Rome, and the Church of the Ara Cœli*, engraved by William Bernard Cooke (1778–1855). In Costello, Volume II, facing p. 117. See text, pp. 221–223. Cooper was not so much attracted to the aesthetic of ruin as other Romantic travelers.

PLATE XIV   *Interior of an Upper Corridor of the Coliseum*, drawn by Colonel James Patrick Cockburn (1779?–1847) and engraved by W. B. Cooke. In Costello, Volume II, facing p. 118.

PLATE XV   *Interior of the Pantheon, Rome*, drawn by David Roberts, A.R.A. (1796–1864), and engraved by Frederick Smith. In Costello, Vol. II, facing

p. 117. Cooper's treatment of the ruins of ancient Rome was largely matter of fact, but the interior of the Pantheon embodied for him an idea which was "one of the most magnificent of its kind that exists in architecture" (see text, p. 225).

PLATE XVI   *Venice*, drawn by James Baker Pyne (1800–1870) and engraved by S. Bradshaw. In Costello, Volume II, facing p. 50. This view of San Giorgio Maggiore, on the island of San Giorgio near the entrance to the Grand Canal, reflects Cooper's vision of the whole of Venice as "a city afloat" (see text, p. 279).

HISTORICAL INTRODUCTION

Gleanings in Europe: Italy, the last of Cooper's European travel books in the sequence of publication, was the fourth volume in the chronology of travels recorded in the series. Its relative position, together with the variant titles under which it originally appeared, is indicated in the following chart:

Chronology	Title in Cooper Edition	Title in American First Edition	Title in British First Edition
14 July–15 Oct. 1828	*Gleanings in Europe: Switzerland*	*Sketches of Switzerland* (1836)	*Excursions in Switzerland* (1836)
20 Aug. 1830–17 July 1832 passim 18 July–11 Oct. 1832	*Gleanings in Europe: the Rhine*	*Sketches of Switzerland. Part Second* (1836)	*A Residence in France; with an Excursion up the Rhine, and a Second Visit to Switzerland* (1836)
1 June 1826–27 Feb. 1828	*Gleanings in Europe: France*	*Gleanings in Europe* (1837)	*Recollections of Europe* (1837)
28 Feb.–29 May 1828	*Gleanings in Europe: England*	*Gleanings in Europe England* (1837)	*England. With Sketches of Society in the Metropolis* (1837)
16 Oct. 1828–11 May 1830	*Gleanings in Europe: Italy*	*Gleanings in Europe Italy* (1838)	*Excursions in Italy* (1838)

Historical Introduction

I

A leisurely progress of two weeks (8 to 22 or 23 October 1828) in an elegant *calèche* brought Cooper and his family from Bern to Florence and the beginning of their Italian sojourn. In Cooper, "the apathy of one who had got to be a little blasé" after eleven weeks of "sublime communion"[1] with the Alps began to give way to delight at the softness, exuberance, and artfulness of the Piedmontese lake district, Milan, Bologna, and a succession of smaller towns in Lombardy. Yet for him these were not the true Italy: both the Piedmont and Lombardy were still too Alpine in landscape and culture, and Lombardy was then in Austrian hands. The "Lower, or true Italy" included Tuscan Florence and points south, and Cooper's way of absorbing it was to concentrate on four of its most celebrated places. The family thus spent nine months in Florence (Letters II–X); four months on the Bay of Naples (Letters XI–XX); five months in Rome (Letters XX–XXVI); and ten days in Venice (Letters XXIX–XXXII). After a residence of eighteen months, they left Italy in May 1830 for Dresden.

Henry James would later write of "the sense of rest and leisure that must in olden summers have awaited here the consenting victims of Italy, among ancient things all made sweet by their age,"[2] and though it was not in Cooper's nature to give complete consent to its seductive atmosphere, Italy induced in him, repeatedly, a mood of *dolce far niente*, a desire "to make a *siesta* of life, and to enjoy the passing moment."[3] In this state of mind, his senses seemed continually caressed. People, objects, places, and events—even the simplest daily rituals—seemed enveloped by a warm glow which softened him, bringing out feelings of admiration, tenderness, and even love. Just how deeply his experience of Italy affected him is movingly evident in his gesture of farewell. He left, his wife observed, "looking

over a shoulder" (295 in the present edition). Later he would
call Italy "the only region of the earth that I truly love" and
would liken it to his own house, and even to "another wife,"
who "haunts my dreams and clings to my ribs."[4] After the publication of his book of gleanings in 1838, he wrote to his friend
Horatio Greenough, "I could wish to die in Italy."[5]

Domestic arrangements, daily rituals, the artful ceremonies
of life in the "capital" cities of Florence and Rome, Italian architecture, the monuments of classical antiquity, painting, and
most particularly the Italian landscape all took special places in
Cooper's itinerary, and all made their contributions to his experience of Italy.

Moderate in their spending, the Coopers lived exceedingly
well in a succession of fine hotels, apartments, and suburban
villas. After a month or so at the Hotel York in Florence, they
moved on 25 November to an apartment in the Palazzo Ricasoli
on Via del Cocomero (now Via Ricasoli), "but a step" from the
Piazza del Duomo. In the spring (1 May 1829), they moved to
the Villa St. Illario, in the hills beyond the Porta Romana. In the
late summer, after ten days at the Hotel delle Crocelle in Naples, they moved on 20 August to the Villa del Tasso, reputedly
Tasso's birthplace and a shrine for Romantic travelers, in Sorrento. In their second winter, after a brief stay in the Hotel de
Paris in Rome, they moved in December 1829 to an apartment
at 50 Via Ripetta, its windows overlooking the Tiber and St. Peter's. And in their second spring, in Venice (28 April–7 May),
after a stay at the Leone Bianco, they took an apartment near
the Piazza San Marco.

In these spaces, Cooper savored with continual delight "the
good things of this world, in the shape of creature-comforts"
(143). In his book, he pays homage to the elegant, even magnificent, "mode of living" in Italian palazzos. At Florence, he cele-
brates the wine of the Ricasoli vineyards, brought daily to his
apartment in the palace, as "among the best of Tuscany" (20);
at Naples, quail, *beccafichi*, and the *lachryma christi* of Vesuvius.
At the Villa St. Illario, he discovers what he takes to be the perfection of the sense of taste: a "single fresh fig . . . after the
soup" (69).

His social life in the cosmopolitan cities of Florence and Rome
had a kindred effect and, with that of Paris, became for Cooper

the model of what society in a true capital should offer. The highest form of civilization in America, he declares, is still the commercial town, and its society is characterized by "a certain absence of taste, a want of leisure and of tone; a substitution of bustle for elegance, care for enjoyment, and show for refinement" (82). By contrast, he evokes the life of the two Italian capitals, in scenic *tableaux*, as a series of ceremonial *fêtes*—a ducal reception, masked balls, the Easter Illuminations, a picnic on Monte Mario—in which people hold gay, leisurely, richly toned and elegant converse with each other, easily and without pretension. Assiduously ignoring the Italy of bohemian "Cafés and valets de place,"[6] Cooper flourished in the company of the emigrés and expatriates who were, he observed in Florence, "at the head of the gaiety of this place" (24). Received as an artist and a man of the world, he cultivated friendships with the families of Louis Bonaparte, the former King of Holland, and of Camillo Borghese, whose family art collection in Rome was one of Italy's finest. At the same time, he kept up his friendships with Horatio Greenough, Gouverneur Wilkins, and John G. Chapman, their conversations leavened by their common attraction to Italian art.

Cooper's interest in this art, indeed, was even more intense and germinal than his interest in the social life of Italy, though both, of course, were related expressions of Italian civilization. Everywhere in Italy, Cooper studied the feats of engineering and architecture: roads, bridges, aqueducts, and port facilities; the ubiquitous walls surrounding towns and cities; palaces, churches, urban houses, and suburban villas. The verbal sketches of these works in *Italy* are so frequent as to suggest at times the notebooks of an architect. During the 1820s, Cooper had in fact become an articulate critic of American architecture.[7] His preference for the Gothic Revival style, however, survived his exposure to Italian architecture. In Rome, he emphasizes, "one sees no Gothic architecture" (235), though he does concede that its function as a "grand" and "magnificent" place in the landscape, if not its virtues as a style, is "nobly supplied" by such masterworks—mostly Baroque—as St. Peter's and the Vatican, the Corsini Chapel in the Church of St. John in Laterano, and the early seventeenth-century Palazzo Borghese.

Cooper's interest in the artifacts of Republican and Imperial

Rome was equally intense and similarly qualified. Their ex-
cavation, begun in the 1740s and continued throughout the
nineteenth century, had engendered the eighteenth-century
classical revival evident in the sculpture, the architecture, the
political ideals, and the literature of the new republic; and none
of these expressions was lost to a generation schooled, as
Cooper's was, in Latin. Yet in his response to the Capitoline,
Cooper shows himself to be, like his Romantic contemporaries,
more aware of the differences than the kinships between the
Roman and the American republics. "We call our legislative
structures Capitols," he argues, "under some mistaken notion
. . . about the uses of the Roman Capitol." The latter, "originally, was a town; then a fortress . . . and, in the end . . . a collection of different objects of high interest, principally devoted
to religious rites" (222). In the ruins and museums of Rome,
Cooper did encounter "objects of high interest," but unlike
Jefferson's generation did not see them as expressions of a civic
ideal to be emulated. In the Vatican Museum, for example, he
is less interested in the sculpted busts and figures of Roman
statesmen than he is in the "precision and nature" (239) with
which classical sculptors had wrought animals.

His classicism is centered on rural and on late-classical aesthetic ideals: thus his continuous interest in the villas and ruined
temples embellishing the Campagna and the bay of Naples; his
excitement over evidence of the ancients' "private life" revealed
in the excavations of Pompeii and Herculaneum; and his interest in Virgil's use of the Baian shore in Book VI of the *Aeneid*.
His choice of the Laocoön over the Apollo Belvedere as "the
noblest piece of statuary that the world possesses" (240), like his
qualified attraction to Baroque architecture, demonstrates his
preference for energy and complexity over classical simplicity
in the plastic arts.

Cooper's most generative experience of Italian art was with
its splendid galaxy of Renaissance and Baroque painting. His
visits to the municipal galleries which displayed this painting
were a regular feature of his itinerary from Milan to Naples to
Venice; and during the winters of 1828–1829 and of 1829–
1830 he had the opportunity for close examination of the paintings in Florence and Rome, where the most extensive collections hung on display.

Cooper was, of course, neither unique nor naive in this interest. The gradual emergence of the picturesque aesthetic in England during the eighteenth century had renewed interest in a corpus of paintings by Raphael and Michelangelo; da Vinci; the Venetian masters (Titian, Tintoretto, and Veronese); the Eclectics of Bologna (Caracci, the "divine Guercino," Guido Reni, and Domenichino); Correggio; and the trinity of Baroque mentors to Romantic landscape painters: Nicholas Poussin, Salvator Rosa, and Claude Lorrain. Rome, with its great collections of this work, had become one of the capitals of Romantic painting. With the rise in popularity of landscape painting in America, Salvator Rosa and especially Claude Lorrain became major influences on American painters. Claude's house in Rome housed John Vanderlyn and later Horatio Greenough. Thomas Cole occupied Claude's studio in 1831 while he ranged the Campagna sketching Claudian landscapes. "Claude, to me," wrote the founder of the Hudson River School, "is the greatest of all landscape painters: and, indeed, I should rank him with Raphael or Michael Angelo."[8]

Cooper was drawn to Italian painting (and to Northern European painting as well) not as a dilettante or critic but as a student of the picturesque. He had already played, and would continue to play, a pioneering role in the application of this aesthetic to the appreciation of American wilderness, to the embellishment of inhabited landscapes, and, above all, to the art of the novel.[9] In the galleries of Italy, Cooper had the opportunity of refining his knowledge of the aesthetic by a study of its models, for, despite its application to other arts, the picturesque was based on values "capable of being illustrated by painting." Unfortunately for modern readers, he chose to reveal little of what he saw there. The reason he offers in his book is that visits to the galleries had been an obligatory staple of travel narratives for so long that "the subject is . . . hackneyed" (10). It is also probable that his knowledge of the painting from etched or lithographed copies made his encounters with the originals less of an epiphany for him than it had been for earlier travelers, "whose pictorial view of landscape . . . can be traced fairly exactly to the actual sojourn in Rome, where the works of Claude and Salvator were to be seen."[10] How Cooper himself employed the picturesque aesthetic in the composition of *Italy* will be shown in Section III of this Introduction, but it is appropriate here to characterize what he does record about his visits to the galleries.

The allusions in his letters and journals as well as in *Italy* suggest that Cooper was deeply interested in treatments of the human figure and that his taste drew him more towards picturesque beauty than towards sublimity in form and subject. He ranked Raphael over Michelangelo among Renaissance painters, because, though Michelangelo's *Last Judgment* is "one of the most extraordinary blendings of the grand and the monstrous in art," it lacks Raphael's "gentleness and sensibility to beauty" (242). In Florence, he commissioned Greenough to sculpt a copy of three cherubs (details from the *Madonna del Trono*, of the school of Raphael), "the beau ideal of childhood mingled with that intelligence which may be thought necessary to compose a heavenly being. . . ."[11] In Rome, he dwells at some length on Raphael's Vatican frescoes and speaks of the *Transfiguration* as one of the "[s]ix or eight . . . most celebrated easel pictures of the world" (238–39). He draws the line, however, at Raphael's more erotic celebrations of beauty. Raphael's painted designs on jars at Loretto, for example, "exhibit the author of the Transfiguration, very much as Ovid betrays his taste in the Metamorphoses . . . ." "[T]he divinity of the school of Raphael," Cooper concludes, "is not the divinity of an anchorite" (266).

Similar tastes informed his responses to Baroque painting. "All Martyrdoms are nuisances on canvass," Cooper declares of Titian's *Martyrdom of St. Peter* in Venice (283), but the author of the still-uncompleted *Leather-Stocking Tales* seems particularly interested in treatments of St. Jerome's visions in the wilderness by Correggio (in Piacenza) and by Domenichino (in the Vatican), both distinguished by their dramatic use of *chiaroscuro*. He is even more interested in the way Baroque painters modeled their spiritually transfigured women, especially Venus and the Virgin of the Assumption. If he drew away from the erotic, he nevertheless appreciated close attention to the female form. The *Venus de Medici* in Florence is "a beau ideal, a goddess if you will, with little character," but the *Venus of Capua* in Naples' Museo Nationale is "exquisitely womanish," a creature of "flesh and blood."[12] The allegorical figures of Guido Reni's *Phoebus and the Hours Preceded by Aurora* (a fresco in Rome's Palazzo Rospigliosi), in whose faces lines melted and flowed into one another, producing what one observer had called a picturesque effect of "pleasing languor, which the union of all that is beautiful impresses on the soul,"[13] moved him to commission John G. Chapman to make a copy.[14] But he paid perhaps his greatest homage to Titian's women, with their "brilliant complexions and fair hair" (275) and a vitality heightened by the "blaze of glory" which the painter's colors produced (282), making special mention of the *Venus of Bartolini* in Florence and the *Assumption* in Venice, "one of the most gorgeous Titians extant" (282). Consciously or intuitively, Cooper seems to have recognized in these women that sensuous ideality he also saw in Italian landscape, as if they were its *genii loci.*

More than the life and art of the cities, indeed, it was the suburban and rural landscapes of Italy which most fully engaged Cooper's intelligence and informed his feelings. The Apennines, the Roman Campagna, and the Bay of Naples were, for most romantic travelers between 1820 and 1880, the climactic experience of Italy. Places Italian painters had drawn for three centuries, they seemed themselves to be immense, exquisite works of art—every tree, body of water, and rock form sculpted to perfection by weather, 'improved' by the signs and artifacts of Italian civilization, transfigured by the luminous softness of Italian light, and enriched by their long association with art and literature. In the Apennines, with their cliffs, gorges, cataracts, and blasted oaks, the traveler viewed a Salvatorian landscape, with overlays from the Gothic fictions of Ann Radcliffe and Washington Irving. On the Roman Campagna, the traveler viewed a landscape painted by Claude both from the place itself and from the descriptions of Horace and Virgil. Perhaps a Claudian *steffage* of trees framed and energized the foreground. In the middleground, Horatian shepherds with oaken staves stood in enigmatic kinship with ruined houses or temples. In the background to the west loomed the dome of St. Peter's, "the monument" (Irving called it) ". . . over the grave of ancient Rome";[15] to the east, the surge of the Alban and Sabine Hills, with the Apennines in the mellow blue distance. Around the Bay of Naples, the traveler viewed what was, or could have been, a Claudian coastal landscape with reminders of Virgil: skies of prodigal softness and tonal variegations; boats on an aqua-marine sea; volcanic upthrusts of land, their outlines softened by time and enhanced by terraced and porticoed villas, monasteries, and villages.

It was on these landscapes that Cooper concentrated in the rural excursions which dominated his itinerary: the transits from city to city, especially those which took him through the Apennines north of Florence, northeast of Naples, and northeast of Rome; the excursion to Marseilles by way of Genoa in the spring of 1829; the walks through the hills around Florence in the early summer of 1829; the "aquatic excursions" from Sorrento to Ischia, Capri, Baiae, and Pozzuoli and the explorations of Pompeii, Herculaneum, Vesuvius, the hills of Sorrento, and Paestum during the late summer and fall of 1829; the weekly horseback rides on the Campagna during the spring of 1830. It was his verbal sketches of these landscapes to which he would give pride of place in *Italy* and in which he would try to concentrate all that Italy had contributed to his mastery of the art of the picturesque.

Savor Italy as he did, however, Cooper did so after a day's work. In Florence, undistracted even by Carnival, he worked steadily on *The Wept of Wish-ton-Wish*, and his excursion to Marseilles was primarily an effort, fruitless as it turned out, to get the finished novel printed there or in Paris. (It was subsequently printed in Florence, by order of the Duke, at the Dante's Head Press). In Florence, too, Cooper began *The Water-Witch*. By September, in Sorrento, he was "on the *middle* chapter"; and by 6 January 1830, in Rome, he had finished this novel, too.[16] By 9 April he was "concocting another"[17]—possibly *The Bravo*, on which he was still at work when he left the country that would "haunt [his] dreams."

II

Cooper wrote of his Italian experience in a variety of ways. One was the journal sequence begun on 13 October 1828, which ends suddenly and inexplicably at Sorrento (7 October 1829), including nothing on Rome or Venice.[18] Another was a series of "finished" landscape sketches incorporated into novels: the Bay of Naples in *The Water-Witch* (1830); Venice in *The Bravo* (1831); and Italy's west coast in a later novel, *The Wing-and-Wing* (1842). He did not begin his Italian travel narrative until 1837, seven years after he had left the country.

When he finally did come to it, *Italy* took about four months of gestation and four months of writing. On 19 November 1836, Cooper wrote to his English publisher, Richard Bentley, offering *England* and suggesting that *Italy* would follow.[19] By 6 March 1837, the book was "under way";[20] by 14 April it was "nearly done."[21] On 8 July, he posted the finished manuscript aboard the *Pennsylvania*, bound for England, where it was published in February 1838.

A tangle of distractions and rebuffs and the insistent need to pay a proper homage to Italy complicated his work on the book. As he wrote it, he was reading proof for *England* and projecting or writing *The American Democrat, The Chronicles of Cooperstown,* and *The History of the Navy of the United States.* He was also embroiled in a dispute with the people of Cooperstown over their claim to Three Mile Point, a piece of family property. The Panic of 1837 and the ensuing depression, furthermore, made him more than usually worried about money, while his publishers were trying to discourage the completion of his travel series because its market had virtually disappeared. A letter from Bentley of 19 February 1837 expressing "the hope that I may shortly have it in my power to announce another Work of Fiction from your pen"[22] must have stung all the more for its indirection.

The rebuffs mounted as Cooper began negotiations for *Italy*. In March, he had offered the book to Bentley for £300 on the grounds that it "will do better with you" than its predecessors.[23] By April, he had reduced his price to £200, "[a]s you say you have not done much" with *France* or *England*.[24] In May, Bentley offered "the sum of £150 leaving the remaining moiety contingent upon the sale of the Work."[25] In July, Cooper received an amended offer of £200, which was paid five months later, in December. *Excursions in Italy* finally appeared in England on 12 February 1838, in a two-volume edition of 1,000 copies, at a price of 21 shillings. On 12 May 1838, the *Bibliographie de la France* announced the appearance of an English-language edition in France, a reprint of the Bentley, publication date unknown.[26]

Meanwhile, in June 1837, Cooper's American publisher, Carey & Lea, refused *Italy* because of the depression and the losses they had already sustained on the series. Three months later, on 8 September, Cooper tried Carey again, explaining disingenuously his contract with Bentley, noting that he had sent the manuscript and would be receiving the sheets from Bentley, and finally suggesting that, "[a]s the entire series makes a complete work, I suppose you would like to have it."[27] The reply was blunt:

We do not know what to say of Italy. Since you were here we have not put to press a single new volume & the success of your last eight volumes, we are sorry to say, presents us with no inducement to go on. We certainly have not made one cent by them thus far to pay us for capital & time employed in them—With such results before us we certainly have no inducement to undertake Italy as a speculation.

Carey & Lea finally conceded, however, that "[i]f you are anxious it should come from the same press as the others, we would be willing to print 750 copies & if it should produce any profit divide it between us."[28] On 28 May, the American edition finally appeared in a run of 1,000 copies, for which Cooper received $200. Until now, except for some passages which appeared in Susan Cooper's *Pages and Pictures*,[29] *Italy* has not been reissued.

Reviewers were hardly more encouraging than the book's publishers. Many gave it the briefest descriptive "notice." Most viewed it almost solely as social criticism, emphasizing its sporadic attacks against the English nobility or its reformist critiques of American culture: the lack of a true capital, the subjugation to a spirit of commerce, the "property patriotism." Few noticed its flaws or its real achievements.

English reviews, which were generally favorable, took mild umbrage at its Anglophobia. Typically, *The Literary Gazette, and Journal of the Belles Lettres* (17 February 1838) found it "pleasing," though "it is particularly against England, and the English, that his spleen and dislike are continually thrust into notice." "Pooh, folly!" it said about Cooper's claims of English anti-

Americanism.[30] Perhaps the most perceptive of the English reviews, in the *Spectator* (17 February), stressed the uniqueness of Cooper's approach to a familiar subject:

> he has natural faculties of observation trained by long exercise to a high degree of excellence; he has habits of analysis and reflection. . . . He has an expansion of mind, arising from habits of extensive speculation. . . . To all which may be added, his nativity, which gives him to see European usages with American eyes.[31]

Not surprisingly, some American reviewers discovered anti-Americanism in *Italy*. "Next to abusing your mother," said a reviewer in *American Monthly* (July 1838), "we can conceive of no more elegant recreation than that of villifying your country." If the author would really "prefer to live in Rome," said the reviewer, perhaps it should be arranged "to furnish him with a charger in the shape of a rail, and a full parade-dress of tar and feathers."[32]

Other Americans applauded, even exaggerated, the Anglo-phobia. Cooper, said *The Hesperian* (July), never missed "a good opportunity of peppering the Britons with grape and canister."[33] *The New Yorker* considered this "habitual sourness" a kind of tonal relief for "the pencillings of Italy."[34]

More perceptive American reviewers heard the dominant tone of the book and considered it the most agreeable and "good natured" of the series. Philadelphia's *National Gazette* (26 May) found that it was happily devoid of "second hand enthusiasm."[35] *The Knickerbocker* (June) thought the "political or personal prejudices" a minor note in a book which pictured the "beauties or grandeur of nature,"[36] though of what these pictures consisted the reviewer did not say.

Cooper was his own most disappointed critic. In the summer of 1838, he confessed to Horatio Greenough: "I have not done justice to Italy, or myself, in the book on that country—I did think to make it a pleasant book of its sort, but the failure is owing to circumstances I could not control. I wanted time to do what I think I could easily have done, with such a subject."[37] Later, when critics began announcing their preference for *Italy* over *England*, Cooper painfully disagreed. In his judgment, there was "no comparison" between the two.[38]

III

When he began *Italy*, Cooper declared that he wanted it to be
"more poetical than the First Part of Switzerland, and a little
unique, and without politics. . . ."[39] Near its completion, he
called it "a *picturesque* book, rather than a political, with a few
more touches of society" than *Switzerland* had.[40] Rightly understood, these phrases reveal much about the kind of book
Cooper worked to compose.

The term "picturesque book" has a large and elusive meaning which must be inferred from *Italy* itself, in the context of
hundreds of travel books which appeared in the first three dec-
ades of the nineteenth century. The pattern of these books is
traceable to the theory and example of the English parson
William Gilpin, whose *Three Essays on Picturesque Beauty* (1792)[41]
may be said to explain and advocate much of what they enact in
narrative form. The *personae* of these books were versions of
the "picturesque traveller," a person of taste and sensibility in
pursuit of cultivation. Their object was the discovery of ideal
"scenes"—buildings, cityscapes, genre scenes, rural landscapes,
wilderness—in which every detail contributed to the complex
aesthetic unity of the whole. In theory, the art of the picturesque travel book was the creation of verbal sketches which
emphasized the pleasingly irregular outlines and textures of
objects (of various kinds and combinations) and the intricate
effects of light, shadow, and color to be found in the great
works of landscape painting, especially those of Salvator Rosa
and Claude Lorrain. In practice, however, and with no warrant
from Gilpin, most of these books fell into a rhetoric of ejacu-
lation and "touzy-mouzy" (dizzied and dizzying enthusiasm)
which dissolved visual nuance.

As narrator of *Italy*, Cooper clearly styles himself as a version
of the picturesque traveler, a "man of sentiment and intellect"
(132) patiently attentive to Italy's natural and inhabited spaces.
The narrative frame of the book is elastic enough to include a
broad miscellany of incidents and reflections, including the *tableaux* of life in Florence and Rome, Cooper's "touches of society." Nevertheless, *Italy*, too, highlights the traveler's pursuit
of the ideal landscape, making the book chiefly a series of excursions punctuated by sketches. Cooper's commitment to the

style of picturesque impressionism is clearly evident in his manner of composing these sketches. In his treatment of form and light in the Italian landscape, moreover, one can see how he tried to make the sketches "a little unique" by avoiding the excessive pitches of emotion which blurred the vision of his predecessors; by attempting to synthesize into his picturesque aesthetic elements of both beauty and sublimity; and by valuing what he saw in terms of a new, symbolic, ideography.

The care Cooper took to compose his sketches according to picturesque principles is amply documented. Like those of *Switzerland,* they are fruits of a remarkable collaboration between Cooper's visual memory and his journal. As in the sketchbook of a painter, the journal consists chiefly of descriptive notes taken on the scene or shortly afterwards, while the impressions of it were still fresh. Some notes—those, for example, on the Simplon Pass and the Piedmont, which Cooper incorporated into *Switzerland,* and those on the Villa del Tasso—are detailed verbal sketches. Usually, however, they are of the character advocated by Gilpin. "A few scratches," Gilpin had written, "like a short-hand scrawl . . . , legible at least to ourselves, will serve to raise in our minds the remembrance of the beauties they humbly represent; and recal[l] to our memory even the splendid colouring, and force of light, which existed in the real scene."[42]

Most of Cooper's journal entries are just such scratches: "Describe position of Naples," for example, "Capri &c. &c. Vesuvius much further from the City than I had believed and differently placed"; or "Beautiful villa of Cardinal Ruffo. Splendid scenery of the Bay."[43] Just how much the latter note recalled Naples to Cooper's mind may be seen in the finished sketch in Letter XIII (109–112). As Gilpin suggests, the note locates "the best point of view" and a few "characteristic features" of the landscape; the finished sketch gives scrupulous attention to matters of composition ("a degree of *correctness,* and *expression* in the out-line"), to "a little *ornament* . . . from figures, and other circumstances," and to "some *effect of light.*"[44]

In such a fashion, Cooper's Italian journal furnished the verbal sketches for much of the book through Letter XVI. Of the first six journal entries—on the Piedmont, Milan, Piacenza and Parma (12–17 October 1828)—Cooper elaborated some in the concluding letters of *Switzerland* and the rest in Letter I of *Italy*. The second group of entries—on the departure from Florence, the sea-passage to Naples, and the view from Sorrento (31 July–? September 1829)—he elaborated in Letters XI–XV; and the four final entries on Sorrento (27 September–7 October 1829), in Letter XVI.

Cooper's effort to make his finished sketches "a little unique" began with an attempt to restore an equilibrium between the play of the mind and the play of the eye. In accord with Gilpin's argument, the sketches "[descend] not to the minutiae of objects" but keep to "general ideas"[45] and thus leave room for both kinds of play. But whatever moods or thoughts it might set into motion, the picturesque, for Cooper, was grounded on scrupulous fidelity to the seen world. Necessarily, this conviction set him against the prevailing conventions of the travel sketch, in which that fidelity had been breached, the facts of the visible world ignored, and the traveler's sensibility given too much play. This conviction is evident in Cooper's criticisms of Byron's Italian writings; of Ann Radcliffe's *Mysteries of Udolpho* (1794), a Gothic novel set in the Apennines; and of such popular travel narratives as John Chetwood Eustace's *Classical Tour Through Italy* (1821), Nathaniel Hazeltine Carter's *Letters from Europe* (1827), Lady Mary Wortley Montagu's *Letters and Works* (1837), Louis Simond's *A Tour in Italy and Sicily* (1828), and Mariana Starke's *Travels in Europe* (1827).[46]

Byron's view of the world, wrote Cooper in a letter, was distorted by a "vapid . . . exhibition of gross affectations, puerilities, caprices and morbid vanity: Duels in which no blood is shed, hair-breadth escapes and adventures in countries that are every day travelled without hazard, and the opinions of a traveller of twenty two who had seen Portugal, the South east corner of Spain, Malta, Sardinia, Sicily and a part of Greece! And this he calls some knowledge of Europe, Asia and Africa."[47]

Cooper did not reject the conventions of Gothicism so emphatically, but in *Italy* Mrs. Radcliffe's novel does serve as a reminder of how these conventions distort visual facts to heighten their dramatic effects. His own experience disconfirmed, for example, his preconception of the Apennines as infested with banditti and dotted with Gothic castles. Early in his sojourn, he discovers the reports of banditti to be grossly exaggerated; towards the end, he remarks that he has "not seen the castles of the romances at all" (268).

His recourse to popular travel narratives, finally, kept him to his promise to include "nothing but the gleanings that are to be had after the harvests gathered by those who have gone before me" (51). But more importantly, these books displayed "no definite notions of distances, surfaces, &c." Mrs. Starke, he observes, fails to consider the physical dimensions of the Vatican when she describes it. Carter is wrong in his statements about matters as diverse as Italian scorpions and the identity of the Rialto in Venice.

Cooper's world is not static. For him, it is by its very nature changeful and various, an elusive collaboration between matter and consciousness. He takes no little delight in its illusions and surprises. The *trompe l'oeil* (or visual mirage), indeed, is as important to *Italy* as the *coup d'oeil* ("a sudden scene of grandeur" bursting "unexpectedly upon the eye")[48] is to *Switzerland*. In Florence, for example, Brunelleschi's Duomo seems to rise "like a balloon" from a "field of roofs" (17). The scale of St. Peter's is so massive that men seem "dwindled into boys" (191), and a marble throne at the far end of the church seems "distant as a cavern on a mountain" (192). Venice is "a city afloat" (279).

Yet unlike the victims of "touzy-mouzy," Cooper refuses wholly to be lost or to lose the reader in such warps. That is why his first impulse is to take account of the visible facts of a place. Of landscapes and buildings he is first a topographer, accurately establishing directions, distances, sizes and contours. He early locates, for example, the seven primary topographical features of the Bay of Naples: Naples in the northeast and Castellamare in the southeast corners of the bay, with Vesuvius between and behind them; the two peninsular arms of the bay; and the sentinel islands of Ischia and Capri west of the bay's mouth. Similarly, his eye for size, shape, materials and function in architecture establishes the visible facts of human artifice. In one of his most telling gestures, he embraces a column of St. Peter's "not," he assures the reader, "in a fit of sentimentalism, but to ascertain its diameter" (191).

For most of his facts, however, Cooper seems to have relied upon guidebooks. In writing up the side trip from Florence to Genoa (Letters VII–VIII) and the stops which he made at Venice, Verona, and Trento (Letters XXIX–XXXIII), he made use of his copy of Engelmann and Reichard's *Manuel pour les Voyageurs en Allemagne et dans les Pays Limitrophes*,[49] in which he had made marginal notes. For the Roman letters, his dependence on the guidebooks of Mariano Vasi was even more extensive— too much so, as it turned out.

The habit of mensuration which allowed Cooper to restore topographical accuracy to the perception of landscape also allowed him, in his "poetical" sketches, to concentrate with greater clarity than previous travelers upon the complex and often only momentary coalescences of form, light, shadow, and color which constitute the picturesque in landscape.[50] These sketches reemphasize the fact that the principles of complexity, variety, and contrast defined by Gilpin and other theorists as the grammar for this language each have manifold visual references. Cooper's sketch of Lago Maggiore, near the end of *Switzerland*, is a glossary of the visual phenomena which make Italy for him so distinctively picturesque. The sheer "multiplicity of . . . objects" in this typically Italian landscape offers one kind of visual complexity. More specific complexities are evident in the "irregular" curve of the shoreline and in the succession of terraces and "bold" slopes leading up from the surface of the lake to the "noble background of the Alps." Visual contrasts and variety manifest themselves in images of villas "buried among fruit trees"; in "castles, or convents, on headlands, or heights"; and in the "strikingly picturesque" groupings of boats "beached in beautiful disorder on the sands" and of the figures of fishermen "anchored on their grounds, or gliding athwart the glassy lake, with all their appliances disposed as one would introduce them into a picture."

Cooper's respect for these complexities of form, in turn, reemphasizes the importance of light—and this, too, patiently observed—as the means of organizing such forms into a coherent landscape. At Lago Maggiore he thus observes the effect of *sfumato*, one of the unique effects of Italian atmosphere: the forms and groupings merge in a "glow," "a dreamy warm mistiness," which softens their outlines and throws back "the chiselled peaks into the distance," so that nearer forms seem bathed in a luminous sea.[51]

Cooper concentrates his study of light on Italy's west coast.

He is particularly drawn to afternoon and evening lights, with their ikonic transformations of form into subtle *chiaroscuros* of glowing gold, silver, rose. At Leghorn, he sees afternoon side-light sculpting the coastal mountains—"piles that buttress the coast"—in sharp contrasts of light and shadow, rendering them "pictures to study." At the same time, *sfumato* mellows these "magnificent" forms with "a bewitching softness, such as perhaps no other portion of the globe can equal" (84). Later, he observes that the atmosphere mellows "every tint and trait" in the landscape; blends "all the parts in one harmonious whole"; and suffuses the picture with "a seductive ideal, that blended with the known reality in a way I have never before witnessed . . ." (112).

Cooper's study of picturesque form and light in Italy, in fact, took him far beyond Gilpin's understanding of the aesthetic. Like Gilpin, he seems to consider the picturesque a beauty roughened by weather, time, or human usage: the kind to be found in the "irregular" curve of a shoreline, for example, rather than in the symmetrical curve of a Chippendale chair or a clipped tree in an eighteenth-century garden; in the "glassy" sheen of a lake dotted with boats and figures rather than in the unbrokenly smooth finish of a mirror. His sense of Italian beauty extends as well to its wondrously soft, spiritualizing delicacies of light and color and to its subtle harmonies between natural forms, human artifacts, and human figures. His departure from Gilpin begins with his perception, in Italy, of a picturesque beauty interfused with elements of sublimity. Italy's "softened sublimity" (109) manifests itself to him not in vast height or depth, the obscurity of night, desolation, or kinetic power (though these are intermittently evident), but rather in vast distances, grand (not stupefying) scale, the luminous obscurity of haze, magnificence of color and form, and the kind of muted power evident in the time-softened, art-embellished volcanic landscape of Naples.

In the book, picturesque beauty and "softened sublimity" blend so subtly that it is difficult to distinguish them except by their effects on the mind. Nowhere is this more evident than in the sketch of Ischia, with its "black volcanic peaks" in the background; its strolling figures lending a graceful "movement of life"; and its "lofty, fantastic, broken fragment-like crags" looming into the foreground as the traveler's boat approaches them, everything suffused with soft light. The adjectives in the sketch evoke its touches of sublimity; the light and motion give it its lovely delicacy. In a contemplative pendant to the sketch, Cooper pays homage to the painter who seems most to have helped him to visualize a landscape which for him epitomizes Italy, the paragon of picturesque landscapes. The "flood of sensations [here poured] on the mind," he declares, awakens the kinds of ideas evoked in "an exquisite landscape by Claude" (132).

Cooper went beyond Gilpin not only in his sense of visual complexity, but also in his sense of the effects of picturesque phenomena upon the mind. His best Italian sketches define the elusive interplay of beauty and sublimity in gatherings of various irregular forms transfigured by light and constantly changing as light and perspective change. At the same time, they also transform landscape into a kind of mute, illuminated text whose images are charged with manifold symbolic significances. For Gilpin, the chief value of the picturesque was the pleasure it gave to the educated eye. For Cooper, its chief value was as the embodiment of ideals which could give peace and nobility to human life. Italy's beauty intimates a subtle, tender, and enduring (if elusive) harmony—a world well-kept. Its sublimity intimates a vast, mysterious splendor—a world imbued with a grand design. And this ideography has significance which is variously ethical, spiritual, intellectual, and cultural.

The chief source of symbolic meaning in the sketches is the interaction between light, landscape, and the mind of the beholder. The effects of this interaction are elusive and changeful, because the order they intimate is manifold and defies fixed definition. At times, the light engenders a feeling of *dolce far niente*, easeful, luxuriant, benevolent. Again (the feeling translating itself into a benevolist ethic), it engenders an experience which Cooper likens to an encounter with "an extremely fine woman," the light softening the landscape as "the eloquent and speaking expression of feminine sentiment" softens a woman's "stateliness and beauty." As you would such a woman, he suggests, "you come to love [the landscape] like a friend" (84, 132). Yet again, it engenders a state of mind akin to the calm repose of sleep or death—some dream-like consciousness in which time is stopped, and the past becomes a tangible apparition "adorned and relieved by a glorious grouping of so much that is exquisite in the usages of the present" (111). Cooper tries to express this state by allusions to magic, witchery, sorcery, and fairy-like presences. In the mountains above Sorrento, the light, the elevation, and the distanced perspective on the abiding "glories of the earth" (141) call forth intense expressions of religious sentiment, affirmations of a divine order manifest in these glories. In the prismatically colored atmosphere of a sunset viewed from Castel St. Elmo, "the whole concave is an arch of pearl; and this . . . is succeeded by a blush as soft and as mottled as that of youth." At one still point in this turning, a "soft rosy tint illumines the base of Vesuvius, and all the crowded objects of the coast, throwing a glow on the broad Campagna that enables one almost to fancy it another Eden" (173–174).

Like so many other Romantic travelers, however, Cooper's most recurrent conception of these intangible harmonies owes less to Protestant orthodoxy than it does to the classical ideal of Arcadia. His Protestantism does perhaps temper his sense of duration in this ideal landscape. *Et in Arcadia ego,* say the death's heads in Northern European painting. The bodies of the naked dead at Campo Santo and the volcanic "cauldron" under Naples offer similar reminders to Cooper, and even his most exuberant sketches are tinged with melancholy. Though Naples has endured for "nearly all of known time" (93), its future is not assured, and its present is not free of "disgusting details"—or of oppression. Nevertheless, the dominant idea suggested by the landscapes is that of a manifold and enduring intercourse between Italian nature and Italian civilization: light, earth, mood, manners, and art all in tender, exalting intimacy with each other.

The composition of the sketches—remarkably consistent for all of the complexity and variety which they encompass—also plays an important role in defining and elaborating Cooper's Arcadian ideal. The backgrounds typically have an amphitheatral shape. In the panoramic sketches, the peaks and faces of the Apennines with their "blue and ridgy" outlines form a "natural wall" (157, 94). More proximate amphitheatres enclose the close-up sketches. The Baian shore repeatedly isolates the life of the bay; cliffs loom even into the foreground at Ischia and

Sorrento; and in Rome, walls and domes create equivalent effects. Each of these amphitheatres has its symbolic function. Appropriately, each isolates the landscape from the rest of the world and at the same time defines the 'scene' for the dramas of interaction between nature, art, life, and mind which take place within it.

By contrast, the foregrounds are usually dominated by figures or buildings rather than by natural objects, and these visibly manifest the kinships between man and nature. The figures are rarely at work; typically they are taking part in a procession or taking their ease, their slow movements at once reflecting their own attunement to the atmosphere and the easeful state of the artist's mind. A sketch of the bay from Capo di Monte, for example, brings into the foreground an assemblage of villagers on a "crescent of sandy beach." The "children sporting on the sands, the costumes and flaring colours of the female dresses," the men with their red caps and "loose trowsers that descend but little below the knee" (123)—all of these details suggest an enlivening intercourse between their village culture, the nature which envelops them, and the artist observing them.

Buildings appear more frequently than figures in the foregrounds and the middlegrounds of the sketches. Like his American contemporaries and successors, Cooper retained a respect for the integrity of objects which distinguishes his impressionism from that, say, of Turner, in whose later paintings objects are dissolved in stormy vortices or annihilated by light. Nevertheless, Cooper tends to image objects diffusely, emphasizing their place in the landscape rather than their discreteness.

Objects, too, thus elaborate his Arcadian ideal, demonstrating the harmonies between nature and Italian civilization. In Italy, Cooper perceives, art embellishes rather than ignores or contests with nature. To accentuate this impression, he tends to de-emphasize foliage, even though he is clearly aware of the picturesque qualities of the poplar, the orange, the olive trees (16, 271). As in the Italian paintings he cites (12, 53), rock forms dominate, especially those of the mountain and the coastal cliff, the architecture repeating these forms in brick and stucco. In the coastal landscapes, Cooper is particularly drawn to the "wasp-nest looking" villages clustered on cliffs at Villa Franca, Ischia, and Amalfi. From Mount Albano, Rome appears the exemplary improvement of a picturesque site. Its suburban temples and villas embellish the prairie-like "wastes" of the Campagna and graduate into the grand "mountains" of capital architecture.

Like many another Romantic traveler, Cooper is drawn, too, to the classical ruins of Rome, Baiae, Pozzuoli, Pompeii, Herculaneum, and Paestum. Yet three things distinguish his interest from that engendered by the aesthetic of ruin and its pendant drama of historical and poetic associations, which peopled ruins with figures remembered from history, hagiography, poetry, and myth. One difference is that his "recollections," with the exception of St. Paul's disembarkation at Pozzuoli (127–128), take the form of reflection on historical fact more fully than the form of dramatic fancy. Just as he refuses to lose himself in the warps of visual impression, so he refuses to lose himself in imagining Cicero in the Forum, for example, or Horace in the Sabine Hills. The second difference is that he never allows his recollections to obscure his response to ruins as visible objects in a landscape. It is only when the ruins are visually uninteresting—"indistinct, and much dilapidated" (129), as at Baiae; or of little "interest directly to the senses" (219), as in the Forum—that he turns to recollections. They are conspicuously absent in his sketches of the still-intact and impressive Pantheon or the Piscina Mirabile, a Roman reservoir near Baiae. On Mount Albano, with a spectacular landscape laid out below him, he makes not even dutiful mention of the Ovid or Horace he knows by heart, or even of Claude.

In Cooper's *Italy*, the picturesque involves a visualizing and a symbolizing more than an associational intelligence. The blendings of rock and architectural forms have an effect as Arcadian as the effect of light:

Pinnacles, peaks, rocks, terraces, that, in other countries, the traveller might feel disposed to embellish by some structure, in his fancy, poetical alike in its form and uses, are here actually occupied, and frequently by objects whose beauty surpasses even the workings of the imagination (166).

IV

Sadly, the finished book could not sustain the high aspirations Cooper had for it. His decision to make it a book "without politics" deprived it, from the beginning, of a major element of that synthesizing intelligence he brought to the matter of Europe. Given Italy's political situation, moreover, a book which avoided politics was itself politically significant. In 1815, the Congress of Vienna had rendered Italy, in Metternich's arrogant phrase, "only a geographical denomination," with Lombardy and Venetia annexed to Austria and the old dynasties—all bound to Austria—restored to the other nine kingdoms, duchies, principalities, and states on the peninsula. Popular anti-Austrian and nationalist sentiment precipitated revolts in Piedmont and Naples in the early 1820s, when Cooper was writing *The Pioneers*; and again in February 1831, ten months after Cooper's departure, in Modena, Parma, and the Papal States. Not until 1870 did Italy finally achieve unification.

In the final letter of the book, Cooper's awareness of Italy's political agonies does finally surface. "Sooner or later," he declared a decade before moderate Italian liberals arrived at the same conclusion, "Italy will inevitably become a single State . . . though the means by which it is to be effected are still hidden. . . . [P]erhaps the wisest way is, to direct the present energies to reforms, rather than to revolutions; though many here will tell you the former are to be obtained only through the latter" (299). But Cooper strikes this note too late to keep his book from appearing to accept, tacitly, Italy's status quo. Having met, for example, in an elaborate ceremony, Leopold II, the enlightened Grand Duke of Tuscany, who was also an Austrian archduke, and having formed a favorable opinion of Leopold's character, he is moved in Letter VI to declare that Italy has made heartening progress in the last eighty years—a tired truism that American colonists had often heard applied to their own situation in the years before 1776. Consider, too, his treatment of Adam Mickiewicz, poet and organizer of the Polish Legion. Like Margaret Fuller twenty years later, Cooper befriended the exiled revolutionary in Rome, and Mickiewicz regularly accompanied the American democrat on the rides about the walls of Rome described in Letters XXII and XXIII. The letters make no mention either of Mickiewicz or of their conversation, though it is tempting to speculate how much of the latter Cooper remembered when he finally made clear his political position on Italy.

Cooper's apolitical treatment of Italy is most problematic in his treatment of human figures in the landscape. As his own later fiction shows, Cooper understood how the picturesque could lend itself to the creation of 'rounded' characters, complex and changeful in behavior and mentality, reflecting social and political as well as physical environments. In *Italy*, however, Italians are simply the ornament of scenes. They are not as phantasmagorical as the figures in earlier travel narratives— not compounds of history, hagiography, and myth. Yet they are flatly conventional creatures of a "poetical" perspective: Virgilian shepherds; priests in solemn ceremonies; colorful beggars; strollers taking the evening light and air. Of such *dramatis personae*, Henry James's remark that an Italy "preoccupied with its economical and political future . . . must be heartily tired of being admired for its eyelashes and its pose"[52] comes uncomfortably close to the mark. Nevertheless, the book's "touches of society" and its depiction of Italy's political environment anticipate by more than sixty years the senses of place which characterize James's own distinguished Italian narratives, *William Wetmore Story and His Friends* (1903) and *Italian Hours* (1909).

Italy's chief flaw is that the pictorial intensity of its landscape sketches is not sustained, as it is in *Switzerland*. By the time he moved to Rome, perhaps unaware of their crucial importance, Cooper had abandoned his journals, and he was thus excessively dependent on guidebooks. When he describes Rome, for example, he turns frequently to Mariano Vasi's *Itinéraire de Rome et de Ses Environs*[53] and at times incorporates Vasi word for word. Here the sketches become infrequent, mostly hurried, and prone to drift into exposition, in the manner of a guidebook. As *Italy* progresses, landscapes omitted loom as large as those included. Cooper 'names' but does not 'do' Tivoli, the *sanctum sanctorum* of rural Rome, and much the same is true of his Venice.

Yet if, on the whole, *Italy* is a less successful book than *Switzerland*, its finest sketches—especially those of the coast from Leghorn to Naples—are indeed "more poetical" than those of

Switzerland. They have a warmth, a complex integrity of impression, and a conceptual coherence which surpass anything in *Switzerland.* They fully reflect Cooper's belief in "the vast superiority of the Italian landscapes" (132), and they are among the finest fruits of his sojourn in Europe.

Picturesque Arcadian Italy became Cooper's paragon of the inhabited landscape. In the book, he confirms its "vast superiority" by comparing it to Swiss and American landscapes. These comparisons, which begin in the closing letters of *Switzerland*, also help him further to codify the elements of sublimity most amenable to the picturesque vision. The Alps' "sublimity of desolation," though ameliorated by "a certain unearthly aspect which the upper glaciers assume in particular conditions of the atmosphere," he concludes, has no lasting value in the education of "the man of sentiment and intellect." The harsh, uninhabitable nakedness of the Alps excites first wonder, then apathy. The "union of the pastoral with the sublime" on the upland slopes of the Alps "astonishes, and it often delights," but the union is too rough and unfinished and the contrast too great, as if nature and civilization had not yet been sufficiently assimilated. "The *refinement* of Italian nature," on the other hand—a refinement produced by weathering, by human use, and most especially by the light—gives rise "to a sublimity of a different kind, which, though it does not awe, leaves behind it a tender sensation allied to that of love" (132).

In contrast to Italy, Cooper concludes, there is "very little of the grand, or the magnificent" in American landscape, but "enough of beautiful nature" to delight the eye, educate the sentiments and the intellect, and inform the arts of the new nation (95). The "property patriotism" which touts the supremacy of the American landscape is simply another form of blindness to the highest values of the visible world, a sign that Americans have not yet understood their natural endowments. Though beautiful, New York is not as beautiful as Naples. Its harbor is a turbid, dullish green; while the Italian coast, including the Bay of Naples, is the color of deep water, a limpid cerulean blue running to ultramarine. In place of the picturesque complexity and curvilinear beauty of Naples' volcanic promontories, bays, peninsulas, and grand islands, New York offers "nothing but the verdure and foliage of spring and summer." New York City is straggling, thinly populated, busy with "commerce, shipping, drays, and stevedores," and situated on a flat, "shaved" surface; Naples is condensed, overflowing with people, leisurely except for its port, and situated on cliffs. "As regards artificial accessories," New York and the Hudson River run to "Grecian monstrosities, and Gothic absurdities in wood"; Naples, to "palaces, villas, gardens, towers, castles, cities, villages, churches, convents, and hamlets, crowded in a way to leave no point fit for the eye unoccupied, no picturesque site unimproved." And "[i]f New York does possess a sort of back-ground of rocks, in the Palisadoes, which vary in height from three to five hundred feet, Naples has a natural wall, in the rear of the Campania Felice, among the Apennines, of almost as many thousands." Inland American landscapes show equivalent flaws in relation to Arcadian Italy. "Our lakes," Cooper argues, "will scarcely bear any comparison with the finer lakes of Upper Italy; our mountains," like the Alps, "are insipid as compared with [the Apennines], both as to hues and forms" (93–94, 96).

Cooper does not intend these comparisons to be denigrating. His motive is to exercise not an anti-national but an extranational standard for the perception and judgment of landscape. The imagination of the artist, Gilpin had observed, "is a magazine abounding with all the elegant forms, and striking effects, which are to be found in nature."[54] If the deficiencies of the American landscape become evident on comparison with the ideal landscape in Cooper's mental magazine of landscapes, so too do its subtle virtues and its possibilities for improvement. In *Italy*, thinking about the "gorgeousness" of American sunsets and autumns, Cooper recalls that "liquid softness in the atmosphere" of autumn (173), a kind of American *sfumato* in whose alchemies might be glimpsed a New World version of the Arcadian landscape. As that version took shape in his mind during the late 1830s and the 1840s, Cooper would come to see that the rough and changeful beauties of America's dominant features—trees (forests, forested mountains) and water (lakes, rivers, cataracts)—required picturesque improvements along the lines of the English rather than the Italian garden, of neo-Gothic rather than Italian architecture. But the principles if not the particulars of this vision were most fully grounded in Cooper's experience of Italy.

NOTES

1. *Gleanings in Europe: Switzerland* (Albany, N.Y., 1980), pp. 5, 278. (Hereafter cited as *Switzerland*.)
2. Henry James, *William Wetmore Story and His Friends*, (New York, [1903]), II, 4.
3. *Gleanings in Europe: Italy* (Albany, N.Y., 1981), p. 21. (Pages subsequently cited in the text refer to this edition.)
4. *The Letters and Journals of James Fenimore Cooper*, ed. James Franklin Beard, 6 vols. (Cambridge: Harvard University Press, Belknap Press, 1960–1968), III, 233; II, 371. (Hereafter cited as *Letters and Journals*.)
5. Ibid., III, 330.
6. Ibid., I, 372.
7. See James T. Callow, *Kindred Spirits: Knickerbocker Writers and Artists, 1807–1855* (Chapel Hill, 1967), pp. 192–215.
8. Louis L. Noble, *The Course of Empire, Voyage of Life and Other Pictures of Thomas Cole . . . , with Selections from His Letters and Miscellaneous Writings* (New York, 1853), p. 171.
9. For Cooper's use of the picturesque, see Donald Ringe, *The Pictorial Mode* (Lexington, Kentucky, 1971); Blake Nevius, *Cooper's Landscapes* (Berkeley: University of California Press, 1976); and Ernest H. Redekop, "Picturesque and Pastoral: Two Views of Cooper's Landscapes," *The Canadian Review of American Studies*, 7:2 (Fall 1977), 184–205.
10. Christopher Hussey, *The Picturesque: Studies in a Point of View* (Hamden, Connecticut, 1967), p. 84.
11. *Letters and Journals*, I, 369.
12. Ibid., I, 397.
13. Uvedale Price, *Essays on the Picturesque . . .* , 3 vols. (London, 1810), I, 65.
14. *Letters and Journals*, I, 404.
15. Washington Irving, *Tales of a Traveler. Works*, Kinderhook ed. (New York, n.d.), I, 377.
16. *Letters and Journals*, I, 389, 400.
17. Ibid., I, 409.
18. Ibid., I, 350ff.
19. Ibid., III, 249.
20. Ibid., III, 258.
21. Ibid., III, 261.
22. Ibid., III, 249, n.2.
23. Ibid., III, 258.
24. Ibid., III, 262.
25. Ibid., III, 258, n.4.
26. *Bibliographie de la France* (Paris, 1838), 2391–2392.
27. *Letters and Journals*, III, 289.
28. Ibid., III, 289–290, n. 1.

29. Susan Cooper, *The Cooper Gallery; or, Pages and Pictures from the Writings of James Fenimore Cooper* (New York, 1881), pp. 200–229, 241–248.
30. *The Literary Gazette, and Journal of the Belles Lettres*, No. 1100 (17 February 1838), 100.
31. *The Spectator*, 11, No. 503 (17 February 1838), 161. This review was reprinted in *Museum of Foreign Literature*, 33 (May 1838), 77–79.
32. *American Monthly Magazine*, 12 (July 1838), 75.
33. *The Hesperian; or Western Monthly Magazine*, 1 (July 1838), 251.
34. *The New Yorker*, 5 (June 1838), 173.
35. *The National Gazette* (26 May 1838), p. 2.
36. *The Knickerbocker*, 11 (June 1838), 560.
37. *Letters and Journals*, III, 330.
38. Ibid., III, 334.
39. Ibid., III, 258.
40. Ibid., III, 261–262.
41. William Gilpin, *Three Essays on Picturesque Beauty*, 3rd ed. (London, 1808).
42. Ibid., p. 51.
43. *Letters and Journals*, I, 379, 380.
44. Gilpin, *op. cit.*, pp. 62–63, 65.
45. Ibid., p. 87.
46. John Chetwood Eustace, *A Classical Tour Through Italy*, 4 vols. (London, 1821); Nathaniel Hazletine Carter, *Letters from Europe* (New York, 1827); Lord Wharncliffe, ed., *The Letters and Works of Lady Mary Wortley Montagu* (London, 1837); Louis Simond, *A Tour in Italy and Sicily* (London, 1828), for which see *Letters and Journals*, I, 374; and Mariana Starke, *Travels in Europe* (London, 1828).
47. *Letters and Journals*, I, 405.
48. Gilpin, *op. cit.*, p. 44.
49. Julius Bernard Engelmann and Heinrich August Ottokar Reichard, *Manuel pour les Voyageurs en Allemagne et dans les Pays Limitrophes* (Frankfurt sur le Mein, 1827). Cited in *Letters and Journals*, I, 362–63, n. 1, and 413–14, n. 3.
50. Cooper's habit of mensuration anticipates by more than a decade what Barbara Novak calls "the mensurational inclinations" of the American luminist landscape painters. See her *American Painting of the Nineteenth Century* (New York: Praeger Publishers, 1969), pp. 92–164.
51. *Switzerland*, p. 293.
52. Henry James, *Italian Hours* (New York, [1909]), p. 111.
53. Mariano Vasi, *Itinéraire Instructif de Rome et de Ses Environs*, 3rd ed. (Rome, 1829). The following is a list of apparent references to Vasi:

Reference:		*Italy*:	Vasi:
Walls of Rome:	year 276	196.3	Vol. I, p. X
	writer	196.12–16	p. X
	writer	196.27	p. 290
	16½ miles	197.9	p. X
Rome:	14 quarters	197.28	p. XII

Circus Maxentius:	1825	207.18	Vol. II,	p. 388
	year 311	207.38		p. 390
	18,000 people	208.24		p. 392
	1560 Roman feet	208.25		p. 390
	240 feet	208.30		p. 390
	not quite 900 feet	208.30–31		p. 393 (837 pieds)
Sacred Mount:	years 261 and 305	214.19	Vol. I,	p. 258
Coliseum:	years 79, 81, 96	216.27–8		p. XVII
	years 523 and 1381	216.31, 35		p. 152
	1641 and 157 feet	217.11,14		p. 154
	285 by 182 feet	217.22		p. 155
Column (Forum):	years 1813 and 608	221.13,19		p. 127
Forum of Trajan:	year 1812	223.12		p. 217
	132 feet	223.14		p. 218
	2,000 by 600 feet	223.26–27		p. 221 (2,000 by 650 feet)
Column of Antoninus:	story and eleven feet	224.1–14		pp. 23–25
Citorio:	year 1748	224.22		p. 26
Pantheon:	year 727	225.8	Vol. II,	p. 312
	132 Roman feet	225.37–38		p. 317
	year 608	226.1		p. 313
Rome:	133 churches	236.7		pp. 628–32
Vatican:	1100 by 800 feet	237.16		p. 515 (180 by 120 toises)
	three statuaries	240.28		p. 560

54. Gilpin, *op. cit.*, p. 61.

Preface.

If the author were required to give a reason why he has written on a country so well known as Italy, he might be puzzled to give any other answer than that he loved the subject, and has been indulging his own recollections possibly more than he will please his readers.

As this, like most other books, must speak for itself, the author has little to add, in the way of Preface, to what has already been published in the work with which his travels commence. He has endeavoured to avoid a pretension which his research would not justify, while he hopes some may be glad to go over again, even this beaten road, in his company.

Cooper's town, 1838.

Letter I.

ALTHOUGH we had breathed an atmosphere of delight from the moment the carriage turned out of the glen of the Doveiria to enter the first really Italian valley, the ardour of expectation and enjoyment was scarcely diminished when we entered the carriage to quit Milan, on our way towards the barrier of mountains that separates the Upper from the Lower, the false from the true Italy. We had certainly some of the architecture, glimpses of the nature, and a multitude of the recollections of the latter, where we then were; but we well knew that there was more beyond, and we were glad to hurry towards it after the two or three days of repose that we had now taken. As yet we had only seen Cis-Alpine Gaul.

Old Caspar mounted his horse with renewed vigour, and he trotted through the southern gate with us, some time before the sun had risen. Although it was only the 15th of October and we were now fairly on the great plain of Lombardy, the morning was so sharp that I found both a surtout and a cloak agreeable, if not necessary.

The streets of Milan, and indeed of all the towns of this part of Italy, have lines of flat stones, a sort of railway, laid for the carriage-wheels; the celebrated Corso having two tracks, in order that the vehicles may not intercept each other. The town walls are of bricks, and a good deal covered with ivy; and as the ditch is imperfect and neglected, they were probably more efficient in the days of the Visconti than in those of Napoleon. Military patroles march the streets at night, and all night, so that the place is orderly and safe. We saw many people with *goîtres* in the streets, peasants most probably from the valleys of the Alps.

We took the route to Lodi, which is about twenty miles from Milan. The road lay the entire distance through meadows and vines. There was little other prospect than that of fertility, for we were in a sea of plain, though the Alps still lifted their hoary peaks along the northern horizon. South, east, and west, the sight was bounded with a fringe of fruit-trees, with, here and there, a gaunt church-tower thrusting up its neck, to mark the site of a village. There was, however, a good deal of irrigation, with canal-like ditches, among the meadows, and occasionally a broad margin of faded verdure around us.

At Lodi we stopped two hours. The inn windows overlooked the market-place, which was teeming with the activity, gesticulation, bawling, humour, and wrangling of low Italian life. One fellow, mounted on a horse, was haranguing a crowd; and, leaning forward, I caught enough to discover that he was a quack dispensing immortality at very modest prices. Suddenly a peasant presented his face, when the fellow extracted a tooth, without dismounting. The operation was performed with great readiness, and, flourishing his prize in triumph, while the poor patient was holding his jaws and kicking right and left with pain, the fellow called on all around him to witness how slight a thing it was to lose a tooth.

Observing great quantities of what I supposed to be small birds, beautifully white and clean, strung on coarse grass, I went down to examine them, thinking they might be some game of which it would be well to know more; but, on inspection, they proved to be the hind quarters of frogs! There were hundreds of strings of them in the market. I know not how the French got their reputation of frog-eaters, unless it comes through the usual English prejudice; for I feel certain that ten frogs are consumed in Italy for one in France. Indeed, frogs are rather an unusual dish in Paris; nor do I remember ever to have seen them anywhere on a private table. The country around Lodi, however, is just suited to such a stock, and, literally, thousands are consumed by the inhabitants.

We were anxious, of course, to examine the celebrated bridge. I found, however, that the people on the spot did not deem the battle so serious an affair as it is usually imagined; and as I have heard, on pretty good authority, that several of Napoleon's battles were fought principally in the bulletins, I went doubting to the river. The stream, you know, is the Adda; it is straggling, and a good deal disfigured by sand-banks. The bridge, six or eight hundred feet in length, is narrow; and the land opposite the town is a low meadow. A few houses on that side mark the approach to the bridge, and the buildings of the town do the same thing on the other. As it would be physically impossible to cross this bridge under the fire of batteries of any force that were in the least well managed, and as the Austrian artillery, moreover, if not the very best, is considered among the best in Europe, I was a good deal staggered with the appearance of things. The result of all my inquiries on the spot was as follows, and I presume it is not far from the truth.

The Austrian army was in retreat, and had thrown the Adda between itself and its enemy. Napoleon arrived in pursuit. Ascertaining that the stream might be forded, he sent a detachment with that object towards a flank of his enemy, and the Austrians retired, leaving a force to protect their retreat at the bridge. Anxious to strike a blow, Napoleon decided to force this point immediately, and ordered the attack. My informant affirmed that most of the Austrian artillery had commenced retiring before the assault was made; and this appears, at least, probable. Finding that his column paused under the fire of the few guns left, Napoleon and his generals cheered them on in person. The French did not get across until the Austrians were too far on their retreat to make the affair decisive, but soon enough to seize some of the guns in the rear; guns that the Austrians probably intended to sacrifice.

I give you this account as it was given to me by one who affirmed he was an eye-witness. Certainly, after seeing the bridge, I shall not believe that one army crossed it in face of another that was not completely disorganised. *Au reste*, it was sufficiently hazardous to attempt it in the face of a couple of efficient guns; and the personal intrepidity of the generals would be abundantly apparent even under such circumstances. It was probably a gallant thing, though by no means the precise thing we are accustomed to believe it.

Lodi is a town of some size, having a population of sixteen or eighteen thousand souls: it is the place in and near which the celebrated Parmesan cheese is made, the environs being chiefly in rich meadows. No Italian, I find, thinks of eating his soup without a spoonful of this cheese, which as regularly forms one of the ingredients as salt. It struck me as a discrepancy in civilisation to eat frogs and not to know how to make good coffee; for we have quite taken leave of the latter since we crossed the Alps.

The country continued much the same beyond Lodi. Towards evening we discerned the towers of a town in the visible horizon, and soon after came to the side of a sluggish stream of some size, lying low between banks that it sometimes evidently filled. The town was on the opposite side, walled, and not immediately on the stream. The river was the Po, which we crossed by a bridge of boats, and, making a little circuit, we drove through a gate-way and entered Piacenza. Ordering dinner, I walked out to look at the place, which contains more than 25,000 inhabitants. It is gloomy, crowded, and dull. Indeed, it is not easy to see how so many towns of this size are kept up on so small a surface. There does not appear to be any commerce worth mentioning; the manufactures are usually on a small scale, and half the people seem idle. There is a small palace belonging to the sovereign, of tolerable architecture. It has fifteen windows in front, while that of the governor of the place has thirteen. I believe the White House has less than either of these; though Piacenza is merely a provincial town, and the duchy of Parma itself contains less than half a million of souls.

Austria has made a very convenient arrangement for the defence of this frontier. She has a right, by treaty, to maintain garrisons in several of the towns that lie in the adjacent territories; by which means she gains so many outworks beyond her own limits. Piacenza is thus garrisoned, as is also Ferrara. This town and its walls are principally constructed of bricks: an unusual thing on the continent of Europe. The walls seem going to decay.

In the evening I strolled into the great square, which I found thronged with people. These towns are so cramped within their fortifications, that walking, except in an area like this, or on the ramparts, is almost out of the question; and as they all have a *place d'armes*, the people have acquired the habit of resorting thither for air and exercise.

There was a silent, gloomy crowd in the square; and as many of the men wore cloaks and were smoking, it reminded me of Spain, a country whose habits may very well have been introduced through the princes. You will remember that, by an intermarriage with the heiress of the Farnese family, this duchy passed into the possession of the Spanish Bourbons. It was a short time in the hands of the Emperor, as an indemnity, and by him again ceded to the Bourbons. Three generations of the latter family next reigned here; but the last gave up his duchy for the ephemeral kingdom of Etruria; one of the bungling jobs at king-making that Napoleon turned off during his own apprenticeship. At the peace of 1814, Marie Louise received Parma in full sovereignty; but this arrangement was subsequently altered, and she now holds it for life, the reversion being settled on the present Duke of Lucca, who is the son of its ancient sovereign, the King of Etruria. At his succession, I believe Lucca is to be annexed to Tuscany. In speaking of the size of the palace, I ought to have mentioned that Piacenza was once a separate duchy; to which circumstance it probably owes that structure.

We were off at six, as usual, and trotted on merrily, through a perfectly level country, though apparently less fertile and less peopled than Lombardy Proper. Until now, since we entered Italy, our course has been generally south; but on quitting Piacenza we diverged materially towards the east, travelling almost in a parallel line with the ranges of the Apennines, whose forms began to loom up, a little, in the haze of the atmosphere.

We had been warned of the necessity of bargaining at the inns for what was ordered; but higgling is so odious, that I had done nothing of the sort, preferring imposition. The last night at Piacenza, however, I left the family in the carriage, and went to look at the rooms myself, asking the price. Under these circumstances, I found that about half as much was demanded as I had hitherto paid. The result showed that our lodgings and supper cost very little more than the breakfast alone, and yet we had a parlour and four good bed-rooms! The next day, at breakfast, I ordered the meal at so much a head, and for so many persons: there was no difference in the service, or in its quality, and we paid three dollars for that which had cost us five the previous day.

We crossed the bed of a torrent that was absolutely dry, but broad, and spanned by a noble bridge that Napoleon had commenced and which his widow has just finished. Nearly everything is constructed of bricks, still. Near Parma we passed an old castellated edifice that excited a good deal of curiosity among us by its name, which is Castel Guelfo. I could get no history of this fortress, but it is fair to presume it had some connexion with the wars of the Guelphs and the Ghibellines. The building stands directly on the road, like a tavern, and in a perfectly level country. The main edifice, which is very high, is ranged around a court; it is about one hundred and fifty feet on each front, and is constructed of bricks and small stones placed in alternate layers of about three feet in thickness. The structure is surrounded by a ditch that is now dry. Three or four low, heavy, awkward towers are attached to the square building; and several appendages are scattered about, without the ditch. The whole is dilapidated, though still inhabited.

We reached Parma very early, the day's work being less than forty miles, over a perfect plain, although it nearly carried us from one side of the duchy to the other. This is a much finer town than Piacenza, and materially larger. We were no sooner housed and refreshed, than we hurried off to see the palace, the theatre, and the other curiosities. The first is an ancient irregular edifice of bricks, with a small, new, stuccoed façade. The theatre is one of the largest in Europe, and, one would think, capable of holding all the *élite* of the duchy. A covered gallery built on arches connects it with the palace, of which it is properly an appendage.

We saw many cockney sights, such as the cradle of the young Napoleon, and other similar wonders; but the duchess herself, of whom I could gladly have stolen a glimpse, was at Vienna, where she passes most of her time. The servants spoke of her as *Sa Majesté*, and told us that she maintained a good deal of state. She has three or four thousand troops, *gendarmes* included; and we saw the garrison here, in coats of sky-blue faced with red.

The Academy of Arts repaid us for the visit. It has many good pictures, one in particular by Correggio, who was a native of the vicinity. Here we met, for the first time, with specimens of architecture that, I believe, are nearly, if not quite, peculiar to Italy. A tower is erected near the church to contain the bells, which is called the *campanile;* and a sort of dome stands at hand, a structure altogether apart, in which the office of baptism is performed. The latter, from its object, is called the *Battistero*.

I have seldom seen quainter or ruder specimens of the Gothic than we found here, in a church of the middle ages. One of the bas reliefs is a car drawn by two horses, of which one is actually placed on the back of the other, from ignorance of all laws of perspective. This is almost as bad as the bas reliefs in the rotunda of the Capitol. But all nations have their Gothic ages; though it is to be hoped ours is to precede, and not follow the golden.

We breakfasted at Reggio, in the duchy of Modena, a place which gives the title of Duke to Marshal Oudinot. The country continued much the same, perfectly level, with the shadows of mountains on our left, and apparently fertile. We reached Modena itself, very early, and had time to look at the sights, the best of which are in the palace of the duke, consisting of pictures. Here we also first saw composition floors, made of stucco, in imitation of marble. When several coats of mortar have been laid, and beaten to a proper consistency, pieces of marble are stuck in it, so as to variegate the surface, and sometimes in a way to form designs. When the whole has indurated and set, the surface is polished. The result is a beautifully mottled floor, richer than any natural stone, much cheaper, and, if well made, perhaps as durable. It would be well to adopt this mode of ornamenting houses in America. We might commence in the public buildings and in large private houses. It has the additional recommendation of security against fire. In a warm climate, however, it is the most desirable; though carpets can be used over the stucco, in winter, as well as over boards. The servants told me that a little oil mixed with bran or saw-dust, and swept over the floor, had the effect of brightening the colours and of rendering the whole brilliant. This process is repeated once or twice a week.

The palace was neat, well kept, and large for the Duchy. Even this structure puts Windsor to shame, so far as the internal arrangements, and the beauty and lightness of the rooms are concerned. Modena is a town of five-and-twenty thousand souls, and, like most of the places of this part of Italy, the wonder is what they find to do. The reigning family was also at Vienna; for all this region, though governed by different princes and held by different titles, is virtually Austrian.

Our next day's march was still easier, extending no farther than Bologna, where we arrived about noon. The frontier of the States of the Pope was passed near the town of Modena, most of the road lying in the new territory. It was on the line of the ancient *Emilia Via*.

Here, then, we were at last on the confines of Lower Italy, and though the Apennines threw up their bold heads between us and our goal, we began to feel as if we had arrived. In the mean time, we sallied out to see the wonders of Bologna.

The streets of this town are lined with arcades, like those of Berne, though loftier, lighter, and of better architecture than the gloomy vaults of the city of the *Burgherschaft*. The architecture is altogether superior. You will be surprised to hear that the same cause has induced this particular mode of building; viz. the snows! Although in the heart of Italy, Bologna, lying at the foot of the Apennines, and on their northern side, is liable to have its streets obstructed with snow. There is a church on a hill, at the distance of a league from the town, and certain pious persons have actually caused a covered walk to be constructed the whole distance to it. It is an arcade open to the south, and protected towards the north by a wall. So much for the climate of Cis-Alpine Gaul!

The pictures of Bologna gave us great satisfaction; but the subject is so hackneyed, that it is seldom I shall enter into details about such things. The wax-work preparations have a horrible truth, and though probably useful as anatomical studies, are odious as spectacles. The same things exist at Paris, in equally disgusting accuracy.

There are two ugly motiveless brick towers in this town, one of which is of great height, and the other is not low, that lean out of the perpendicular in the way to make a spectator shudder. They have not much more beauty than the chimneys of a paint manufactory, and seem to have been built precisely for the reason that boys often pile bricks, with one leaning over the other, or just to ascertain where a line drawn from the centre of gravity will fall without the base. These babyisms on a large scale are apt to succeed the noble conceptions of a great nation, when in its decline. I believe, however, there is some pretence of utility connected with the best of these extraordinary freaks, and some pretensions to workmanship.

Bologna gives one an idea of the riches of Italy, in palaces and the arts. Its venerable and celebrated university is on the wane; but there are noble remains of its former wealth, learning, and importance. Many of the first families of Italy still reside here, and its society is said to be very desirable. But what can one who passes a day in a tavern tell you of these things that is worth knowing?

Letter II.

CASPAR paid me a visit, after dinner, with an ominous face and a more ominous report. He had ascertained that not less than twenty carriages were to cross the mountains next day. This augured badly for our comfort. In the first place, we might have a famine, or be brought to chestnuts, the true diet of the Apennines; and moreover, there was but a single house within a day's work of Bologna where we could possibly sleep. The ex-dragoon affirmed that nothing could pass him while actually in motion; but they who travelled post had the advantage of not stopping at all, and of course would win the plate. Nothing remained to be done but to get the track at starting, and to throw ourselves on our speed with at least the hope of distancing all the *vetturini.*—We accordingly drove through the gates of Bologna, before the day had fairly dawned. The inquiry of Caspar, whether any one had preceded us, was satisfactorily answered, and, cracking his long whip, the happy fellow trotted merrily to the foot of the first ascent. The road carried us very soon into the mountains, and here we bade adieu to the sea-like plain of Upper Italy.

For the first two or three hours we did little else but ascend; but it was evident that the piles were not Alpine. The road, however, was excellent, and though the country was scarcely grand enough to be imposing, or sufficiently soft to be pleasing, it had a peculiarity in its features that served to keep attention alive. We found the inn on the edge of what may be called the first considerable plateau—if any portion of mountains that are a succession of rounded caps can thus be termed. We were the first arrived, and were rewarded for our diligence by getting the first breakfast. If it was the best, our successors were to be pitied, for it consisted of execrable coffee, bad bread, tallowish butter, and greasy chops. One seldom sees a meaner repast in a log-house on the American frontier. Inferior as it all was, the laughing Caspar assured me those who came after us would fare worse, for we had consumed all the milk;—"*et les voilà*," he added, pointing down the mountain to a train of carriages that were dragging their weary way up the ascent. By this time we were ready to move, and away the dragoon trotted, chuckling at his own management as much as at our success.

The region we were now in had a wildness and a character that, to us, were entirely novel. Most of the mountain-tops were bald; and, indeed, as far as the eye could extend, west and south, it beheld nothing but a species of elevated downs, that were however much broken into irregular valleys and hills. There was a little forest, here and there; but, in the main, nakedness was the prevailing characteristic of the view. As I sat on the carriage-box, I could see the road leagues ahead of us, winding its way among the ascents, and forming an object of high civilisation amidst the otherwise rustic and quaint peculiarities of the wilds. I can best compare the view to the backgrounds which the old Italian masters sometimes put to their religious subjects, and of which treeless hills, rocks, winding paths, and picturesque towers compose the materials. Of the latter, however, there were no signs in this portion of the Apennines.

Soon after quitting the inn, an expanse of water showed itself to the north-east, quite in the horizon; for in that direction we could still overlook a vast reach of hazy, and of nearly indistinct plain. Judging by the map, the land was the Bolognese, with the country near Ravenna, and the water the Adriatic! As this glimpse was quite unexpected, it came upon us with the agreeable variety of a surprise.

Just after the water disappeared, a swarthy, picturesque-looking peasant passed us, on a brisk trot, eyeing the carriage keenly as he went by; he then leaped into a cross path, that led in nearly a direct line towards the winding ascents of the road, that were plainly visible at the distance of two or three miles, but to reach which we were compelled to make a long *détour*. A valley and a wood were between us and these ascents, and unpleasant thoughts began to suggest themselves at this little incident. I had heard of families borne off into these very Apennines by banditti, and held for ransom, failing of which they had been murdered. Robbers would have full an hour to do their work in; for the peasant, who had just left the tavern, must have understood the order of our march, and be certain that our party would be unsustained by any other for that time at least. Then there were a startling sagacity and a suspicious observation in the dark rolling eye that had so closely scanned us; and, all together, the fellow had about him an air of premeditation and design.

We were four men, and, with a pistol apiece, might have made a good defence; but I had not even a penknife or a cane, and Caspar had nothing but his whip! At times, I was disposed to laugh at my own apprehensions; but the heavy responsibility that I felt continued to render the matter serious. Still I was unwilling to alarm the females, and preserved silence, determining to halt in season if I detected any symptoms of an ambuscade before us. With this purpose I kept a vigilant look-out on the formation of the ground; and though I was not so much alarmed as to fancy every bush an enemy, no bush was left unexamined.

At length we began to descend, and I cheered Caspar up to a pace that would at least render aim a little uncertain. I now determined, as the road was excellent, the instant a shot was fired, to cause the postilions to set off on a run, and leave the issue to our speed. The fall of a horse, it is true, would undo us; but we must trust to fortune. As the postilion, unless an accessary, is generally the first victim in such an affair, I got ready to jump on the pole, and to spring into his seat should the ex-dragoon fall. The *fourgon* speaking for itself, and being a visible temptation to robbers, I had hopes too, by abandoning the baggage, at least to save the females. All these plans were duly arranged in my own mind, that no advantage might be lost in the confusion of a surprise.

While busy fancy was at work in this manner, during which time we passed over two or three of the most uncomfortable miles I ever remember to have travelled, we came to the foot of the long descent. Here, happily, was a house or two, and a group of men in the road, with five or six yokes of oxen, ready to assist us up the winding and sharp acclivities that lay in front. Foremost among these honest people was my dark-eyed peasant, who had run across the open waste merely to give notice of our approach, and to notify to the neighbourhood the number of oxen that would be required!

This was the first serious alarm I had felt about Italian banditti, and, I may add, it was the last; though I believe we were subsequently in situations where less indifference than this incident served so much to create would have been more prudent. As fear, though particularly contagious, excites no sympathy after the danger is passed, I kept my own secret.

By the help of the oxen we toiled our way up as steep ascents as one sees in Switzerland, though by no means as long; after which we had a succession of hills and valleys, through the same naked region as before. Towards the close of day we reached a village, or rather a hamlet, near which is a remarkable burning field that we dared not stop to examine, on account of our pursuers. The inn was soon in sight, and old Caspar pointed to it with his whip and grinned. Then he cast a glance of triumph back at the long winding road that might be seen for miles. Half a league in our rear three or four carriages had come into view, for it would seem that their owners too had bethought them of the night and its wants. The evening was lovely. [Mrs. Cooper] was on the carriage-box with me, enjoying its blandness, and we were all full of a sort of racing excitement, and laughing at our success. At this very moment, when the inn could not have been half a mile from us, *click clack, click clack*, was heard close to the carriage-wheels. A courier, in the usual livery, galloped past us, flourishing his whip in bravado, and before we could get there he dashed up to the door of the inn! In a few minutes, however, we were there too; and when I went into the house, the fellow was leaning coolly in the door. My inquiry for rooms was answered by showing me two or three mean closets, without fireplaces or comforts of any sort. As the house was tolerably comfortable, I demanded better apartments. All the rest of the house was taken by the courier at the door, who was in the service of Lord Lansdowne. The plot was apparent at once. The rogue had entered into an arrangement, pretended or real, with the innkeeper, and rooms were to be sold at an advance. I had a slight acquaintance with Lord Lansdowne, and had half a mind to wait his arrival and trust to his known courtesy for accommodations; but, preferring independence to being placed in controversy with a courier, Caspar was ordered to proceed. The innkeeper felt disposed to change his tactics when he saw the carriage departing; but I was not inclined to humour roguery, and we went our way.

There was an inn about two leagues farther, and the road was good. It is true, Caspar shrugged his shoulders when he mentioned it; but I thought the best accommodations of even an inferior inn, in our sole possession, might be better than the worst of the place we had just left in the midst of a crowd. Our departure caused long faces; but the example probably did no good, the house possessing a monopoly.

The moon had risen, and the night had grown chilly, before we reached the other inn. It was a single house, in a sort of heathy country, the very type of solitude. Here, however, we were joyfully received. Mounting by a narrow flight of steps, we were shown into the *sala*, a room of some size, lighted from above, and surrounded by bedchambers. In one corner there was a fireplace, and a faggot was soon in a bright blaze. The beds were homely but clean, and I took care to secure one for each of us, with the proper number of apartments. This was the first house we had entered that had a truly distinctive Italian character, and we submitted to some wants, the more readily, from the circumstance. The woman of the house was all assiduity and attention, and it was not long before our supper made its appearance. Our great desire was to dispose of this, and to get quietly into our own rooms, before any more of the rejected travellers should arrive from the other place. None came, however, though we had one or two alarms, and we ate our chickens fried in oil undisturbed. Secure of the supper, we strutted about our *sala*, admiring the novelty of the situation, gazing at the wild waste from the windows, and setting all couriers at defiance.

I have since been told that this very inn was the scene of many robberies and murders that were perpetrated with the connivance of the parish priest, and which were subsequently discovered. The host had however been changed, and we were now in honest hands. Certainly no house could be better situated for deeds of violence; and there was even something in its internal arrangements so retired and gloomy as to aid such practices. Altogether, we enjoyed the excitement of the incidents, preserved our place on the road, had an entire house to ourselves, gained two leagues in distance, and considered ourselves the gainers.

We kept the track in the next day's racing. Much of the way was descending, and the southern faces of the Apennines, like those of the Alps, were more genial and fertile than the northern. I ought to have said that we entered Tuscany near the place where the alarm had been given by the peasant. I shall take this occasion to say that, with a slight exception, on entering France and the Milanese, the custom-house officers have given us no trouble between this and London, although we have passed through eight different states, and entered the ninth. We have uniformly met with civility: nor have the *douceurs* been heavy; and what is more, they have followed, and not preceded, the politeness.

To-day we passed a spot where high poles lined the road; a precaution to enable travellers to keep it, in the deep snows. This was Alpine, and yet the spot was on the brow of the southern margin. We strained our eyes, in the hope of getting a glimpse of the blue Mediterranean, but in vain.

The grasping courier galloped past us again; but we now regarded him and his *bidet* with indifference. The olive soon appeared, a meagre, formal, insignificant tree in a landscape, with a pale and stinted leaf, making altogether a miserable substitute for the apple, though an evergreen. Still one looks at it with pleasure; as one does also at the orange, the pomegranate, the fig, the date, and other trees of Oriental associations, though none but the fig has much beauty. Even the supper of the previous night, though saturated with oil, savoured of Italy, and was so much the more agreeable than the lame imitations of French cookery we had met with previously. Having asked one of my servants how they fared in the mess of old Caspar, she laughed and told me that ever since we had left Berne, the postilions and domestics, out of the large towns, had fared better than the masters; this little attention to the caste of *voituriers* being a tribute to their power. On this hint, I had the curiosity to visit their table, and I found the statement literally true. Old Caspar laughed heartily at the exposure, and altogether the whole party, which included the domestics of two or three other travellers, appeared to think it a capital joke. What renders the palpable conspiracy more absurd, is the fact that the servants figure in the bills for the merest trifles,—at a franc or thirty sous a meal, I believe. On my remarking that the people of the house had made a mistake apparently, having served both us and them with the wrong breakfast, the whole party, my own people included, burst out in a fit of merriment, that showed how much they enjoyed the blunder. *"Ce sont de grands coquins, ces aubergistes, monsieur,"* observed Caspar, by way of apology.

At length we reached a descent that communicated, by a gorge, with the valley of the Arno. Soon after the city of Florence appeared, seated on a plain, at the foot of hills, with the dome of its cathedral starting out of the field of roofs, like a balloon about to ascend. We crossed a part of the plain, between groves of olives and mulberries, went beneath a sort of triumphal arch, erected, I believe, in commemoration of the completion of the great road that we had just been travelling, and entered the gate of the city. A few pauls were given to the custom-house officers, and the carriage rolled freely along the broad flat stones, with which all the towns of Tuscany are paved, the gutter being in the centre of the street. We proceeded to the Hotel York, a house which is so called from the cardinal of that name, took rooms, and unloaded the *fourgon*, for the first time since quitting Berne.

It was but a step to the cathedral square, and I was no sooner dressed than I ran out to feast my eyes with its wonders. The buildings had a mottled look that displeased me, being faced with differently coloured marbles; but the magnitude of the church is imposing. The *campanile* has the same fault; though, a finical thing in itself, it can better bear finery. The baptistery is near by, and altogether the spot has the charms of magnificence sustained by those of association. The servant pointed out a particular stone, on which Dante, it is said, used to seat himself in the cool of the evening, in order to breathe an air less confined than that of the streets.

This night I first learned to respect a musquito. If Buffon had in view the comparative merits of these insects when he broached his theory of the inferiority of the animal nature of America to that of Europe, there is more apology for the extravagance of the supposition than is commonly thought among ourselves. Luckily we had musquito nets,—a thing I never saw at home, by the way,—and though they were full of holes, the creatures were too large to find their way through them. One fellow did get in, however, and he made as much noise as the horn of a mail-coach, at the distance of half a mile. The next morning poor Lucie, who I fancy had no net, looked as if she had the small-pox.

Letter III.

As it was our intention to pass the winter here, old Caspar was discharged, and we took lodgings. Florence is full of noble hotels, which are termed palaces in the language of the country, and few families still retaining a sufficient portion of the ancient wealth to occupy the whole of such huge edifices, apartments are let in them, furnished, or not, as it may happen, on the French plan. Hunting for lodgings gives one a good idea of the domestic economy of a place, for we entered some twenty or thirty of these palaces with this object. Rooms are unusually cheap, notwithstanding the number of strangers who resort to the place, for the town has shrunk to less than half its ancient population, and probably to a tithe of its ancient magnificence.

We become fully impressed with the changes that time produces, not only in things, but in the moral aspect of the world, by seeing a town like Florence. In our age, the man who should dream of making an inland place, in the heart of the Apennines, the focus of trade, would be set down as a simpleton; nor could any powers of combination or of wealth now overcome the efforts of those who would naturally resort to more favourable positions.

These old merchants, however, men who truly ennobled commerce, and not commerce them, have left behind them more durable remains of their ascendency than can be seen in almost any other place. As they were not particularly pacific, the constant struggles of factions in the streets induced a style of architecture that is almost peculiar to Florence, for every palace is a sort of fortress. We took an apartment in one that belongs to an ancient family who still inhabit a portion of the building, and as our rooms are on the street, we may be said to occupy the fortress. The great gate is of iron, and the great stairs, of course, massive and solid. The lower floor is occupied only for the offices and stables. Then comes what is called a *mezzanino*, or a low story, with small windows, but which has some very good rooms. Above this is our apartment, with ceilings nearly twenty feet high, large rooms all *en suite*, and windows to look out of which we ascend two steps. The walls would bear considerable battering, though the position of the house protected it from any danger of such a nature. Forty or fifty stout-hearted retainers, and the number would not be great for the old Florentines, must have been able to stand a respectable siege in such an abode.

You will ask me what are my impressions, on finding myself entrenched behind such works, with a thousand recollections of the Medici and the Strozzi, and the Capponi, to awaken the love of the romantic and interesting? Alas! I am filled with the consciousness of the impotency of man, who, after rearing these piles, and guarding against the violence and ungovernable passions of his fellows, is obliged to allow that all his resources cannot keep out the musquitoes.

We have two noble bed-rooms, besides several smaller; a large drawing-room, and a larger dining-room; a good cabinet for myself; an ante-chamber, and baths, offices, &c.&c. all furnished, for the moderate sum of sixty dollars a month. We have ten good rooms in all, besides the offices.

Our hotel has a small court, and, I believe, a garden; though I have not had access to the latter. By the side of the great gate is a small hole in the wall, closed in general by a shutter. At eleven o'clock every day, people come to this shutter and rap, and it is opened by a steward of the family. The applicant puts in an empty flask and a paul (ten cents), receiving in return a flask filled with wine. In this manner, I understand, most of the great families of Florence now dispose of the products of their vines! It would be curious to learn if the Medici carried on this trade. The wine of our palace is among the best of Tuscany, and I drink it with great satisfaction; the more so because its cost is about four cents the bottle. It is positively much better wine than half the claret that is drunk in Paris. Twice a week, a donkey appears in the court, dragging a little cart filled with flasks from the estate, and carrying away the "dead soldiers." We are, however, a little above the market, as our wine commands fully a cent a flask, or about four mills a bottle, more than most of the Tuscan liquor.

We burn in our lamps oil that you would be happy to get on your lobsters and salads. In other respects the market is good, and cloths are both fine and cheap, finer and cheaper than I remember to have seen them anywhere else, and yet they are imported! The shopkeepers are moderate in their wishes, preferring the *dolce far niente* to the more terrible *energies* of trade.

There is a sleepy indolence in these Italians, that singularly suits my humour. They seem too gentlemanlike to work, or to be fussy, but appear disposed to make a *siesta* of life, and to enjoy the passing moment. The Tuscans seem full of sentiment, and though the poor, as is the case all over the continent of Europe, are very poor, the class immediately above them have as much satisfaction, I fancy, as they who dream dollars and talk dollars from "the rising of the sun unto the going down of the same." If you ask me if I would exchange populations and habits, I shall answer, we cannot afford it. It would check our career short of perfect civilisation. We have arts to acquire, and tastes to form, before we could enter at all into the enjoyments of these people; one half of their pleasures depending on recollections that possibly may have had their origin in the *energies* of the first of the Medici; and there are things that must be created, but which give more satisfaction in after ages than during the period of their formation. For myself, I begin to feel I could be well content to vegetate here for one half my life, to say nothing of the remainder. All who travel know that the greatest pleasure is in the recollections; and I fancy that nations in their decline enjoy more true happiness than nations in their advance.

Of course, I have visited the Venus, and the Pitti, and all the other marvels of art that Florence contains. These things have been so often described, that my remarks shall be limited to such gleanings as others appear to have left, or as are suggested by my own passing feelings. The tribune of the gallery contains the most precious collection of ancient art, perhaps, in the world. Everything in it is a *chef-d'œuvre* in its way; though I am far from seeing the necessity of believing that every old statue that is exhumed is an original. When I was introduced into this place, I felt as if approaching the presence of illustrious personages, and stood, hat in hand, involuntarily bowing to the circle of marble figures that surrounded me, as if they were endowed with sensibilities to appreciate my homage. You are not, however, to suppose that a love of art was so much at the bottom of this reverence, as association. There was a set of engravings in my father's house that represented most of the antique statues, and for these I had imbibed the respect of a child. The forms had become familiar by years of observation, and the Venus, the wrestlers, the dancing faun, and the knife-grinder, four of my oldest acquaintances on paper, now stood before my eyes, looking like living beings.

Florence is walled, but it is in the style of three or four centuries ago, and the defences may be set down as of no account in the warfare of our own times. There is a citadel, however, of a more warlike character, reserved, I suspect, for state purposes. The walls are picturesque, but, failing of the great military object, they are next to useless, as they are not provided with promenades. *Au reste*, they are a little *Jerichoish*, or as I have already described those of Morat to be.

Economy, the galleries, the facility with which one obtains lodgings, caprice, and the court, unite to make Florence a favourite residence with strangers. The court has a little more of air and pretension than it might otherwise possess, from the circumstance of the sovereign being an archduke. Tuscany, however, is a respectable state, having nearly a million and a half of subjects, with Lucca in reversion.

Among the strangers the English and Russians predominate; especially the former, who are found in swarms, on the Continent, in all the most agreeable places of residence. The policy of the Tuscan government encourages diplomatic appointments, and I believe all the great courts of Europe have ministers here. The French, Russians, English, Austrians, and Prussians have ministers plenipotentiaries, and many others *chargés d'affaires*. All these things contribute to render the place gay; nor is it without brilliancy at times, the little court appearing at the festivals and other ceremonies with sufficient pomp. I shall not philosophise on these things, but I fancy they do more good and less harm than is commonly thought by us democrats. I have often compared the *agréments* of this little town with those of one of our own larger cities. New York, which is four times as large as Florence, and ten times as rich, does not possess a tithe—nay, not a hundredth part of its attractions. To say noth-

ing of taste, or of the stores of ancient art, or of the noble palaces and churches, and the other historical monuments, the
circle of living creatures here affords greater sources of amusement and instruction than are to be found in all the five great
American towns put together. Every one appears to be at leisure, and the demon money seems to be forgotten, unless, indeed, he occasionally shows his talons at the gaming-table. An
evening party offers the oddest collection of human beings
imaginable; for the natives of half the civilised countries of the
world appear to have met on neutral ground in this little capital, the government having the liberality to tolerate even men
of political opinions that are elsewhere proscribed. I met at a
soirée, lately, besides a proper sprinkling of Tuscans, and Italians from the other parts of Italy, French, Swiss, Germans from
half a dozen states, English, Russians, Greeks, Americans from
several different countries, Dutch, an Algerine, an Egyptian,
and a Turk. There were, in addition, sundry adventurers from
the islands of the Mediterranean.

This is the age of cosmopolitism, real or pretended; and Florence, just at this moment, is an epitome both of its spirit and of
its representatives. So many people travel, that one is apt to ask
who can be left at home; and some aim at distinction in this era
of migration by making it a point to see everything. Of this
number is a certain Count di V[idua], whom I met in America
just before leaving home. This gentleman went through the
United States, tablets in hand, seeming to be dissatisfied with
himself if he quitted one of our common-place towns with an
hospital unexamined, a mineral unregistered, or a church unentered. It struck me at the time that he was making a toil of
a pleasure, especially in a country that has so little worth examining. But, a short time since, I dined with my banker here. At
table, I was seated between the Marchese G——, a Sardinian,
and the Baron P[oerio], a Neapolitan. Alluding to the locomo-
tive propensities of our times, I mentioned the ardour for
travelling, and the industry I had witnessed in the aforesaid
Count di V[idua]. Signor G—— told me that he knew him intimately, having himself visited all the North of Europe in his
company, previously to which his friend had explored Greece,
Egypt, Northern Africa, and the West of Asia, by himself.
"When he left the United States," continued Signor G——, "it

was to go—where?" "To the West Indies and Mexico." "True; and from the latter he came through Columbia to Brazil, where I was at the time. He left me there to cross the Andes, and I cannot tell you what has become of him."—"Why do you not come to the East Indies?" said an Englishwoman to me the same evening, and to whom I had been introduced as to a lady who lived in that part of the world, but who had taken a run from Calcutta to pass the summer in Switzerland, and the winter in Italy.—"I fancy few mere travellers get as far as Hindostan?"— "Oh, we have them occasionally. Now, the winter before I left home, we had one for several weeks in our own house: he only left us to go to the Himalayah mountains, and return a few months before I sailed."—"An Englishman, of course?"—"No, indeed; an Italian."—"Pray, ma'am, was it Count Carlo di V[idua]?"—"Yes, it was."—"And may I ask what has become of him?"—"He left Calcutta to go to Ceylon and Manilla, on his way to China." So much for our own times!*

The strangers are at the head of the gaiety of this place, few of the Florentines *receiving* much. In this number may be included Prince Borghese, the brother-in-law of Napoleon, an amiable, well-intentioned, and modest man, who has abandoned Rome, his proper country, to reside here, where he maintains a good style, opening his palace periodically for the reception of all who choose to come. Then we have, besides the regular exhibitions of the town, rival houses in two English theatres, with amateur-performers; at the head of one of which is Lord B[urghersh], and at the head of the other Lord N[ormanby]. At the latter only, however, can one be said to see the legitimate drama; the other running rather into music,—an experiment not to be idly attempted in Italy.

We have seen Shakspeare in the hands of these noble actors once or twice, and found the representation neither quite good

---

*This unhappy gentleman subsequently lost his life by falling into a boiling spring in the island of Batavia! He was probably the greatest traveller that ever lived; having, so far as the writer can learn, visited every country in Europe, Persia, Palestine, Egypt, and all northern Africa; nearly, if not every country in America, and most of the East! By adding New Holland and the islands, he would have seen the world.—Would he have been any happier for all his toils and dangers? It may be doubted.

enough to please, nor yet bad enough to laugh at. Occasionally, a character was pretty well represented; but the natural facility of the other sex in acting was sufficiently apparent, the women making out much better than the men. It was like all private theatricals, well enough for a country house, but hardly in its place in the capital of Tuscany. We had a specimen of the feeling of the English towards America, as well as of national manners, the other evening, that is worth a passing notice. One of the players sang, with a good deal of humour, a comic song, that attempted to delineate national traits. There was a verse or two appropriated to the English, the French, the Germans, &c. &c. and the *finale* was an American. The delineations of all the first were common-place enough; the humour consisting chiefly in the mimicry, the ideas themselves having no particular merit. But the verse for the American seemed to be prepared with singular care, and was given with great unction. It represented a quasi Western man, who is made to boast that he is the lad to eat his father, whip his mother, and to achieve other similar notable exploits. I do not know that I am absolutely destitute of an appreciation of wit or humour, but, certainly, it struck me this attempt was utterly without either. It was purely an exaggerated and coarse caricature, positively suited only to the tastes of a gallery in a sea-port town. The other verses had been laughed at, as silly drollery, perhaps; but this was received with—how shall I express it?—a *yell of delight* would not be a term too strong!

No one is more ready to give proper credit to the just-mindedness and liberality of a portion of the English than myself; but the truth would not be told, were I to leave you under the impression that their tone prevails even among the better classes of their society, in relation to ourselves. You will remember that this song was not given to the pit or galleries of an ordinary theatre, but to a society in which there were none beneath the station of gentlemen, and that I should deem this caricature altogether beneath the intelligence and breeding of the company, were it not for the singular rapture with which it was greeted. It is a much more laughable commentary on this extraordinary scene, that, just as it was finished, the Count di—— leaned over and whispered to me that the dislike and "*jealousy*" (I use his own words) of the English for the Americans seemed inappeasable! I observed that the side of the room that was chiefly occupied by the people of rank was mute, the nobles maintaining a cold and polished indifference; but in the other end of the *sala*, which was filled with half-pay officers and the *oi polloi* of the travellers, the *yell* was quite suited to the theme. One might have fancied it the murdered father shrieking under the knife of the parricidal son.

At the *receptions* of Don Camillo Borghese, as the Romans style him, one sees most of the strangers. These entertainments are *dansantes*, and, as the rooms are large and the music noble, they are imposing; though the company is far from being of the purest water. As a proof of this, a noisy party preceded us, the other evening, the young men calling out to each other, "Where is the fat man?"—"Now for the fat man," &c. the prince being almost unwieldy from his size. Waltzes are the favourite dances; though no people know how to waltz but the Germans—or, indeed, to play the necessary airs, but their musicians. It has struck me that I have seen no people who had the organ of *time*, but the Germans and the negroes of America: and a waltz without the utmost accuracy in the movement is a ridiculous dance. I have observed that the young women of condition in France and Italy were not often permitted to join in this dance, by their mothers, with men as partners, unless the latter were near connexions; and as the latter arrangement cannot well be made in a public ball, none joined in the waltzes here.

As a specimen of the sort of *omnium gatherum* that Florence has become, I will give you a list of some of the notables that were seen, recently, in the first row of the Pergola, the principal opera-house, here. First, there was the Count St. Leu, as he is styled, or the ex-king of Holland. Near him was the Prince de Montfort, his brother, or the ex-king of Westphalia. In the same row was Mrs. Patterson, once the wife of the last-named personage. At no great distance was Prince Henry of Prussia, a brother of the reigning king. In the same line, and at no great distance, sat Madame Christophe, ex-empress of Hayti, with a daughter or two. In addition to these, there was a pretty sprinkling of chiefs of revolutions, *littérateurs* of all nations, ex-ambassadors, and politicians *en retraite*, to say nothing of mere people of fashion.

The winter has come upon us sharply, ice forming freely in the ditches around the town, and skates being brought into requisition. I have seen snow impending over us, in falling clouds even, but it vanishes before it reaches the ground: though the Apennines are occasionally powdered. Once, and once only, a little has lain in the streets, but not long enough, or in sufficient quantities, to enable one to say it has covered the stones. Still it is snapping cold, and we find our good wood fires as comfortable as in New York.

Letter IV.

G[OUVERNEUR] W[ILKINS] has been here, and we have made a run together down to the coast. We parted in June last, you will recollect, in Amsterdam, he on his way to Moscow, and we on ours to Rome, where he is likely to arrive before us, as he is off already in that direction, and we still linger here on the banks of the Arno. The little excursion we made together is worthy of a passing word.

We left Florence in W[ilkins]'s carriage, an excellent bachelor-like vehicle, on as cold a noon-tide as one often meets with in New York, even north of the highlands. These Apennines, which form a magnificent backbone for Italy, give the country a great diversity of climate, serving as a wall to heat it in summer, and as repositories of snow to cool it in winter. We were closely curtained and had the glasses up, and went *ventre à terre* over the paved roads, and yet had great difficulty in keeping ourselves warm.

The first halt was at Pistoja, a town of some size, in which we amused ourselves for half-an-hour in looking at a church or two, as well as at some pictures. Taking a little refreshment, we proceeded at the old pace, and drove into the gate of Lucca, just as night had set in. Shivering with cold, for this little capital is in the heart of the mountains, we made our way into a room, and only began to recover the natural hue of our skins, when a dozen cones of the pine, well filled with resin, were in a bright blaze. These and a plentiful supply of faggots brought back the congealed vitality, whose current had almost frozen. A good supper and good beds reconciled us to life.

We were up betimes, and went forth to explore Lucca. The town stands on a plain, a mountain basin, and is walled in a semi-modern fashion. If good for nothing in the way of defence, the ramparts make an excellent promenade. We visited the churches and pictures as usual, and then took a fancy to examine the palace, a long, unornamented edifice in the heart of the place. The duke is travelling, and, pretty much as a matter of course, is out of his own dominions, which, though one of the most populous countries of Europe, possessing three hundred and thirty souls to the square mile, has not one hundred and fifty thousand people. When it is remembered that a large portion of even this small territory is mountain and nearly uninhabited gorges, you may form some notion of the manner in which the little plain itself is peopled. The town has only twenty-two thousand souls; but as we walked on the ramparts and overlooked the adjacent country, it seemed alive with peasants of both sexes, labouring in the fields. They resembled pigeons gleaning a stubble, literally forming lines of twenty or thirty, working with hoes. Indeed, the agriculture was gardening.

Lucca was a republic down to the period of the French Revolution, about which time it was given to his sister Eliza by Napoleon, as a duchy. I believe the palace is owing to her taste, and to the expenditure of an Imperial princess. We found it Parisian in style and arrangement, and in these particulars, I thought, superior even to Windsor. Nature has fitted the French to excel in mantua-making, upholstery, and philosophy.

After passing the morning in this manner, we took flight for Pisa. These republics must have had warm neighbourhoods formerly, for the distance between the two towns is only a single relay. The respective plains are separated by a noble pile of the Apennines, a mountain that is isolated, and which serves admirably as a party-wall between the capitals. The first glimpse we had of Pisa was of its tower and domes, the houses and walls lying so low as scarcely to come into the view. There was a line of respectable aqueduct, leading from the mountain, however, to give notice of the proximity of civilization. The country, too, was fertile and well cultivated, but much less so than that of Lucca.

Pisa is a place to be seen, for it was once of note, and has curious remains of its former power. There is a palace, and the Tuscan court is here at this moment, passing a few weeks in it every winter. The town, notwithstanding, is dull and half-depopulated, noble houses being to be had for prices almost nominal.

The chief interest of Pisa is concentrated in a single corner, where the cathedral, the baptistery, the Campo Santo, and the leaning tower are all to be found within a few feet of each other. They are all within the walls, as indeed is a good deal of vacant ground; both Florence and Pisa, like Rome, appearing to have shrunk from their ancient dimensions.

You probably know that it is a disputed point whether the tower, or *campanile*, was built at its present inclination, or whether it sunk on one side from a defect in the foundations. I shall take side with those who espouse the former opinion. By looking at an engraving you will perceive that this tower is composed of seven distinct compartments, externally, each being ornamented with its own columns. Internally it is merely a circular flight of steps, that lead to the gallery of the bells. Now the four lowest of these compartments lean materially, the two next less, and the last is almost, if not absolutely perpendicular. I think these facts go to show that the tower was built in this form; for had it sunk when only half completed, it is scarcely probable that the artist would have persevered: he would have taken down the materials and laid the foundations anew. Then there is no crack, no dislocation of the columns, not the least derangement of the parts within or without, to denote a violent change of position. The principal reasons for supposing that it has sunk since erected, are the manner in which one side of the foundation appears to be buried, and the fact that there is an ancient painting which represents the tower as upright.

As for the first of these facts, it strikes me that an architect silly enough to erect such a monstrosity would be as likely to begin his folly at the bottom as anywhere else. The painting may be explained. It is a fresco picture of the town, in the cloisters of the Campo Santo, and no part of the tower is represented but the summit, which appears above the adjoining buildings. I have told you already that this summit is perpendicular, or so nearly so as to have that appearance when abstracted from the rest of the tower. Besides, the tower itself leans but one way, and taken in two positions, it of course presents nothing extraordinary. Now the view in the picture is precisely in one of these positions, or *en profil*. You will remember, moreover, that the bit of tower seen in the painting is but small, and that it is an accessory in which foreshortening would not be much attended to had the artist been equal to such an attempt: but, in fact, the whole work is of no great merit, and the entire perspective is indifferent.

I am of opinion that this tower was built as it now stands, until a point was reached where the architect thought it necessary to vary the line, which, it would seem, he did twice before reaching the summit. Caprices of this sort are not unknown; most men, indeed, fancying it a greater achievement of genius to make a thing that is extravagant than a thing whose merit consists in its exquisite fitness. A thousand will exclaim at the manner in which cloth, or a bit of lace, is represented in a picture or a statue, to one who will fully feel the beauty and repose of the expression of either.

The effect of the leaning tower, when standing in the upper gallery, is what one might imagine. It requires a slight effort of reason to look down without a sensation of fear; for it is like looking over a precipice. The view is fine, and for the first time in twenty years I got a sight of the blue waters of the Mediterranean. We saw the island of Gorgona, and overlooked a sea of plain. Had the day been finer, we should have enjoyed the prospect more.

The cathedral is a droll medley of beauty, and of a barbarous taste. The dome struck me as low and mean, and some of the details as good as others are bad. But these are subjects of which I say little, too many folios already existing on such matters. I liked the baptistery very much.

As for the Campo Santo, who has not heard of it? It is contained within cloisters, the monuments being under cover, and the space occupied by the bodies is not larger than a considerable court in a palace. In this place one might pass weeks in agreeable but melancholy contemplation. In the baptistery we saw a priest by the font, muttering something, and drawing near, found he was baptizing a child. Religious rites, under establishments, get to be rather common-place.

There are few spots in Europe of superior interest to this corner of Pisa; and yet there is a little chapel on the quay, called *Santa Maria della Spina*, that is worthy to be here, the tradition running that it is the repository of a thorn from the crown of the Saviour. It is a miniature edifice of marble, and one of the most grotesque little things I have ever seen, in its way; quite equal to the celebrated town-house of Louvain. The style is termed here *il Gotico Moresco*, to distinguish it from *il Tedesco*, or what is here called the German Gothic. There is a good deal of Moorish architecture in Tuscany, or that which approaches it, if not quite pure, the court of the Medici palace at Florence being in this Oriental style. I think it singularly beautiful in its place, especially for cloisters and courts. The chapel in question is of black and white marble,—a taste that suits its general quaintness, but which impairs the majesty of severer architecture.

After passing the night in Pisa, we galloped across the wide plain to Leghorn. The sea-air was grateful, even in winter, and I snuffed the odour of this delightful sea with a delight that was "redolent of joy and youth." We got into a very good inn kept by a Scotchman, and soon exhausted the wonders of the place. It is not easy for one who has not been in Europe to appreciate the difference that exists between its capitals and its commercial towns. Leghorn is rather an interesting town, and has even a few respectable points of poetic interest; but it had an atmosphere of trade, that struck us forcibly on entering it. It has canals within the walls, is fortified, and has some very good streets.

We ordered dinner, and hurried off to the port. Here we feasted our eyes on the different picturesque rigs and peculiar barks of this poetical sea. Long years had gone by since I had seen the felucca, the polacre, the xebec and the speronara, and all the other quaint-looking craft of the Mediterranean: for, whatever may be said of the utilitarian qualities of our own vessels, poetry has had no more to do with them than it has had to do with anything else in the land. I do not believe we are without poetic feeling as a people; but we are sadly deficient in the ordinary appliances of the art. As we strolled along the mole and quays, we met several men from the Levant; and an Algerine Rais was calmly smoking his *chibouque* on the deck of his polacre.

Observing the eagerness with which I surveyed these objects, our *laquais de place* declared, it was a pity we had not been in Leghorn ten days earlier, as we might then have found a ship worth seeing, the Delaware, American man-of-war. We sneered at this information, and asked him what a people like the Americans could produce that was worth examining? "I thought so

too, gentlemen," he answered; "but the Delaware was the finest
ship that has ever been at Leghorn, as every one admits." "Of
course her crew were black?" "Not so, signore: *I expected that too;*
but they were all as white as we are:" which perhaps was not so
literally true.

The only people in Europe who have a respectful opinion
of the Americans are those who see their ships: and these are
getting to entertain notions that are a little extravagant the
wrong way.

Leghorn was the first sea-port that I had entered since leaving Holland, and its delicious odours were inhaled with a delight that no language can describe. I had been living in an atmosphere of poetry for many months, and this was truly an
atmosphere of life. The fragrance of the bales of merchandize,
of the piles of oranges—of even the mud, saturated as it was
with salt—to say nothing of the high seasoning of occasional
breathings of tar and pitch, to me were pregnant "with odours
of delight." Still I found that residences in European capitals,
and among the Alps and Apennines, is creating a strong dis-
taste for all the more common appliances of commerce. Leghorn seemed vulgar and mean, after Florence, with its pretty
little court, its museums and its refinements; and the only
things that interested us were the sea, the port, the picturesque
vessels, the fragrance, and a cemetery for the Protestant dead.

The island of Gorgona was looming in the haze, a hummock
of rock, and it is said there are days on which the mountains of
Corsica are visible from the mole. There is also a noble dark
pile at no great distance from the town, which is, appropriately
enough, called Monte Nero. Its side is garnished with country-
houses, and there is a church near its summit that is in great
repute among mariners, as a shrine at which offerings are to be
made for deliveries from the casualties of the sea: I believe its
name is that of Our Lady of the Storms. These Catholics have
certainly got all the poetry of the religion.

We went to the Protestant cemetery, which contains many
American graves, and among others that of Captain Gamble,
who died here, in command of the Erie, about ten years ago.
This gentleman, one of four brothers in the service, had been
my messmate on Lake Ontario some twenty years before, and it
was startling to find myself unexpectedly standing over his

grave in the other hemisphere. On examining the monuments near, I was still more startled at reading the name of "Tobias Smollett" on one of them. He is known to have come to Italy to terminate his worldly career. The "Siste Viator" applies with force to those who speak English, and who find themselves unexpectedly standing over such a grave!

We soon exhausted the sights of Leghorn and returned to Pisa, where we slept. The weather was intensely cold, and we sat shivering over a bad fire until it was time to retire. I would advise no consumptive person to come to Italy, in the expectation of finding a more genial climate than can be got in America. The West Indies offer many more suitable spots for the malady; and a man of science at Paris has told me that the temperature of St. Augustine is known to be more mild and equal than that of any other place in the world, of which there are authentic journals of the changes of weather. Every one here tells me that the patients usually come to die; a fact to which the Leghorn cemetery bears ample testimony. It were a worthy object for the government to push St. Augustine, if for no other purpose than to render it comfortable to invalids.

The next day we returned to Florence, by the great route, reaching the gates of the town in time to dine. The weather had become more mild, and we were struck with the beauty of the peasant girls, many of whom were sitting in the sun, and a fair proportion of whom had pretensions to some of that pastoral prettiness of which the poets delight to speak. These were the first females of the class, however, that had the smallest claims to beauty, which it had been my good fortune to meet with in Europe, out of England. Hitherto I had seen occasional exceptions, but on this road we actually met with rural beauties in crowds. I attribute the circumstance to their employment; for most of them were plaiting straw for hats.

Letter V.

A LITTLE circumstance that is scarce worth mentioning has drawn me from my privacy, and induced me to appear at the court of Tuscany. When the resolution to be presented, was taken, a letter was addressed to the great chamberlain, with a request to have an audience of the grand duke, and of the princesses of the family, of whom there are three of an age to have establishments; and I received an answer that I should be presented on the occasion of a festival that was at hand, when there was to be a grand drawing-room. Accordingly, the sword, and steel buttons, and lace were early provided; for I was given to understand that these were indispensable paraphernalia. Were the thing to be done over again, I should ask permission to appear in the full dress of my own country: for if a Turk can be received in this manner, why not an American? My attire, however, was not much out of the ordinary way, being merely a black coat, breeches, and vest, with lace at the cuffs and frills, steel buttons and a sword, with a dress hat. Still, I make no doubt, had a proper representation been made, I might have been received precisely as one goes to the White House; for the rule is, that each person shall appear in the full dress of his own country.

As we have no minister in Italy, I escaped the necessity of offering an apparent slight; for in no ordinary circumstances would I be presented by an American minister: it is not his duty, and one can get along quite as well without him as with him. I did think of asking the minister of Russia to do me this favour, for he would have been the most natural substitute for one of our own; but, on reflection, I determined to put myself altogether in the hands of the regular officer of the court.

The great chamberlain, the Marchese Corsi, had directed me to be at the Pitti at an early hour in the evening, where I was to inquire for him. The King of England is lodged much less like a monarch than the Grand Duke of Tuscany, who inhabits a palace fit for an emperor, although it was originally constructed, or rather commenced, by a merchant. As every one is admitted to see its pictures, I had often been in the building; but this was the first occasion on which I had entered the regular reception-rooms.

Of course I was punctual, and on ascending the great stairs, I found them, the galleries, and the ante-chambers crowded with lackeys in the royal liveries. Beyond these, again, was a party of the noble guards, a sort of *gardes du corps;* and still farther in advance, was a room in which the young pages of honour, sons of the first houses of Tuscany, were amusing themselves after the fashion of their time of life, with certain practical jokes on each other. One of these was the young Baron [Ricasoli], the owner of our own palazzo, and, although just at the moment he was very busy in exercising his wit on one of his companions, he no sooner recognised me, than he good-naturedly abandoned his fun to come and offer his services. I told him I wished to find the Marchese Corsi, and he pointed to one of the chamberlains of the court as the person to whom I ought to apply.

I saw through the long vista of rooms, that a crowd was present, and that everybody was in high dress. The chamberlain to whom I applied was in scarlet, and seemed to be in waiting for stray courtiers like myself. As soon as I preferred my request to be conducted to Signor Corsi, he asked me, with a little point of manner, if I were an American. The answer was in the affirmative, of course, and, for a rarity, my national character appeared to be in my favour. This gentleman very obligingly led the way through two or three large rooms full of courtiers, and presented me to the grand chamberlain, who was in a small apartment that contained merely a dozen people. After a short conversation, I was desired to wait a little, for the appearance of the royal family. On looking round, I perceived that my companions were the secretaries of the different legations, and as I knew several of them, we fell into discourse. I observed that my presence caused a little surprise, and apprehensive that it was my duty to retire to the crowd in the outer room, I took an opportunity to question an English acquaintance on the subject. From this gentleman I learned that my presence in this particular room was a little out of rule. He said this delicately, but with sufficient distinctness. The family was in an apartment still further removed from the crowd, where it was in the practice of receiving the heads of the different legations; and the subordinates, with the ministers of state, had their place in the little room in which we then were. My informant added, that several of his countrymen were among the courtiers, waiting to be presented. This information was no sooner obtained, than, supposing I had misunderstood M. Corsi, I withdrew.

In a minute, however, I was summoned back to the side of the great chamberlain, who told me that the grand duke was about to enter the room. I explained my error, by intimating that I had been led to suppose myself where I ought not to be. On this hint, the great chamberlain indirectly, but very politely, gave me to understand that *he* was master of the ceremonies at the court of Tuscany, and no one else. Of course I had no objection to make, and was resigned to my honour. But at this moment the Count Fossombrone, the first minister of state, a respectable old man of an excellent character, entered, and took his station near the door. The rest of us were ranged in a circle, the Marchese Corsi nearest to the premier, and I at his elbow.

You probably know that the Grand Duke of Tuscany is also an Austrian Archduke. The scale is so graduated, that I believe he ranks higher, as a cadet of the Imperial House, than as sovereign of this beautiful and respectable little state. At any rate, his usual style is that of His Imperial and Royal Highness, Leopold, &c. &c. His sister and daughters are also styled Archduchesses; although the latter are as yet mere children.

Tuscany came into the possession of the House of Austria by an arrangement with France. At the death of John Gaston, the last of the Medici, in 1737, Louis XV. succeeded, as the descendant of Maria di Medici, the wife of Henry IV. About the same time, Francis, the reigning Duke of Lorraine, had married the heiress of the Hapsbourgs, and was elected Emperor of Germany. Lorraine lying within the Rhine, at a short distance from Paris, and since the conquest of Alsace actually *enclavé* by the French territory, it was very desirable to possess it. The death of John Gaston offered a favourable occasion, and the family of Lorraine, durably transferred to the thrones of Austria, consented to exchange its ancient states for those of Tuscany. As regards extent and richness of territory and population, France made a hard bargain; but high political considerations balanced the account. Tuscany was remote, while the possession of Lorraine threw back the eastern and most vulnerable frontier of the kingdom at once to the Rhine. The marriage of Francis, moreover, would have left the future head of the House of Austria in occupation of a territory almost in the heart of France, without this arrangement, or a violent seizure. France stipulated that Tuscany should never be merged in Austria, as a state, however, but that it should be governed by a cadet of the family. Thus, when Joseph II. died without issue and was succeeded by his brother Leopold, then Grand Duke of Tuscany, the second son of the latter, Ferdinand, became sovereign of Tuscany. His son Leopold II. is the reigning duke; and, of course, he is a nephew of the emperor, and stands next in succession to the Imperial throne, after the two sons of the emperor, and before the Archdukes Charles, John, Regnier, Anthony, &c. &c. &c. Thus, though we are about to see the sovereign of Tuscany, it is an event by no means improbable that he may one day become Emperor of Austria, as happened to his grandfather, and predecessor in the grand duchy.

I had hardly come to an understanding with the Signor Corsi, when the members of the family entered the little room in which we were ranged. The grand duke, a man of good stature and of an amiable countenance, came first. He was dressed in the uniform of an Austrian officer, or in a white coat and scarlet pantaloons, embroidered in gold, with military boots; and he wore the star and badge of the Golden Fleece, &c. He appeared to be about thirty.

On entering the room he addressed himself to Count Fossombrone, his minister, with whom he conversed a few minutes. He then turned with a look of inquiry to the Marchese Corsi, who made a sign to me, mentioned my name, and retired a few steps. The conversation lasted about five minutes, commencing with the usual questions as to my route, the length of time I had been in Florence, and civil expressions of satisfaction at seeing me at his court: it was held in French. The grand duke left on my mind a strong impression of integrity of character; a quality far more to be prized than any other. One proof of the simplicity and justness of his mind was so striking, and so very different from what I had just escaped from in Paris, that it deserves to be recorded. "They tell me you are the author of many books," he said; "but as it has never been my good fortune to meet with them, I can say no more to you on the subject, than that I have heard them well spoken of by those who have." Here was a civil thing, united with an honesty that did equal credit to his tact and his truth. He left me with renewed expressions of his satisfaction at seeing me at his court, and then made the circuit of the secretaries and *attachés*.

While the grand duke was talking to me, the two grand duchesses, and the Archduchess Louisa, appeared in the room. I say, the grand duchesses; for there is a dowager as well as a reigning grand duchess. These ladies are sisters, and nieces of the King of Saxony, the eldest having married the late grand duke, not long before his death, and being childless. The three followed each other, speaking in succession to those who had been previously addressed by the grand duke, and waiting until he had done. As our conversation had lasted a little longer than common, the three princesses were standing in a line behind the grand duke, when the latter left me. They were all in high court dresses, and had their trains borne by chamberlains.

Each of the princesses spoke to Count Fossombrone, in passing; and when the grand duke moved on, the reigning grand duchess approached me. There was no introduction in words, M. Corsi merely bowing towards me, to prevent any mistake. I dare say you think I now got some compliments on a work of fiction or two: no such thing—the subject was not alluded to by either of the princesses. They had treated letters with high distinction, by the especial notice they conferred; for, as I afterwards understood, the outer rooms were filled with men of rank waiting to be presented; but they avoided all allusion to the subject. With the two grand duchesses I had, for the circumstances, a good deal of conversation, and one of them quite won my heart by the manner in which she alluded to my children, of whom she had accidentally heard something. The archduchess said least; but the two grand duchesses were not only disposed to talk, but were everything that was amiable.

I had a droll specimen of the influence of favour on this occasion: for the family had no sooner passed on, than I had to receive nearly the whole diplomatic corps; the rays of royalty

illuminating the secondary planets as the moon receives brilliancy from the sun.

The rest of the reception was conducted in the same mode,
the grand duke going through all the rooms; but the ladies
were less particular. The latter sat down to cards; where I observed that the refreshments they received were taken from the
pages, and handed to them by the chamberlains.

Among the company was M. Eynard, the celebrated Swiss
Hellenist. He wore the military jacket of the Swiss militia, with
a Greek cross on the sleeve. There were several Englishmen of
rank present, in yeomanry uniforms; and one, Lord——, told
me his was that of a lieutenancy in the militia—an office he had
formerly held. I mention these things, as so much misconception
exists in America on the subject. The wisest way to go to court,
here, would be to go in the full dress of Washington; but nothing is in better taste than to go in a militia uniform, if one happened to be entitled to wear it. The mistake is in flourishing
these *quasi* military titles on the card, and in ordinary life, and
in believing they are out of place on occasions like this. We get
most of these things *sens dessus-dessous*, and fancy ourselves criti-
cally right, when we are singularly wrong. The well-known
story of Napoleon and General —— *may* be true, but I greatly
question it, as it is opposed to the spirit of European feeling;
and it sounds very much like one of those inventions that float
about American society, and are taken for gospel. I have known
a dozen similar tales, in great vogue, which are certainly false.
Ignorance of European life is so very general in America, and
the susceptibility to European opinion so very keen, that we are
to make great allowances for what is rumoured in such matters.

After remaining some time in the drawing-room, I was stealing off; when I perceived the grand duke moving slowly towards me, followed by a large circle of courtiers. I got into an
angle of the room that happened to be empty at the moment,
and close to a door, thinking I should be passed unseen, as I did
not like the appearance of pushing myself on his notice, after
the extreme civility of the first reception. With such an intention, however, a worse position could not have been taken; for
on entering the room, happening to glance his eye aside, the
grand duke saw me, and turning short, I was literally cornered.
Those who kept near the person of their sovereign, some fifty

in all, formed a semicircle, extending from the outer side of the door across the room, and we were left alone, literally in the corner. At first, the grand duke had his back turned towards the rest of the company; but recollecting the awkwardness of the position, he changed it so as to face his subjects.

The conversation lasted, I should think, twenty minutes. His imperial highness was very curious as to America, and though there were great modesty and politeness, mingled with a singular and commendable sincerity, in his manner, he asked a hundred questions, while, of course, I did nothing but answer them. He inquired into the number and size of our towns, the habits of the people, and the general state of the country. Some of his notions were, as usual with most Europeans, vague and false; but, on the whole, he appeared to me to know more about us than most of even the learned in this hemisphere. His geographical attainments struck me as being very respectable; and what gave me more satisfaction than anything else, was the simple integrity apparent in all his sentiments.

The Osages had passed through Florence not long before, and had been fêted and fed, as at Paris. The grand duke inquired if I had seen them, and, on being answered in the affirmative, he wished to know whether I believed them to be chiefs of importance in their tribe, and enquired their motive in coming to Europe. Now, it would not be agreeable for one who fancied he had seen a hero, to hear he had only seen a common man,—or who thought he was entertaining a saint, to discover that his attentions were lavished on a sinner. But catching some of the sincerity of the grand duke, I told him what I really thought: viz. that these savages could not well be principal chiefs, as the agent of our government would scarcely permit such to visit Europe; and that I believed the whole thing to have no connexion whatever with religious conversion, but to be merely a speculation of the Frenchman who managed the affair. This explanation was taken in good part, and I thought the grand duke had even anticipated some such reply. Princes so seldom get truth, that its novelty sometimes pleases them.

With one of his questions, which was personal to myself, I was both startled and amused. *"De quel pays êtes vous, vraiment?"* he asked, laying particular emphasis on the last word. Had he not discovered too much knowledge of America previously, I might have suspected the old difficulty of colour was a stumbling-block; but as this was out of the question, suspicion was drawn another way. I believe the simple solution of this unusual question to be as follows:—Not long before, I had taken an opportunity to expose the motives and policy that had given rise to the systematic and enduring abuse of the English press on America. Any one might have accomplished this duty, for such it had actually become; but, favoured by circumstances, my own publication had made its way in Europe, where most American books would never have penetrated. As a matter of course, I had been blackguarded,—for the Anglo-Saxon race seems to take natural refuge in blackguarding when it can neither refute nor disprove. By way of weakening my testimony, a report had been industriously circulated that I was a renegado Englishman, and an honest indignation for unmerited national calumny was ingeniously imputed to personal disaffection and personal discontent. As half-a-dozen of these rumours had fallen under my eyes in the public journals, I was at no loss to understand the drift of the grand duke's inquiry; and this the more especially, as he awaited the answer with evident curiosity. Determined to set him right on this subject, which if of no importance to the state of Tuscany, was of some importance to myself, I told him, with commendable particularity, I was a native of the small state of New Jersey, a territory lying between the two great states of Pennsylvania and New York; though a citizen of the latter from infancy. He wished to know if New Jersey was an original state, and whether my father had not been an Englishman. On this hint, I added, that my family had migrated to America, in 1679, from England certainly, but I had every reason to believe that I was the first member of it, in the direct line, who had been out of the country since; and, moreover, that Pennsylvania, New Jersey, and New York were original states in the heart of America, and that more than a hundred men of my name and blood were at this moment among their citizens. I believe this satisfied the grand duke: for so general is the disgust created by the English system of calumniating, that I have often had occasion to observe that the inhabitants of other countries are usually pleased to find the islanders put in the wrong.

It was not an easy matter to answer all the questions of this prince without misleading him, for etiquette prevented more than direct and brief replies. He was curious on the subject of luxury, and had many exaggerated notions concerning the magnificence of our nation. He seemed surprised when I told him we had no scenery to compare with that of the Mediterranean, and that nearly all of the American coast, in particular, was tame and uninteresting.—"But your lakes?"—"Are large, sir, without question; but so large as to resemble views of the ocean, and with coasts that are far from striking. We have many beautiful little lakes, it is true, but nothing to compare with those of Italy and Switzerland."—"Your rivers?"—"Are large and beautiful."—"And your mountains?"—"Are much inferior to those of Tuscany, even."

But I cannot recall all that passed in this long conversation, of whose outline, rather than of its details, I have endeavoured to give you some idea. It terminated with the usual expressions of civility on the part of the grand duke, and the hope that Tuscany would prove an agreeable residence to us. Throughout the entire evening, I was under the impression that I had been treated with more than usual distinction, on account of my country; a source of distinction so very novel in Europe, that I deem it worthy of being recorded.

Like most of the Austrian family, Leopold II. is a man of kind heart and affections, and, I believe, a strictly honest prince. In many public acts it becomes necessary to separate the absolute sovereign from the individual; though the world is constantly guilty of the injustice of confounding them, while it is apt to overlook the divided responsibilities of aristocracies;— a polity that probably works more positive wrong than any other, since a large part of the crimes of despotisms are merely excesses of those in places of trust. But Tuscany is a mildly governed country, and though it cannot be free from the vices of a *want* of publicity, it is free from their opposite—the vice of a too great publicity, or that of confounding the necessities of the community with the rights of individuals. The most insidious enemy of monarchy is aristocracy, which destroys while it pretends to support. Still, it is the natural goal of every nobility, and it has struck me there is a secret instinct which teaches this important truth to the sovereigns of our time. A country may be so far advanced as to wish for democracy; but this is the fact under few despotic governments; while all the nobles of Europe pine to become political, or true, as well as social aristocrats. In such a state of things, there is nothing violent in supposing that an absolute prince would regard an aristocrat with more distrust than he regards a democrat; for the polity of the former is an impossibility to him, while there is a constant and natural gravitation towards the latter. At all events, in my own intercourse with princes and aristocrats, I think I have discovered in the former greater liberality, a more confirmed deference for the facts of a country and less theoretical ardour in favour of systems, a higher tone of philosophy with less apparent selfishness, than in the latter, considering the aristocrats as a body, and not regarding the occasional brilliant exceptions. As respects affability and absence of hauteur, the advantage is altogether with the prince, for it depends on a law of nature. I believe, that as we are farther removed from competition and jealousy, the greater the spirit of humanity and charity becomes.

Letter VI.

THE carnival commenced early this year, and we have now been a month occupied with its harmless follies and gaieties. Our little capital has shone forth in new colours, and a round of masked balls, at the different legations, has been one of the principal sources of amusement. I was present at the one given by M. de Vitrolles, the minister of France, and shall describe it, in a few words, that you may form some idea of the manner in which these things are managed in Italy.

Although a mask is not indispensable, one is expected to wear some symbol of the folly of the hour. I was told that a little silk cloak, that fell no lower than the elbows, lined with red, and furnished with tassels, was much used by the *juste milieu*, and was the very minimum of admissible costume. Provided with one of these, then, and otherwise dressed as usual, I presented myself among the crowd at the "*Hôtel de France.*"

Perhaps half the company was masked; the rest appearing in every sort of dress that fancy, usage, or caprice dictated. A town like Florence offers, on such an occasion, a greater variety of national costumes than one of the larger capitals; for the society is more than half composed of travellers, who come from all the countries of Christendom. The ball-room, as a matter of course, presented a brilliant *coup d'œil*, the more especially as all the women were in high fancy-dresses. There was the usual sprinkling of Greeks, Egyptians, Turks, and magnificos, with a large proportion of *bonâ fide* military uniforms. Among others, I saw an Englishman of my acquaintance, a Sir —— ——, in a coat of a cut that reminded one of the last century. On inquiry, he told me that he had belonged to the guards in his youth, and that he never travelled without his old coat, which he found still very useful on occasions like the present. This is the sensible mode of getting along; but our provincial sensitiveness makes us afraid of a militia uniform. Lord —— was also here, in his jacket, as a lieutenant of yeomanry. Again, in the course of the evening, a group of Englishmen collected in the centre of the room, and began to talk of their own country. They were all in uniforms, perhaps ten of them, and all belonged to what they called "the household brigade." The rest of the company shrugged their shoulders at this invasion of the English guards, which was not exactly in good taste; but a cluster of finer young men could not easily have been found. Several of them were six feet two or three, and among the Italians they looked like giants. It resembled a ring of our own Western boys, for a novelty, well dressed.

Soon after the company had assembled, a party appeared beautifully attired in the Polish costume, and danced a polonaise. Both the men and women wore boots, and the dresses were singularly striking. The movement of the dance was slow, and had some slight resemblance to that of a quadrille, though it was much more German and theatrical. The dancers were chiefly Italians; but the master of ceremonies was, I believe, a Pole.

After I had been some time in the room, I found I was the object of general attention. Every one turned round to look at me, until, suspecting something was wrong, I asked an acquaintance what could be the cause of so much and so unusual observation. "You have no cloak," he answered. Sure enough, the apology for a costume that had been thrown over my shoulders had fallen; and the want of it, in that assembly, was just as much a matter of surprise, as wearing it would have been under other circumstances.

"*Vive la folie, mon cher!*" cried the eloquent Baron ——, as he saw me pick up the fallen garment; "*il faut être aussi fou que le reste du monde, ce soir.*" This gentleman was enveloped in a white domino, without a mask; his fine Neapolitan eye rolling over the scene, like one who enjoyed its gaiety. The blending of colours formed one of the attractions of the evening, the white dominos, in particular, greatly aiding the effect.

Looking over the company, I was led to speculate on the probable consequences of the extraordinary blending of nations, that is the consequence of the present condition of Europe. Fifty years since, none but the noble and rich travelled; and even of this class, not one in ten could fairly be said to have seen the world. At that time, the Alps were crossed only with difficulty, and at a heavy expense; and the roads and inns, generally, were so bad, that a journey from Paris to Rome was a serious undertaking, and a residence in either town involved a total change of habits for the inhabitant of the other. To-night a young Englishman of my acquaintance civilly asked me if he could do anything for me in London. "I'm going to take a run home for a month or six weeks," he added, "and shall be back before you go farther south." He thought little more of the journey than we think of an excursion from New York to Washington. His father would have taken more time to prepare for such a journey, than the son will consume in making it.

One evident and beneficial effect of this commingling is certainly the general advancement of intelligence, the wearing down of prejudices, and the prevalence of a more philosophic spirit than of old. In a society where representatives from all the enlightened nations of the world are assembled, a man must be worse than a block if he do not acquire materials worth retaining; for no people is so civilized as to be perfect, and few so degraded as not to possess something worthy to be imparted to others.

It would be morally impossible for Europe to retrograde to the coarseness and open oppression that existed eighty years since, without the occurrence of some violent revolution: nor is it any longer easy for any particular community so far to isolate itself from the general sisterhood of states, as to retain many of the flagrant abuses that outrage the spirit of the age. There is still something to gain in these particulars, beyond a doubt; but the progress is steadily onward, and twenty years more of peace and of continued intercourse will create a standard of moral civilization below which no people can fall and keep its place in the scale of nations. This is the right sort of public opinion; not one which invades the sacred precincts of private life, subjecting the sentiments and actions of individuals to the supervision of a neighbourhood, and giving birth to a wrong as great as any it removes,—but a controlling judgment that settles great principles, and throws its shield before the wronged and the feeble —a public opinion that benefits all without doing injustice to any. In this respect, Europe enjoys an immense advantage, from which we are almost entirely excluded by position. I think the effect very apparent, when one comes to analyze the modes of thinking of the two hemispheres; and in nothing is this effect more obvious than in the circumstance to which I have had occasion so often to allude in these letters, of the manner in which opinion precedes facts here, and facts precede opinion with us. This, after all, when one has made a proper allowance for the influence of time on physical things, is the great distinctive feature between the people of most of Europe and the people of America.

We have the carnival in the streets as well as in the palaces, and most of all in the theatres. Balls are given nearly every night in some one of these public places, and I have been to two or three in masks, but always in domino. On several of these occasions I have attempted to mystify countrymen of our own; but Jonathan is usually as innocent of joking as he is of Hebrew. One evening I attempted a conversation with a tall Yankee, whom I had seen before, and succeeded in getting him a little aloof from the company; when he started up suddenly from his seat, and plunged into the crowd, leaving me delighted with the success of my awful communications. You will judge of my astonishment at hearing him tell a mutual friend next day of the abrupt manner in which he had escaped some impudent trull, who had endeavoured to get him beneath *a chandelier where the grease might fall on his new coat*—a plot of which I solemnly assert my innocence. My greasy friend was revenged by a party which got round me, and quizzed me at such a rate, that I took shelter from them, by putting my mask in my pocket, and going into the box of the Count St. Leu, who was not in mask. My tormentors, however, were not to be driven off so easily; for two of them followed me, keeping up a round of pleasantries about America and the Indians until I was glad to be quit of them. Later in the evening, one of these gentry met me in the crowd, and removing his mask a little, he showed me the face of Prince Napoleon Bonaparte, the eldest son of the count—a young man of great personal beauty and of singular cleverness. I masked again, and we took a seat apart, and began to discuss the usages of our respective countries. Both agreed that the world was little more than a masquerade, and my companion related the following anecdote, among other things, as a proof of the truth of our truisms.

You will remember that when King Louis abdicated the throne of Holland, it was in favour of this very son, who was a titular monarch for the few days that intervened between the retirement of his father and the incorporation of the country with France. Though a mere boy, he was condemned to listen to many congratulatory addresses on his accession, his whole reign being distinguished by little else. One morning he was required to receive a deputation, just as he had prepared to discuss a quantity of *bons-bons*, on which he had set his heart, and of which he was particularly fond. While the courtier was dwelling on the virtues of the retired monarch, the weight of his loss (that of the *bons-bons*) oppressed him even to tears; and "you will judge of my surprise," he added, laughing, "at hearing all the courtiers bursting out in exclamations of delight *at the excellence of my heart*, when I expected nothing better than a severe rebuke for my babyism!" This, he said good-humouredly, was the first of his masquerades.

1. *Florence*, drawn by William Callow and engraved by E. Brandard

11. *Dream of Arcadia* (c. 1838) by Thomas Cole

III. *Bandits on a Rocky Coast* (17th c.) by Salvator Rosa

iv. *Entrance to Sorrento*, drawn by James D. Harding and engraved by
S. Fisher

Letter VII.

A SUDDEN call drew me from Florence during the carnival, and put me unexpectedly on the road to Paris. As I went alone, I took the mail, or *malle-poste;* a species of travelling in great request for those who are in a hurry. The mail is always attended by a guard, who accompanies it from one great town to another. His duty it is to see it properly delivered by the way, and to receive contributions that offer on the route. The contractor is permitted to take one or two travellers in his carriage, which is purposely disposed so as to receive them.

I took my place accordingly as far as Genoa, and we left Florence just as the sun was setting, with our lamps lighted. As we drove through the gate of Pisa, I observed a dragoon dashing along, on each side of us, and was then told that frequent robberies had rendered this escort necessary, until we got out of Lucca. There was a *contadino* inside, a respectable farmer, who was going a post or two down the Arno, and his eye glistened with delight as he regarded the dragoons. "Those are the boys, signore," he observed to me. "Nineteen of them put five hundred Neapolitans to flight here during the late wars." I wonder if there be a people on the globe that does not think itself the salt of the earth! Near Salins, last year, as we approached Switzerland, the postilion gravely pointed to a fort, which he affirmed had surrendered to five-and-twenty French, though garrisoned by two hundred Austrians. One can hear of such prodigies anywhere, though they are obstinately uncommon in practice, "even Providence," as Frederick expressed it, "being usually on the side of strong battalions."

We drove through Pisa at midnight, and reached Lucca before day. On the confines of this little territory we got some beautiful scenery, the road descending and climbing *à la Suisse*, offering occasional glimpses of the sea. Massa, the capital of the duchy of that name, was little more than a straggling village, seated on a hill-side, but picturesque and Italian; and Carrara, which aspires to the title of a principality, and which is so well known for its statuary marble, is not much more. Both the small states belong to the Duchess Dowager of Modena, and at her death will come under the government of the Duke of Modena, extending his possessions, which already join them, to the sea.

Here the Apennines approached the Mediterranean, until we soon saw their noble piles forming capes and headlands, impending over the blue element. It was altogether a wild and picturesque road, running among and over mountains, along the margin of torrents and through frowning gorges, with occasional openings toward the Mediterranean, that seemed like the breaking away of clouds in winter. One of the most extraordinary features of the scenery was the manner in which grey villages were stuck like wasps' nests against the acclivities, resembling romantic structures placed in the most picturesque positions on purpose to produce an effect. Fifty of these dusky hamlets rose like bas-reliefs, or embossings, from the brown sides of the mountains; and some of them seemed perched on pinnacles that the foot of man could hardly scale. I had never before seen anything, in its way, half so wild and romantic as the rustic hamlets in the distance; though a few that we entered completely destroyed the charm on the near view.

At Spezzia an indentation of the coast brought our carriage-wheels fairly into the water; and after this we began to ascend. Just as night closed, we were buried in the mountains, and I composed myself to sleep. A jog from the *conducteur* awoke me, while we were driving through a gallery that equalled the boasted cuttings of the Simplon. Looking out, I found we were on the coast again; and passing village after village in quick succession, we reached the gates of Genoa, amid a crowd of donkeys, and of market-people of both sexes, who profited by our arrival to enter the town.

You are to remember that I have promised nothing but the gleanings that are to be had after the harvests gathered by those who have gone before me. My task, therefore, is less one of minute and close description, than of desultory findings. This peculiarity may cause occasional meagreness of facts, and some apparent eccentricities of thought; for while I pretend to have gathered no more of what has been left by others than has come in my way, most of what I have actually seen is necessarily un-recorded, and matters of opinion are commonly uttered when I have found reason to differ from the multitude.

At Genoa I remained two days. To the peculiar attractions of a port, and that too a port of the Mediterranean, were added the magnificence and glories of a capital. Every one has read of the palaces of this town, the *Strada Balbi* probably having no equal, in its way, in any other European capital. It is not wide, is without side-walks, and but for the structures that line its two sides, would offer nothing remarkable. For more than a mile, however, it is a succession of edifices, that, in any other country but Italy, would be deemed fit for royalty. The Faubourg St. Germain has more large hotels, certainly; but the architecture is better here, and the material much superior to that in use in France. I should think that in the material point of gardens, the French capital has greatly the advantage. I entered several of these fine houses, which were generally remarkable for their marbles, staircases, and paintings. That of Serra is known all over Europe for a saloon that is covered with mirrors which reflect its half columns in a way to give it the air of a fairy palace. This room, when well lighted, must present an extraordinary sight; though it is rather small for its style of ornament. I have seen many rooms decorated in this mode, but never one with the blended magnificence and simplicity that are to be observed here. Generally the effect has been that of a toy,—a sort of German prettiness, or German conceit; but there was none of this in the Serra palace. The master of this noble house is not *compos mentis*, though quiet and harmless. He was seated over a brazier, in an ante-chamber, in the company of the ladies, as I passed through; and he rose politely to return my bow, muttering some words of compliment. It may be that he has a simple satisfaction in this amusement, but it struck me painfully. The antics of the carnival were acting in this fine street.

I saw the palace of the King, and some of the pictures; that of the Feast of Cana in particular. But the town, the scenery, and the port most attracted me. Genoa lies at the base of a hill, around the head of a large cove, which has been converted into a fine harbour by means of two moles. One quarter of the town actually stands on low cliffs that are washed by the sea, which must sometimes throw its spray into the streets. Its position con-

sequently unites the several beauties of a gorgeous capital with
all its works of art, the movement and bustle of a port, the view
of a sea with passing ships and its varying aspects of calms and
tempests, with a background of stupendous hills;—for at this
point the Alps send out those grand accessories to their magnificence, the Apennines. The place is fortified, and the nature of
the ground requiring that the adjacent hill should be included,
the *enceinte* is large enough to contain all Paris. On the side of
the cliffs and at the moles, are water batteries; the entire port is
separated from the town by a high wall, which, while it does little more in the way of defence than protect the revenue, offers
a peculiarly beautiful promenade, which overlooks the busy
and picturesque little haven. Towards the land the works are
more regular, and are intended for defence. The ascent is
rapid after one is out of the streets; and the walls, flanked by
forts, follow the line of a ridge, that is shaped like an irregular
triangle, which by falling off precipitously towards the country,
supersedes the necessity of ditches.

I took a horse and made the circuit of the walls. The day was
mild, but had passing clouds; and some of the views towards the
interior were of an extraordinary character. A deep valley separated us from the district around the works; and there were
several fine glimpses, in a sort of wild perspective, among the
recesses of the mountains. I scarcely remember a scene of more
peculiar wildness blended with beauty, than some of these
glimpses offered; though the passing clouds and the season
perhaps contributed to the effect. The inland views resembled
some of the backgrounds of the pictures of Leonardo da Vinci.
Indeed, it is only in Italy, and among its romantic heights with
their castle-resembling villages and towns, that one first gets an
accurate notion of the models that the older masters painted.

Seaward, the prospect from the apex of the triangle was truly
glorious. The day was mild, and twenty sail were loitering
along, quaint in their rig, as usual, and wallowing to the heavy
ground-swell. Here I got almost a bird's-eye view of the town,
port, and offing, with the noble range of coast southward, and
a pile of purple mountains whose feet were lined with villages.
I scarcely remember a day in Switzerland that was more fruitful
of delight than this. As I descended to the highway, one of the
royal equipages, a coach and six, with scarlet liveries, went by

at a stately pace, followed by another with four, and several outriders. It added to the brilliancy of the foreground of the picture.

The large space between the town and the walls was nearly waste; though there stands a citadel, overlooking the former in a way to suggest the idea of offence, rather than of defence. The streets in general are Moorish in width, many of them positively not being more than eight or ten feet in breadth. I had one or two encounters with donkeys loaded with panniers, a passage being frequently quite a Scylla-and-Charybdis matter. As the houses are six or seven stories high, it is like walking in the fissures of a mountain to walk in these streets. Of course carriages never attempt them. Still, Genoa has many fine avenues besides the Strada Balbi.

I saw more street devotion in Genoa that I had previously witnessed in Italy, men on their knees in the streets being rather an unusual sight in Florence. The gambols of the carnival were much as usual; though Italian humour is both richer and stronger than that of France. This is in favour of the people, and shows that they have had a place in the world; for I take it the French are wanting in this peculiar quality of the mind from the all-absorbing moral as well as political superiority of the court. The humour of France is nearly all military, as might be expected; and in this they are unequalled.

Letter VIII.

I BELIEVE I fancied business called me to Paris, as much to make the passage of the Maritime Alps, as from any real necessity; for here I am back again at Florence, after an absence of less than three weeks, the journey unaccomplished.

I took the *malle-poste*, again, on the afternoon of the third day, and left Genoa for Nice, with no other companion than the *conducteur*. As we whirled round the cliff that forms the western point of the port, I looked back with longing eyes at *Genova la Superba*, and thought that it well deserved the title.

Now commenced one of the most extraordinary roads it was ever my good fortune to travel. It ran for a long distance on the very margin of the sea, the carriage literally rolling along the beach in places. I cannot recount the names of all the pretty little fishing and trading hamlets that we galloped through in this manner; but they were numberless, and now and then we had a town. The shore was fairly lined with them; while the mountains, inland, soon began to tower upward to an Alpine magnitude. This was the commencement of the Maritime Alps; and the following day we were to turn their flank along what is aptly enough termed the *corniche* road.

Imagination cannot portray bits of scenery more picturesque than some that offered on the beach. Wild ravines, down which broad and rapid torrents poured their contributions, opened towards the hills; and bridges of a singular construction and of great antiquity frequently spanned them in bold and imposing flights. Many of those wide arches were half ruined, adding the aid of association to their other charms. As for the beach, it was principally of sand; and wherever a hamlet occurred, it was certain to be lined with boats and feluccas, some lying on their bilges, and others shored up on their keels, with perhaps a sail spread to dry. How some of these crafts, vessels of forty or fifty tons, in the absence of tides, were got there, or how they were to be got off again, exceeded my skill at conjecture; though the *conducteur* affirmed that they sailed upon the sands, and would sail off again when they wished to put to sea!

Here and there a prettily-modelled felucca was on the ways. Altogether, it was an extraordinary passage, differing entirely from any I had ever before made. Night overtook us a little before we reached Savona, and for several hours we travelled in darkness. We had left Noli before the day dawned; and when it came, it opened on an entirely different scene. The beach was deserted,—or rather, there was no longer a beach, but the coast had become rocky and broken. The land was heaving itself up in gigantic forms, and on our right appeared a peak that bears the name of *Monte Finale*. It was the last summit of the Alps!

The huge background of mountains protects all this coast from the north winds, and the sun of a low latitude beating against it, joined to the bland airs of this miraculous sea, conspire to render all this region precocious. Even the palm was growing in one or two places; and, though only in the first days of March, we felt all the symptoms of a young spring. This harmony between the weather and the views contributed largely to my pleasures.

Although the coast had become so broken, we occasionally descended to the margin of the sea. At Ventimiglia we passed a torrent of some width; and this was a point that the King of Sardinia was fortifying extensively, as it completely covered one flank of his Italian possessions. Farther on, we passed a small town called Mentone, which is in the principality of Monaco. This little state lies *enclavé* in those of Sardinia, contains some six or eight thousand souls, and has passed into the possession of the French family of Valentinois. Why it was preserved through the eventful period of the late wars, I cannot tell you; but three or four of these pigmy governments have shared its fate, let it be for good or for evil. Among them are Lichtenstein, St. Marino, Knyphausen, and Monaco. The last, however, is not strictly independent, but is under the protection of Sardinia, and is without foreign relations; or it is an independent and sovereign state *à la mode de nullification*.

A little distance from the town we passed a new building, erected by the prince for a country-house. It was not much larger than an American dwelling of the same sort, and, barring the Grecian monstrosities and the shingle palaces, not more respectable. The grounds were small and naked of trees, and altogether it was the most comfortless and unpretending abode of the sort I have seen in Europe. But the Prince of Monaco resides chiefly in France, cannot properly be considered royal, and, I dare say, values his French peerage as highly as his Italian states. We passed barracks that were said to contain an army of twenty men.

Soon after quitting Mentone, the road began to wind its way across the broad and naked breast of a huge mountain. This was, in truth, the point where we crossed the Maritime Alps, the rest of our mounting and descending being merely coquetting on their skirts. The town of Monaco appeared in the distance, seated on a low rocky promontory, with the sea laving one of its sides, and the other opening towards a pretty and secluded port. The whole of this coast is as picturesque and glorious, however, as the imagination can paint: and then the associations, which are Oriental, and sometimes even Scriptural, come in to throw a hue over all. I observed to-day, while we were traversing one of the heights or promontories of the coast, a polacre rolling at her anchor, while boats were carrying off to her oil and olives, from the spot where the latter had grown. To give you a still juster notion of the nature of this region, as I sat leaning back in the carriage this afternoon, the line of sight, by clearing the bottom of the carriage window, struck another vessel under her canvass, at the distance of half a league from the shore. We might have been, at the moment, a thousand feet above the sea. Some of the panoramas, seen from these advanced eminences, were as magnificent as land and water could form; and this the more so from the hue of the Mediterranean, a tint that is eminently beautiful. Indeed, one who has seen no other sea but that which is visible from the American coast, can scarcely form a notion of the beauty of the ocean; for there the tint is a dull green, while in most other parts of the world it is a marine blue. The difference, I think, is owing to the shallowness of our own seas, and the depth of those of this hemisphere, —and, perhaps, also to the magnitude and number of the American rivers.

After climbing a league we reached the summit of the pass, which was a sort of shoulder of the range, and had a short distance of tolerably level route. From this elevation we caught a glimpse of a deep bay, with a town at its head called Villa Franca; and one of the most extraordinary of all the wasp-nest-looking villages I had yet seen presented itself. It literally capped the apex of a cone, whose sides were so steep as to render ascending and descending a work of toil, and even of risk. I should think that a child that fell from the verge of the village must roll down two hundred feet. On this extraordinary pinnacle were perched some fifty or sixty houses built of stone, and resembling, as usual, one single and quaint edifice, from the manner in which they were compressed together. The *conducteur* deemed this village the most extraordinary thing on his route, and when I asked him what could have induced men to select such a position for a town, he answered, "The bears!" Protection was unquestionably the motive, and the village is probably very ancient. My companion thought there must be a well of great depth to furnish water, and he added, that the inhabitants were chiefly shepherds. It is necessary to see a landscape embellished by towns, convents, castles and churches, occupying sites like this, to form any accurate notion of the manner in which they render it quaint and remarkable.

We now began to descend, and for a long distance the road wound down the breast of the mountain; though it was far from being remarkable as an Alpine pass. At length we reached a sort of basin on a level with the sea, which held the city of Nice; the county of that name lying on both sides of the Alps, and having been entered near Mentone.

A good supper and a bed were the first requisites; but, finding that the *malle-poste* did not proceed until the next afternoon, the following morning I set about examining the exterior of this celebrated refuge of the valetudinarian. The town is of some size and well-built, being divided into two parts by a high bit of table-land, or a low mountain, which is near the sea. I ascended this eminence, and got a bird's-eye view of its *entourage*. The port is small, and, I should think, in part artificial,—for it is like a dock, with a narrow entrance, from a coast that was a perfectly unbroken and regular curvature. The vessels lie as in a basin, though within a few yards of the open sea, from which they are separated by a low beach. There were a good many crafts in port, partaking of all the picturesque beauties of the polacre, latine-rig, felucca, Lombard, &c. &c. Among the rest, I was struck with a beautiful little schooner, that had so much of a ship-shape and knowing air about her, that I was just about to inquire whence she came, as an English ensign was set on board her. She was the yacht of an English naval captain, in which he is in the habit of making short excursions in this glorious sea. If there is a man on earth I envy, it is he! This craft was about thirty tons burthen, well found, and as neat as a marine's musket.

I walked across the port, and thence around the nearest headland, by a winding foot-path, and came out at the mouth of the harbour of Villa Franca, which, I was told, is a haven much used by the Sardinian men-of-war. To me the place seemed stagnant and deserted, and I returned to Nice by the same path. Strolling along the quays of the latter, I found more of those signs of Oriental life, which never fail to transport me in spirit to the regions of a fabulous antiquity. Among other things, I saw a great number of large jars, intended to hold oil, which at once explained the manner in which the forty thieves were secreted,—a difficulty that always destroyed the illusion of the tale. Many of these jars were quite large enough to hold a man; though the attitude he would be compelled to assume might be none of the most agreeable for an ambuscade.

The orange-trees in this vicinity were covered with fruit; but the oranges themselves were sour and unpalatable. On the whole, the situation of Nice, which is almost entirely sheltered by mountains towards the north, must render the climate generally mild; and the proximity of the Mediterranean, no doubt, lends a blandness to the air. But, on the other hand, the sudden changes and cold blasts that certainly do occur among all mountains, cannot but make it a little precarious for consumptive people. If the scirocco, the greatest drawback of this region, blows home at this remote point, it will be an additional objection. I believe that the present condition of the world, and the great facilities for travelling, are bringing other places more into notice, and Nice and Montpelier are in less request than formerly. Still, judging only from my own hasty and imperfect surveys of both, I should recommend Nice much sooner than Pisa.

After dinner, which, for the first time since I came to Europe, was made at a *table d'hôte* filled by men in trade,—a set that struck me as singularly professional on so long an abstinence from the luxury of the craft,—we left Nice for Antibes. The road ran along a level and fertile country, among orange-groves and olive-trees, until we reached a broad and straggling river called the Var, across which was thrown a rude, long, wooden bridge. Near the middle of this bridge was a gate that marked the frontier of France. At the opposite side of the river, we encountered a custom-house, where my luggage was examined. This was done in a very civil and *pro formâ* manner; and the *douceur* that was offered, as an acknowledgment of this favour, was declined. The circumstance deserves to be recorded.

It was dark when we reached Antibes, a walled and garrisoned town, that occupies a low promontory which forms a pretty little haven. This place is known in the history of Napoleon, who landed in a meadow about a league from it, where he encamped for the night, in the celebrated expedition of 1815. An officer, with a few men, was sent to summon Antibes; but they were captured and confined in the town. The moments were too precious to be lost in discussing the matter, and the next day the Emperor moved on, leaving his agent, as the lawyers say, "to abide the event of the suit." The coast is generally low in this vicinity, and the brigs found good anchorage in an open roadstead. The descent was made at an unprotected point, and as we passed it next morning the *conducteur* showed me a tree under which Napoleon passed the night. It is now generally understood that his arrival was expected, and that the army was in a great measure prepared to receive him. "*Le Petit Caporal!*"

From Antibes to Cannes we were at no time far from the coast. The latter is a small town on the strand, and the harbour is little more than a roadstead. As we approached Fréjus, the ruins of an ancient aqueduct were seen on the adjacent plain; and as this is a place of great antiquity, I could gladly have passed a few hours in it. But the *malle-poste* stops for nothing, except at designated points; not even to eat. To supply the place of a breakfast, however, I ran into a shop and bought a famous *biscuit de Savoie*, fancying that one ought to get a cake of such a name good so near the frontier of Savoy itself. At the first mouthful it crumbled into dust, and I discovered that the good

woman of the shop had sold me her sign! Swallowing a little water at a fountain to wash away the *débris*, I ran ahead and examined an amphitheatre that is still standing in the skirts of the
place. It is small, but far from being a total ruin, most of the
seats being still to be traced quite distinctly. *Feste, Farina e
Forche,** seems to be a political maxim as old as Italy itself; for
wherever any traces of ancient Rome are to be found, one usually meets with a theatre or an amphitheatre. These noble traces
of a remote civilization, in a retired place like this, had far more
interest for me than the personal adventures of Napoleon.

At Fréjus we quitted the coast, for I was tied, for better for
worse, to the letter-bags. Our road now lay across a hilly and far
from inviting country to Draguignan. We had the cork and the
olive for companions, the latter having suffered severely by the
frosts of the previous winter. This was the commencement
of the mountainous and retired region into which Napoleon
plunged when he marched from Antibes, and in which he was
lost to observers, for a few days, previously to his brilliant *coup
de main* at Grenoble. Hitherto I had seen little of the real rusticity of France, for everything around Paris and on the great
roads leading to it is conventional and *maniéré*. Draguignan
proved to be literally *une ville de province*, but we got a reasonably good dinner.

From Draguignan to Aix it was, again, night-work; though
we got to the latter place in time to enjoy a bed for a few hours.
Aix is an ancient and a celebrated town, but it offers little to interest a stranger. I passed a few hours in it, undecided whether
to pursue the road to Paris, or to turn again towards the coast,
where, I was given to understand, the object of my journey
could be effected as well as in the capital. I fear a longing for
the blue Mediterranean had its influence on the decision, for I
had turned my back on it reluctantly; about noon I got into a
diligence and was on my way to Marseilles. I saw little of the
beauty of Provence, for a less attractive region than that we
drove through is seldom seen. Indeed, I feel persuaded that
few countries offer less to the eye of the mere passer-by than
France; the tastes of the people being little given to the picturesque, and, like the cookery, in which bad imitations of art mar

*Festivals, bread and the gallows.

the natural qualities of the viands, the provincial attempts to resemble Paris destroy the country without properly substituting the town. Nothing, in short, has the simplicity and nature of rural life until one gets as low as dirty *blouse* and *sabots*. Between coarseness and mannerism the chasm is wide indeed.

It was *Mardi Gras*, and as we drew near Marseilles, we met the population making the usual promenade on the highway; there being a sort of *corso* just without the town. There was the usual number of buffoons and patched faces, a good line of plain carriages, and very many pretty women. Indeed, the women of this town struck me as being much handsomer, generally, than those of the North of France.

I remained ten days at Marseilles, which is little besides a commercial town; but which, by its pretty port, beautiful coast, and its movement, offers enough to amuse one for a short time. The new town is built in a good style, with wide straight streets; but the old town, like all the places of the middle ages, is narrow, crowded, and dirty. The port is natural, but has all the appearance of an artificial dock, the gates excepted. The entrance does not exceed two hundred feet; and yet the basin within, which lies surrounded by the town, will contain five hundred sail,—vessels of any size, I believe, finding sufficient water. There is a good roadstead, almost a port, outside of this again, and capital anchorage behind an island, on which stands the Lazaretto. As the quarantine laws of this sea are extremely rigid, it is something to enjoy moorings so secure and picturesque.

An Egyptian frigate of French construction, however, was lying in the port; and certes, if such cruisers are fobbed off on the Pasha, he may look forward to many more Navarinos; this being one of your regular wafer-sided and spider-kneed crafts.

I might write a long description of Marseilles—and the place merits it in its way; but such is not my cue,—which, you will always remember, is rather to deal with things that others have omitted. The time was spent in preparations to return to Florence, and, anxious to be afloat again on the Mediterranean, I looked out for something about to sail in that direction. Luckily a large English brig offered, and I took passage in her. This vessel was of four hundred tons burthen, had a crew of eighteen men, and was commanded by a half-pay naval officer, who was, in part, owner. She had just been in the French transport service, in the expedition to Greece; as, indeed, had been the case with several American vessels in the port. One needs no better evidence than this fact, of the want of aptitude for the sea in the people of the country; the government not being able to transport a few thousand men across a small and tranquil sea, without drawing on the maritime enterprise and resources of foreigners, and, in our instance, of a people in the other hemisphere! One such circumstance is worth a folio on political economy, and, coupled with the fact that France lies between two seas, sufficiently proves that the bias of the national character is to *terra firma*.

One of the *mauvaises plaisanteries* of Jack is to sing songs at the expense of the soldiers. Our crew were heaving round on the capstan, accompanying their tramp with some pretty rude poetry, one line of which was, "A soldier's wife is a sailor's ——." You will judge of my surprise at hearing this well-known and pathetic sentiment suddenly travestied by the substitution of "Yankee's" for "soldier's," and "Englishman's" for "sailor's." A young Englishman on board felt ashamed of this coarse proof of national antipathy, and he endeavoured to explain it by saying, that the people of the brig had had a quarrel with the crew of an American which lay within hearing. It might have been so; but abuse of America flows so easily from the English tongue, that it was probably owing to the old grudge. I felt gratified, however, in the reflection that on board an American of the same size such coarseness and vulgarity in the people would not have been tolerated. I question if it would have been so in this brig, had the master been on board; but, at the moment, he was ashore; for though a good hater as respects America, he kept up a manly discipline.

We were towed out of the harbour some distance into the roads, when the brig was cast, with a light but fair wind from the north-west. This was the commencement of a *mistral*,—a breeze that has much reputation in this part of France, on account of its freshness, as well as for its invigorating properties. We took things leisurely, however, aboard the brig, and the night had passed before we were up with Toulon. The next morning, on turning out, I found a gallant breeze, and our vessel rolling through it as fast as a kettle bottom, a narrow spread of canvass and short masts would permit. Being in light ballast, we got along about seven knots, with the wind over the taffrail, while I am persuaded the brig had nine in her.

It is at all times a delicate matter to give a hint to a sea-officer; but I could not refrain making some inquiries about the light sails. The boom-irons were not on the yards, with a fair wind, and fifteen hours out! By dint of jokes, however, I got an order to have them put on. This was about ten in the forenoon. At meridian two were on, and then the order was countermanded. The master had methodically and deliberately taken the sun, and worked up his longitude; and, judging from his position, he thought we should reach Leghorn in the night, if we carried more sail. While he was at work with his quadrant, we had the peaks of the Maritime Alps, and those of Corsica, both glittering with snow, in plain sight. The chart lay spread on the companion-way, and taking the bearings of the land by the eye, I guessed our position—if guess it might be called—within ten miles. Now all this an American master would have seen at a glance; and, I will engage, his quadrant would not have budged, though all his cloth would have been spread. Not so with our methodical mariner: he took counsel of his instruments, and the boom-irons were sent down again, in spite of several broad hints from me, that one might always lie-to after he had made his run, and that Gorgona would be a capital land-fall, if he was afraid of overrunning his reckoning, in the dark. It would not do, however; the irons were sent down, and instead of making more sail, we unbent a top-gallant-sail to mend it. The wind began to fall, and just at sunset we were up with the head of Corsica, with the topsails flapping against the masts. Belonging to another parish, I could only shrug my shoulders. It is too late in the day to deny the seamanship of the English, who, in some particulars, are probably our betters; but the *go-ahead* properties of the Yankee, and the go-by-rule habits of the Englishman, are every day lessening the distance between the wealth and power of the two people.

The evening was pleasant, and as we gradually rolled past the land, I had a calm pleasure in looking at it. The northern extremity of the island is an attenuated bluff, low in comparison with the ice-covered mountains behind it, seemingly sterile, and with but few signs of habitations. A small rocky island forms an advanced work. Against this, and against the bluff itself, the sea was beating in sullen surge; and we were near enough to see its spray, and to note the marine birds hovering over their nests. The sun set while I was lost in the contemplation of this scene, and of the rocky and indented coasts beyond.

The master of the brig was a respectable man, and he endeavoured to compensate for his want of energy by entertaining me with the marvellous riches of the "nobility and gentry," —a subject of which Englishmen of his class seldom weary. He commenced with an account of the value of the plate of the Duke of Northumberland, who had just been appointed lord-lieutenant of Ireland, and who had paid a premium of 90,000*l.* to get it insured between London and Dublin. As the rate was a half per cent. this made the plate itself worth 1,800,000*l.*! But Englishmen of this class do not often stick at trifles on such a subject,—and yet they coolly accuse us of exaggerating! Another of the tales of my shipmate was an account of a Mr. W —— P ——, who had got 500,000*l.* a year by his wife, and who was in the habit of losing whole streets in London on a game of cards. And yet this man, with all his imagination about guineas, never bethought him of the necessity of a ship's having boom-irons to make a passage, which is making money. We can talk more "dollar" than the English in a given time, I believe; but we have no parallel to their cool accumulations of tens of thousands a year in the way of incomes.

I got into my berth about nine, and waking up in the morning, I soon discovered that we were pitching instead of rolling. Going on deck, I found the brig under double-reefed topsails, on the wind, and Gorgona just visible in the haze on our weather-bow, the vessel heading to the eastward. In other words, the wind was blowing hard, directly in our teeth. The boom-irons would have carried us up to our port before this change occurred. An hour later, we passed an English brig running before it, and the master manifested a wish to follow her, as she was in ballast,—a sign that freights were scarce in Leghorn; but I encouraged him to stand in, with the assurance that Monte Neve would give timely notice of the dangers of the coast. By three the wind had moderated, so that we carried whole sail, and it hauled sufficiently to enable us to head up to the point where I thought the town lay; though it became so thick, we could not see half a league. Suddenly, the coast appeared; our master became alarmed, and hove-to his brig. At that moment, a boat came in sight, and a pilot soon jumped aboard of us. Had we stood on, we should have made the mole without fail. Instead of shortening sail, the pilot steered straight for the mole-head, under both topsails. We weathered it by about fifty yards, and shot in astern of a tier of vessels that lay moored behind it. These vessels were Americans and English, and they rode by anchors ahead, while they were steadied by fasts run out to the mole. These fasts were slackened as we came sweeping in, and we ran over them, gradually losing our way by backing the maintopsail, and fetching up on the bights of the hawsers. I never witnessed bolder or better handling of a vessel of that size, for we came up to the mole-head with four knot way on us. Nothing was parted. A hawser was thrown upon the mole; a line or two, fastened to the ties, steadied us, and brought us head to wind; a kedge was carried off into the port, up to which we hauled, where we dropped a bower-anchor, and by hauling in on the stern-fasts we were moored. We could not take the outer berth, for it was occupied, and we thus became the fourth vessel in the tier. Altogether, I repeat, it was one of the prettiest things I ever witnessed, albeit it was performed by an Italian. I fancy Columbus must have had some such men with him.

The public coaches of Italy are peculiar. If a sufficient number of passengers are ready, (in our case four sufficed,) a small carriage is sent off with them, drawn by post-horses. In this mode I got up to Florence next day, paying about five dollars for myself and man, a distance of sixty miles.

Letter IX.

THE season soon became sufficiently advanced to give us a sight of an Italian spring. The birds of passage had flown, some north and some south, but all in quest of pleasure. The members of parliament had run up to London to take their seats, the peers excepted, for they can do their duty by proxy. As for the Russians and French, they had chiefly gone to Naples, or taken refuge in the mountains. The poor political exiles, of whom Florence has a large number, are still seen walking on the shady sides of the streets, but filled with lassitude and *ennui*. The town is as hot as Philadelphia.

We left our palazzo within the walls, and went to a villa, called St. Illario, just without them. All the eminences around Florence are dotted with these retreats, many of which are large and princely. That we occupy is on a smaller scale; but it has numerous rooms, is near the town, and has many conveniences. Among other recommendations, it has two covered belvederes, where one can sit in the breeze and overlook the groves of olive-trees, with all the crowded objects of an Italian landscape.

But, to give you some idea of the region in which we dwell: The valley of the Arno, though sufficiently wide, and cultivated chiefly with the spade, is broken by many abrupt and irregular heights, the advanced spurs of the ranges of the Apennines that bound it. On nearly all of these eminences, stands a stone edifice topped by a belvedere; sometimes with, and sometimes without terraces; here and there a tree, and with olive-groves beneath. The whole country is intersected by narrow roads leading up the heights; and these lanes usually run between high walls. They are commonly paved to prevent the wash of the rains, and nothing can be less attractive than the objects they present; though we find the shade of the walls beginning to be necessary as the season advances. To obtain a view, one is obliged to ascend to some one of the look-outs on the hills, of which there are a good many; though the rides and walks on the level land, that lies above and behind us, occasionally furnish us glorious glimpses. We are much in the habit of going to one of these places, which is rightly enough called *Bellosguardo*, for a better bird's-eye view of a town is not often had than this affords of Florence. In addition, we get the panorama of the valley and mountains, and the delicate lights and shades of the misty Apennines. Some of the latter I rank among the best things in their way that I have seen. These mountains are generally to be distinguished from the lower ranges of the Alps, or those whose elevation comes nearest to their own, by a softer and more sunny hue, which is often rendered dreamy and indolent by the sleepy haziness of the atmosphere. Indeed, everything in these regions appears to invite to contemplation and repose at this particular season. There is an admixture of the savage and the refined in the ragged ravines of the hills, the villas, the polished town, the cultivated plain, the distant and chestnut-covered peaks, the costumes, the songs of the peasants, the Oriental olive, the monasteries and churches, that keeps the mind constantly attuned to poetry.

The songs of Tuscany are often remarkable. There is one air in particular that is heard on every key, used to all sorts of words, and is in the mouth of all the lower classes of both sexes. The soldier sings of war to it, the sailor of storms and seas, the gallant of his adventures, and the young girl of her love. The air is full of melody, a requisite of all popular music, while it has the science and finish of a high school, and is altogether superior to anything of the kind which you might fancy in use by the same classes of society at home. It is withal a little wild, and has a *la ral lal la* to it, that just suits the idea of heartiness, which is perhaps necessary, for the simplicity of such a thing may be hurt by too much sophistication.

I first heard this air in the town, at a particular hour every evening. On inquiry, I found it was a baker's boy singing it in the streets, as he dispensed his cakes. I often hear it, as I sit in my belvedere, rising from among the vines or olives, on different heights: sometimes it is sung in falsetto, sometimes in deep bass, and now and then in a rich contr'alto. Walking to Bellosguardo, the other day, I heard it in a vineyard in the latter key, and getting on a stone that overlooked the wall, I found it came from a beautiful young *contadina*, who was singing of love as she trimmed her vines: disturbed by my motions, she turned, blushed, laughed, hid her face, and ran among the leaves.

This is not the only music I get gratis. One of the narrow lanes separates my end of the house from the church of St. Illario and the dwelling of the priest. From the belvedere, which communicates with my own room, we have frequent passages of civility across the lane with the good old *curato*, who discusses the weather and the state of the crops with unction. The old man has some excellent figs, and our cook having discovered it, lays his trees under contribution. And here I will record what I conceive to be the very perfection of epicurism, or rather of taste, in the matter of eating. A single fresh fig, as a corrective after the soup, I hold to be one of those sublime touches of art, that are oftener discovered by accident, than by the investigations of knowledge. I do not mean that I have even the equivocal merit of this accidental discovery, for I was told the secret, and I believe French ingenuity had got pretty near it already, in the way of the melons. But no melon is like a fig; nor will a French fig, certainly not a Paris fig, answer the purpose at all. It must be such a fig as one gets in Italy. At Paris you are always offered a glass of Madeira after the soup, the only one taken at table; but it is a pitiful substitute for the fig. After communicating this improvement on human happiness, let me add that it is almost destructive of the pleasure derived from the first, to take a second. *One* small, greencoated, fresh fig, is the precise point of gastronomic felicity in this respect.

But the good *curato*, besides his figs, has a pair of uneasy bells in his church tower, which are exactly forty-three feet from my ears, and which invariably ring in pairs six or eight times daily. There are matins, noon-tide, angelus, vespers, and heaven knows what, regularly; to say nothing of extra-masses, christenings, funerals, and weddings. The effect of the bells is often delightful when heard in the distance, for they are ringing all over the valley and on the heights, morning, noon, and night; but these are too near. Still, I get, now and then, rare touches of the picturesque from this proximity to the church. The *contadini* assemble in their costumes beneath my belvedere, and I have an excellent opportunity of overlooking, and overhearing them too.

The *Lingua Toscana* applies rather to the people of the towns than to the rural population, I fancy; for these worthy peasants speak a harsh *patois*. Walking in sight of the *duomo*, lately, with a gentleman of Florence, I desired him to put a question to a group of peasants; and I found that, while he was perfectly understood, he had great difficulty in understanding them. The aspirated words of Florence itself are well known to all who have been in Italy. We had a droll proof of this just before we left the town; for desiring my man to give our address to a shopkeeper, he gave, "Il Signor [Cooper], *Hasa Rihasole, via del Hohomero.*"*

One of the most picturesque of our relations with the church arises from the funerals. Lounging in the clerical belvedere lately, we saw torches gleaming in a distant lane. Presently the sounds of the funeral song reached us; and these gradually deepened, until we had the imposing and solemn chant for the dead, echoing between our own walls, as if in the nave of a church. It is necessary to witness such a scene to appreciate its beauty, on a still and dark night, beneath an Italian sky.

In one of the dreamy walks that I take in company with a Florentine, I strolled near a league along the road to Rome. The country is broken; the road winding among naked and abrupt hills, that constantly remind me of the scenery that one usually finds attached to subjects painted from Holy Writ. On a small bit of table-land, that rises in one of the valleys, is a Carthusian convent; and finding ourselves beneath its walls, my companion proposed entering.

The ascent was easy, and the outer gate open. We saw no one, but, following a carriage way that resembled the approach to an ancient castle, we soon reached the door that communicates with the cloisters. Here we accidentally met with a lay brother, who amused himself with cooking for the worthy fathers, and our application for admission was favourably, but silently received. The place was the image of solitude and silence; not a soul besides the lay brother was visible, and even he soon disappeared.

Casa Ricasoli, via del Cocomero. The aspirations are gutteral, and have a touch of the Moresco-Spanish about them.

You may imagine the effect of strolling through vast, tenant-less, echoing, monastic cloisters, corridors and halls, on a sleepy Italian day, grateful for the shade and coolness, but wondering for whom these vast edifices were constructed. We positively entered, remained an hour, and left this structure without see-ing a soul but the lay brother. The gates were open, apparently, for all who chose to enter; the chapel, sacristy, and cloisters were all accessible, not a door or a gate requiring the hand, and yet no one was visible. We departed as we had come; and the only evidence we had that there was a fraternity within, was to be found in a list of the fathers who were to perform certain masses, which was suspended in the chapel, and on which the priests were all designated by the Latin abbreviation *Dom.* or *Dominus.* As we returned along the highway, however, a Car-thusian, dressed in his white robe, was seen mending a pen at a window of his small tenement: for each father has a tiny house to himself, with a garden and yard; the rules requiring that they shall live separately, and deny themselves, as much as may be, the comforts and solace of speech. These habitations form a court, all opening on the cloisters, of which they compose, in fact, the several sides. A covered gallery makes the usual means of intercourse within, while the distinct character of the struc-tures is only apparent from without. The gardens lie between the small houses, or apartments.

Letter X.

THE great Florentine fête was celebrated a short time since. One of the ceremonies is so peculiar, that it may amuse you to have a short account of it. There are several considerable squares in the town, but the largest is that of Santa Maria Novella. At the festival of St. John, who is the patron saint of the city, an imitation of the ancient chariot-races is held in this square, which affords the most space. The games are called the *corse dei cocchi*. There are two small obelisks on opposite extremities of the square, and the temporary circus is constructed by their means. A cord is stretched from one to the other; a sort of amphitheatre is formed by scaffoldings around the whole, the royal and diplomatic boxes being prepared near the goal. As there is much scenic painting, a good parade of guards both horse and foot, a well-dressed population, and a background of balconies garnished by tapestry and fine women, to say nothing of roofs and chimneys, the general effect is quite imposing.

The falling off is in the chariots. The ancient vehicle was small and had but two wheels; whereas these were large and clumsy, had four wheels, and unusually long and straggling perches,—an invention to keep them from upsetting. In other respects the form was preserved, and the charioteers were in costume.

Four chariots, to use the modern language, entered for the race. The start was pretty fair, and the distance twice round the obelisks. If you ask me for the effect, I shall tell you that, apart from the appliances,—such as the court, the guards, the spectators and the dresses, and perhaps I might add the turns,—one may witness the same any fine evening in New York, between two drunken Irish cartmen who are on their way home. There was certainly a little skill manifested at the turns, and it was easy to see that betting should have been on the outside chariot; for those nearer to the obelisks were obliged to go considerably beyond them before they could come round, while the one farthest from the poles just cleared them. This outside chariot won the race, the charioteer having the sagacity not to make his push before the last turn.

After the chariot-races, we had the *corsa dei barberi*, or a race between barbs. The horses were without riders, and the track was the longest street of the town. To this amusement every one who could went in a carriage, and the *corso* of vehicles was much the most interesting part of the exhibition. Two lines are made, and the coaches move in opposite directions through the same street, on a walk. Of course, everybody sees everybody,—and pretty often the somebodies see nobodies, for the mania to make one on these occasions is so strong, that half the artisans are abroad in carriages, as well as their betters. The royal equipages moved in the line, the same as that of the milliner. When we were well tired of looking at each other, the grand duke went into a gallery prepared for him, and the race was run. The latter does not merit a syllable; but so strong is the rage for sporting, that I heard some Englishmen betting on the winner.

But the amusements of the evening were really fine. They consisted of fireworks and illuminations, besides an odd scene on the river. It is only for a few of the summer months that the "Silver Arno" deserves its reputation; for I scarcely know a more turbid or dingy stream during the period of high water. Indeed, it brings down with it from the mountains so much yellow earth, that "Golden Arno" would better express its tint. But, at this season, it is placid and silvery. Care has been taken to make it a river all the year round, in the town at least, by raising a dam just at the suburbs, which causes the water to fill the bed between the quays even in the dry months. Below this dam, it would be possible for an active man, aided by a leaping-staff, to jump across the channel. This is the common character of the Italian rivers, which, fed by the mountains, are turbulent torrents in the winter, and ribands of water in the hot months. Many are absolutely dry in mid-summer.

We were kindly invited to witness the fête on the Arno, from the palace of the Comte de St. Leu, the windows of which overlook the river. The party was small, but it contained several members of the Bonaparte family. Among others was the Comtesse de Survilliers, or, a name she is better known by, *la Reine*

Julie; and that fine young man the Prince Napoleon, with his wife, the Princess Charlotte, so well known in America. The Prince and Princess of Musignano, with their children, made up the family party.

I believe I have not spoken to you of the Comte de St. Leu. He is one of the handsomest men of his age I have ever met with; but it is the beauty of expression more than of features, though the latter are noble and regular. I can scarcely recall a more winning countenance; and his manner, though calm and dignified, is kind and unpretending. I should think his stature materially above that of Napoleon, though he is not of more than the middle height, and his figure is compact and square. The Comte de Survilliers is short, inclining to fat, and, though rather handsome, particularly as to expression, is not by any means so striking in appearance as his brother. The Prince of Canino (Lucien) is taller than either, thin, and has a decided Italian countenance, one that is shrewd, quick, and animated. The Prince de Montfort (Jerome) is short and slight, and resembles his brother Lucien more than the others. He is said to have most of the expression of Napoleon; but I should think, judging from the busts and likenesses, that Louis has most of the noble outline of the Emperor. The whole family, so far as I have known them, are certainly very intellectual and well-informed. The Comte de St. Leu lives here in a good style; having a fine villa, where I dined lately, and this palace in the town, which is altogether suited to his rank and past life. He is styled "your majesty" by those around him, as was the Countess of Survilliers; and a little, though not much, of the etiquette of royalty is maintained in his intercourse with others.*

---

*Joseph has taken the title of Survilliers from a small village on the estate of Morfontaine, which was once his property. Louis gets that of St. Leu also from an estate. His wife, Hortense, is styled the *Duchess* of St. Leu, while he is called the Count. Lucien has been created Prince of Canino, by the Pope; and his eldest son, Charles, has obtained the title of Prince of Musignano, in the same manner. Jerome has been created Prince of Montfort, by his brother-in-law, the King of Bavaria. Joseph has no son, but two daughters,—the Princess Musignano, and the Princess Charlotte, the widow of her cousin Napoleon, the eldest son of Louis. Lucien has many children, by different wives. Of these the writer has seen the Prince of Musignano, the Princess Hercolani, the Princess Gabrielli, Lady Dudley Stuart, and Mrs. Bonaparte Wyse. Jerome has several children,—one by Miss Patterson, and the others

As for the fête, it consisted of a display of boats, with a multitude of coloured paper lanterns. The former were filled with company, and as they floated about, with their lights and music, they made both a singular and a pleasing exhibition. There were extremely fine fireworks on one of the bridges, which terminated the amusements. One sees the influences of climate in the Italian fireworks generally, which are brilliant beyond comparison. On returning to the villa St. Illario, we found that the dome of the cathedral was illuminated; and you may judge of the effect produced by showing the outlines of so noble a piece of architecture at night, by the aid of artificial and well-disposed lights. It looked like a line-engraving of fire.

Notwithstanding the constant practice of men, one is constantly surprised at the ignorance of the commonest laws of philosophy that is betrayed on such occasions. I have often seen the gardens of the Tuileries illuminated, when the torches have been placed on the pedestals of the statues, but in plain view; the eye necessarily taking in the flame, to the exclusion of all the minor light. Were these torches concealed in a way to exclude them from the view, while their rays fell on the statuary,—a thing easily enough done,—the effect would be infinitely more agreeable, though perhaps less vulgarly flaring. I remember to have once beheld a drop scene, at a theatre, formed of mirrors. A flood of light was on and near the stage, and, as a matter of course, the audience, instead of seeing itself when the curtain fell, as was the intention, had a glorious view of the reflection of a thousand lamps and candles! Had the lights been so disposed in the boxes, as to illuminate the audience, while they were not

---

by the Princess of Wurtemberg. The family is generally distinguished for abilities. *Madame Mère* was a slight attenuated old lady, with little remains of beauty, when seen by the writer, (the winter of 1829–30,) except fine black eyes. It may be true that she had the talents of the race; but, in several interviews, she did not manifest it. A good mother, and, under her peculiar circumstances, an energetic one, she certainly was; but, beyond this, it is probable her reputation was factitious. She possessed a bust of her husband that was strictly Bonapartean, not one of her sons bearing any material resemblance to herself. In any ordinary situation she would have passed for a respectable country lady,—one who came so lately into the great world as not to have acquired its usages, or its appearance. Her French was Italian, and her Italian far from good. She was quiet, simple, and totally without pretension, however,—in short, *motherly*.

seen from the stage, the desired effect would have been produced. Franklin, speaking of some of the coarse contrivances of French industry, pithily remarks, that "a respectable *instinct* would be better than such a *reason!*"*

Still, the illuminations of architecture are usually good; and I remember one particular thing at Paris, that is quite unrivalled in its way. The Hotel of the Legion of Honour is the ancient Hôtel de Salm, of which Jefferson speaks so much in praise, in his letters. It is a low building, though a very pretty one; and on the occasion of the great fêtes it is the practice to raise a tall spar from the roof, and to hoist at it an imitation of the star of the order, formed by coloured lamps. This star, seen on a dark night, shining, as it were, in the heavens, is, in its way, the prettiest thing I know.

We have also had the Corpus Domini, which is the great Catholic fête of the year. The royal family walked in the procession, as usual; and there was a parade of the Knights of St. Stephen, in their robes,—an order of chivalry that, I believe, had some connexion with the suppression of the piracies of the barbarians from Africa.

The heat in July became intense, and we began to think of quitting Florence, where we had then been nearly nine months. I found the sun intolerable out of the shade; and the hills, which render the valley cold in winter, have the effect of converting it into an oven in the summer. Accordingly, I announced an intention to depart, and soon had occasion to remark that birds of passage like ourselves have little hold on those we employ beyond their gains. Two of our Florentine domestics conducted themselves in such a manner, as soon as they ascertained the day we were to quit the place, that I was

---

*On a particular occasion the writer was invited to take a seat *with the critics*, in the Park Theatre. As an interlude, two dancers exhibited, one in front of a large gilded frame that had gauze in it, and the other behind it; the aim being to produce the effect of reflection. Both backs and both faces being exhibited at the same time; the writer, in his capacity of critic, felt himself bound to hiss; whereupon he was himself incontinently hissed down. What! tell a New York corps of critics, that a man looking into a glass did not see the back of his own head! The writer merited his castigation, and seizes this occasion to admit how far he was behind the Manhattanese philosophy.

compelled to discharge them; and, as this occurred on the third day of their respective months, both demanded an entire month's wages! This, you will perceive, was just doubly their time. I resisted, and gained both my causes; and it is to be hoped that these people are the wiser for their defeat.

A little occurrence that took place soon after our arrival in Florence is worthy to be related, as it may serve to put other Americans on their guard, and to let you understand the nature of European intrigues. We commenced housekeeping with a man-cook, a housemaid, and two footmen, with the Swiss maid whom we brought with us. One of the footmen was discharged for drunkenness, within a fortnight, and I did not think it worth while to fill his place. The other proved an excellent servant, but a great scoundrel. It was not long before [Mrs. Cooper] complained to me of the bills of the cook, which, on examination, turned out to be about double what they were at Paris, though Florence has a reputation for cheapness. The housemaid, who was a Lucchese woman, offered her services, and the man being discharged, she was promoted to the kitchen, and her place was otherwise filled. Her name was Bettina.

About this time, a poor Neapolitan, who had fallen under the notice of [Mrs. Cooper] just before her confinement, came to return her thanks for certain little comforts she had received. "You got the money I sent you?" asked [Mrs. Cooper]. "Si, signora."—"How much?"—"Three pauls, each time, signora."—Now these three pauls should have been ten pauls, or a francescone each time, and Bettina had been the messenger. On demanding an explanation, the newly-made cook admitted the fraud, giving as a reason for keeping back seven-tenths of the money, that she thought it was too much for the Neapolitan. Notwithstanding this flagrant dereliction, there was something so *naïf* in her confessions, that the woman was not discharged. But some dissatisfaction caused [Mrs. Cooper] to change the milkman. A day or two after this change, the milk for the coffee was found to be turned. Bettina was sent for, and she attributed it to the bad milk of the new milkman. When she went out, Luigi the footman quietly observed that he happened to have a little of the milk put away cold for the tea, and by setting it before the fire in the breakfast-room, we might soon ascertain whether it was really bad or not. The experiment was made, and the milk proved to be good. Bettina was again examined, and on my threatening to take her to the police, she confessed that the old milkman had bribed her to put vinegar in the new milk. Of course she was now discharged.

As Luigi had hitherto behaved perfectly well, and had gained a reputation by his expedient, his counsel was attended to, and he was permitted to put a friend of his own into the kitchen. The explanation of the whole is as follows:—The man-cook, though *out of reason* a rogue, was got rid of by a combination between Luigi and Bettina; Bettina next lost her place, by the management of Luigi, who reaped the advantage of his intrigues, as I afterwards learned, to the tune of about two hundred francesconi, beyond his wages. When he obtained his discharge, he actually had the audacity to chase my little son with a carving-knife, threatening to cut his throat. He was paid his wages regularly every month, and towards the close of the time half-monthly, at his own request,—an expedient to prevent stoppages, as I subsequently found, on account of his frauds,— and I owed him a dollar when he was sent away. This he refused, claiming ten; and before the cause was decided, he claimed his entire wages for the whole nine months, affirming I had paid him nothing! In other respects he proved to be a thorough villain.

I do not tell you this as a specimen of Tuscan or Italian character, but as a proof of the impositions to which strangers are liable. After an experience of nine months, I am disposed to think well of the Italians, who seem a kind, and who certainly are a clever people; but the great throng of strangers in these towns loosens the ordinary social ties, by releasing the evil-disposed from many of the usual responsibilities. It may be taken as a general rule, I think, that travellers, unless greatly favoured by circumstances, see the worst portion of every country; the better classes, and the well-disposed, waiting to be sought, while those of the opposite character must seek acquaintances and connexions where they are least known, and where it is easiest to practise their deceptions.

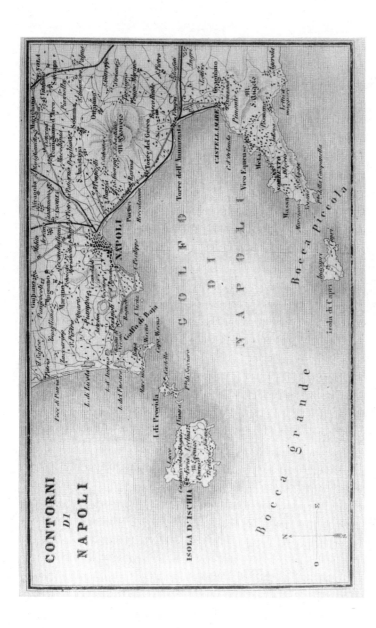

v. Map, Bay of Naples, from P. E. Sacchi, *Descrizione di Napoli e Contorni*

vi. *A View of Naples*, drawn by Claude Joseph Vernet and engraved by Nicolet

VII. *Bay of Naples* by John Gadsby Chapman

VIII. *Pozzuoli*, drawn by James Duffield Harding and engraved by W. R. Smith

Letter XI.

T HE time for quitting Florence having arrived, I wrote to ask an audience of leave of the royal family. The answer was favourable, the grand duke naming the following morning at the Pitti, and the grand duchess an hour a little later at the Poggio Imperiale, a palace just without the walls, and in the immediate vicinity of St. Illario.

Ten was the hour at which I presented myself at the Pitti, in an ordinary morning-dress, wearing shoes instead of boots. I was shown into an ante-chamber, where I was desired to take a seat. A servant soon after passed through the room with a salver, bearing a chocolate-cup and a bit of toast,—a proof that his imperial highness had just been making a light breakfast. I was then told that the grand duke would receive me.

The door opened on a large room, shaped like a parallelogram, which had the appearance of a private library, or cabinet. There were tables, books, maps, drawings, and all the appliances of work. The library of the palace, however, is in another part of the edifice, and contains many thousand volumes, among which are some that are very precious, and their disposition is one of the most convenient, though not the most imposing as to show, of any library I know.

The grand duke was standing alone, at the upper end of a long table that was covered by some drawings and plans of the *Maremme*, a part of his territories in reclaiming which he is said to be just now much occupied. As I entered, he advanced and gave me a very civil reception. I paid my compliments, and made an offering of a book which I had caused to be printed in Florence. This he accepted with great politeness; and then he told me, in the simplest manner, that "his wife" was so ill, she could not see me that morning. I had a book for her imperial highness also, and he said it might be left at the Poggio Imperiale.

As soon as these little matters were disposed of, the grand duke walked to a small round table, in a corner, near which stood two chairs, and, requesting me to take one, he seated himself in the other, when he began a conversation that lasted near an hour. The prince was, as before, very curious on the subject of America, going over again some of the old topics. He spoke of Washington with great respect, and evidently felt no hostility to him on account of his political career. Indeed, I could not trace in the conversation of the prince the slightest evidence of a harsh feeling, distrust, or jealousy towards America; but, on the other hand, I thought he was disposed to view us kindly, —a thing so unusual among political men in Europe as to be worthy of mention. He left on my mind, at this interview, the same impression of simplicity and integrity of feeling as at the other.

He observed that fewer Americans travelled now than formerly, he believed. So far from this, I told him, the number had greatly increased within the last few years. "I used to see a good many," he answered, "but now I see but few." I was obliged to tell him, what is the truth,—that most of those who came to Europe knew little of courts, that they did not give themselves time to see more than the commoner sights, and that they were but indifferent courtiers. He spoke highly of our ships, several of which he had seen at Leghorn, and on board of one or two of which he had actually been.

I found him better informed than usual on the subject of our history; though, of course, many of his notions had the usual European vagueness. He seemed aware, for instance, of the great difficulty with which we had to contend in the revolution, for the want of the commonest munitions of war, such as arms and powder. He related an anecdote of Washington connected with this subject, with a feeling and spirit that showed his sympathies were on the right side of that great question, on whichever side his policy might have been.

We had some conversation on the subject of the discovery of America, and I took the occasion to compliment him on there having been a Florentine concerned in that great enterprise;*

*Americus Vespucius.

but he did not seem disposed to rob Columbus of any glory on account of his own countryman, though he admitted that the circumstance in a degree connected his own town with the event.

At length he rose, and I took my leave of him, after thanking him for the facilities that had been afforded me in Tuscany. When we separated, he went quietly to his maps; and as I turned at the door to make a parting salute, I found his eyes on the paper, as if he expected no such ceremony.

Two or three days from this interview, we got into our carriages, after dinner, and went down the valley of the Arno at night, to avoid the intense heat of the days, which, Americans as we were, completely overcame us all. We reached the gates of Pisa just as the sun rose, and stopped a few hours to see the curiosities.

By twelve we were completely melted with the heat, and were glad to get into our comfortable seats in the carriages again: I say, carriages, for I had hired an extra conveyance at Florence, our little flock having increased too much in size, though not in numbers, to be conveniently put into one, as formerly.

We were all in our corners, half sleeping, half waking, when, about five miles from Leghorn, the whole party revived as suddenly as people awake from a doze. We had passed into the current of the sea air, and it acted on our spirits like a bath. I have known these veins of invigorating humidity drawn along the coast almost as accurately as the sands, so that one did not feel them two hundred feet from the water; but on this occasion we met the salt air at least a mile from the sea, though I never knew the effect greater or more sudden. Even the horses appeared to feel it, for they began to trot merrily, and soon brought us to the door of the Locanda San Marco.

The honest Scotchman who keeps this inn gave us a large airy apartment, whose windows overlook both the sea and the mountains; two objects at which I never tire of gazing. As for the rest of the party, to whom the Mediterranean was entirely new, they had eyes for nothing else; and really, for those who had now passed years excluded from any sea finer than the North Sea, the bright glittering blue expanse was an object to be gazed at. To this was to be added the luxury of Italian rooms at the commencement of August; and, taking all together, I do not remember a happier party than we were for the two or three days we remained in this inn.

I have frequently spoken of the difference between commercial towns and capitals; a distinction that you, who never saw any other than towns of the former class, will not readily comprehend, but which it is essential to know in order to understand Europe. I had the same embarrassment on first coming to this hemisphere, for it is quite common here to speak of our towns as being *purely commercial*. A short experience, however, has shown me so much, that there is nothing I now perceive sooner, or which strikes me with greater force, than the peculiarities of these places that are entirely devoted to trade. If you ask me what these peculiarities are beyond the outward signs of commerce, I shall answer, a certain absence of taste, a want of leisure and of tone; a substitution of bustle for elegance, care for enjoyment, and show for refinement. Leghorn and Marseilles have betrayed these visible signs of their pursuits more particularly after a long residence in Florence; though neither of these towns is so obnoxious to the charge as any one of our own large maritime towns. I think, however, that all our own great towns, while they are unquestionably provincial, as any one will allow who has lived in a real capital, have also many of the distinctive marks of the better towns of Europe that these have not. When a European speaks of New York as a provincial town, notwithstanding defer to his greater experience (unless he happen to be cockney); for, rely on it, such is peculiarly the character and appearance of your Gotham.

Walking through the streets of Leghorn, a shop filled with statuary, Venuses, Apollos, and Bacchantes, caught my eye, and I had the curiosity to enter. If I was struck with admiration on first visiting the tribune of the gallery of Florence, I was still more so here. On inquiry, I found that this was a warehouse that sent its goods principally to the English and American markets: I dare say Russia, too, may come in for a share. Where the things were made I do not know, though probably at Carrara; for I question if any man would have the impudence to display such objects in the immediate vicinity of the collections that contain the originals. Grosser caricatures were never fabricated: attenuated Nymphs and Venuses, clumsy Herculeses, hobbledehoy Apollos, and grinning Fauns, composed the treasures. The quantity of the stuff had evidently been consulted, and, I dare say, the Medicean beauty has lost many a charm for the want of more marble.

The day after our arrival, we were refreshed with a delightful sea-breeze; a luxury, after being heated in Florence from April to August, that must be enjoyed to be appreciated. I can only liken Philadelphia to the latter town in this respect. On visiting the port, I found only one American, though three lay in the roads. Time was, when thirty would have been a trifle. There were ten Englishmen behind the mole, and a good many Sardinians lay scattered about the harbour. Of Tuscans there were but few, and these all small. Three Russians were laid up on account of the war with Turkey! They were fine-looking ships, however. Rowing under the bows of the Yankee, I found one of his people seated on the windlass, playing on the flute; as cool an act of impudence as can well be imagined for a Massachusetts-man to practise in Italy.

I inquired for a conveyance to Naples, and the result was my engaging a Genoese felucca, for one hundred francesconi, for my own exclusive use. This vessel was about thirty tons burthen, and of beautiful mould. She was decked, and had a hold, but no cabin. In lieu of the latter, the quarter-deck, with the exception of a small space aft for the play of the tiller, &c. and a narrow gangway on each side, was covered with a painted tarpaulin, having a rounded roof like the tilt of a waggon, stretched on large hoops: the space beneath was sufficiently large, and as the covering was ample, and high enough to walk under, it gave us a room far preferable to one below. She was latine-rigged, carrying two sails of that description, and a jib. This little craft had a complement of ten men! I have myself been one of eleven hands, officers included, to navigate a ship of near three hundred tons across the Atlantic Ocean; and, what is more, we often reefed topsails with the watch.*

*The present Commodore ——, when a young man, commanded a merchant ship for a short time. On one occasion, inward bound, the yellow fever broke out in the vessel. Most of the crew died; and all on board, with the exception of the young captain, had the disease. The tasks of tending the sick and of

Having engaged the felucca, we passed another day in gazing at the hazy Apennines, whose lights and shadows, particularly the noble piles that buttress the coast to the northward, rendered them pictures to study; and in driving along the low land that lies between the sea and Monte Nero, where we fairly rioted in the pleasures of the cool breezes. But the entire northern shore of this luxurious sea, in summer, is one scene of magnificent nature, relieved by a bewitching softness, such as perhaps no other portion of the globe can equal. I can best liken it to an extremely fine woman, whose stateliness and beauty are relieved by the eloquent and speaking expression of feminine sentiment.

The next day, at noon, we embarked, and took possession of our new lodgings. The wheels had been taken from the carriage, and the body of the vehicle was placed athwart the deck, so as to form a forward bulk-head. W[illiam] had the interior for a state-room. Roberto was put into the hold. There were tarpaulin curtains at both extremities of the tilt, and by the aid of a few counterpanes we subdivided the interior as much as was necessary. Each person had a mattress at night, which pretty well covered the deck; while, piled on each other, they made comfortable sofas during the day. A table, eight or ten chairs, with a few trunks and stools, completed the furniture. Of course, we had the necessary articles of nourishment and refreshment, which our own servants prepared. I never dared to look at the kitchen, but I dare say it was quite as clean as that we had left at Florence.

With this outfit, then, the little *Bella Genovese** got her anchor, with a light wind at north-west, about five in the afternoon, and began to turn out of the harbour. In half an hour we had made three or four stretches, which enabled us to weather the head of the mole, when we stood to the southward, with flowing sheets.

---

taking care of the ship consequently fell on the latter. He cooked, nursed, made and shortened sail, managed the helm, and, after several days of severe labour, brought his vessel safely up to the Hook. What is more extraordinary, he twice reduced the canvass to reefed topsails, and spread it to the royals. Of course, he brought everything to the windlass.

*The Beautiful Genoese.

By examining the map, you will perceive that our course lay between a succession of islands and the main, in a south-easterly direction. Of these islands Gorgona and Capraja were in sight on quitting the port, and our first object was to run through, what here is called, the *canal* of Elba; a streight between that island and the head-land, or cape of Piombino. The wind was so light that our progress was slow; and when we took to our mattresses, Leghorn was but two or three leagues behind us.

On turning out next morning, early, I found the felucca close hauled, beating up for the channel, with a fresh breeze at the southward. The brown mountains of Elba formed the background to windward; Porto Ferrajo lying about two leagues from us, directly on our weather-beam. The prospect of beating through the pass, against the lively little sea, which would be certain to get up, was not pleasant to the ladies; and I ordered the padrone to tack, and stretch in under the land.

We fetched in just beneath the cliff, or promontory, that forms the north-eastern extremity of the town of Porto Ferrajo, a rocky eminence of some elevation. It was crowned by the government house, which had been the palace of Napoleon during his insular reign. My object had been to get into smooth water, by making a lee; but this near view of a place so celebrated was too tempting to be resisted, and I determined to beat up into the bay, even if we should run out again without anchoring. This bay is several miles deep, and at its mouth near a league wide; the land being chiefly mountain and *côtes*. The promontory, on which stands the town, makes a bend on its inner side, like the curve of a hook; and this, aided a little by some artificial works, forms a beautiful and secure little harbour, of which the entrance is towards the head of the bay, the water being everywhere deep, with bold shores.

By ten o'clock we had weathered the mouth of the little haven, and the wind still continuing foul, I determined to run in and anchor. This was accordingly done, and I had called to a boat to come and put us on shore, when the padrone announced the appalling news of there being a quarantine of fifteen days between Elba and Naples! We immediately hauled out of the harbour, and only waited to breakfast, before we went to sea again. While discussing this meal on deck, the padrone was discussing matters with a brother of the craft, on board another felucca; and he came to me to say, that, though there *was* a quarantine of fifteen days between Elba and Naples, there was none at all between the Roman states and Tuscany, or the Roman states and Naples; and that, by running into Cività Vecchia, we might get clean bills of health, and all would be plain sailing. —So much for a Mediterranean quarantine! I accepted the terms, and we landed.

Porto Ferrajo is a small crowded town, populous for its size, containing five thousand souls, lying on the acclivity on the inner side of the promontory. It is pretty well fortified, though the works are old, it being walled, and having two little citadels, or forts, on the heights. It was garrisoned by five hundred men, they told me; and there were two hundred galley-slaves kept in the place. The town was clean enough, the streets having steps, or narrow terraces, by which we ascended the hills.

The arrival of a party of strangers created a sensation; for, with the exception of the brief interruption of the presence of Napoleon, there are few more retired spots in Europe than this. We went to the best inn, which bears the imposing title of the *Quattro Nazioni*. It was far from bad, and it gave us a reasonably good dinner; furthermore, it promised us four beds and a sofa, should we pass the night there. The art of colouring the bricks of the floors has not reached this inn; for the room in which we dined had a sofa and seven mirrors, while the floor was of coarse, dirt-coloured bricks full of holes. Ireland and America are not the only countries in which discrepancies in style occur. In short, England is the only country where they do not; and even in England there is something inappropriate, in seeing three or four powdered lackeys, and a well-appointed equipage, before the door of a mean, dingy town-house of bricks, with three or four windows in front, and quite destitute of all architectural taste.

I had some conversation with the people of the house concerning their late sovereign. Napoleon arrived in the evening, and remained in the frigate until next day. One of his first acts was to send for the oldest known flag used by Elba, and this he caused to be hoisted on the forts; a sign of independency. He was not much seen in the town, though he often rode out on horseback, and a carriage-road around the head of the bay was pointed out as his work.

We found it so agreeable to be on a spot to which travellers do not resort, that, I think, the felucca would have been discharged, and we should have remained on this island two or three months, had good accommodations offered. There were also some hints of malaria that did not encourage this notion.

While at the inn, I saw what the Italians call a *tarantola:* not a spider, but the lizard which bears this name. Perhaps nine-tenths of the Italians fancy the bite of this animal mortal; though it cannot bite at all, I believe. It is a perfectly inoffensive lizard, living on insects, and is found in America, where no one ever hears of its poison. It is, however, a most disgusting-looking object; which is probably the reason it bears so bad a name. The scorpion of Italy, also, is not in favour. We found several at St. Illario, but they are not dangerous in this latitude; the sting being about as bad as the bite of a spider. Both these animals are held in great respect by ordinary travellers; Mr. Carter, among others, dwelling on their horrors. This amiable and well-intentioned man saw more important things through quite as mistaken a medium.

After dinner we walked up to the head of the promontory to see the house of Napoleon. It stands conspicuously, is low and small, being composed of a main body and two wings, showing a front, in all, of ten windows. The entire length may have been ninety feet, or a little less; but the other dimensions were not on a proportionate scale. It was now inhabited by the governor of the island, and we could not obtain admission, as he was at dinner. Near this building is another, that stands on the street, against the acclivity, and which has a better air, as to comfort. It has but one principal story, but it showed fifteen windows in a row. This was the house occupied by *Madame Mère*, we were told.

We might have lingered longer on this height, which overlooks the sea, but I found the wind blowing fresh from the north-west, which was as fair as could be desired. Hurrying down to the port, I directed the felucca to be got under way. This order was a commencement of the difficulties of Mediterranean navigation. I was covered with protestations of the impossibility of putting to sea in such weather, blowing as it did. At this I laughed, telling my padrone that I was an old sailor myself, and was not to be imposed on in this manner. The wind was fair, and we could make a lee behind Elba in an hour if we found too much sea; but to this he would not listen. I then pointed to the females, and asked him if he were not ashamed to pretend fear, when they wished to go to sea. This touched his pride a little, and, after a good deal of wrangling, I got him out of the port, just as the sun was setting.

We found the wind fresh outside, but as fair as could be wished. Our course was to double the eastern end of the island, where there was a narrow passage between it and a small rocky islet, the place of which Napoleon is said to have taken possession with a corporal's guard, as soon as he was established. It was a dependency of the new empire. This act of his has been laughed at, and is cited as a proof of his passion for conquest; but it strikes me as more probable that he did it to prevent an unpleasant neighbourhood. The insignificance of the spot had caused it to be overlooked in the treaty by which his sovereignty over Elba had been retained, and it belonged to him only *by construction*. Political constructions are useful to the managing; and as it is probable he already meditated the events of 1815 in 1814, it was a measure of forethought to occupy a spot that might otherwise have proved embarrassing in the possession of spies.

When I pointed to this passage to leeward, the padrone pointed to the sky to windward. There was a lively sea on, but the little felucca skimmed it beautifully. The people, however, began to murmur, and [Mrs. Cooper] begging that we might have no difficulty, they were permitted to take their own course, which was to run across the streight, under the lee of Piombino, where we anchored, at nine.

At day-light next day, the wind being still fair, but very light, we got under way, and stood to the southward, having lost at least forty miles of our run, by stopping in at Piombino. About eight, the wind came ahead, and we made several stretches, until ten, when it fell calm. There was a small rocky islet, about a mile from us, and we swept the felucca up to it, and anchored in a little sandy bay. The padrone said this island was called

Troia. It contained about thirty acres, being a high rock with a little shrubbery, and it was surmounted by an ancient and ruined watch-tower.

We landed and explored the country. Our arrival gave the alarm to some thousands of gulls, and other marine birds, who probably had not been disturbed before for years.

W[illiam] undertook to ascend to the tower,—an exploit that was more easily achieved than the descent was effected. He found it the remains of a watch-tower, of which this coast has hundreds, erected as a protection against the invasions of the Barbary corsairs. The sight of such objects brought the former condition of these seas vividly to the mind. With one coast peopled by those who were at the head of civilization, and the other by those that were just civilized enough to be formidable, preferring constant warfare, the habits of slavery, and the harem, one can understand the uses of all these towers. Difficulties existing between France and Algiers just at this moment, several of our French acquaintances had tried to persuade us there was danger in even making this little voyage; and when at Marseilles, lately, I witnessed the departure of a brig, which was accompanied by the prayers of hundreds, her sailing having been actually delayed some time on the same account! The impression of the risks must have been strong, to prove so lasting. As to the tower on the little island, it could only have been used as a look-out to give notice of the approach of corsairs, and as a protection to the coasters, for there were no people to take refuge in it.

The north wind made at noon, and we embarked. We had a good run for the rest of the day, at the distance of a league or two, from a coast lower than common; off which there were many islets, and some banks of sand visible. The channel lay near one of the latter, which might have offered some danger, had we stood on the previous night. The padrone pointed to it with exultation, asking me how I should have liked to be laid on it in the dark. I pointed into the offing, and inquired, in turn, if there were not water enough for the Bella Genovese between the sands and Monte Cristo, a small island that was dimly visible to the westward, and which lies about half way between Corsica and the main. My Genoese shrugged his shoulders as he muttered, "As if one would like to be out there, in a little felucca, in a mistral!" It was quite obvious this fellow was no Columbus.

Just before sunset we came up with a high headland that looked like an island, but which in fact was Monte Argentaro; a peninsula connected with the continent by a low spit of sand. Behind it lies one of the best harbours for small craft in Italy, and the town of Orbitello. Directly abreast of it, and at no great distance, are several small islands, and we took the course between them. This was delightful navigation, at the close of a fine day in August, with a cool north wind, and in such a sea. We ran so near the mountain as to discern the smallest objects, and were constantly changing the scene. On this headland I counted seven watch-towers, all in sight at the same moment, and all within the space of a league or two. Including Elba, we must have seen and passed this day, in a run of about twenty miles, some twenty islands.

The wind died away with the disappearance of the sun, and when we took to the mattresses it was a flat calm. I was awoke, next morning, by the creaking of the yards; and rising I found we were working up to Cività Vecchia, with a foul but light wind,—a business we had been engaged in nearly all night. The Roman coast commenced as soon as we were clear of Argentaro, and we were now stretching in towards it, approaching within half a mile. It was low; and the watch-towers, better constructed than common,—a sort of martello tower,—were so near each other as completely to sweep the beach with their guns. They appeared so well that I attributed them to Napoleon, but the padrone affirmed they were constructed a long time since.

Cività Vecchia soon became distinctly visible. It lies around a shallow cove, with an artificial basin within it, and a mole stretching athwart the mouth of the cove. There is good holding-ground off the mole, and against easterly or north-easterly weather a good roadstead, but not much better than is to be found anywhere else on the west side of the boot. At ten we doubled the mole and ran into the port, where we found about fifty vessels, principally feluccas.

We landed and went to an inn, a miserable place at the best. Here we ordered breakfast; but the coffee, almost always bad in

Italy, is getting to be worse as we proceed south, though better in the large towns at the south than in the small ones at the north. There was no milk, and even fish was difficult to be had.

Cività Vecchia is small, but not dirty. There is an ancient mole, and a basin that once contained Roman galleys. The bronze rings by which they made fast to the quays still remain! To my surprise I was told there was an American consul here. He proved to be a consular agent, appointed by the consul at Rome; and I found him in a shop weighing some sugar, with a cockade in his hat as large as a small plate. He was civil and useful, however, for he obtained our passports, which had been taken from us on landing, without delay, and was serviceable in getting the necessary papers for the felucca.

After breakfasting and walking through the little town, we were anxious to proceed, for there was not time to look at some curious objects in the vicinity, and as for the town itself it was soon exhausted. By dint of two hours of pretty hard work I got the padrone on board, and compelled him to get under way. We beat into the offing at five, and then made a fair wind of it. The run this evening was delightful. The wind soon hauled and blew fresh from the land, leaving us perfectly smooth water, and we glided along at the rate of seven knots, so near the shore as to discern everything of moment. Among other objects we passed a fortress of some magnitude. At first the land was high, but, as the day declined, it melted away, until it got to be a low waste. This, we knew, was the water-margin of the celebrated Campagna of Rome; and about nine the padrone pointed out to us the position of Ostia, and the mouths of the Tiber. He kept the vessel well off the shore, pretending that the malaria at this season was so penetrating as to render it dangerous to be closer in with the wind off the land. As this was plausible, and at least safe, I commended his caution.

I was singularly struck by the existence of this subtle and secret danger in the midst of a scene otherwise so lovely. The night was as bright a starlight as I remember to have seen. Nothing could surpass the diamond-like lustre of the placid and thoughtful stars; and the blue waters through which we were gliding, betrayed our passage by a track of molten silver. While we were gazing at this beautiful spectacle, a meteor crossed the heavens, illuminating everything to the brightness of a clear moonlight. It was much the finest meteor I ever saw, and its course included more than half of the arch above us. The movement, apparently, was not swifter than that of a rocket, nor was the size of the meteor much less than one of the ordinary dimensions. Its light, however, was much more vivid and purer, having something intense, and much beyond the reach of art, in it. Soon after this beautiful sight, we retired to our mattresses.

Next morning we were off the Pontine Marshes, with Cape Circello, the insulated bluff in which they terminate, and the islands of Ponza and Palmarola, in sight. The latter were the first Neapolitan land we saw. The wind came a-head and light, as had invariably been the case since we left Leghorn in the morning. We gave ourselves no uneasiness on this account, feeling almost certain of a shift to the westward; a change as ancient as the Romans, this being their zephyr, which blows in summer almost daily in this part of the Mediterranean. From the sea the Pontine Marshes did not present an appearance sensibly different from that of the coast near Ostia. Both were low, and in some places reedy; and yet we saw dwellings along them immediately on the coast. One large, naked, treeless house, we were told, was the residence of a cardinal. There was even a small town visible, though nothing of importance, immediately next the marshes. The lowest part of the Pontine Marshes, however, is not on the coast to the west of them, but on the south, near Terracina; the stream that passes through them, as well as the canal, having that direction. The margin of the marshes next the sea, I take it, is higher than their centre, the drains running north and south.

A favourable slant of wind enabled us to double Cape Circello at noon, when we opened the Gulf of Gaeta, Terracina, and all the grand coast of that vicinity. The volcanic peaks of Ischia loomed in the distance, and the zephyr coming fresh and fair, we soon raised other objects of interest along the Neapolitan shore. Our course was, as near as might be, to the southeast, across the mouth of the gulf, and, as the coast receded, the fine mountains fell away in haze; but our mariners having an instinct for the land, we got better views than might have been expected, as we did not make a perfectly straight wake.

Towards the middle of the afternoon we had the town and

citadel of Gaeta abeam, dimly visible. A thunder-storm among the mountains produced a magnificent effect, though it frightened the padrone into shifting his sails, and even spars, for he sent down the old ones, and sent up a lighter set. We lost time unnecessarily by this precaution, for the wind did not increase. He showed me, however, two Neapolitan gun-vessels struggling through it, two or three leagues in shore of us; and we had the consolation of knowing that, had we been in their places, our smaller sails might have been of use.

Just before the gust appeared, I discovered a conical isolated mountain to the south-east, looming up in the haze. It proved to be Vesuvius. We saw it over the nearer but lower land of Baiæ and its vicinity. As usual, the wind fell at sunset, and finally it shifted. We had a little rain, and went to sleep uncertain of the result.

The next was the sixth day we had passed on board the Bella Genovese. Going on deck at sun-rise, I found the felucca contending with a head wind, but luckily in smooth water. On our right, lay high dark mountains thrown into picturesque forms, with a shore lined with hamlets and towns. This was Ischia. Ahead was another island, of the same character, resembling a gigantic sea-wall thrown before the bay. This was Capri. On our left, lay a small, low, level island, teeming with life; and to the north and east of us, opened the glorious Bay of Naples, with thousands of objects of interest, that, by their recollections, embrace nearly all of known time.

The wind blew directly in our teeth, and we beat up the whole distance, making short stretches close in with the western, or rather northern side of the bay. The multitude of things of interest we saw and passed, rendered the time short, though it took us three hours.

As the day opened, and we advanced farther into this glorious bay, we could not help exclaiming, "What dunce first thought of instituting a comparison between the bay of New York and this?" It is scarcely possible for two things composed of the same elements to be less alike, in the first place; nor are their excellencies the same in a single essential point. The harbour of New York is barely pretty; there being, within my own knowledge, some fifty ports that equal, or surpass it, even, in beauty. These may not be in England, a country in which we seek every standard of excellence; but the Mediterranean alone is full of them. No one would think of applying the term pretty, or even handsome, to the Bay of Naples; it has glorious and sublime scenery, embellished by a bewitching softness. Neither the water nor the land is the same. In New York the water is turbid and of a dullish green colour, for in its purer moments, it is, at the best, of the greenish hue of the entire American coast; while that of the Bay of Naples has the cerulean tint and limpidity of the ocean. At New York, the land, low and tame in its best months, offers nothing but the verdure and foliage of spring and summer, while the coasts of this gulf, or bay, are thrown into the peaks and faces of grand mountains, with the purple and rose-coloured tints of a pure atmosphere and a low latitude. If New York does possess a sort of back-ground of rocks, in the Palisadoes, which vary in height from three to five hundred feet, Naples has a natural wall, in the rear of the Campania Felice, among the Apennines, of almost as many thousands. This is speaking only of nature. As regards artificial accessories, to say nothing of recollections, the shores of this bay are teeming with them of every kind; not Grecian monstrosities, and Gothic absurdities in wood, but palaces, villas, gardens, towers, castles, cities, villages, churches, convents, and hamlets, crowded in a way to leave no point fit for the eye unoccupied, no picturesque site unimproved. On the subject of the scale on which these things are done, I will only say, that we tacked the felucca, in beating up to the town, under the empty windows of a ruined palace, whose very base is laved by the water, and whose stones would more than build all the public works on the shores of our own harbour, united.

The public mind in America has got to be so sickly on such subjects, that men shrink from telling the truth; and many of our people not only render themselves, but some render the nation, ridiculous, by the inflated follies to which they give utterance. I can safely say, I never have seen any twenty miles square of Lower Italy, if the marshes and campagnas be excepted, in which there is not more glorious scenery than I can recall in all those parts of America with which I am acquainted. Our lakes will scarcely bear any comparison with the finer lakes of Upper Italy; our mountains are insipid as compared with these, both as to hues and forms; and our seas and bays are not to be named with these. If it be patriotism to deem all our geese swans, I am no patriot, nor ever was; for, of all species of sentiments, it strikes me that your "property patriotism" is the most equivocal. Be on your guard against the statements of certain low political adventurers, who are as notorious for abusing everything American, while in Europe, as they are for extolling them, when in America.

I am far from underrating the importance of fine natural scenery to a nation; I believe it not only aids character, but that it strengthens attachments. But calling a second-rate, or an inferior thing, a first-rate and a superior, is not making it so. There is, in America, enough of beautiful nature, coupled with the moral advantages we enjoy, to effect all necessary ends, without straining the point to the absurd; but there is very little of the grand, or the magnificent.

We got up with the head of the mole, (the only harbour of Naples being the small basin behind this mole,) about noon, and immediately landed and sought an inn. As we drove along the streets, we met one of the royal equipages, a coach and six, and one of four, with a portly, well-looking man, with a Bourbon face, in the former. It was the Prince of Salerno, a brother of the king. Our guide took us to the hotel *delle Crocelle*, one of the principal inns in the Chiaja, where we found excellent and roomy accommodations.

Letter XII.

Y ou know the conditions on which these letters are written. I shall go on, in my own desultory manner, gleaning what it appears to me others have left, and speaking of such things only as I know from experience I should most like to have been set right in, did I depend on reading for my own information.

Our first night at Naples was absolutely delicious. There was a young moon, and everything was soft and lovely. It reminded us of an evening in August at New York, when people walk without their hats, and enjoy themselves after the intense heat of the day. But Naples has one great advantage over our own town. It lies literally on the sea; for the bay has all the advantages of the sea itself, and scarcely ever wants its refreshing influence. In the deep ravines of streets, one is entirely sheltered from the sun, and on the shore, one feels the air from the water. We have built a northern town in a southern latitude, though not without some excuse for it.

But the two towns are as unlike as their scenery. One is condensed, the houses clinging, in places, to rocky cliffs, some of the streets actually lying a hundred or two feet above their immediate neighbours; while the other is straggling, and has a surface shaved down nearly to a water level. One is overflowing with population; the other, properly peopled, would contain five times its present numbers. One is all commerce, shipping, drays, and stevedores, the particles of taste and beauty existing in fragments; the other all picturesque, the trade and the port forming the exception.

Immediately beneath our windows, here, is a line of seabeach, of more than a mile in extent, that has no sign of trade about it beyond the boats of fishermen, which lie scattered on the sands and shingle as if disposed there for the study of the painter. But I must not anticipate.

Vesuvius alone disappointed our expectation. It appeared low and insignificant compared with the mountains we had seen, filled the eye less in the view than we had imagined, and was altogether differently placed. As to its height, it varies essentially by the rising and falling of the crater, and I am told it is several hundred feet lower now than it was a year since. Indeed, one well-informed person says, its last great fall exceeded a thousand feet. You may easily imagine, however, that a mountain that could bear such a loss must be of respectable dimensions. I should think the present height of Vesuvius not far from three thousand feet; but there are peaks behind Castel-a-mare of double this altitude. The summits of Ischia and Capri are also high, and the whole southern shore of the bay is a noble outline of mountains.

Vesuvius, and indeed Naples, stand differently from what I had thought. The bay itself may be near twenty miles in depth, and its width varies from about fourteen, to something like eighteen miles, it being a little wider at its mouth than at its head. The general direction is east a little north, perhaps east-north-east. Now, the head of this bay, though irregular, is square, rather than rounded. Of the two, it presents a convex line to the water, rather than one that is concave. Naples stands at the north-east corner, and Castel-a-mare at its south-east, distant from each other about fifteen miles in a direct line; and Vesuvius occupies the centre, a little nearer to the first than to the last. All idea of danger to either of these places from lava, is an absurdity. They have reason to apprehend earthquakes, and internal convulsions, but nothing that comes out of the crater can ever harm either. Even Portici, which stands on the base of the mountain itself, is deemed to be reasonably safe.

The hazards of this volcano are easily estimated. Lava, the only serious cause of danger, breaks out of the sides of the mountain. It resembles the boiling over of a pot, and its descent can be calculated like that of water. The interposition of a ravine offers an effectual barrier. As to the stones and other fiery missiles that are projected into the air, they necessarily fall in the crater, or on the sides of the mountain; and their flight does not much exceed that of a bullet, at the most. It is probably two miles in an air line, from the limits of their fall to the nearest habitation, if we except the Hermitage, which is near half that distance. The ashes certainly are borne to a great distance; but they do good rather than harm, greatly fertilizing the surrounding country. Vesuvius is, in fact, as far from Naples as the heights of Staten Island are from New York, and the water actually lies between them.

One of our first visits was to Pompeii, which lies, perhaps, more properly at the head of the bay than Castel-a-mare, though they are not far asunder. The distance between the summit of the mountain and Pompeii is about five miles; the direction is from north-west to south-east, Vesuvius lying most northerly. This, of course, brings Pompeii on the side opposite to that of Naples, and about one half nearer to the crater. But lava could no more touch this place, than it could touch Naples, the formation of the land carrying it more towards the water. The road winds round the head of the bay, which has a succession of hamlets, villas, towns, and palaces. Indeed, I scarcely know a spot that is more teeming with population than the base of this terrible mountain. It is true that there is a broad belt of broken rising ground between the sea and the regular ascent, of three or four miles in width; but even this is dotted with habitations, and the lava *does* find its way across it. We saw two or three towns and villages in ruins, from the great eruption of 1822. The lava had passed directly over houses, when they were strong enough to resist it, and through them, when not. Of course, that which had cooled, remained, and it is not easier to fancy a more complete picture of desolation than these black belts of ruin present in the midst of a moving population;— even the road had been cut through them. These towns are populous, Torre del Greco having twelve or thirteen thousand souls, Castel-a-mare more, and Portici several thousands. The celebrated palace at the latter is so placed that the public highway passes directly through its great court, a singular caprice of royalty.

I think we were all a little disappointed with Pompeii. Perhaps our expectations were wrought up too high, for, certainly, I have approached no place in Europe with the same feverish excitement. Still it is an extraordinary thing to see even these remains of a Roman town, brought to light, as they have been, in their ancient appearance. As some popular errors, however, exist on the subject of this place, and touching the catastrophe by which it was overwhelmed, I shall first endeavour to tell you what I have ascertained on these points on the spot.

You probably know that, while all this region afforded geological evidence of a volcanic origin, as is the fact with Ischia, Sorrento, and so much more of it to-day, including Naples itself, there was no historical account, prior to the great eruption, of there having been an active volcano. The peak of Vesuvius has now three distinct summits, separated by tolerably deep valleys, and it is probable that these three peaks were formerly united in one, the separation being owing to the explosion. Lest you should form an erroneous notion of the present appearance, however, of this celebrated mountain, it may be necessary to add that the cone, or the peak, which is actually called Vesuvius, is so much higher and more conspicuous than the others, that its form of a cone is not much impaired by the fact, not at all as seen from many points, particularly from the direction of the sea. The three mountains, too, if they can be so termed, stand near each other, on a common base, their dividing valleys, or ravines, not descending more than a few hundred feet, and they are entirely insulated from the ordinary ranges of the Apennines.

The great eruption, which occurred in the year 79, was preceded by the usual signs, but, there being no crater, or, at the most, only an old one, the first explosion was necessarily tremendous. Pliny describes the smoke as resembling a gigantic pine, which rose to a vast height, and veiled the sun. He meant a pine of this region, or what is sometimes called a stone pine, of which many are now to be seen in Lower Italy. It is a tall tree, with an umbrella-shaped top, very different from any pine we have, and which resembles the smoke of a fire, before it is driven away by the wind. Boiling water, pumice stones, ashes, and heated sulphureous air, accompanied the explosion, and lava succeeded. The wind must have been at the north, for Pliny the elder lost his life on the beach near Castel-a-mare, by inhaling the heated gas, a distance of at least seven miles from the crater. As no one else near him appears to have suffered, his death, it is to be presumed, was owing to a particular condition of the body; defective lungs, most probably. The people of Pompeii had time to remove many of their effects; but the greatest of the popular errors has arisen from a misapprehension of the nature of the interment. Even now, the buildings are scarcely covered, and the dirt, or ashes, that lie on them, is so light, that it may be shoveled like dry sand. The country is principally in the vine, and there is a light soil of course; but, this removed, in dry weather nothing can be more easily worked than these ancient ashes. Now, every object of any elevation, such as the towers, must have been left above ground. These would serve as landmarks; and, as very few things are found in the houses, it is probable that their owners dug into them, after the alarm was over, and took away everything of value that could be found. The few human remains prove that the danger was not instantaneous, or without notice; for thousands would have been destroyed in such a case, instead of one or two hundreds.

It is usual to say that the site of Pompeii was discovered about eighty years since. This may be true as respects the generation then in being, but could not be true as to very many that went before it. Discoveries of this nature are a little equivocal. If a man of letters stumbles on any ancient remains, or a fine valley, or a statue, he calls himself a discoverer, though thousands in the neighbourhood know all about them; the latter do not write books on the subject. The ashes are only about eighteen feet deep, and the walls, in some places, are even higher than this. The temples, amphitheatre, and even some of the houses, must have exceeded this height. It is probable that adventurers have been down into these ruins, in places, in every age since the accident occurred, though the state of intelligence has prevented the facts from being published. A Neapolitan poet who wrote near two centuries since, alludes to the towers as visible in his time. Nothing but alarm could have prevented the people from clearing away the ashes, and taking possession of their town again; for the expense could not greatly exceed that of clearing the streets of New York after a hard winter.

To me, much the most interesting object at Pompeii is the amphitheatre. It is complete with the exception of its ornaments, and the marble seats, of which just enough remain to prove that they once existed; their disappearance demonstrates that the place had been pretty thoroughly explored, probably soon after the eruption. This amphitheatre stands by itself, in a corner of the town, against the walls, and is large for the place.

Were those of Rome, Verona, and Nismes, and one or two more, not in existence, it would be thought prodigious.

The houses of Pompeii, you will readily conceive, were low, and they had the flat roofs, of cement, that are still used in all this region, the shape being a little rounded so as to turn the water. I should think few of them could have been destroyed by the weight of the ashes immediately, though time would be certain to cause their beams to rot. Most of the dwellings were connected with shops, but there are enough of a better sort, to give one a very respectful opinion of the luxury of the Romans. They are built around courts, which, in this mild climate, would answer all the purposes of halls for most of the year, and which, probably, were often veiled from the heat of the sun by awnings. The diminutive size, and the want of light and other conveniences of the sleeping-rooms, however, rather detract from our estimate of ancient comfort. The scale on which the places of public resort existed, such as the amphitheatre and theatres, the forum, temples, and baths, coupled with the showy character of the greater, and the meaner character of the more private, apartments of the dwellings, I think, leave an impression against the *individuality* of the people. I do not know whether the public *meddled* as much among the Romans, as among us Anglo-Saxons, but the inference seems to be pretty fair, that the man lived voluntarily more before it than is our practice.

Here I first saw a small fragment of the Appian Way. This road was far from straight, making deviations from the direct line to communicate with towns and posts, as well as to avoid natural impediments; as is proved both here and at Pozzuoli, as well as in other places. It entered Pompeii by the Naples gate, and left it near the amphitheatre. It has been uncovered for some little distance in the former direction; and, as usual, it was bordered by tombs. Cicero somewhere speaks of sitting with a friend in a certain seat, without this gate, near to a particular tomb, reading one of his Offices. The seat and tomb are both there!

Pompeii certainly offers a multitude of objects of intense interest, (but which I shall not describe for the thousandth time;) but whoever fancies he sees in it a disinterred town that needs only to be peopled to be perfect, has an imagination more fertile than mine. It wears the aspect of a ruin. It is true that the modern towns and villages of this region are not without something of the same appearance; for the absence of visible roofs, the apertures of the windows, which, when open, show no glass, —and open they generally are in summer,—and the dun hue, conspire to give them a look not unlike that of this Roman city. But Pompeii has still more of this character, from the manner in which its temples were destroyed, (as is thought,) by a severe earthquake a few years previously to the eruption. The broken columns, and the other fragments, sufficiently testify to this fact.

The walls are well preserved, and I walked for some distance on them. The summits of their towers have principally disappeared, for they must have risen above the ashes, and were probably the towers spoken of by the poet mentioned, the Romans seldom building any other. They have a strong resemblance to the walls of the towns of France, which were used before artillery was much improved. The inscriptions, signs, scribbling on the walls, and divers other little usages of the sort, certainly produce a startling effect, referring as they do to the most familiar things of an age so very remote, and in a manner of so little design. These things savour more of peopled streets, than the houses.

The Neapolitan government keeps slowly at work, disinterring. Its deliberation has been idly censured, as are many other things of this nature, by inconsiderate travellers; but I believe it prudent and even necessary. The town is probably near half disinterred, and it would be possible to lay it entirely bare in a twelvemonth,—perhaps in a single month; but it would be at the risk of injuring paintings, as well as of loss by frauds and haste. A small piece of coin mixed with ashes and cinders, or a child's toy, is easily overlooked in a scramble. This much derided deliberation is probably in the interest of knowledge, besides the fact that nothing presses. A house had been laid open just before our visit, that showed the necessity for caution. Among other curious things, in its court was a small fountain, ornamented with shells, which came out as fresh and uninjured as if they had just been put together. Another house nearly adjoining, has a similar fountain. In both cases the courts are rather small, though one of the buildings has the appearance of a dwelling of some pretension. You will understand that these courts did not receive carriages, like ours, or rather like the European courts, but they were a species of domestic cloisters, by which the light was admitted, and by means of which the communications with the different rooms were maintained. In a few instances there were small gardens in addition to the courts; but I suspect that the street which contains most of the good houses remains to be opened. Looking about at the forum, theatres, and temples, I find it difficult to believe that such edifices would have been erected for the uses of those only who dwelt in habitations like most of these which have already been disinterred.

It would be possible to render Pompeii immeasurably more interesting than it is at present, by roofing a few of the houses; or by covering them with arches, and using them as places in which to exhibit the different articles found there, and which are now assembled in the Studio at Naples. Perhaps one of the buildings might be nearly furnished in such a manner. I think, as things now are, the ruins lose in interest by the absence of these articles, and the articles by the absence of the ruins. There would be a certain inconvenience in this arrangement, it is true, but I think it would be more than compensated for, by the intensity of the interest that would be created, to say nothing of the greater distinctness that would be afforded to our idea of the ancient domestic economy.

Pompeii once stood on a low promontory, and was a port, but the land has made in a way to throw the sea back, fully a mile. Through this low bottom the Sarno now flows into the bay. In the present state of the entrance of the river, no vessel could approach the town, it being difficult to get a common boat into it when there is any wind. A portion of this stream was led through the town, and the water still flows in the artificial channel beneath the houses and temples!

Our guide went through the usual routine tolerably well, but he had obtained a droll jumble of languages from the different strangers who frequent the place. With *him* the conversation was principally in Italian and French, while among ourselves we occasionally spoke English. Ambitious to show his knowledge, he called out to me, as I stepped into a building to examine it, with a strange confusion of grammar and tongues—"*Eh! Signore; celui-là sono tutti shops.*"

Returning from Pompeii, we stopped to visit Herculaneum. This place, in very many particulars, is of far greater interest than the other. It was much more important of itself, and, instead of being barely covered with ashes and cinders, it was indeed, buried; the distance between the pit of the theatre that is opened, and the surface of the ground, being about seventy feet. Lava did the work here, and as every thing was covered while the rolling mass was in a state of fusion, the fiery fluid found its way into every crevice, cooling around them, so as to preserve the forms of the things it enveloped.

You know that Herculaneum was discovered by digging a well. Since that time, which was more than a century since, the hole has been enlarged so as to disinter the entire pit of the theatre, and galleries have been cut around it, enabling one to examine nearly all of that particular edifice. Owing to the formation of the ground, this city has been covered very unequally, not only as to depth, but as to substance. The lava is a hundred feet deep in places, while, towards Resina, the covering is very like that of Pompeii, and not essentially deeper. This thin and light coat of earth, however, is unfortunately over the suburbs, rather than over the town itself. A portion of these suburbs have been laid bare, and the result has been the discovery of several houses, and even portions of streets, that are very like those of Pompeii. One is called a villa, that is not much, if any, inferior to the well-known villa of the latter town.

It is fair to presume that this region was much visited by earthquakes, previously to the great eruption. A pent volcano is certain to produce calamities of this nature, and we know from history, that the earthquake of 63 did great injury to these two towns in particular. Slight earthquakes are even now quite common. To this cause is probably owing the lowness of the dwellings; those of Herculaneum, that are quite laid open, being no higher than those of Pompeii. There were also a forum and a temple opened, but parts have been filled again in receiving the *débris* of new diggings. Some apprehensions for the town above may have caused this provision; as Portici and Resina both stand, more or less, over the buried city.

We descended into the theatre by a passage cut through the lava, and explored its neighbourhood by torchlight. The stage, proscenium, consular seats, orchestra, and lobbies, are open;

and it was a curious sensation to wander through such places under such circumstances. The general appearance was that of a mine; but when the eye came to scrutinize the details, and to find that the place was once actually a populous city, which exists as near as possible in its ancient condition, embedded, filled, gorged with lava, a feeling of awe and of intense admiration comes over one. I think this place, out of all comparison, the most imposing sight of the two. Pompeii offers more to investigation, and more for the gratification of common curiosity; but there is a sublimity in the catastrophe of Herculaneum, a grandeur in its desolation, that has no parallel. One is like examining a mummy carelessly prepared, in which the mass has been so far preserved, it is true, as to show a general but a hideous likeness to humanity, while the other is opening one of those graves that, owing to some property of the soil, preserves the body with most of the peculiarities of the living man. The lava and the stone of the edifices are so intimately united, that one does not, at first, distinguish between them in those places where the separation has not been made; and I cannot describe the effect on the feelings, when it is suddenly ascertained that the hand is actually resting on a portion of a human structure.

As the light descends by the large opening that was made around the well, the stage and pit of the theatre, with all its more principal parts, are sufficiently obvious. But even this excites a sensation different from any other ruin (the word is misapplied, for every thing is nearly as perfect as on the day when the catastrophe occurred) when the frightful interment is contemplated. Judge for yourself of the appearance of a large and even elegant structure, placed in the bosom of rocks, eighty feet beneath the surface, and of the crowd of associations that press upon the mind at contemplating such an object. Of the magnitude of the edifice you may form some notion by that of the proscenium, which is set down in the books at one hundred and thirty feet in length, the rest of the building being in proportion of course. It is said this theatre would hold ten thousand people, but the number strikes me as extravagant. When it was first opened, everything that was not liable to be removed, or destroyed, by the motion and heat of the lava, was found as it stood at the moment of the disaster. Thus the stage had all its permanent decorations, though some were displaced and injured, such as bronzes, alabaster columns, &c. These fragments have been preserved in the museums. You know that the celebrated equestrian statues of the Balbi came from Herculaneum.

I have only given you my first impressions on visiting these two remarkable places, as volumes exist filled with their details, arranged with care, and collected with accuracy. To the American, to whom a quaint chimney-top, half a century old, is a matter of interest, I should think few objects in Europe would present more attractions than either; for though much older and even better specimens of ancient arts and ancient manners are certainly to be found, none others exist surrounded by so many of the evidences of familiar life.

The entire base of Vesuvius, which in former times, as now, seems to have been a favourite residence, offers the same species of remains, wherever a shaft is sunk or an opening made, though there are but two or three buried cities. Many villas and hamlets have been discovered, and I have seen one or two of them in the distance. A much more wonderful thing, as is said, I know not with what truth, is the fact, that Pompeii stands on lava, which in itself covers another town. This may be true, for the site might induce the occupation of the spot; but if true, what a miserable figure human annals make!

On returning from this visit I witnessed a droll scene beneath our windows. There is a small garden, with a pavilion, directly opposite the hotel. It stands on the margin of the sea, is enclosed with a high wall, and is the property of the crown; the royal children frequently coming to it to take exercise. While we were seated in the balconies, enjoying the sea-breeze, a carriage and four, with a *piqueur*, and the royal liveries, drove to the door of the pavilion, and set down a gentleman and a lady, with a boy and a girl, the latter about six, and the former perhaps four years old. These were two of the younger children of the king. They went together into the house. It was not long, however, before they all came out again. A crowd had collected by this time, and every one stood uncovered, the guards, at the gate of the garden, with presented arms. The children were lifted into the hind seats of the carriage, an open barouche, with great respect, and their attendants were about to take the front seats, when the little creatures sprang on them, with the zest that forbidden pleasures are apt to excite. The gentleman and lady remonstrated without success; the sight of the horses overcoming the sense of etiquette. The boy, in particular, was for driving. The lady then entered the carriage, carefully avoiding seating herself on the hind seat, and finally succeeded in persuading the girl to take her proper place; but his royal highness, the Conte d'Aquila, for such is the appellation of the boy, resolutely refused to budge. At last, the whole affair consuming several minutes, the gentleman entered, seated himself by the side of the lady, took the young prince in his lap, and whispered his remonstrance; but all in vain, the little fellow struggling manfully to get a sight of the horses again. Tired with his pertinacity, he was put, by respectful violence, in his proper place, the servant closed the doors in haste, the coachman whipped his horses, and the equipage dashed off, with the obstinate little prince pinned by force on the precise spot that etiquette enjoined he should occupy. The whole time the crowd was uncovered, and the soldiers stood at presented arms.

Deference to royalty is carried very far here. W[illiam] and myself were strolling in one of the public buildings lately, and I stopped to read a proclamation. While carelessly running my eyes over it, a sentinel ordered me to take off my hat. It was commanded that the royal proclamation should be read uncovered. As this was a little too much in the spirit of Gessler, I preferred not reading any more to submission.

I do not mention these things to deride them, for they have their use, though proper substitutes exist; but simply as touches of the country. I wish there was a little less of this abstract deference for station and authority here, as I sincerely wish there were a good deal more of both (under certain limitations of common sense) in America. Society loses nothing by causing those who do not know how to reason, to feel. Besides, there is great danger that, in the absence of respect for station, men will get to have a respect for mere money, which is the most abject and contemptible of all conditions of the mind, to say nothing of its direct tendency to corruption. I should deem it a *pas en avant*, could we hear it said at home, "That fellow is proud of his descent, his manners, his knowledge of the world, his conversation, his connections," his any thing, in short, instead of the vulgar accusation of being "purse-proud."

Letter XIII.

Having determined to pass the remainder of the season in the vicinity of Naples, we have been employed, for the last week, in looking for a house. Our aim has been the vicinity of the town; so far from it, as to escape its confusion and noise, and yet so near as to possess its conveniences. The occupation has enabled us to see more of the modes of ordinary life, than a traveller usually gets in a hurried visit. At the same time we have given glances at the different objects of curiosity as they presented themselves.

The Bay of Naples, which is truly *"un pezzo di cielo caduto in terra,"* * is surrounded by country houses, of which a large number are to be let. We may have been in fifty of them, and we find them possessing very generally a common character; large edifices, with spacious, sometimes vast apartments, terraces that overlook the sea, and furniture that is rich though commonly decayed. Some of the chairs and tables that we have found in these places, appear to be more than a century old, being carved, gilded, and heavy. We entered houses, that are palaces in extent, in the size and in the number of the rooms, that were utterly destitute of conveniences on the score of furniture, but which were not without a certain air of comfortless magnificence. The views were almost always fine, though perhaps a majority of the situations had objections on account of their vicinity to roads, hamlets, or dusty thoroughfares of some sort or other. Others, again, were more modern, were freshly and even elegantly furnished, but they were too dear. The rents were generally high, for this is the very season when the villas are frequented; the Italians of condition, like the French, sel-

*"A little bit of heaven fallen upon the earth;" the common Neapolitan saying.

dom visiting their country houses, except for a short time in midsummer, or near the vintage. The latter is their *villeggiatura*. These residences around Naples, however, are not, of course, the old baronial hotels on the estates, but merely temporary retreats. The gardens are seldom of much extent, or very well kept, though there are exceptions.

One of the places that we visited in the course of our inquiries, was so remarkable as to merit a particular notice. It was the villa of Cardinal Ruffo; not the prelate who was so celebrated in the revolutionary movements of the last century, for he, I believe, perished at the time, but one of the same dignity, name, and family.

Naples, I have told you, in part occupies broken ground. A volcanic rock tops the city; and here is placed the well known castle of St. Elmo; a citadel, or fortress, that can almost send its shot down the chimneys of the place, as well as possessing a formidable range for its fire, in the way of marine defence. The view from this castle is singularly beautiful, and, owing to the proximity of the town, and the formation of the land, one can vary it in fifty ways, by slight changes of position. I know no other capital that possesses such a look-out, as it were, in its bosom; that of Montmartre, though fine and even extraordinary, from its extreme contrasts between town and country, wanting altogether the softened sublimity which reigns all through this region. Immediately below the citadel stands a convent, which is now converted into an hospital, I believe, on the extremest verge of the cliffs; for the part of the town that lies nearest the sea, or the south-western quarter, is placed on terraces, which are separated by perpendicular walls of tufa. From the balconies of this convent there is a terrific bird's-eye view of the more level quarter of the town;—terrific, after all, is not precisely the word I ought to use, for, as I have so often intimated, there is a softness thrown around every natural object here, that lessens all the harsher features of the landscapes. From this convent I looked into the streets, which resembled narrow ravines, and not even the sounds of a town proverbially noisy, ascended to our ears. It required no great stretch of the imagination to fancy the venerable fathers seated at their windows, now contemplating the mites beneath them, engaged in the boisterous and selfish pursuits of their lives, now turning their looks upwards at the serene calm of the blue vacuum, through which, as habit has taught us to imagine, lies the path to heaven. This is the poetical side of the picture, for, were the truth known, I dare say the sight was as often gloating on the baskets of green figs, and luscious grapes, and other delicious objects, that are always to be seen in the streets, as on any thing else. Before proceeding to the villa, I shall add, that we went through this convent, which amply repaid the examination, by its scented and carved sacristy, its picture by Spagnoletto, and its "incense-breathing" chapels. Some of its passages and apartments were the very quintessence of pious architecture, being cool, fragrant, rich, quaint, and clerkly. Really, one occasionally finds in Italy religious retreats, that are so suited to the climate, the dreamy existence of the country, and the priestly tastes, that there are moments when a monkish feeling comes over me, and even a monkish life has its attractions. I believe, however, that I was not created for vigils and fasts.

The villa of Cardinal Ruffo lies on a terrace a little lower than this convent, facing more to seaward. I do not know the precise elevation of these rocks, but I think St. Elmo cannot be much less than four hundred feet above the bay, if it be any less, and the villa is about two hundred and fifty to three hundred. The garden is pretty, extensive, and is well shaded with trees and shrubs, though the motive appears to be, principally, to exclude the objects in the rear. The house is extensive, though low, standing also on the verge of the cliffs. It was in good order, neat, and reasonably well furnished, having just been occupied by an Englishman of rank. But no language can do justice to the scene which presented itself, when we reached its balconies. I shall attempt to describe it, however; for, having heard so much of the beauty of this spot, you will feel some desire to get more distinct ideas than can be gained by general eulogiums.

You know the position and magnitude of the bay, and the exquisite beauty of its water. No American who has never been off soundings, can appreciate the latter beauty, I repeat, for I know of no blue water in all America. Our most limpid lakes are nearer the colour of amber than any other, and the entire coast is a sea-green. The Mediterranean, on the other hand, is unusually blue, and its bays and gulphs appear to have as deep a tint as the open sea.* The house commands a view of all that part of the bay which lies in the direction of Capri, the opposite coast, with the open sea, in the distance. The foreground was the lower terraces, and the portions of the town that were not hid by the cliffs, on the side of the Chiaja.

The bay itself was asleep, with its bosom dotted with a thousand boats, and crafts of different sizes. The deathlike calm that pervaded everything was in exquisite accordance with the character of the entire view. The mountains were dreamy, the air was filled with a drowsy repose, while the different objects of historical interest over which the eye rather lingered than glanced, gave the whole the semblance of a physical representation of things past, adorned and relieved by a glorious grouping of so much that is exquisite in the usages of the present.

Of fishing-boats alone, I feel certain of being within bounds when I say, they were out in hundreds. A long line of them stretched away from near the town, in the direction of Capri, not one of which appeared to have motion. Clusters of them lay scattered about in every direction, and the sails were drooping on board of vessels of nearly every sort of rig known in this picturesque sea. These elements of beauty might have been assembled elsewhere, though scarcely in such numbers and in so much perfection; but you will remember that, besides the peculiarities of the vessels, their varieties, the boats, the union of sublime land and glorious water, there was also a coast teeming with places over which history, from remote antiquity, had thrown its recollections and its charms. That bewitching and

---

*Soon after the return of the writer to this country, he was shown a view of the Bay of Naples, painted by Mr. Chapman, which was taken from a spot near the house he had inhabited most of the time he dwelt on its glorious shores. On being asked if it was faithful, he answered, "Perfectly so, *except that the artist has not done justice to the hue of the water, which is not sufficiently blue.*" He was then told, that the ordinary criticism was to complain of the element *as being too blue for nature.* The same objection is often made to the skies of Italian and Grecian landscapes, and to the other tints, as exaggerated. All this is a consequence of judging of Nature by a rule that is applicable only to her laws under particular circumstances. These hues certainly vary, but the writer has often seen the lakes of Switzerland and the bay of Naples almost as dark as ultra-marine itself.

almost indescribable softness of which I have so often spoken, a blending of all the parts in one harmonious whole, a mellowing of every tint and trait, with the total absence of everything unseemly or out of keeping, threw around the picture a seductive ideal, that blended with the known reality in a way I have never before witnessed, nor ever expect to witness again.

Travellers often come to this place on a hasty visit, and, encountering bad weather, or an unpropitious state of the atmosphere, they go away with false notions of the comparative excellence of things. We have now been ten months in Italy, and, certainly, had we gone away without visiting this portion of the country, we should have formed no accurate opinion of Italian nature. Had we come here during the bad weather, it is equally probable that, by transferring to a time of the year when no nature is seen to advantage the descriptions that refer to the more genial months, we might have felt disposed to accuse those who made them of exaggeration and fraud. Even now, the atmosphere is not of extraordinary purity. It has a sleepy haziness about it, that I find in admirable harmony with the season and the region; but experience has taught me to distinguish between months, and to look for its most peculiar and its greatest charm at a still later season of the year.

It is not an easy thing to find a residence for a family that has no material objection. The price was the great obstacle to taking the villa of Cardinal Ruffo, and we reluctantly turned our eyes in another direction. We had now been three weeks in taverns, and one must experience it to feel the relief that is afforded by getting out of these public places into a private dwelling with a family. Our inn, notwithstanding, offered fewer objections and more attractions than any I was ever in. It was nearly empty at this season—a great advantage in itself, was well kept, had noble rooms, and overlooked the bay.

The choice was finally made at Sorrento, a town of a few thousand inhabitants, directly opposite to Naples, and at the distance of eighteen miles. The house we took has a reputation from having been the one in which Tasso was born, or, at least, *is said* to have been born; and although it is not the villa of Cardinal Ruffo, it is little inferior to it in scenery. The greater part of the plain on which Sorrento stands is surrounded in a half circle by mountains, the segment facing the bay. The whole formation is volcanic, large fissures of the tufa appearing in the shape of deep ravines in various places. Advantage was taken of the accidental position of these ravines, so as to form a deep natural ditch around most of the place, which stands on the immediate margin of the plain. This plain is six or seven miles in length, is a continued village, very fertile, and extremely populous. Its elevation above the bay varies from one to two hundred feet, the verge being a perpendicular cliff of tufa nearly the whole distance. Sorrento lies near the south-western extremity, the heights overlooking it. The house we have taken is on the cliffs, within the walls, and in plain sight of every object of interest on the bay, from Ischia to the promontory of Vico, Castel-a-mare and a short reach of the coast in its vicinity excepted.

Having settled the material point of a residence for the remainder of the warm months, we passed a few more days in looking at sights. I shall say nothing of the Museum, and of similar things, for you can read of them at any time, but confine myself to what has struck me as peculiarities. The first of these shall be the Campo Santo, or the place of interment. A large proportion of the people of Naples die in the hospitals; and even of those who do not, perhaps half are unable to leave means for their interment. A place has accordingly been provided for those who are interred at the public expense and this is the spot to which we will now go.

The Campo Santo is a short distance from the city, enclosed by high walls. There is a chapel near the entrance, with a few rooms for the use of the officials. As I understand the arrangement, the earth was removed from the entire area, when the cavity was walled up into three hundred and sixty-five separate vaults. As there is, however, so much of that soft material in this vicinity, I am not certain that the desired number of vaults has not been cut in the tufa, the effect being the same in the two cases. Each vault has a large hole in the centre, that is covered by a stone fitting closely. This stone has a ring, and a movable lever, with its fulcrum, all of which are on wheels, is in readiness to remove it. Each night the lever is applied to a new ring, and a stone is removed. At an appointed hour the dead arrive in covered carts. Our guide affirmed that, after the religious service, they were then *dumped*, to use a New York term, from the cart into the hole; and judging by what I witnessed, I think this probable. The bodies are next sprinkled with quick lime, and the stone is replaced and closed with cement. At the end of the year, little is found besides bones, which are removed to a bone-house, or vault, kept for that purpose. The hole, however, is not closed for twenty-four hours, the fees paid by the curious being an inducement to keep it in readiness to be opened during that time.

When W[illiam] and I presented ourselves, we were received by a cadaverous-looking priest and sexton, on whose appearance this constant communication with the remains of mortality had produced anything but an aspect of devotion. Our wishes being known, after examining the place generally, we were desired to look into an open vault: it was quite empty, and indeed clean. The lever was then applied to the ring of the covering of the vault last filled, and a more revolting and hideous spectacle has been seldom witnessed than the one we saw. Seventeen dead bodies were lying naked beneath the hole, in a way that I can only compare to the manner in which Jack-straws fall! If they had not actually been dropped from the cart, no care had been taken even to lay them side by side, but they were placed just as chance had ordered it. A few rags served as apologies to decency, and even these were not always used. Whether they were actually brought from the hospitals in this state, I cannot tell you: the guide affirmed that they were; but one cannot confide in the information of guides.

While the poor meet with the fate of the "unhonoured dead," the taste of the Neapolitans of means is for gorgeous funerals. I have met several in the streets, in which there was more of pageantry than about any private ceremonies of the sort I have ever witnessed. Led horses are one of the standing honours of a gentleman,—I presume, from some connexion with a chivalrous origin. We observe the same usage, even to this day, in all our own military funerals of field-officers. The body, I find, is often exposed here, as in other parts of Italy, though I have not yet seen it on any of the great occasions just named.

Naples has a corso in the Toledo; but at this season the carriage promenade appears to be by the Chiaja, and along a road that leads to the south-western point of the bay. This is one of the most delightful drives in the world. The road follows the strand for two miles, having houses and villas on one hand, and the water on the other. It passes the Villa Reale, one of the prettiest gardens imaginable, and the celebrated gallery of Pozzuoli, or the grotto, as it is usually called. This passage, which is of great antiquity, is of immense convenience, though of no great cost or labour, the rock through which it is cut being soft. The effect on looking through it is singular, for it is never empty, during the day at least; and as a proof of its utility, it smells like a stable. The reputed tomb of Virgil is on the side of the hill, immediately over the entrance of this grotto. The best reason for believing it to have been erected in honour of the Great Mantuan, is, that if it be not his tomb, no one can say whose tomb it is. After all, Virgil had a tomb, he died here, and this is an ancient work. It may be the tomb of Virgil.

The mole of Naples, and the entire strand from the Castel Nuovo, near it, to the eastern extremity of the town, offer extraordinary exhibitions. This was the region of the Lazzaroni; and finer-looking or merrier vagabonds than those who are now found in it, it is not easy to meet. The streets that they frequent, and in which they may be said to live, lie in this quarter, and are altogether unique. Brawling, laughing, cooking, flirting, eating, drinking, sleeping, together with most of the other concerns of life, are all transacted here beneath the canopy of heaven. The throng resembles the quays of Paris in the neighbourhood of the Pont Neuf during a fête, with this difference, that as *everybody* of a certain class appears to be out in the French capital on such occasions, the streets of Naples also include every *thing*. The serenity, and, what is of more influence, the security of the weather, convert the streets into dwellings; and if these people have lodgings at all, they must be far less agreeable than the open air.

The veritable Lazzaroni, however,—the houseless fellows who look to Abraham's bosom as their first regular lodgings,— have greatly diminished of late years, if they exist at all. Murat made soldiers of them, and otherwise gave them something to do, and they are now less averse to regular employment than formerly. I saw many at work, quite as near a state of nature as our Indians in a war dress, the paint and feathers being so much the more in favour of the latter. The only garment was a pair of very unsophisticated breeches, that did not cover a fourth of the thighs. The colour, as may be imagined from exposure under such a sun, was not essentially different.

The day we arrived, while the felucca was hauling into her berth, I observed a pair of feet, soles uppermost, just out of water, not far from the shore. Watching them for some time, they gradually sunk, when a swarthy face came up in their place. This was one of the Lazzaroni getting his dinner from the smaller shell-fish. A long resident here tells me that these people can exist in summer on incredibly small sums; such as three or four *grani* a day. Coarse bread, grapes, and most fruits are cheap; "and recollect," added my friend, "when you give a Neapolitan beggar a *grano* (which is less than a cent) you give him a meal." The figs are delicious, and I make it a point to eat one of the luscious little green fellows, with a blood-red interior, every day immediately after the soup. This has got to be a matter of conscience with me. The water melons are much like our own, and about the same price; but the musk melons are greatly inferior to those of New York. The peaches seem to be merely tolerable. Notwithstanding this, fruits are abundant, and, so far as the markets are concerned, better than ours; though he who judges of the fruits of New York from the public-houses and the markets, knows nothing about them. We have tried the ices in the Toledo, and, notwithstanding their reputation, think them greatly inferior to those of other towns we know. Contoit need not hide his head in comparison with anything, in the way of simple creams, that are to be found in Europe. But I have found good coffee in one café here, and it is the first I have found in Italy. The house is kept by a Frenchman.

Naples and New York lie within a few miles of the same latitude. There are marked differences between the climates, certainly; and yet there are also, at this season in particular, marked points of resemblance. Our proximity to the West Indies gives us some advantages as regards the markets, as does the mixed character of our temperature. I believe America to be almost the only country in which the peach and apple come to perfection in the same field without resorting to forcing.

The streets of Naples at night are like our own, or rather like one or two in America, when there is a bright moon, and there has been a warm day. The absence of side-walks here, and the greater throngs, make the difference. But I know no place that offers a scene like this towards the setting of the sun. Imagine the effect in a street, or perhaps on the side of a hill, where the houses are six or seven stories in height, the windows all opening on hinges, and having balconies, and these balconies filled with people enjoying the cool air. I have literally seen streets with scarcely a balcony unoccupied. Fancy also the pleasure of sitting in such a spot, at such an hour, and overlooking a town like Naples, and such a bay! Most of the houses that face in the right direction, and which stand on the hill-sides, possess this advantage.

The common public vehicle for single passengers is a sort of sulky, which is driven by the passenger, the keeper standing behind him and using the whip. It goes with great velocity; and what struck me as daring in streets so crowded and with chance drivers, the horses have no bits, being entirely controlled by a noseband, like a halter, to which the reins are attached.

The population of Naples is generally short, and both sexes, as a rule, incline early to obesity. This applies particularly to the class of the *bourgeoisie*. But I have never seen so fine a display of muscle anywhere else as among the labourers of this place. The habit of ascending and descending the precipices of the coast gives to all the porters on the bay an extraordinary development of the muscles of the legs. Those of Genoa have a reputation in this respect; but I think them, though of larger proportions in general, inferior to those of Naples, or rather to those of the Bay of Naples.

Letter XIV.

WE did not get into our residence at Sorrento until the 20th of August, and here we have now been several weeks. Everybody is delighted with the place, and I think we have not in any other abode, in or out of Europe, enjoyed ourselves so much as in this. The house is not particularly elegant, though large; but as it has a name, and may be taken as a specimen of an Italian country abode, I shall describe it.

To begin at the foundation, ours rests on narrow shelves of the cliffs, which cliffs, just at this spot, are about one hundred and fifty feet in perpendicular height, or possibly a little more. It has a treacherous look to see the substratum of a building standing on a projection of this sort; but I presume sufficient heed has been taken to security. Of this substratum I know but little, though there appear to be two or three stories down among the cliffs. All the dwellings along these rocks, many of which are convents, have subterraneous communications with the sea, the outlets being sufficiently visible as we row along beneath the heights. The government, however, has caused them to be closed, without distinction, to prevent smuggling.

The house forms two sides of a square, one running inland, and the other standing on the extreme verge of the cliffs, as you will readily understand when you remember that the foundations rest on the places I have just mentioned. We occupy the principal floor only, although I have taken the entire house. There is a chapel beneath the great *sala*, and I believe there are kitchens and offices somewhere in the lower regions; but I have never visited any portion of the substratum but the chapel. We enter by a gate into a court, which has a well with a handsome marble covering or curb, and a flight of steps fit for a palace. These two objects, coupled with the interest of Tasso's name, have been thought worthy of an engraving. From the *loggia* of the great stairs we enter into an ante-room of good dimensions.

Inland is a still larger room, in which we dine, and another within that again, which is the only apartment in the house with a fireplace. By the presence of the chimney, it is fair to presume the kitchen is somewhere at hand. This room W[illiam] has for a bedroom. Seaward, two or three vast ante-chambers, or rooms *en suite*, lead to the *sala*, which faces the water, and is a room fifty feet long, with width and height in proportion. The furniture is no great matter, being reduced to the very minimum in quantity; but it is not unsuited to the heat of the climate and a *villeggiatura*. There are old-fashioned gilded couches and chairs, and a modern divan or two to stretch our limbs on. There are also some medallions and busts, antiques: one of the former, on what authority I cannot say, is called an Alexander the Great. The windows of the *sala* open on the court, on the street, and on the sea. A street that leads among convents winds toward the great landing and the bay.

Towards the water there is a little terrace, which forms the great attraction of the house. It is only some fifty feet long, and perhaps half as wide; but it hangs over the blue Mediterranean, and, by its position and height, commands a view of three fourths of the glorious objects of the region. It has a solid stone balustrade to protect it, massive and carved, with banisters as big as my body. This renders it perfectly safe, as you will understand when I tell you that, hearing an outcry from P[aul] the other day, I found him with his head fast between two of the latter, in a way that frightened me as well as the youngster himself. It was like being embedded in a rock.

As I sit at the foot of the dinner-table, I look, through a vista of five large rooms, by means of doors, at the panorama presented by Naples, which town lies directly across the bay, at the reputed distance of eighteen miles; though I see St. Elmo so distinctly, that it appears not half as far. Of course, when seated on the terrace, the view is infinitely more extended. The sea limits it to the west. Ischia, dark, broken, and volcanic, but softened by vegetation and the tints of this luxurious atmosphere, comes next: then Procida, low, verdant, and peopled. The misty abrupt bluff of Misenum is the first land on the continent, with the Elysian fields, the port of the Roman galleys, and the "Hundred Chambers." The site of delicious Baiæ is pointed out by the huge pile of castle that lies on the hill-side, and by the ruined condition of all the neighbouring objects of curiosity, such as the Sibyl's cave, the lake of Avernus, and the bridge or mole of Agrippa. Behind a little island called Nisida, the bark of St. Paul must have sailed when he landed at Puteoli, on his way to Rome. The palace of Queen Joan, the grotto of Pausilippo, the teeming city, and the bay dotted with sails, follow. Then the eye passes over a broad expanse of rich level country, between Vesuvius and the heights of the town. This is the celebrated Felice Campania, with Capua in its bosom; and the misty background is a wall of broken rocks, which in form are not unlike our own palisadoes, but which, a grand range of the Apennines, have probably six or seven times their height. These mountains, at times, are scarcely visible, just marking the outline of the view in a sort of shadowy frame, and then, again, they come forth distinct, noble, and dark, the piles they really are. On particular days they do not appear to be a dozen miles from us. I have seen them already, more than once, glittering with snow, when they are indeed glorious. The base of Vesuvius, a continued hamlet of white edifices, including palaces and cottages, with its cone for the background, follows; and a pile of dingy earth, or ashes, just marks the position of Pompeii.

There is a little room partitioned off from the terrace, that I use as a cabinet, and where I can sit at its window and see most of these objects. The distance impairs the effect but little; for so great is the purity of the atmosphere, at times, that we have even fancied we could hear the din of Naples across the water. In all this, too, I have said nothing of the movement of the bay, which is getting to be of great interest.

Our communication with Naples is daily, and exceedingly regular. Large boats, carrying a single latine sail, and, at need, pulled by fifteen or twenty oars, leave all the places on this side of the bay with the dawn, at which hour there is almost always a wind from the northward. They make the passage sometimes in two hours, and it is usually made in four. About noon, the zephyr springs up, and we see our little fleet bearing up from under the town, spreading as it advances, one steering in this direction, another in that; for there are a dozen havens, or landings, on our side of the bay. We usually get the papers and letters by two o'clock. I have one boatman in pay, and this man brings me even dollars with rigid honesty.

We are in the midst of antiquities. The foundations of a large edifice are visible in the limpid water, directly beneath the terrace. They are said to have belonged to a temple of Neptune, and there are caverns in the cliffs, at no great distance from these ruins, which are supposed to have belonged to them, for they have evidently been intended for baths. We appropriate them to their ancient use, seldom suffering a day to pass without bathing in them. The place can only be approached with a boat, and we go in a body, there being accommodations for us all. A large circular cavern, arched like an oven, is the room of the ladies. The water passes in and out of it, by means of two channels cut in the rock (tufa), and an orifice serves for a window. There is a seat cut in the stone all round the circle, and a beautiful soft sand has collected on the bottom, so as to render the water of the desired depth. A ship might float against the cliffs on the outside. I land the ladies at the window, where there is sufficient room to receive them and to answer the purposes of the toilette, and then I pull round to the entrance of the gallery by which the sea enters. This gallery is crooked, of sufficient height to walk in, and has a narrow *trottoir* by the side of the water, along which one can walk. Midway between the sea and the circular bath, is a deep cut about twelve feet long and half as wide, and five feet deep. This is my bath, while W[illiam] has one near the entrance; both of us occasionally striking out into the bay. All these works are artificial, and perfectly retired; and you may fancy what a luxury it is to bathe daily in sea-water, sheltered from all eyes, as well as from the sun. The circular bath is about fifty feet in diameter, and twenty in height above the water. We have a little difficulty in landing sometimes, on account of the sea; but it is not one day in ten that we cannot effect it.

Carriages here are nearly useless. There is but a single wheel-track, of a few miles in extent; and that runs, the whole distance, through villages, or between high dead walls. When we wish to make excursions on the land, we walk in the ravines that form the ditches of the place, a most picturesque and remarkable promenade, or we take to the adjacent hills. Sometimes donkeys are commanded, but we usually prefer our own feet.

On the water we do better still. I have a good and safe boat, that one man can manage with ease, and in which W[illiam] or myself commonly pull the family for an hour or two, under the cliffs, of an afternoon, or when the bay near us is in shadow. Then there is a handsome pinnace with two lug sails and six oars, that can be had any day for a dollar. In this we cross the bay, or go to Pompeii. For longer excursions, I get the *Divina Providenza*, one of the crafts that ply to Naples. This vessel, in which we have weathered a heavy gale, is pulled by twenty oars in a calm, sails fast, and costs me just five Neapolitan dollars a day!

Our daily excursions under the cliffs are peculiarly Italian. We cannot move until the day is drawing towards a close; but about four, the shadows of the rocks are thrown so far on the water as to form a complete protection against the rays of a fierce sun. At that hour, too, it is commonly a flat calm, and we glide along sometimes with a boatman, but oftener by ourselves, as far as a rocky point, where are the ruins of a palace, or of a temple, (tradition has it both ways,) and where, by rowing through a rocky arch, we can enter a little haven of a very extraordinary character. At this place the boat is almost in a cavern. Here we land and get new views of the unrivalled bay. Every excursion that we make, we return more and more delighted with the region in which we dwell, and deriding the opinions of those who pass eight or ten days on the Chiaja, or in Santa Lucia, running from sight to sight at any season of the year that may offer, and then go away fancying they have seen the country of Naples!

There is a good deal of the *"dolce far niente"* in all this; but it is a feeling admirably suited to this luxurious climate, and to a country of recollections. In other places one is obliged to submit to much toil and some privation, in order to see many objects of curiosity; but they are assembled around the noble amphitheatre of this bay in such numbers, that one is only obliged to turn his head to get a view of them. If more curious, he can approach them in a boat, shaded by an awning, without at all deranging the *"far niente."*

And yet we as much affect the inland walks, as this lazy navigation. Our excursions are of two sorts, which may be divided into the "donkey" and the "non-donkey." In the "non-donkey," we roam over the hills near the town, which are covered with fruit-trees, and are intersected with paths, the kind and gentle peasants smiling as we pass, never offering rudeness of any sort.

There is a spot called *Capo di Monte*, a term that always designates the best look-out of a neighbourhood, from which I think one finds the prettiest bit of scenery, in its way, I have ever met with; nor do I remember any picture that surpasses it. The landings on this coast are necessarily made on some small beach, or at a ravine which admits of an ascent to the plain, or *piano*, above. At Sorrento there are two, the "large" and the "little" landing.* The latter is in the heart of the town, and has a sort of wharf, at which one can embark in smooth water. This is the port of the *Divina Providenza*, but all the craft, big and little, are hauled on the beach at night; the other is a crescent of sandy beach, lined the whole distance with the houses of fishermen. It is at the verge of the town and without its walls, extending to the mountain, which here juts out into a low promontory, forming a protection against the sea. The *Capo di Monte* is so placed as to have this landing for its fore-ground. The view of the beach strewed with crafts of different sizes, including boats, to the number of a hundred,—the domestic groups between them and the houses,—the children sporting on the sands, the costumes and flaring colours of the female dresses, with nets spread to dry, and all the other little accessories of such a spot that you can so readily imagine,—make a perfect Flemish picture. The men usually have a shirt and loose trowsers that descend but little below the knee; and they wear a Phrygian cap, that is oftener red than any other colour. The pleasure of a residence in such a spot is enhanced by the circumstance that, on the continent of Europe generally, the inhabitants of these country towns, though they are often large, seldom affect the airs of a capital, but are mere assemblages of rustics, and not children in wigs and hoops, like those of our own small places. Here, the distinctions between a capital, a country town, a village, and a hamlet, are all freely acknowledged and maintained; but the aspiring qualities of our population will not submit to this.

The great number of beggars that torment one like gnats was at first a drawback on our pleasures. It was no unusual thing to have a dozen of them in chase; and, if unprovided with change,

*"*Marina Grande*," and "*Marina Piccola*," or the "*Marinella*."

we were often harassed by them until we returned to our own gate: for the poor Neapolitans, unlike the beggars of Paris, are not often provided with change. We have got relieved from them, however, by mere accident; and as the incident is characteristic, it is worth mentioning.

Walking one day on the terrace that overhangs the bay, I happened to cast my eyes over the balustrade into the street, where there is a public seat that is much frequented by idlers, immediately beneath our *drawing-room* window. It was occupied at the moment by an old fellow with a lame leg, as fine an old mendicant as one shall see in a thousand. This man was enjoying himself, and keeping an eye on the gate, in expectation of our daily sortie; for we had been a little irregular of late, and had given our tormentors the slip. Seeing me, the beggar rose and pulled off his cap. As I had no change, I called a servant to bring me a *grano*. This little ceremony established a sort of intercourse between us. The next day, the thing was repeated. As I usually wrote in the cabinet of a morning, and walked on the terrace at stated hours, my new acquaintance became very punctual; and there is such a pleasure in thinking you are making a fellow-creature comfortable for a day at so cheap a rate, that I began to expect him. This lasted ten days, perhaps, when I found *two*, one fine morning, instead of the *one* I had known. The other *grano* was given, and the next day I had *three* pensioners. These three swelled like the men in buckram, and were soon a dozen. From that moment no one asked charity of us in our walks: we frequently met beggars, but they invariably drew modestly aside, permitting us to pass without question. We might have been a month getting up to the dozen; after which, my ranks increased with singular rapidity. Seeing many strange faces, I inquired of Roberto whence they came; and he told me that many of the new visiters were from villages five or six miles distant, it having been bruited that, at noon each day, all applicants were accommodated with a *grano* apiece by the *American admiral*. By this fact alone, you learn the extreme poverty of the poor and the value of money in this country.

We went on recruiting, until I now daily review some forty or fifty *gaberlunzies*. As my time here is limited, I have determined to persevere, and the only precaution taken is to drive off those who do not seem worthy to be enrolled on a list so eminently mendicant; for a good many of the wives of the fishermen began to appear in our ranks. A new-comer from Sta. Agata, a village across the mountains, had the indiscretion lately, as he got his *grano*, to wish me only a hundred years of life. "A hundred years!" repeated the king of the gang; "you blackguard, do you wish a signore who gives you a *grano* every day, only a hundred years? Knock him down! away with him!" "*Mille anni, signore,—* a thousand years; may you live a thousand years!" shouted the blunderer, amid some such tumult as one would see around a kettle of maccaroni in the streets of Naples, were its contents declared free. "A thousand years, and *long* ones too."*

*The writer kept up his mendicant corps until he left Sorrento, there being no less than ninety-six paraded in the court the day he departed. Many of these poor people came ten miles! Some of them, he was told, passed the last week of his residence in Sorrento, in order to receive the pittance more at their ease.

Letter XV.

OUR aquatic excursions have extended, by this time, to the whole coast of the bay. We have visited all the islands, and nearly every object of interest, from Ischia to Capri. As some of the pictures may amuse you, we will make a short cruise in company over the same ground.

We embarked at the *Marina Grande*, in *La Divina Providenza*, with our twenty-one oars (the odd one falling to the share of the padrone), and your humble servant at the helm. The day had just opened, and the bay was radiant, while all the mountains stood out distinct and clear. This was a sign of northerly weather, and of a pure sky. We had now been more than a month on the bay, and scarcely a drop of rain had fallen. At our first arrival, we had frequently distrusted the day; but our acquaintances laughed at the omens, and told us to go forth in security, on occasions when I should have expected a thunder-shower. The advice is good, and in no instance have we suffered. As the season advances, however, we perceive symptoms of change, and we are told that, ere long, we shall see rain.

Our boatmen made the water foam, and we soon saw the dark pile of Capri looking out from behind the western headland, and the shore of Massa. When one is at Naples, this fine island appears to lie directly in the mouth of the bay; but, in fact, it is posted, like a sentinel, at one of its corners, and Ischia is at the other.

Our course was north-westerly, for the headland of Pausilippo, which lay about eighteen miles distant, directly across the bay. We pulled several miles before we caught the land-breeze, which soon sent us in under the romantic coast for which we were steering. Passing between Pausilippo and Nisida, the island that is said to have been the temporary retreat of Brutus after the death of Cæsar, we hauled up into the little bay beyond, which is that of Baiæ. Here the town of Pozzuoli stands,

on a low projection that runs into the water. There is little, perhaps no doubt, that this is the Puteoli of Paul. I thought of this
apostle and of his perilous voyage as we rounded to at the quay,
and pictured to myself the sort of vessel in which he had arrived, nearly eighteen centuries since, in the same harbour. She
was called the Castor and Pollux, (what a thing to know even
her name!) the ship of Alexandria, that had wintered in Melita,
and which put into Syracuse, where she lay three days. Thence
"we fetched a compass, and came to Rhegium." This is the Reggio of Lower Calabria, which lies nearly opposite to Messina.
"And after one day, the south wind blew, and we came the next
day to Puteoli." We learn some curious facts by the simple narrative of the apostle. He sailed, first, in a ship of Adramyttium,
bound to some port that lay on the way to Rome. This was a
regular convoy of prisoners; and we may gain some idea of the
means of communication between the different parts of the
empire, and of the relative insignificance of Jerusalem, at that
period, by the circumstance that no direct conveyance offered.
It has been objected to the authenticity of the Books of the
Apostles, that the Roman writers did not speak of Christ. That
the Jewish writers did not, (the well-known allusion of Josephus
being generally admitted to be an interpolation,) must be ascribed to his appearance conflicting with their own notions of
the Messiah. There certainly *was* a sect called Christians, who
took their origin from a reputed Christ, and these facts *must*
have been known to the contemporary Hebrews, and yet *they*
are silent. But with the Romans it was different. The means of
communication were so few, and Jerusalem was so unimportant
in the eyes of the mistress of the world, that the philosophers
who prided themselves in an elaborate system of mythology, in
which an attempt is made to personify the attributes of the
Deity,—a system that bears some such mystified relation to
divine truths, as the black-letter notions of an old-school lawyer
bear to abstract justice,—did not think such provincial opinions
of sufficient interest to occupy their time and attention. On this
point an error is sometimes committed by confounding the
importance of Christianity at a later day, with the importance
previously to, and immediately after, the Crucifixion.

Paul was put into a ship of Alexandria, in "Myra, a *city* of
Lycia." At Lasea in Crete, they put into port, although the ves-

sel was large enough to hold two hundred and seventy-six souls. Here there were serious notions of wintering! When they did put to sea again, it was merely with the intention of running as far as Phenice, another port in the same island. They took a moment to do this, when "the south wind blew *softly*," but were "caught" by the gale, that drove them up into the Adriatic, as is commonly thought, but into what was, more probably, no more than the Ionian sea. When they struck soundings, "four anchors" were let go by the stern. There are still relics of this usage, the smaller craft carrying many light anchors. I have seen as many as eleven on the deck of one small bark on the Lake of Geneva, and seven or eight are the common number. They lie in a row bristling on the forecastle. Anchoring by the stern is an old expedient: Nelson did it at the Nile. These anchors, however, are a proof that the vessel, notwithstanding her "two hundred three score and sixteen souls," was small; as was also the fact that the crew, who were about to desert, were lowering *the* boat under the plea of carrying out anchors from the bows in a gale of wind!

The seamen of the Mediterranean appear to have had the same practice of running into port, at every adverse turn of the wind, in the time of St. Paul, that they have to-day. An ordinary run from Palestine to Puteoli, in a good ship, would not exceed six or eight days, and here we find men wintering by the way, and putting into half a dozen ports, besides attempting to make several they could not enter. The ships of Alexandria were probably among the best of the sea, and yet even the one in which Paul arrived saw fit to winter in Malta, bound to Italy!

We passed close to a fragment of the ancient mole, which is commonly called the Bridge of Caligula, and which probably was used as a part of it; but I thought more of this arrival of Paul, as the different objects presented themselves, than of the luxury of Rome, and of all her emperors united. "Where are the doctrines that Saul of Tarsus taught, and where now is Rome!"

The whole shore of Baiæ is a succession of antiquities, or of natural curiosities. Puteoli, judging from its remains, was a place of some size; and this is the more probable from its proximity to the Baian shore, a spot devoted to taste and poetry. We saw the remains of the amphitheatre, and of various temples; but the ruins were indistinct, and much dilapidated. We walked, also, to the Solfatara, which may be termed the pulse of Vesuvius. When it is quiet, the mountain is deemed dangerous; but when it is in action, the volcano is thought to be in subjection. The distance between the two cannot be less than fifteen miles. This is a sort of low crater, out of which smoke and heat escape through cracks in the surface, rather than by a regular orifice. The surface is not unlike that of a brick-yard; and a large stone cast on it, gives a hollow menacing sound. The idea of breaking through into a mass of burning sulphur accompanies the experiment, though the crust is really too thick to make it at all dangerous.

In the Solfatara, we were joined by Mr. Hammett, the consul, who had come from Naples by land, to join our party. To this gentleman, whose education and long residence in Naples so well qualify him for the office, we have been indebted for a great deal of local information, and information that we prize the more as it is always, on such occasions, a source of happiness to exchange the marvels of a *laquais de place*, for the more accurate and chastened knowledge of a gentleman.

With this addition to our party, we re-embarked, and pulled across the bay, the distance of a mile or more, to the Lucrine Lake. The water was smooth as a mirror, and as our swarthy people, each of whom stood with his face towards the bows of the speronara, pushed their heavy oars, I could almost fancy we were in a Roman galley, passing from one villa of Baiæ to another. It is scarcely possible to imagine a region that was once so renowned for its luxury and magnificence,—so teeming with historical associations, temples, palaces, baths, bridges, groves, and gardens,—that has more completely changed its character, than this. Of remains, and those of a nature to establish localities, there are abundance. It might be difficult to find another place in Italy, out of Rome, where so many are crowded into so small a space; but they are hidden, require to be sought, and all the glories of the past, so far as mere outward appearances are concerned, are completely supplanted by the present negligent and half-wasted aspect of the whole shore. The Lucrine Lake has almost disappeared, little remaining beyond a sort of pond in the sands; but, in its place, a natural curiosity has thrust itself, which serves strangely to add to the jumble of wonders that this extraordinary district offers. It is a small cone, or mountain, of volcanic embers and sand, which was forced upwards by a convulsion of nature, in 1538, and which is properly enough, in such a neighbourhood, called *Monte Nuovo*. It may be two or three hundred feet high, and has a sterile, naked look, the meagre verdure it possesses being altogether of a different hue from that of the rest of the soil. We can see this cone from the terrace at Sorrento.

We did not stop at the Lucrine to eat oysters, but followed a tangled path, between the upstart hill, and some of the more venerable heights that once groaned beneath palaces and Roman villas, to the shores of Avernus. Why Virgil chose this spot as the entrance to hell, I cannot tell you; unless it were for its reputed depth. It is a circular sheet of dark water, with shores that rise on every side except that by which we approached, and which are deserted and tangled. The ruins of a temple stand in the solitude, erected, it is said, in honour of Pluto.

Agrippa is thought to have cut a canal from this lake to the sea, in order to form a port. The cost of such an undertaking at present would not be great, and it would make one of the best man-of-war harbours in the world; easy of access and of defence, and as snug as a *boudoir*. But to need a harbour, a people must have ships.

The path conducted us to the Sibyl's Cave, a long narrow cavern cut in the rocks, beneath the palaces and villas, and which leads to nothing. These cuttings are curious as connected with the religious rites of antiquity, and Virgil probably had an eye to them in his descent to the nether world. We found a Styx within them, and seeing no Charon, but one who offered to carry us on his shoulders, we returned to try another route.

We retraced our steps to the beach, and visited some hot springs and remains of baths, which, right or wrong, have the reputation of once belonging to a country palace of Nero. The frequent occurrence of ruins in all this region is to me a constant matter of wonder. They embrace all ages, down to our own. Here is a broken pile on a rock,—it is a retreat of Tiberius; that on the opposite peak was inhabited by some Goth. This is the dilapidated residence of a Bourbon; yonder is a fallen citadel of the barbarians; and temples to all the gods of antiquity, with remains of churches erected in honour of the Ancient of Days, dot the eminences and valleys!

We embarked and proceeded to Baiæ itself, a mere hamlet, to-day. Here are some tolerable remains, one in particular of a temple in honour of Venus, and also the heavy pile of citadel that is visible from Sorrento. We lingered on this site of Roman taste and indulgence several hours, and finding the day on the wane, bethought us of the coming night. The consul recommended Ischia, when we embarked with a light wind, and made sail in that direction. We glided immediately beneath Misenum, which, for a novelty in this part of the world, is a high *sandy* bluff; though all the Baiæan shore is more or less of sand. We looked into the little port, where the Roman galleys formerly lay, and whence Pliny departed when he proceeded to Stabia, to meet his death from the volcano. It is a small circular haven, with a very shallow draught of water at present, the padrone saying that the *Divina Providenza* would find little enough for her wants. It was in part artificial, and the remains of the works are still distinctly to be traced.

We hauled up to windward of Procida, sailing through an element so limpid that we saw every rush and stone on the bottom in five fathom water. Having opened the channel between the two islands, we bore up for the town of Ischia, where we arrived a little before sunset. Here a scene presented itself which more resembled a fairy picture than one of the realities of this everyday world of ours. I think it was the most ravishing thing, in its way, eye of mine ever looked upon. We had the black volcanic peaks of the island for a background, with the ravine-like valleys and mountain-faces, covered with country-houses and groves, in front. The town is near the southern extremity of the land, and lies along the shore for more than a mile on a bit of level formation; but, after passing a sort of bridge or terrace, which I took to be a public promenade, the rocks rose suddenly, and terminated in two or three lofty, fantastic, broken fragment-like crags, which make the south-eastern end of the island. On these rocks were perched some old castles, so beautifully wild and picturesque, that they seemed placed there for no other purpose than to adorn the landscape. By a curvature of the land, these rocks sheltered the roadstead, and the quaint old structures were brought almost to impend over our heads. The whole population seemed to be out enjoying themselves after the heat of the day, and a scene in which a movement of life was so mingled with a superb but lovely nature, it is indeed rare to witness. Until that moment I was not fully sensible of the vast superiority of the Italian landscapes over all others. Switzerland astonishes, and it even often delights, by its union of the pastoral with the sublime; but Italian nature wins upon you until you come to love it like a friend. I can only liken the perfection of the scene we gazed upon this evening to a feeling almost allied to transport; to the manner in which we dwell upon the serene expression of a beloved and lovely countenance. Other scenes have the tints, the hues, the outlines, the proportions, the grandeur, and even the softness of beauty; but these have the character that marks the existence of a soul. The effect is to pour a flood of sensations on the mind, that are as distinct from the commoner feelings of wonder that are excited by vastness and magnificence, as the ideas awakened by an exquisite landscape by Claude are different from those we entertain in looking at a Salvator Rosa. The *refinement* of Italian nature appears to distinguish it as much from that of other countries, as the same quality distinguishes the man of sentiment and intellect from the man of mere impulses. In sublimity of a certain sort, more especially in the sublimity of desolation, Switzerland probably has no equal on earth; and perhaps to this is to be added a certain unearthly aspect which the upper glaciers assume in particular conditions of the atmosphere; but these Italian scenes rise to a sublimity of a different kind, which, though it does not awe, leaves behind it a tender sensation allied to that of love. I can conceive of even an ardent admirer of Nature wearying in time of the grandeur of the Alps; but I can scarce imagine one who could ever tire of the witchery of Italy.

Climate has a great influence in bringing about these results. As the greater portion of the United States lies south of Naples, you may wish to know why we do not possess the same advantages. We want the accessories. A volcanic formation puts all competition at defiance in the way of the picturesque. This feature alone frequently renders mountains of no great elevation in themselves sublime, while others of twice their height are

tame. We want the water, the promontories, the bays, the peninsulas, the grand islands, and lastly, we want all the quaint and
time-honoured forms that art assumed, in this region, three
thousand years ago, seemingly never to abandon them.

Our attempts to obtain lodgings at the town of Ischia were
unsuccessful, and we shaped our course for a villa on the coast
two or three miles distant, where we were received. Our *couchée*
was a little unsophisticated, most of the party using mattresses
on the floor; but we had brought tea with us, and made a good
supper. Italy pays the penalty for the warmth that is thrown
around its landscapes, in having little milk, the article, of all
others, in which its great rival Switzerland abounds. Wine can
be had anywhere, as may oil; but the excellent tribute of the
cow is hard to be got. We found maccaroni, however, which is
as much a standing dish in Naples as rice in Carolina.

Arrangements for the night were soon made. Everybody had
a mattress; though I afterwards found that Gelsomina slept in
an open gallery, and Roberto in the cellar. The idea of putting
two people in the same bed, even if married, scarcely ever
comes into the heads of the Europeans of the Continent; nearly
every bed-room of the least pretension, if intended for the use
of two, having its two beds. I have seen double-beds in Italy, it
is true; but they were as large as small houses. That peculiar
sentiment of the Western American, who "wondered that any
man should be such a hog as to wish a bed all to himself," appears never to have suggested itself to a people so destitute of
"energy."

We took a light breakfast, and left the shores of Ischia just as
the sun rose. The island is volcanic, and blocks of lava, looking
as fresh as that at the foot of Vesuvius, lie along the margin of
the sea; and yet no tradition, or history, speaks of the volcano as
active! These visible proofs of the imperfection of our records,
and of the course of time, have a tendency to create new views
of things. I am glad to hear that theologians and philosophers
are beginning to see the possibility of reconciling the text of
sacred history with the evidences of science, and to be of a mind
in believing this world vastly older than the vulgar understanding of the Mosaic account has, hitherto, led us to think. You are
not to infer, however, that I believe the lava of Ischia so very
ancient; the five thousand years will very well suffice for all the

geological phenomena that I am acquainted with, and which lie on the surface of the earth.

The morning was calm, and we pulled towards the western point of Procida. This is one of the few islands of this region that is without any mountain. It is extremely populous, though quite small, having a good deal of shipping. We landed on the point, and, by way of exploring the island, walked to the town. It is the fashion to see a Greek character in this people, who were originally a Greek colony (as indeed were those on the adjacent main); but we saw no more than the same swarthy, dark-eyed race that throngs the streets of Naples.

Re-embarking at the port, we pulled towards the promontory of Misenum, and landed behind the bluff, directing our galley to proceed and meet us near Baiæ. Nearly every foot of the shore, for several miles, was now historical, offering, amid a fatiguing sameness, and a sterility of surface, some relic of antiquity. An ordinary traveller, in passing along this place, would see as little to please him, or to attract his attention, as in any part of Italy I know; and yet Pompeii itself is scarcely more pregnant with recollections. The Elysian Fields of Virgil are now a tangled brake; the *Mare Morto* is dead enough, and is scarcely worthy to be called a pool. Some imagine that the first was a place of interment for the wealthy, converted by the imagination of the poet into an arena of souls; and that the *sea* was merely an inner basin of the port of Misenum, transformed by the same subtle process into the Styx. It is more probable that the imaginations of other people converted the Elysian Fields of the poet into this, and the inner basin, if inner basin it ever was, into his Styx. It struck me that the popular notions about this place are altogether too sublimated for a true poet, and that the popular genius, instead of that of Virgil, has been at work here.

The remains of the Romans are in better keeping. The Piscina Mirabile is a stupendous work, and almost perfect; and it puts all modern reservoirs to shame. It is under ground, vast, and contains arches and piers fit for the foundations of a palace. My respect for the Roman marine has never been very profound; but, if it be true that this place was intended to water their fleet, I know no modern nation that, under similar circumstances, would be likely to effect the same object on a scale so magnificent and noble.

The supposed prisons of the Hundred Chambers have the same character of vastness and durability. But everything Roman appears to be of this nature, and, in studying the remains, one is constantly provoked to make comparisons to the prejudice of us moderns. Were Naples to be deserted to-morrow, and this entire region depopulated, it is my opinion that they who visited the country a thousand years hence, would still find remains of the Romans, where every trace of the Neapolitans had disappeared. As for ourselves, the case is still worse. A period as short as that during which the country has been occupied, would probably obliterate every mark of our possession. We have a few forts, and a sea wall or two, that might resist the wear of a few centuries; but New York would not leave a trace, beyond imperishable fragments of stone, in two hundred years. Something may be ascribed to climate, certainly; but more is owing to the grand and just ideas of these ancients, who built for posterity as well as for themselves.

After looking at ruins, if works almost as perfect as they were the day they were completed can be so termed, we embarked, and made sail for the point of Pausilippo, with a light but fair wind. The little island of Nisida, which once had its villas too, is now the Lazaretto, and was filled with travellers in quarantine. The breeze served to carry us half across the bay, and it then deserted us. Our galley put out its oars, and we swept in towards the cliffs, on as lovely an evening as ever fell on this *pezzo di cielo*. Just as the day closed, the black mass of Capri became shut in by the head-lands of Massa, and we approached the rocky shore of Sorrento beneath the light of a placid moon. Before nine, we were all safely housed in the *Casa detta del Tasso*.

Letter XVI.

To Capri we went in the six-oared pinnace. This island, which, as you know, stands sentinel at one side of the bay, as Ischia does at the other, seen at Naples appears to lie in its mouth. This is owing to the position of Naples itself, which is placed at the northern corner of the gulph; Vesuvius, as you have been already told, occupying the bottom. I repeat these things, for, my own notions having been all wrong about them, I have fancied yours might be so too.

Capri is divided into two mountains by a deep gorge, or valley, in which stands the town. The southern mountain is the highest, and is truly a noble object, as one approaches the spot. It rises almost to a peak which is, probably, two thousand feet high; and the ruins that crown it are said to have belonged to a castle of Frederick Barbarossa, and to stand on the site of a villa of Tiberius! There is a tradition that Tiberius had many villas on this remarkable little island; which may be true, as there are numberless remains. At all events, the place was in favour among the Romans, Augustus passing much of his time here, towards the end of his career.

The lowest of the mountains is called Ana Capri, and can only be reached by actually ascending a flight of steps cut in the rocks, of half a mile in length, which ascend by a zigzag. P[aul] was mounted on a donkey; and, making a line of pocket-handkerchiefs, which I fastened to the girth, the ladies were greatly aided in this fatiguing ascent. The picturesque seems exhausted in such beautiful spots. Here we had the bay; the teeming and magnificent coast for leagues; the path, itself a curiosity, with a little chapel, at which the devout were kneeling as we passed. A thousand recollections crowded on the mind. Among other beautiful objects, were the different crafts, of which a fleet lay becalmed under Vesuvius.

The English seized Capri, and held it for some time, while

Murat was king. Several unsuccessful attempts were made to re-take it, and one finally succeeded, under Lamarque. That officer surprised the place by scaling the rocks of Ana Capri, in the night; and, once in possession of this elevated plain, he was in possession of the entire island.

We found Ana Capri a hamlet of cottages. Every building had the low circular roof of cement; and, as is the case with most of the houses of this region, those in the towns and the villas excepted, they were all of one story, like the buildings of Pompeii. A dread of earthquakes has probably introduced this style; though Naples has unusually high houses. Several streets of the capital, however, at this very moment, have beams between the buildings which are said to be departing from the perpendicular, in consequence of the working of the fires beneath. One of these fine mornings, the whole of this "little bit of heaven fallen upon earth" will probably fall into the cauldron beneath it; and then travellers will come to see it as an object of frightful desolation! Such was probably the fate of Sodom and Gomorrah. I wonder if New York will ever experience a similar calamity.

Besides the cruise to Capri, we have made two to Pompeii, the first of which was attempted in a fresh breeze and a heavy sea. When we had got half way, W[illiam], who, though a very bad sailor, swims like a fish, began to make some inquiries about the probability of his art being required in landing; when we learned from the boatmen that any attempt to approach the shore would most likely put us all in the water. I had been told we might ascend the Sarno, about a mile, to the ruins of the town, and, quite like a mariner as I contend, had presumed on smooth water in port. It appeared, however, on inquiry, that there is a bar at the mouth, and that in a flat calm the rollers sometimes make crossing it hazardous. Nothing remained but to down-helm, and haul up again for the Marina Grande. We were rewarded for the excursion, notwithstanding, by enjoying the bay in a tumult. The heavy seas that set into it, are not unlike those of the ocean in moderate weather; and, since the season has advanced into October, we have witnessed the waves dashing against our cliffs in a manner to send the spray upon the terrace.

The next expedition was better timed, and we reached the

mouth of the river in good season. Here we found so little water, that the boat grounded a cable's length from the shore, and
the only way to enter was for the crew to jump into the water,
when, by watching the roll of the ground-swell, and lifting, they
succeeded in forcing us over the bar.

The Sarno is about as wide as the Bronx at West-Farms, and
much such a river. Like the Bronx, it meanders through low
meadows, all of which have probably been formed since the
destruction of Pompeii. We could not get quite up to the town,
as it was; but, leaving the boat, we walked, by a footpath, to the
highway, entering the ruins on the side of the tombs. In this
visit we examined the walls, and entered more into details than
at the former. The progress of the workmen had been slow;
but an entire house, and that of some importance, had been
opened in the interval. I endeavoured to find some traces of the
port, unsuccessfully; but, judging from the present appearance
of the country, I think there can be little question that the town
stood on a low promontory, and that the haven lay considerably
below it. Excavations in the right spot would very probably
bring to light a mole.

We left Pompeii, on this occasion, an hour sooner than we
should otherwise have done, on account of an approaching
gust. For nearly two months, and this in August and September, we had seen nothing resembling a storm in the bay, and
scarcely any rain. Indeed, I can safely say, after having now
passed near a twelvemonth on this side the Alps, that I have
witnessed neither thunder nor lightning that would attract any
attention in America. This may have been a peculiar season;
but, after all I had been told, especially by the English, I had
expected something of the sort particularly awful. While we
were among the ruins, however, there was every symptom of
something better than common in this way, or certainly better
than anything we had yet seen; and fearing a swell would get
up on the bar, I hurried the party off to the boat.

We got out of the Sarno better than we had come into it, and
were soon in the bay. The wind was light at the north-west, and
as we stretched over, under the promontory of Vico, the heavens in the direction of Pausilippo became lowering and grand.
A polacre was beating out of the bight of Castel-a-mare, and
was tacking, about half a league to windward of us. Just as she

filled, with her head to the northward, I observed that she was starting her tacks and sheets, or whatever else these nondescript craft term their gear. I ordered our own lugs to be taken in, and the oars shipped. It was a grand moment, for I scarcely remember a more beautiful opening of a gust, and the effect was greatly increased by the sublimity of the surrounding land. As for the bay itself, it reminded me of a beauty covered with frowns. The water curled and foamed, but retained its limpid blue; and there were openings between the lurid and wheeling clouds through which the void of heaven gleamed brightly, and of its deepest tint, giving one the idea of nature in a mask.

The stroke-oarsman of the boat advised me to pull in under the promontory, as near as we could go. I hesitated about complying, for the sea was getting up fast, and if we found it irresistible, there was no alternative but drowning; for the rocks impended over the water almost to the height of a thousand feet. This noble pile is, in truth, one of the finest objects in its way that I know on any coast. The man, however, explained himself. He said, that the squall would not blow "home," against the rocks, and that, contrary to the general rule, we should find smoother water, and less wind, by running to lee-ward. As this was plausible, and matters were becoming awkward where we were, I followed his direction, and in a few minutes we were as close under the beetling precipice as we could conveniently go. I confess I had doubts of the experiment; but it succeeded perfectly. We got ahead with tolerable speed, had no other than a fair rolling sea, and came out handsomely into the bay of Sorrento within half an hour. I was not sorry, notwithstanding, when I again saw the polacre showing his light sails to windward.

With similar symptoms we should have been deluged with rain in America, and yet we were barely sprinkled. The wind was fresh inshore, and violent a league or two in the offing; for the polacre bore up before it, until she had run a mile or more; and yet we did not ship a gallon of water, or "catch crabs" with a single oar. These Sorrentines are noble boatmen, as bold and as skilful as any I have ever met with; athletic, active and steady, while they understand their waters perfectly. Much as I have boated with them, and on two or three occasions I have seen them in serious weather, I have never seen any praying to saints, or a disposition to do anything unworthy of mariners. I consider the common population of this country, by nature, one of the finest I know.

The weather, soon after this excursion, changed, and interrupted our boating. The siroccos set in, in earnest, and for two or three weeks we had a continuation of strong south winds, occasionally accompanied by rain. The influence of these winds is one of the great drawbacks on an Italian residence. I can tell in my bed if there is a shift of wind to the westward, and no language can describe the cheering effect the changes produce on my feelings. We have had one or two days, in which the house has actually appeared to roll with me, like a ship at sea; and the depression of the spirits, at such times, is really awful—second only to a London November-day.

This is the season in which the vessels arrive from Sicily, and the other southern ports, with wheat. For a fortnight there was scarcely a day in which a dozen, and sometimes twenty sail, did not pass directly before us; for they haul close round the Cape of Campanella, and run into Castel-a-mare, where the great warehouses of the kingdom are placed. Some of the public works of this nature are on a scale that is vast for the extent and commerce of the nation. There is a single storehouse on the bay, by the side of the road that leads from Naples to Portici, designed to be used in cases of quarantine, I believe, that is one of the largest constructions I have ever seen. Its length cannot be much less than half a mile. I counted the windows, and, estimating the distance between them, made it out to be considerably more than two thousand feet. But Europe is full of buildings that to us appear marvellous by their magnitude and riches, and Italy, in particular, before all other parts of it.

The passage of these vessels gave an entirely new appearance to our side of the bay; and the daily arrival of our own little fleet, which sometimes comes staggering along half under water, adds to the interest. Roberto went to Naples a few days since, on business of his own, and he became so thoroughly frightened by the fury of our lovely bay, that the poor fellow, in preference to running the same risk over again, actually made a *détour* of forty miles, by the way of Castel-a-mare and the mountains, in order to get back again to his duty. But the *Bella Genovese* can testify that he is a miserable sailor.

Our siroccos have not been perpetual, but some glorious autumnal days succeeded the equinox. We have profited by them to explore the interior of the peninsula on which we live, for the heat can now be borne even at noon-day. You would laugh to see us start on one of these excursions. Half a dozen little donkeys are paraded at the gate, with two or three swarthy drivers. As soon as the ladies are seated on their beasts, in a species of pack-saddle, W[illiam] and I mount, with our feet just clear of the ground, and away we go, by dint of kicks, thumps, and applications on the flanks from the drivers. Once in motion, we are by no means certain of the direction; for if urged beyond their humours, the little long-eared gentry will put their noses down, and carry one of the ladies just where he pleases. Cries of distress are constantly made; one being run into a church door, another into the window of a hovel, or a third is scampering down the road at a "will ye nill ye" pace. We have a good deal of this amusement for the first mile or two, after which we commonly get on better. No one thinks of laughing at our appearance; for it is as much expected that one should ride on a donkey here, as that one should ride on a horse with us.

We have been on all the heights in this manner. One of our visits was to a ruined convent, a *Camaldoli*, on the mountain that separates the *piano* of Sorrento from that of Vico. These *Camaldoli* are always placed on heights; St. Bruno, the founder of the order, being directed by a dream, or a vision, I believe, to adopt the plan. The effect is poetical and good; for I cannot imagine a finer stimulant for religious meditation, than a broad view of the glories of the earth; and this the more especially, if it be chastened by a knowledge of the things practised on it. One gets, in this way, an idea of what things might be without sin to contrast with one's knowledge of what things are. In boyhood, my feeling on such places was ever to fly, in order to cull the beauties by again approaching them; but, as life glides away, I find the desire to recede increase, as if I would reduce the whole earth to a picture in a camera obscura, in which the outlines and general beauties are embraced, while the disgusting details are diminished to atoms.

The view from the eminence north of the *piano*, like every other view in this region, is magnificent; but one cannot go amiss, in this respect, in a country in which rocks, plains, water, mountains, and life, are blended in the affluence that distinguishes Naples. The convent-buildings are chiefly destroyed, for there has been a great suppression of monastic orders in this country; but the chapel still stands. It is used as a barn, and was half full of hay. Still the altar-piece, a very good picture, remains!

There is a seat on the verge of the cliff, that overlooks the plain of Sorrento, as one would overlook a garden from the belvedere of a house, or a ship's decks from her mizen top. Here we were particularly struck with the resemblance of the houses to those of Pompeii, all the roofs being low, with the species of dome-like curvature, to turn the water, that has been before mentioned.

An excursion in the opposite direction proved to be still finer. We went up the heights, behind Sorrento, by a Swissish road, half stairs, half path, until we gained a country that had a more pastoral character than usual. A hamlet on the summit, that overlooked the Mediterranean towards the south, and at an elevation of near, if not quite, a thousand feet, is called St. Agata. Some small rocky islets, at no great distance from the coast, and around which the sleeping billows, in their incessant rolling, just raised a circle of white, are called the Islands of the Sirens; it being assumed that these are the Islands where Ulysses encountered those sea ladies; and one of them is said to contain the ruins of a temple. They are mere rocks, not larger than that on which we landed near Piombino. Can these ruins once have been the abode of nymphs, who seduced the wanderer from his path, on anchoring accidentally near them?

There is another *Camaldoli* on the summit of the land, between St. Agata and Massa, or about mid-way between the Gulf of Salerno and that of Naples. I passed a morning lately in a memorable manner, in exploring it on foot, and alone. The day was fine, it was the Sabbath, the air from the west, invigorating, just cool enough to be agreeable, and full of life. The ruins command a noble view, as usual; but so does every eminence around us. One looks abroad here, in the full security of beholding objects that are either sublime or beautiful, and commonly both, for the two are so blended as to render it doubtful which most prevails. I cannot describe to you the precise nature of the sensations with which I passed this morning. It was the Sabbath of man, and it appeared to be also the Sabbath of nature; one of those holy calms that sleep on the earth, as if the vegetable world united with the animal to worship the great Source of all. As I flung myself carelessly from height to height, and across downish uplands, every new point that presented itself exhibited the great temple in a new and lovelier aspect; and as I descended from the glorious solitude, (for the only habitations are in the hamlets, or on the plains,) I felt as if I could almost become a monk, in order to remain there for life. The conventual buildings were, as usual, vast, and much of them still remains. Had it been my fortune to suppress monasteries, I should certainly have commenced the work in the cities and on the plains, and have left those on the hill-tops to the last; for I have a difficulty in believing that the tenants of such abodes can do anything but adore God. At least, this is the passing feeling; though I dare say one gets to be *blasé* as respects a fine view, as well as a fine sentiment. At all events, we are pretty certain the devil can climb, as well as crawl: though most of our American devils, I believe, are of the *genus* demon, *species* reptile.

We never ramble in this manner without exclaiming against those who visit Naples, perhaps in the bad season, pass a rainy week or two in sight-seeing, fagged and even fatigued with wonders, and then go away and pretend to describe its nature, its variety, its purity of atmosphere, its pearly lustre of sky, and all its other glorious peculiarities. The environs of Naples are quite another region to-day, than on that on which we arrived; though they have always been lovely. Even a sirocco cannot spoil their charms; for while, like other beauties, they have their good and bad-looking days, the last are merely the bad looks of a Venus. I have never seen the bay when it did not present an object of admiration and rare perfection.

You will be surprised to learn that we also riot here in the good things of this world, in the shape of creature-comforts. The liquor of the country is good, the lachrima christi of Vesuvius being really a choice wine. Then the beccafichi are delicious, and plenty at this season, Sorrento being the very nucleus of their sports: they cost a grano apiece! The quails, too, just now, are as good as can be, very plenty, and quite cheap. They are caught in nets extended among the trees, flying in large flocks. By some caprice in the bird, Capri is a favourite stopping-place with them, and thousands are sent weekly to the market of Naples. By a caprice of man, these birds compose a material part of the revenues of the bishop,—at least so I hear; though I find it odd that so small an island should have a bishop at all. But Sorrento is an archbishopric; its diocesan is a learned man; and they tell me there are near a dozen bishops in the capital, and in its immediate neighbourhood.

While on this subject, I will mention that we have lately had a religious procession, in which an image of the Virgin has been made to take a more prominent part than I have ever before witnessed. She has gone from altar to altar, followed by half the pious of the town, among whom have figured nearly the whole of my corps of gaberlunzies. There are so many churches and convents in this small town, that an inhabitant whom I questioned lately had no idea of their numbers. "There might be twenty, there might be fifty."

While walking on the terrace a few days since, I saw a priest coming up the road from the Marina Grande. He was accompanied by an ecclesiastic, who was chanting in concert with the father. A little distance behind these, came one of the swarthy bare-legged fishermen of the place, carrying on his head the usual flat willow basket, on which it is common to display the fish, and on which, it appeared to me, he then had his game. As he kept a short distance in the rear, I supposed he did not like to pass the others, who were engaged in some religious office. Curiosity induced me to watch the party, and, as it drew near, I discovered the chant was that of the dead. When near enough to be distinguished, I saw on the basket the body of a little girl about six years old. It was dressed in white, with gay ribands; and across its mouth lay an oblong nosegay, or what was more probably an imitation of a nosegay. The flowers contrasted strangely with the pallid colour of death. I called to me a Sorrentine servant, and asked an explanation. The girl was the daughter of the fisherman, and this was literally *le convoi du pauvre*. It was even worse than the interment of the Isle of Wight, though the manner of the priest was more reverent. I was told the body would be taken to a church, stripped of its attire, and cast into a hole, in common with all who are interred in the same manner. *Cast* was the word; but it is to be hoped it was lowered. I did not go to see the process, for I particularly dislike obtruding the curiosity of a stranger on the religious ceremonies of a strange people. The rude and indifferent manner in which Protestants ordinarily violate the sanctity of Catholic worship, does quite as much discredit to those who practise, as to those who tolerate it; though, in the plenitude of self-complacency, we followers of Luther are a little too apt to throw all the blame on the latter. I believe pious Catholics are as much shocked by the practice, as pious Protestants would be, were the case reversed.

We have now followed this dreamy mode of life so many weeks, that, coupled with the invigorating airs of October, the desire to enter into a little more activity begins to beset us. Boating is a lazy occupation, unless one handles the oar; and even sight-seeing, usually an extremely laborious business, on the shores of this luxurious bay is deprived of half its wear and tear.

I have forgotten to mention, by the way, that our own house is one of the wonders of the district. Most travellers honour us with a call, much to the advantage of Roberto's pocket, for he acts as master of ceremonies. Luckily, there is nothing to show but the *loggia* and the stairs, which one passes in entering, the great saloon, and the terrace. The latter is worth the trouble of mounting a flight of steps to see, and I believe most of the curious go away satisfied. There is, however, a medallion in the great saloon that has the reputation of being an Alexander the Great. It is an antique, I believe; but how far it deserves to be called an Alexander, I cannot say. It is the head of an enthusiast, rather than of a man of intellect; though I think one rarely finds any of the very magnificent bumps and foreheads about the truly distinguished. There are also a bust of Bernardo Tasso, the father of Torquato, and a medallion of Julius Cæsar, representing him as a youth. The Bernardo is probably authentic, as the family of the duke is said to be connected with that of Tasso; but Roberto shows the others, without remorse, as beyond cavil.

Of course we retire when the admirers of Tasso come to look at his residence; but taking a peep the other day at a visitor, I recognized a young Austrian, Baron ——, whom I had seen at Florence, and I went out to speak to him. We chatted together half an hour; and I mention the circumstance, because my companion betrayed a feeling that I find is very prevalent here, on the subject of the recent accession of General Jackson to the presidency. This feeling first discovered itself by some questions relative to the age of the new president; for when I mentioned that he was already an old man, I thought my acquaintance was surprised, not to say disappointed. His expectation evidently was that our democracies had taken the predicted course, and that we were already tasting the sweets of a military despotism. A military despotism, forsooth, in a country containing 2,000,000 square miles of surface, and an army of 6000 men!

I found that the exaggerated, electioneering trash of the opposition prints at home had made an impression, and, as is usual with most men, that which was ardently desired was readily believed. It is not easy for one living in the retirement of America, for all America is but a *villeggiatura*, and Wall Street worse than retirement, so far as the great political questions and knowledge of the day are concerned, compared with the activity, principles, and designs of Europe;—it is therefore difficult for one dwelling in the retirement of American life to form a correct notion of the opinions that float about here in reference to ourselves. An eminent Neapolitan, a man of singular shrewdness and of high political station, lately asked me seriously, what was the object of the English in making their descent on Washington in 1814. As I supposed a *coup de main* of that nature, under the peculiar circumstances, spoke for itself, I was as much surprised at the question as he could possibly be with the answer; for when I explained to him that Washington at that time was an open, straggling village, of some eight or nine thousand souls, of whom a good portion were black slaves, —that it covered a surface of nine or ten square miles, without works and without a garrison,—and moreover that its capture would have no more influence on the result of the war, than the seizing and holding for twenty-four hours of any other inland place of the same magnitude,—he expressed his astonishment. I was given clearly to understand, that it was viewed differently in Europe; and, owing to the influence of our enemy, I now believe the war of 1812 is better known here by this use-

less expedition than by anything else, notwithstanding all our
own notions of the matter.

You are to feel no surprise at this; for the influence of England, at this very moment, singularly controls opinion in
America itself, of which I have just seen an absurd proof, connected with this very subject. A New York journal, one of those
patriotic organs of sentiment which are constantly sneering at
the institutions, reserving their indignation and *energies* for the
defence of the illustrious cats and dogs of the country, (which,
by the way, are generally much inferior to the cats and dogs of
Europe,) has just been quoting the statements of a British officer in relation to the campaigns of New Orleans and Washington, as proof that some of our own previous notions in reference to both were untrue. Now, this very officer who affirms he
was at Washington, calls it a place, apparently, of about sixty
thousand souls, and passes some architectural strictures on the
wings and *main body* of the Capitol, the latter of which at that
time had never been erected! Some of our people will swallow
an English camel, when they strain at an American gnat.

Letter XVII.

You may be surprised that I have said so little about Vesuvius. Notwithstanding my silence, we have not passed a day, scarcely an hour, unless at night,—and many hours of the latter even are an exception,—without having this beautiful mountain under our eyes. I say beautiful, for, including its base, loaded with towns, palaces, ruins, villages, and villas,—its sides seamed with ravines, and occasionally smiling with verdure, or dark with forests,—and its cone of cinders,—it forms altogether an object of great attraction. By day, there is usually a light cloud of smoke rising from the crater, and hovering above it; and by night, occasional flashes illumine the sky and the mouth of the mountain in the way that the fire of a forge brightens and sinks in the darkness. I do not think we have seen any positive flame; but of late we have had brighter gleamings from beneath than are usual.

The heat of the weather had hitherto prevented an attempt to ascend; but W[illiam] and myself determined, not long since, that it was time to make the excursion. To this end we crossed the bay to Naples, and passed the night in town, having also an early start in view. Accordingly we drove to Portici, where we breakfasted. We then mounted our horses, under the protection of a guide of reputation, and proceeded. The ascent for four or five miles is gradual; the road, an indifferent one at the best, and nearly impracticable for wheels, leads at first through vineyards, then among copses, and often along water-courses, or across beds of ancient lava. The summit of the mountain is the cone of which I have spoken. Its form is regular, though the edges are broken, some portions being much higher than others, though the side nearest Naples and the bay, just now, is tolerably even. I believe the perpendicular height of the lowest part of this cone is about eight hundred feet; though it varies materially at different times. From its base, a ridge runs in a westerly direction for the distance of a mile, when it falls away rapidly towards the plain. The form of this ridge is favourable for the ascent as well as for safety, since the land is lower near the cone than at its extremity, and before lava could flow on the latter, it would run down the sides of the ridge both north and south of it. On the extremity of this ridge, which forms a sort of inland promontory, stands the celebrated Hermitage.

We reached this place in less than three hours after quitting Portici, the ascent in its immediate neighbourhood being sharp, but not long. The building is a simple stone structure, with a small chapel connected; but it has all the peculiarities of a tavern, rather than of a religious residence. One who had the appearance of a monk lived there, and administered to our wants, for which consolations we punctually paid. His whole manner was that of an official of the bar, rather than of the altar. In consequence of there having been a few robberies between the Hermitage and the cone, a small guard of soldiers was stationed at the former, with instructions to send one man with each party of travellers.

We remained half an hour at the Hermitage, took a cup of wine, and enjoyed the view, which was magnificent; but, as it was embraced in that from the crater, I shall not speak further of it here. There are some fine trees in front of the buildings, and, altogether, a lovelier spot could not be desired for a recluse. The distance, in an air line, between the summit and the Hermitage, must be about a mile; and although it *sounds* dangerous to live so near the crater, I would as soon be at this spot in an eruption, as in any of the towns at the base of the mountain, though these lie at five or six times the distance. A little explanation will render the matter clear. Lava, from which most of the danger has arisen in modern times, *cannot* touch the Hermitage, on account of the formation of the ridge; and, as for the red-hot stones and cinders that are always flying into the air, they ascend in nearly perpendicular lines, and their descent is necessarily much the same. In point of fact, they rarely fall at any distance from the crater. It is these, indeed, of which the cone is entirely composed, and from the base of this cone the Hermitage is distant about a mile. The *quasi* hermit, therefore, is just that space out of the line of fire.

We left the spot on horseback, and rode near half a mile, by a pretty path, through a wood, and nearly on a level line. We then emerged upon a plain of lava, which lies materially lower than the wood, and from which the heated metal has evidently flowed north and south. This low plain serves as a ditch to the promontory or ridge of the Hermitage. No lava can possibly cross it until it is filled; an event not likely to happen soon, as the lava flows off at each side. Winding our way across it, we soon came to its eastern margin, and dismounted. Here we left the horses, and prepared for the struggle that was to follow.

The ascent is rather steeper than the sides of a pile of gravel would be, supposing it to have been formed by the falling of the material on a given place, without a force sufficient to change its outline. It appeared to me to be at an angle of about fifty or fifty-five degrees with the plane of the horizon. As the cinders yield with the weight of a man, the foot sinking often to the instep, it is a severe task to get up this place. We went at it coolly, but steadily, stopping to take breath after short efforts; and I believe we were about twenty minutes in reaching the summit. The cinders were warm in spots, and a sulphurous smoke issued from the cone in a great many places that we passed. I was too experienced a traveller to run myself out of breath, as the moment of enjoyment approached. Having got within a few feet of the top, I paused to recover breath; poor W[illiam], who had commenced with fury, being still a hundred feet beneath me. The guide waited my leisure; but the guard, whose duty compelled him to go no further than the foot of the cone, but who, being on his first excursion, chose to ascend also, lay panting on the rim of the cone, or crater, as I put my foot by his side.

This was another novel and beautiful *coup d'œil*. As the place was very different from what I had expected to see, I shall endeavour to make you understand what it really is. It appeared to me that the depth of the great crater, at the place where we stood, was a little more than half of the descent of the cone itself, on its exterior; though its edge is ragged, and at one spot was two or three hundred feet higher than that which we had reached. This edge of the cone, or crater, overhung its sides in nearly the whole circuit, and the distance round it was near or quite a mile. It follows, that the diameter of the crater must be about a third of a mile. Its bottom was like a floor of clay, resembling that of the Solfatara, smoke issuing from its crevices. Vivid streaks of brimstone gave it wild, unnatural tints. It seemed quite as level as an ordinary brick-yard, viewed from our stand. A little on one side of this circular plain, rose a small cone, which might be a hundred and fifty or two hundred feet high, formed of the same materials as the outer cone, with an orifice perhaps some eighty or a hundred feet in width. This was the living, or true crater. Out of this spot issued all the smoke, fire, stones, and cinders of the ordinary workings of the mountain, of which, in truth, it is the safety valve. This little haystack-looking cone was nearer to the eastern and southern edges of the great crater than to the northern and western, and it is altogether too low to be visible to any except those who ascend to the place we occupied. The red-hot stones must therefore be propelled upwards many hundred feet, perhaps six or eight, to be seen at Naples or Sorrento, where we have often seen them, however, of late.

The scene that broke upon us, as we arrived, was one of the most extraordinary I ever witnessed. At that instant an ordinary cloud enveloped the summit of the cone, shutting out the whole view, with the exception of the crater and the surrounding objects, and casting a sombre tint on everything. It is probable a few rays from the sun struggled through this vapour, which was not high above our heads, though it seemed to descend half way down the cone, for the streaks of sulphur looked brighter and more unnatural than afterwards. The yellow tint they cast around them, the unnatural, or rather supernatural effect, coupled with the gaping crater, the rumbling of the volcano, and the occasional explosions, combined to give the spot a resemblance to the entrance of the infernal regions. If I could fancy I was obtaining glimpses in at the glories and calm radiance of heaven, when I looked upon the high Alps, looming above the Niesen and cut off from the lower world by a belt of vapour, I had no difficulty in now fancying that I stood on the threshold of hell. Virgil died about half a century before the volcano resumed its action, or he certainly would never have taxed his imagination to use the Lake Avernus, Mare Morto, and Elysian Fields of the Baian shore as machinery for his epic, when Vesuvius presented objects so much more worthy of the subject. The Campagna was as good an Elysian Field as heart

could wish, and the crater a Tartarus equal to the epic. It is
true, there is no Styx; but the monk I saw at the Hermitage
would answer every reasonable purpose of a Charon.

The *"facilis descensus Averni"* would, also, have been physically
true, supposing the crater always to maintain its present form;
for the circuit of the rim, or upper edge, is not made without
hazard, as poor W[illiam] was near demonstrating, in the workings of some of his *goatisms*. The crater, however, changes its
appearance at every great convulsion; though the one I have
described, I am told, is its general character.

You may be surprised to hear it, but the volcano itself attracted very little of my attention for the first half-hour after we
reached the edge of the crater; nor did it at any time, while on
the mountain, fill the first place in my admiration, or even
thoughts. Still it was not idle. Five minutes scarcely intervened
between the explosions, which were much greater than I had
anticipated witnessing. They were preceded by a heavy rumbling, and went off like the puffs of a safety valve to a huge
steam-engine, though unaccompanied by any hissing. The
reports were not altogether unlike those of artillery; the blowing of a whale had also some resemblance: though neither of
these noises was, in all respects, like that of the volcano. Stones
were hurled several hundred feet into the air, and fell on or
near the little cone, which was constantly growing by these ac-
cessions. Cinders, smoke, and flame accompanied each explosion. There were many minor reports, that sounded like the
crackings of a great conflagration. Occasionally, large stones
fell on the plane of the great crater, at some distance from the
little cone; but, I think, any one upon it might easily have
avoided them. They sounded, on the plain, like stones cast on
the Solfatara.

We did not descend into the crater, though there was a spot
where it might be done; but W[illiam] was too much exhausted
by the ascent, and I saw little to be gained by it but the right to
say we had done it. The explosions were so frequent as to render it impossible to ascend the little cone, and look into the real
crater; the fate of Pliny menacing all who did it, as the vapour
was constantly rising in sudden and violent puffs, inhaling
which would probably have been fatal.

My principal enjoyment, moreover, proceeded from the

view, with its extraordinary contrasts. To the west, we had the
bay, with the islands, the gulf of Gaeta, an exquisite blending of
land and water, and the sea; while southward, the Apennines,
and the Sorrentine shore, with the gulf of Salerno, through
vistas in the peaks, formed altogether a lovely panorama. Then
most of the Campagna Felice stretched beneath my eye, like an
Eden, walled by mountains. It was a Swiss view in extent, embellished by a true Italian radiance. Naples lay, like a town seen
in a camera obscura, against its hills, a brilliant accessory, and
the sails that hovered near the port resembled specks. A heavy
Russian frigate was riding off the mole, and her fair proportions were distinctly visible through the pure medium, though
diminished and fairy-like. I say, the pure medium; for the
clouds came and went repeatedly, frequently shutting us in for
minutes, and then sailing away, like birds, towards some other
peak. The contrasts of these moments were sublime; for while
nothing could be more infernal than the crater in its gloom,
aided by the accompaniments of the volcano, nothing was more
soft and radiant than the picture the earth presented when the
veil was removed. The body sympathized with the mind; for
the clouds brought the chill of a fog, which the sun relieved
by its genial warmth as the vapour departed.

I could have passed the day on the mountain with pleasure;
but W[illiam] unaccountably betrayed a physical debility that
was extraordinary for one of his active habits, and we descended, after passing a couple of hours on the summit. The
descent of the cone was an affair of five minutes. All we had to
do was to keep the body perfectly erect, and to throw the leg
forward freely; the rapidity of the fall causing us to go down
some six or eight feet each step. The shock was completely destroyed by the yielding of the cinders; and, in addition to preserving the perpendicular, the only precaution observed was to
stop occasionally, in order not to acquire too much momen-
tum. At the foot of the cone we mounted, and proceeded to
Portici, without halting at the Hermitage.

The next morning, previously to returning to Sorrento, the
consul accompanied us on board the Russian frigate. This vessel is called the Princess of Lowerz, after the wife, by a Morga-
natic marriage, of the Grand Duke Constantine. She is a noble
frigate, though not very elegant. Her crew appeared sturdy;

but the officers had not sufficiently the air of Russians of rank to prove that the service is in favour. No nation will ever have an efficient marine unless its sympathies are strongly with it, as men removed from the public eye, on the high seas, will not exert themselves sufficiently on any other terms. It is a proof of a want of this sympathy, when men of the upper classes avoid the service. This is one reason why the French marine has never done anything in proportion to its cost. The nation knows so little of maritime affairs, that anything passes for good; and the public feeling is altogether with the army. Thus, France has been completely mystified with the affair of Navarino; while England says as little about it as may be. Any seaman can appreciate a battle, in which twelve line-of-battle ships are ranged against a few heavy frigates, forts of no strength, and a maze of corvettes. Vessels of the quality of those of Ibrahim could not, at anchor, be brought to act on any one point in sufficient numbers to overcome a fleet like that under Sir Edward Codrington, if indeed it could be done on the high seas. I see, by a trial now going on in England, that the flag-ship fired less than three rounds in this general engagement!

Letter XVIII.

THE season having advanced far enough to remove all apprehension of malaria, we sent notice to our friend Mr. Hammett, at Naples, and prepared to visit Pæstum. On the appointed day the consul appeared, and, the next morning, after an early breakfast, we left *la Casa detta del Tasso*, on donkeys as usual, and took one of the mountain paths that led towards the gulf of Salerno. We had often explored these very heights, and had often admired the loveliness of the view, as from the elevations we overlooked both bays, and all the radiant scenery, but never more so than on this occasion. The shores of this promontory, on the gulf of Salerno, are, as a rule, much higher than those of the bay of Naples, though they cannot well be more precipitous. At the highest point of the road we dismissed the donkeys, and prepared to make the descent on foot, followed by a man to carry the night-sack and the cloaks. The place to which we were going, and, in particular, the path which leads to it, has great local celebrity, and that deservedly, among the lovers of the picturesque, under the name of the *Scaricatòjo*, which signifies, I believe, a place to discharge at, or a landing. W[illiam], who justifies his Pennsylvanian descent by a love of puns, termed it the "Scare-you, the toes, oh!"—and really it is one of the last places on the coast I should have expected to find a marine landing at. The precipice is very high, many times higher than that of Sorrento, and almost as steep. We went down it by a zig-zag, half stairs and half path, or what —— would call an *amphibious* road, wondering what there could be at the bottom, but the sea. We did find, however, a landing just large enough to receive a boat or two, and the site of a small house, in which two or three custom-house officers live; for so great is the jealousy of this government, in matters of revenue, that every spot at which a boat can throw its crew ashore is closely watched.

At the *Scaricatòjo*, we took a small boat with a pair of oars, and launched upon the water, bound to Amalfi, which lies some six or eight miles further up the gulf towards Salerno. Our party consisted of five; and these, with the two oars, gave us more freight than would have been agreeable in a blow; but fortunately there was scarcely any air, though the cradle of old Neptune was lazily rocking, as it is ever known to be, gale or calm. Occasionally, as we rounded the cliffs, the send of the sea would carry us close in, giving us the appearance of one of the bubbles, though in fact there was no risk.

I had often rowed under mountains, in Switzerland, though not often so immediately beneath rocks of the same elevation, for some of the peaks between Amalfi and the *Scaricatòjo* are said to be six thousand feet high. This is almost equal to Mount Washington, and all, too, in the distance of a mile, or even less, of base. In Switzerland, certainly, one sees cottages, and even churches, convents, and chateaux, on the spurs of mountains; but I do not remember to have ever met with habitations of the same pretension so crowded on rocks so nearly perpendicular, as was the case to-day, a few miles before we reached Amalfi. Some of the country houses seemed to us, who were floating beneath, to be absolutely stuck against the rocks; though I dare say there was ample room for safety, and even for gardens. Just before reaching the town, a convent appeared built *into* the cliffs, in a most picturesque manner, the wall of rock rising above the buildings half way to the clouds.

Amalfi is in a sort of a gorge, and certainly has as few commercial facilities, in the way of a port, as any ordinary mile of sea beach. Beach it has, and that, in a region like this, is distinction enough to form a town; for the light craft most in use by the ancients could be hauled on it—an effectual mode of security. I never before witnessed a scene of wrangling, begging, vociferations, and rapacity, equal to that which followed our landing on the beach of Amalfi. Men, women, and children beset us in schulls, particularly the two latter, until we were compelled to use strong measures to get rid of them.

Amalfi would seem to have been built for pleasure, for the situation is beautifully picturesque; though, the beach excepted, and a gorge in the mountains that permits of a better path than is usual here, were the only two practical advantages

I could discover about its site. You may imagine the effect of a town of some size, clinging to rocks between mountains and the sea, with churches, convents, and villas, stuck about on shelves, according to caprice or accident. These people are the very opposites of us Americans in their urban economy; for while we level mole-hills with the sagacity and zeal of speculators, they perch themselves on cliffs, and people ravines like poets. We may have the best of it, considering a house as an *article*, in which a room must contain but *two* windows, since the *third* curtain will prevent its letting; but they have greatly the best of it, considering a house as a place, in which one is to indulge in his individuality, and in pleasant thoughts. I believe we make money faster than any other nation, while we spend it with less satisfaction. A copy of the lost Pandects of Justinian was found at Amalfi, in 1137. I wonder where the Pandects of Trade were found?

As our time was short, we ordered a large boat with six oars, and left Amalfi within an hour, taking some refreshments with us. The country changed materially as we approached the head of the gulf, the peaks becoming lower and less perpendicular, and the shores generally more accessible. In the direction of Calabria the coast appeared low, the Apennines retiring inland, though their blue and ridgy outlines were visible in the haze. A lad who pulled the stroke oar, and who answered most of our questions, amused us greatly with his *patois*. Signore, he invariably pronounced like *snore*;—"*S'nore, si; s'nore, no;*"—as you may suppose, to W[illiam]'s great delight.

We found Salerno seated on the strand, with hills behind it, and an amphitheatre of mountains in their rear, again. It occupies some such situation on the gulf of Salerno as Naples occupies on her own bay, though less picturesquely surrounded in some respects, while it is more so in others. The southern, or rather the eastern, shore of the gulf, especially, is comparatively tame, on account of the flat land bounding the water. The place of our destination was in that direction, still distant some five-and-twenty or thirty miles. Salerno is little more than a roadstead, for vessels of any size; though it has a mole of some extent, behind which smaller craft can lie. The sciroccos have a full rake into this bay; but against all winds from west, northerly round to south-east, there is a tolerable protection.

As the great post-road from Naples to Calabria, (the ancient Appian Way) passes through Salerno, we here took a carriage and three horses, with which we proceeded, as soon as possible, towards Eboli. The road was excellent, and the scenery enchanting. I can scarcely recall more beautiful pastoral glimpses, of glades and meadows, all relieved by noble oaks, than we passed this evening. The population, too, appeared admirably suited to increase the effect. The dresses were in the highest degree picturesque, though a little rude, and we met few men who did not carry guns. Some even wore short swords. I believe the practice has arisen from the violence of the banditti, who formerly frequented the mountains. The danger of descents by the Barbary corsairs, too, on a coast so favourable, may have had its influence. A pointed, high-crowned hat, occasionally decorated with ribands, leathern gaiters rising to the knees, a jacket a little *à la hussar*, with a gun thrown into the hollow of the arm, at all events, made a man fit for a picture. Although we were not actually in Calabria, the peasants more resembled Calabrians than Neapolitans.

We did not get to Eboli until after dark. The carriage stopped at an inn without the walls, which had once been a convent. On examining it, we found it little more than a coarse drinking-house, with a table and two or three chairs placed in each cell, most of which were reeking with wine, and the bed-rooms quite as unpromising. It was clear the ladies could not sleep there, and yet it was the best public-house Eboli afforded. From this awkward and uncomfortable situation we were extricated by the kindness and forethought of the consul. That gentleman had bethought him, before leaving Naples, of addressing a note to the Prince of Angri,—who is not only lord of Eboli, but the proprietor of most of the adjacent country,—and had received, in reply, a letter addressed to all the Prince's dependants or stewards, commanding them to put any of his numerous houses at our disposal. The head manager of the estate lived in Eboli, and to his dwelling Mr. Hammett and myself forthwith proceeded. On reading the letter, we were told the castle of Eboli should be immediately put at our disposition, and that we had only to go and conduct the ladies up to it. This we did not require two invitations to do.

Eboli is a small crowded town, lying against an acclivity, at the foot of the Apennines, and is crowned by the castle, which occupies, as was usual in the middle ages, the highest site. The place is walled, and the streets are rather rapid and irregular. Most of the ancient castle has disappeared, though a few towers remain; but, in its stead, a spacious and comfortable hunting-seat has been erected. We entered a spacious court, and were conducted by a private way to a large sala, in which a fire was lighted, in a brazier placed in the chimney. Around this we gladly gathered, for the cool air of the Apennines was beginning to chill us. A supper was prepared, and we were furnished with good beds and excellent rooms. All was done with great assiduity, and with a profound desire to do credit to the lord of Eboli; two or three servants remaining always in the castle, whither, however, the owner seldom comes, and then only to pass a few days.

In the morning I rose betimes, and went out on a terrace to look at the scenery, for the darkness had hid everything from observation the previous night. The elevation of the castle gave it a commanding view, and we were enabled to see most of the country through which we were to travel to reach Pæstum, then distant from us twelve miles.

Eboli stands on the verge of the great plain, that stretches leagues along the sea at this place. This country was probably once fertile, and, of course, healthful, like the Campagna of Rome, or it never would have been occupied as the site of such a town as Pæstum. It is now nearly deserted; though there are a few hunting-seats scattered about its surface, which may be occupied in the cool months. Among others is Persano, a house belonging to the king, and which was much frequented by the late sporting monarch, Don Francesco. The sea was visible in the distance; and the site of Pæstum might also be discerned, across a wide reach of plain. This plain was much covered with small trees in the foreground, though it was more naked nearer to the sea.

After breakfast we left the castle of Eboli, grateful for its hospitality, and very sensible of the politeness by which it had been accorded. The road, for some distance, was beautiful; but it gradually led us upon the plain, where soon little was visible besides bushes. Persano was passed, lying on our left; and then, for miles, it was a country that, while it was not positively pleasant, offered nothing that was positively disagreeable.

Peasants soon began to appear that seemed not only out of their region, but almost out of their hemisphere. The physical peculiarities were certainly European; but in size, tint, and almost dress, they might have passed for Esquimaux. Sheep-skins with the wool on were the favourite jacket; and some actually wore blankets, like our own Indians. The sallow hue made us shudder; for one saw it was not owing to climate and habits, acting through centuries, but to disease. Had the same individual been so happy as to pass his days on the adjacent mountains, the springs of life would have remained pure: his colour might have been dark under this fierce sun, but it would not have denoted disease; and his days, though numbered, would have reached the allotted time of man. As it was, the fabulous adventurers of the Bohan upas were not more certainly doomed than these poor wretches. The rice fields of Carolina are kind in comparison with these wastes; for those kill, and there is an end of it; and, unlike these, they do not much injure those whose hard fortune compels them to dwell there, but merely those who yield to cupidity, and not to necessity.

On reaching the Silaro, we found the bridge broken, and we had to cross in a boat. The carriage was swamped, and buffaloes were procured to drag it out. In all this country, buffaloes appear to be used instead of oxen. The plains abound with them, and we saw them at work in all directions. Of course, you are naturalist enough to know that the animal familiarly called the buffalo in America, and which furnishes the sleigh-skins, is not the buffalo, but the bison; the real buffalo differing little from the ox. At Florence oxen are employed, and oxen too of a breed I was very desirous of getting sent to America. They are of a cream colour, a little inclining to the dun, and, besides having a handsome form, are admirably suited to a warm climate, and are the fastest walkers I have ever seen in the yoke. I have frequently walked by their sides, at a quick pace, and have generally found them as nimble as I am myself; nor do I remember ever to have seen one lolling. They are said to fatten kindly, and have a good carcase, though certainly they are a little longer-legged than our own. Their weight might fail a little in the heavy toil of a clearing; but there is a vast deal of lighter American labour in which their qualities would come admirably in use. I was told the breed is Hungarian. I question if the cows

are very good milkers; though this may be the result of hus-
bandry and climate, for milk is far more precious and scarcer
in Italy than wine, as I have already told you, and good pasture
is very scarce—almost unknown.

Passing a house or two of the Prince of Angri, we trotted on
by a straight even road, for a league or two farther. The country had become more wild and sterile, though it could be hardly
termed a desert. It had the appearance of neglect rather than
of barrenness, and, like the Campagna of Rome, doubtless has
gotten the upper hand of industry, by having been so long permitted to go uncultivated. The coachman stopped the carriage
by a copse of bushes, and told us the spot was the scene of a
recent robbery and murder. A newly-married English couple
were going into Pæstum, when their carriage was stopped at
this place. A lad was stationed with a musket by the copse, while
two or three others appeared in the road by the horse's head.
This lad wanted nerves for his task; for on the Englishman's
remonstrating, most probably against his holding the gun
pointed, he fired, and shot man and wife through their bodies,
as they sat side by side. Both were killed, or both died of the
wounds, and the robbers were subsequently taken and executed. A hamlet, against the Apennines, was pointed out to us
as the place in which they had lived. It was said, murder formed
no part of their original intention. Since that time, however,
the police has been much more active, and no robbery has occurred. As for ourselves, the affair of the "runner" between
Bologna and Florence has completely removed all uneasiness
on the subject.

A few yards beyond the thicket of the robbers, we came to the
ruined fragments of a gateway and of walls, and then entered
within the precincts of the ancient city of Pæstum. There are
three or four modern houses within these walls, one or two of
which are of respectable dimensions, belonging to the proprietor of the country, and they injure the effect, although, in the
season when one may sleep here with impunity, they contribute
to the comfort of a visit. It would have aided the general effect,
had the site of the city itself been left to its solitude, and the
dwellings might have stood without the walls as well as within
them.

The history of Pæstum is not very well settled. It is popularly said to have been built by a colony of marine adventurers, who named the place after their own particular god, Neptune.* The temples that remain are certainly of very remote antiquity; probably little less ancient, if any, than the Pyramids of Egypt. The Romans got possession of the place, of course, and Augustus is said to have visited the very temples that are now standing, as specimens of ancient architecture! The Saracens destroyed the town about a thousand years since, and it has lain the whole of the intervening time virtually a waste. So completely was the place forgotten and lost, that standing on the coast, and at no great distance from what must have been the great road into Calabria, since the time of Appius Claudius, at least its site was unknown, to the reading and travelling portion of mankind, until the year 1755, when a painter of Naples, who was out sketching from nature, blundered on the ruins, and brought them into notice. This sounds extraordinary in the ears of an American; but a little explanation removes half the causes of wonder.

In the first place, Pæstum, though it stands within a mile of the sea, lies on the eastern side of the gulf of Salerno, and away from the track of all but the small vessels of the adjoining country. The temples are not high, and when first seen by the painter, were said to have been nearly buried in vines and trees. A common Italian is so much accustomed to see ruins, that the peasants of the neighbourhood would not be struck by their existence; things to which we have been habituated appearing always as things of course, and occasioning no surprise. Besides, Pæstum was never a place much noted in history, but is principally remarkable for containing a rare specimen of architecture in its ruder state, and for the durability of its works. Perhaps the ruins, concealed in tangled brakes, required the keen eye and cultivated tastes of an artist, to attract the attention necessary to draw them from obscurity. How many hunters, land surveyors, and even land speculators, saw the Falls of Trenton before they were spoken of beyond their own neighbourhood! I can well recollect the time when I first heard of them as a thing that would well repay the trouble of walking a mile or two to see; and yet it may be questioned if all Europe has a cascade

*Ποσειδῶν.

that so well merits a visit;—certainly it has not more than one or two, if it has any.

The size of Pæstum is easily to be seen by the remains of its walls. The guide-books say these walls were once fifty feet high; though I saw nothing that would have led me to believe them so lofty. Parts remain, notwithstanding, in a tolerable state of preservation. Their circuit is stated at two miles, the form being elliptical; and this would give, on the shortest side, a diameter a little exceeding half a mile, which is about the real distance. We have few villages, containing fifteen hundred souls, in America, that do not cover as much ground as this; although we have no edifice to compare with the temples that have stood on this spot, near two thousand years, *as ruins*, even in the largest towns. One of the gates still remains; but it may be questioned if it is as old as the temples. There are also the remains of an amphitheatre, or of a theatre, and of many other edifices that belonged to the civilization of that remote age. It is probable the theatre was Roman.

It sounds odd to speak of antiquity as being comparatively modern, because it was Roman; but comparing the temple of Neptune with anything else of the sort, in Italy, would seem quite out of the question. Its history and its style prove it to be one of the most venerable specimens of human art of which we have any knowledge. The Pyramids themselves are scarcely older. And yet, standing a few hundred feet in its front, and examining the structure, one can scarcely fancy that he sees a blemish on its exterior. The lightning has scathed it; but time appears to have wrought nearly in vain on its massive columns. Some of the interior columns are gone, it is true, and a little of the pediment is broken, but scarcely more than is absolutely necessary to give the structure the air of a ruin.

The temple of Neptune is thought to be the oldest of the remaining edifices of Pæstum, and it certainly is much the finest, although that called of Ceres belongs to a more advanced taste in architecture. The rudeness of the former, however, accords so admirably with its massiveness, as well as its antiquity, that I believe few people hesitate about giving it the preference. To me, it was much the most impressive, and I had almost said the most imposing, edifice I know. The mind insensibly ran back to other ages as I gazed at the pile, which, like the fresh-looking lava of Ischia, appeared to laugh at human annals. Three centuries since, I said mentally, Columbus discovered half the world, astonishing the inhabitants of the two hemispheres equally, by bringing each to a knowledge of the other. At that period, which more than swallowed the entire history of my own country, this temple lay buried in vines and brambles, the haunt of serpents and birds. Seven centuries would take us back to the period of the English Conquest, when England itself was a nation scarcely emerged from barbarism. Four or five more might carry us back to the age when marauders from the East laid waste the sickly town that had succeeded the city of the original colonists, when the past, to even its people, seemed remote and obscure. Four or five centuries more would take us up to the Romans, who came to see this temple as an object of wonder, and as a curious relic of distant ages. Another thousand years would probably bring us to the period when the priests officiated at the altar, and homage was paid to one of the attributes of Divine power, through the mysticisms of heathen allegory. What a speck does the history of America become in this long vista of events—what a point the life and adventures of a single man! And yet even this temple does not reach to the last great convulsion, when the earth was virtually destroyed, and animal life may be said to have taken a new commencement: at the next even the temple of Neptune will disappear.

Some astronomers, by calculating the epochas of a particular and a remarkable comet, that which was last seen in 1681, suppose it possible that it may have struck the earth about the time of the Deluge, causing that phenomenon, and producing most of those physical changes that certainly have altered the face of the earth, destroying many of its animals, and which may have actually given it new revolutions. Admitting that this theory is substantially true,—and it is as likely to be so as any other that has been broached,—we may regard the temple of Neptune as one of the best specimens of architecture that succeeded the new civilization. At all events, it is something even to fancy one has seen a work of human art that may be esteemed a standard of human skill three thousand years ago.

A good deal has been written about the scenery of Pæstum, which is certainly not unsuited to the ruins. It would be better without the half-dozen modern dwellings, perhaps; but the mind takes little heed of these intruders, when once occupied with the temples. There is something too engrossing in the study of structures like these, to admit of interruption. The plain is not a desert, but it is covered rather with the luxuriant vegetation of weeds, that associate with the spot the idea of wildness, instead of that of solitude. In this respect, the Pyramids are the most sublime; for there nature, and even vegetation, appear to have gone to decay, while the works of man endure. Still, there are a homeliness and familiarity in the wastes of Pæstum, that suit the nature of the ruins better, perhaps, than a plain of sand. The site of each class of ruins is suited to its particular character. This is a town, and the fancy endeavours to people its streets, to crowd the altar, and to imagine the thousand familiar objects and scenes that once enlivened its avenues. The tangled brake, the wild flower, the luxuriant and negligent vine, while they are eloquent on the subject of solitude, comport well with such recollections. In Egypt the grandeur of the desolation, with the interminable and sterile plains, better suit the magnificence of the works, and the mystery that conceals their origin and history. *Au reste*, the moral of the *entourage* of Pæstum is different from that of the Pyramids; for the Apennines form a distant but beautiful amphitheatre on one side, while the blue Mediterranean on the other, the "eternal hills," and "the great sea" of antiquity, exhibit all the glories of their nature, as they hover over and around these memorials of man.

We sat down to the most disgusting and the nastiest meal at Pæstum I ever saw served; but nothing besides wine would seem to be fit for use at the place. Our host did credit to the latter; and he frankly admitted that, without plenty of good warm liquor, life was a slippery tenure on this plain. What a happy apology for one who takes kindly to the remedy! Several miserable-looking wretches, in whom life seemed to be withering hourly, came round the hovel, and he pointed to them as proofs of the truth of his theory.

We did not return to Eboli, but proceeded direct to Salerno, on our return, reaching that place just as night closed. The inn at this place struck me as being more thoroughly foreign and strange than any I had yet been in. The grand *sala* was in the centre of the house, and almost without external light. It also answered the purposes of a kitchen; the travellers, who were seated around the vast room; eating by dim lamps, enjoying the advantage of whetting their appetites by the aid of the flavours of the different dishes. We succeeded in obtaining three rooms, in one of which, that afterwards served me for a bed-room, we contrived to eat a very unscientific supper.

After a better breakfast the next morning, we proceeded by land, taking the road to Pompeii. The route was beautiful, running over mountains and through gorges, with brilliant views of the sea; for we had now to cross the broken range of the Apennines, that separates the two bays, and which forms the promontory of Sorrento. The cliffs near Salerno were truly magnificent, and a hermitage or two on their giddy shelves put everything of the sort we had seen, even in Switzerland, to shame.

One of the great charms of Italy is the manner in which the most picturesque sites are thus occupied. Pinnacles, peaks, rocks, terraces, that, in other countries, the traveller might feel disposed to embellish by some structure, in his fancy, poetical alike in its form and uses, are here actually occupied, and frequently by objects whose beauty surpasses even the workings of the imagination. Of this character was the extraordinary scene already mentioned, in the island of Ischia. Then the softness of the atmosphere and the skies throw a charm over all, to comprehend which, one must be acquainted with the effect of light in low latitudes.

There were a great many small isolated towers standing along the ridges and sides of the mountains, which, I was told, were used for the field-sports of the King, though in what way I cannot tell you. The mountains between Castel-a-mare and Sorrento also have several. If I understood the explanation, they are not intended for hunting or shooting-seats, for which they are too small and too numerous, but merely as stands to shoot from! This may be set down as royal poaching.

Our visit to Pompeii was short, though we nearly made the circuit of the walls. The amphitheatre is built against these walls, at one end; for, standing on its uppermost point, I found I looked out of the city. The house of the fountain was now

completely disinterred, and we saw a few small domestic articles that had been found in the ashes. I was more strongly impressed than ever, at this visit, with the notion of restoring and
furnishing entire one of the best of the houses; a thing that
might be done from the Royal Museum with tolerable success.
Even a respectable approach to the truth would be infinitely
interesting.

I must still think that a portion of the town of the greatest interest, as respects private dwellings, remains to be explored. I
believe that the street parallel to that of the Appian Way will
yet, when opened, offer some dwelling suited to this plan of restoration, and that by proper care the walls and paintings may be
preserved. It would be better to open a house with this express
intention, than to attempt restoring one of those that has long
been exposed to the air.

From Pompeii we went to Castel-a-mare. This town stands
near the ancient site of Stabiæ, which was also destroyed by the
eruption of the year 79. The King has a favourite country palace on the heights behind the town; it is called *Quì si sana,** a
name that answers to the *Sans Souci* of Frederic, though of a
different signification. We saw, a short time since, the royal
squadron on its way from Naples to Castel-a-mare, the King
having several vessels that he uses as yachts. One was a ship,
and there were also a brig and a schooner. There is a schooner
now lying at Naples, that was seized under the decrees of
Murat, which was formerly appropriated to the same purposes.
Since my arrival here, I have heard an interesting fact coupled
with these seizures, on authority so good that I give it credit.

When the proposition to seize these vessels was made to
Murat, he resisted it, on the ground that it was a species of pira-
cy, a breach of faith that could not be tolerated for a moment by
any independent nation, and *that immediate war would be the consequence.* His minister knew America better than his master:
*"America will not declare war, sire, for it is a country of traders, and
these are men who will not consent to lose their present profits for the
maintenance of a principle.* It is true, in the end something will be
done, for no nation can submit to such an aggression; but at
present it will be nothing but talk. Hereafter, Naples may have

"Here one is cured," literally translated.

to make compensation; but your majesty needs money, and we can consider this as a forced loan." The counsel was followed, and we now know how true was the minister's prediction. This person was wrong in his general estimate of the American nation, but perfectly right in that of its merchants, who have the character common to all in trade. They never look beyond the day. It is our misfortune to have no towns but trading towns, and, consequently, no collected influence to resist their published opinions and interested clamour, which are fast tending to a misconception, and to a displacing of all the interests of life. Thus it is we find men treating commerce, which is merely an incident of human affairs, as a principal, and struggling to make everything, even morals and laws, subservient to its ends, and this, too, without a due regard to means. This class of citizens overawe those presses which have the greatest circulation, and by acting in concert, and with available means, form a powerful, and, more especially, a clamorous resistance, to anything that thwarts, or which they fancy thwarts, their interests. The commercial class of America, as a class, will ever be found in opposition to any administration that loyally carries out the intention of the government; for that intention is indissolubly connected with great principles, whereas their bias has ever been to expedients that are temporary and fluctuating, or to the policy that suits the prevailing interest of the hour. Trade, liable to so many vicissitudes and sudden reverses, never can have any higher code of principles.

I cannot express to you the sensations which crowded my mind as, seated on the mole at Naples, I regarded the schooner in question; a vessel that had been wrested, without even the pretence of legality, from an American citizen, to contribute to the pleasures of the king of this country. Of what avails it that one is an American? His property is taken from him by violence, his person outraged, and if he complain so as seriously to bring in danger the relations of his country, the chances are more than equal that his character would follow his property, if no other means offered to protect, as it is termed, the interests of trade. What aggravates the wrong, is the fact that a large portion of the class who have given this false direction to the public policy are not even Americans, but foreigners who assume the American character merely to advance their fortunes, and who are always ready to throw it aside when there is a question of national pride, or of national disgrace.

For myself, a near view of the effects of these wrongs, and a consideration of the policy and feelings that have succeeded them, has destroyed all confidence in the protection of my native country. I deem the national character of no more use or service to me, as a traveller beyond the influence of his own laws, than if I were an Esquimaux. I know that others of more experience,—I may say, of *bitter* experience,—have the same feeling. I declare solemnly, were I a merchant, and were my vessel seized by any power of sufficient force to render a contest with it of momentary importance to trade, that, so far from believing myself protected by my flag,—unless, indeed, I could call to my immediate succour some of those gallant and right-feeling men who command the cruisers, who are ready enough to assert the honour and rights of the flag, but who are oftener reproached than commended, however, when they *do* discover a proper spirit of this nature,—I should conceive I had made a good escape by compromising with the aggressor for one half, instead of appealing to the government for protection.

There is a great deal of vapouring in the papers about the protection of the flag; but I am perfectly persuaded that my feeling is the feeling of a large majority of the Americans abroad. I do not believe one in ten has the smallest reliance on the spirit, wisdom, patriotism, or justice of the government at home. By government, I mean that body which alone possesses any efficient authority in such cases, which is Congress. Were I personally to be brought under the displeasure of any of these governments, I would sooner seek the protection of a Russian, or even of a French, than of an American minister, unless my personal relations with the latter were such as to render me confident of his support. On those diplomatic men who look forward to political advancement at home, I should have no dependance at all, as a rule, (I admit the character of the individual might influence his conduct,) for such men, as a class, regard the clamour of the most clamorous, far more than either principles or their duties.

This is a sore spot in the American character, and a blot on the American name. I once thought differently, for I followed my feelings rather than my knowledge; but observation and reflection have taught me to think as I now think. What renders the consciousness of this false policy most of all bitter, is the certainty that the heart of the nation is sound, its bones and sinews being as ready as those of any people on earth to maintain a true and a spirited policy. But they are neutralized by the congregated and arrogant interests of trade. Let any wrong of this nature be fairly laid before the nation, in the spirit of honesty and truth, and nine men in ten will be ready to avenge the honour or to justify the rights of the republic; but politicians do not, or will not see this truth, and they invariably point to the towns and the presses of the merchants. I have had several conversations on this very topic with diplomatic men in Europe, and have not found one who was not under this malign and unmanly fear, and insomuch unfit for his trust.*

This is not the popular manner of regarding these things, I know; but I am writing to tell you what, at least, I conceive to be, under the deepest conviction of my responsibilities as a man, the naked truth. The day will come when these opinions will be believed, the political ephemera of the hour having withered, died, and become forgotten, notwithstanding the charlatanism and laboured industry of the Tacituses of the day.

---

*The experiment of a right course has since been tried. A President of a strong will has made a tardy attempt to rescue the honour and character of the nation, and, favoured by circumstances, he has partially succeeded. The treaty with France has not been complied with, according to either its spirit or its letter; but it has been enough to satisfy those who had lost all hope. It has not been complied with, because the money stipulated to be paid with interest has not been paid according to those stipulations, making a difference against the claimants of more than a million. But what was the course of Congress, under the circumstances of a violated treaty, in addition to the original outrage!

Letter XIX.

THE November of Sorrento proved a rough visiter, and we were driven to cluster around the solitary fire-place of the *Casa detta del Tasso*. We resisted every inducement to remove, until the *tramontana* got to be so marrow-chilling, that the alternative lay between total defeat and flight. We chose the latter, preferring abandoning the place we loved so well, to being chilled into mummies. The cold might have been resisted, had the house been in good repair, and suited to a winter's residence; but, as the cook had possession of one of our two fire-places, the other proved insufficient for our wants. This letter is consequently written from Naples. You are not to fancy a freezing cold by this account, but one that was excessively chilling; and this the more so, from the circumstance that our house was fully exposed to the north winds, standing, as it did, on the northern edge of the plain, with the entire bay between us and the Apennines.

The day we quitted Sorrento, the wind blew so heavily from the east, that the people of the *Divina Providenza* looked surprised when we presented ourselves at the *Marinella*, in readiness to embark. They knew the bay better than I did; for, judging by the force of the gale and sea *within* the curvature of our shore, I thought we might make the passage without any risk. Finding us ready to proceed, however, the fine fellows made no objection, but stood out boldly into the gulf. At the distance of a mile or two from the cliffs, we took the whole force of the wind; and really there were a few minutes when I thought of putting back. All our previous boating was a fair-weather frolic, compared to this.

The wind drew through the pass between Vesuvius and Castel-a-mare like a pair of bellows, and the sea, at times, almost laid our little speronara on her side. The vessel, however, was admirably handled, and, by watching the sheet, which was eased off in the puffs, we wallowed across the opening, luffing up to our course handsomely, until we made the lee of the mountain. Here we literally found a calm, and were compelled to use the oars! We had no sooner swept by the base of the mountain, however, than we took the breeze again, stiff as ever, but without the disagreeable attendant of rough water. Notwithstanding the delay of the calm, we made the passage in a little more than two hours.

We are in private lodgings here. Of course, you understand by private lodgings, not a dwelling that differs from a tavern, with a *table d'hôte*, only in name, but an *apartment*, as it is termed, in which we have everything, from the kitchen to the parlour, to ourselves. The American "boarding-house" does exist in Europe, certainly, but it is scarcely in favour. We are near the mole and the Toledo, and have been passing the month in doing Naples more effectually than we could do it in the first visit.

The place is inexhaustible in street amusements. I never tire of wandering about it, but find something to amuse me at every turn. In one quarter, the population appear literally to live in the open air, and we have driven through a street in which cooking, eating, wrangling, dancing, singing, praying, and all other occupations, were going on at the same moment. I believe I mentioned this in the first visit, but I had not then fallen on the real scene of out-door fun. The horses could not move off a walk, as we went through this street; and their heads, suddenly thrust into the centre of a *ménage*, appeared to produce no more derangement than a puff from a smoky chimney in one of our own kitchens.

But the mole is the spot I most frequent. Besides the charm of the port, which to me is inexhaustible, small as the place is, we have all sorts of buffoons there. One recites poetry, another relates stories, a third gives us Punch and Judy, who, in this country, bear the more musical names of Pulcinello and Giulietta, or some other female name equally sonorous, while all sorts of antics are cut by boys. The shipping is not very numerous, though it has much of the quaintness and beauty of the Mediterranean rig. The vessels of war lie behind the mole also, and they show, plain enough, that the fleet of Naples is no great matter. The ships of the line could scarcely cope with modern frigates; and one or two of the latter, though prettily moulded vessels enough, are not much heavier than large sloops of the present day.

A daughter of the King, the Princess Christina, has just married her uncle, the King of Spain, and a frigate is about to sail with a portion of the royal *trousseau*. I have visited this vessel, which is a pretty ship, and I feel persuaded that this nation, with its materials, could it bear the expense in money, might easily become a naval power to command respect in this sea. The country is all coast, has an uncommonly fine population, in a physical sense at least, and wants only the moral qualities necessary to carry out such a plan.

The weather changed soon after we came to Naples, and it has taught us what is really meant by Neapolitan skies. Until the middle of October, I had no notion of the extent of their beauty, which, though not absolutely unknown to us, is of a kind that we know the least. There is a liquid softness in the atmosphere, during the autumnal months, that you must have observed, for we are not without it in America. By this, however, I do not mean, the bright genial days of September and October, that are vulgarly praised as the marks of a fine autumn, but the state of the air, which renders everything soft, and lends prismatic colours, in particular, to the horizon, morning and evening. These colours are quite unlike the ordinary gorgeousness of an American sunset, being softer, more varied, and quicker in their transitions. I have often seen them, in October and November, near the American coast, when at sea, in latitudes as low as 40°: but they are by no means frequent on shore: still we have them, though seldom, perhaps never, in the perfection they are seen here.

You will smile at my old passion for fine skies and landscape scenery, but I have climbed to the castle of St. Elmo a dozen times within the last month to see the effect of the sunset. Just as the day disappears, a soft rosy tint illumines the base of Vesuvius, and all the crowded objects of the coast, throwing a glow on the broad Campagna that enables one almost to fancy it another Eden. While these beautiful transitions are to be seen on the earth, the heavens reflect them, as the cheek of a young girl reflects the rose in her bosom. Of the hues of the clouds at such moments, it is impossible to speak clearly, for they appear supernatural. At one time the whole concave is an arch of pearl;

and this perhaps is succeeded by a blush as soft and as mottled as that of youth; and then a hundred hues become so blended, that it is scarcely possible to name or to enumerate them. There is no gorgeousness, no dazzling of the eye in all this, but a polished softness that wins as much as it delights the beholder. Certainly, I have never seen sunsets to compare with these, on shore, before this visit to Naples; though at sea, in low latitudes, they are more frequent, I allow.

I presume these are the peculiar charms of the Italian skies, of which the poets and painters have spoken from time immemorial. The American who runs in and out of Naples nine months in the year, although he may see beautiful transitions of light in the heavens, can know nothing of these particular beauties unless he happen to hit the right months.

I have said nothing of the Museum, which contains the articles found at Pompeii and Herculaneum, because travellers have written so much about them, that little remains to be said. We have witnessed the slow, nice, and one might almost say, bootless task of unrolling the manuscripts found at the latter place, and it certainly speaks well for the patience of mankind, and of the disposition of this government to encourage learning. I say, found at Herculaneum, for I believe none have been found at Pompeii, nor would they be burned like these had any been found there.

All the manuscripts of the ancients appear to have been kept on wooden rollers: if any were folded in the manner of the modern book, I have not seen them. The heat of the lava has reduced the parchments or papyrus of those found at Herculaneum to a state so near that of cinder or ashes, that a breath of wind will commonly separate the fibres. Still they exist in scrolls, and the object is to unroll them, in order to get a sight of the writing. Fortunately, an ancient manuscript's legibility does not depend at all on the chirography of the author. As printing was unknown, of course all works that were thought worthy of publication, if such a term can properly be applied to such a state of things, were properly written out by regular copyists, in a large fair hand, that was nearly as legible, if not quite as legible, as large type. If anything remarkable is ever to be discovered among the manuscripts of Herculaneum, we shall be indebted to this practice for its possession. As yet, I believe nothing of particular merit, or of particular value, either in the way of art or history, has been found.

To return to the process, which is sufficiently simple in practice, though difficult to be understood from a verbal or written description. The wooden scroll is secured, in a way that admits of its turning, at the bottom of a small frame that a little resembles one of the ordinary frames on which females extend their needle-work. This frame is secured. Threads of silk are attached to screws in the upper part of the frame, and their lower ends are made to adhere to the outer end of the manuscript, by means of the white of eggs and goldbeater's skin. These threads, of which there are several along the edge of the manuscript, are tightened gently, by means of the screws, like fiddle-strings, and then the workman commences separating the folds by inserting the thin blade of a proper instrument. If the manuscript has a hole, or it yields, it is strengthened by applying goldbeater's skin. It is gradually—and very gradually, as you may suppose—unrolled by tightening the threads, until a piece is raised as high as the frame, where it is examined by a man of letters and carefully copied. The letters, owing to the chemical properties of the ink, are more easily distinguished than one would at first imagine. The colour is all black, or a dark brown; but the letters are traced by a species of cavities in the substance,—or perhaps it were better to say, by offering a different surface,—for the whole fabric is almost reduced to the consistence of gossamer. The unrolled manuscript has more or less holes in it, and the vacancies in the text are to be guessed at.

We saw people busily employed in all the stages of the process. Some were mere mechanics, others scholars capable of reading the Latin, and of detecting the more obscure words, as well as of comprehending the abbreviations. The first copy, I believe, in all instances, is a fac-simile; after which it is turned over to a higher class of scholars, to have the vacuums in the text conjectured if possible, and for commentaries and examination.

This operation has now been going on for years, with extraordinary zeal and patience. The Americans who travel in this country are a little too apt to deride the want of "energy" in the government, and a large class falls into the puerile mistake of fancying it patriotism to boast of what we could do under the same circumstances. Certainly, I shall not pretend to compare the benefits of any other political system, *as a whole*, with those of our own, nor do I object to throwing the truth into the teeth of those who ignorantly contemn everything American; but we have our weak spots as well as our neighbours, and I very much question if any Congress could be found sufficiently imbued with a love of learning, or sufficiently alive to its benefits even to our own particular and besetting motive, gain, to persevere in voting funds, year after year, to carry on the investigations that are now making in Naples. Neither a love of the fine arts nor a love of learning has yet made sufficient progress in America to cause the nation to feel or to understand the importance of both on general civilization, without adverting to their influence on the happiness of man, the greatest object of all just institutions. We have too many omissions of our own to throw about us these sneers indiscriminately.

The number of manuscripts that has been found in different places is said to exceed two or three thousand; though it is probable many are duplicates. The greater portion of them, too, are past decyphering; as would have been the case with all, had the ancients used no better paper than the moderns. England, it is true, might possibly resist an eruption; but as for France and America, and Germany, and Italy herself, the heat of the volcano, in an ordinary time, would almost destroy their cobweb fabrics, if exposed to it anywhere near the crater.

The collection of familiar articles found in the ruins, and collected in the museum, is of great interest; but the publications concerning them are so minute, that a description by me is unnecessary. I was much struck with the beauty of the forms, and with the classical nature of the ornaments. Thus, the weights of steel-yards, and many other things of the most familiar uses, are in the shape of heads, most probably busts, and possibly commemorative of the distinguished men of the country.

America might do something in this way that should speak well for the sentiment and tastes of the nation. Alter the coin, for instance, which is now the ugliest in Christendom. The same may almost be said of the flag; though it is not an easy matter to make one uglier than some one sees here. Could the miserable hermaphrodite yclept Liberty that now disfigures the American coin be replaced by the heads of those citizens who have become justly eminent, the expedient would be a worthy substitute for that of statues and medals. To have one's head on the coin, would possess all the advantages of a patent of nobility, free from the evils. To prevent abuses, the solemn votes of the States might be taken, unanimity as States required, and the honour postponed until the party had been dead half a century. This, you know, is the mode in which the Romish Church makes saints. These honours might be graduated too, giving to the most illustrious the honours of the gold, to the next those of the silver, and to another class those of the copper coin. The *quasi*, or ephemeral great, might still figure on the bank notes, as they do to-day. We could begin with Washington and Franklin, two names of which Rome herself might have been proud, in the best days of the republic. The copper coin might, in due time, take most of the Presidents, on which, I fancy, they would very generally be placed by posterity. Perhaps old John Marshall might work his way up to the silver; though I fear original thinkers are too rare in America to resist the influence of fifty years. *The American* jurist is yet to make his appearance.

What should we do with Jefferson under such a plan? Put him on the gold—certainly not. He was too much a party man for that. Even Franklin would get there as a physical philosopher, and not as a moral philosopher, or even as a politician; for as the first of these last he was too mean, and for the second too managing. John Jay might get up to the silver; certainly, had he not retired so early; and as to integrity and motives, he merits the gold. Jefferson might get on the silver, but I fear it would be with some alloy. Poor Hamilton, whose talents and honesty deserve the gold, would fail after all; or, at least, he would get on the *reverse* of the coin, because he was elsewhere on the wrong side.

A great deal of poetic justice might be thrown into the scheme, you see. I fear we should have to import a few hogsheads of *cowries* from Africa, for the *oi polloi* of American greatness. It clearly would never do to trust the decision to Congress, as every man in it would vote for his neighbour, on condition that his neighbour voted for him. The coin might want *rolling*, but it should not be *"log-rolling."*

To treat a grave matter seriously, the tastes of the ancients are fast producing an influence on the tastes of the moderns; most of the beautiful forms that are embellishing the bronzes of France and Italy being directly derived from models found at Pompeii and Herculaneum.

One is a little puzzled with the moral evidence of many of the articles in the Museum. It is not easy to say whether they prove extreme depravity of taste and great dissoluteness of manners, or extreme innocence and simplicity. Taking Juvenal and Ovid as guides, it is to be feared the first is the true solution. The proofs are of the most extraordinary kind, and quite on a level with those which Captain Cook found in some of the South Sea Islands. But the world of the nineteenth century, in decency, whatever it may be in facts, is not the world of any other era. The frescos of Andrea del Sarto, in the *loggie* of churches even, and the tastes of the *Divine* Raphael himself, to say nothing of that of his scholars, sufficiently show this.

It is startling to see *rouge*, play-tickets, knives, spoons, and other familiar things, that were used two thousand years ago. Every one is surprised to see how little these articles have been changed. As to the *rouge*, it is not surprising, for it is a relic of barbarism, and nations cease to use it as they approach nearest to the highest civilization. It is said that no lancets have been found; from which some infer that bleeding was unknown to the ancients, who may have used leeches and cupped. Forks, also, are said to have been unknown. I do not remember to have seen any. Of course, there was no silver-fork school; a singular blessing for a common-sense people.

I think it quite evident, from the articles in the Museum, as well as from the houses in Pompeii, that the ancients were much in advance of the moderns in many matters, and as much behind them in others. In most things pertaining to beauty of forms, and what may be termed the poetry of life, the advantage would seem to have been with them; but it is scarcely exaggerated to say, that one may detect the absence of the high morality introduced by Christ, in a great portion of their habits. Domestic life does not appear to have been enjoyed and appreciated as it is now; though I confess this is drawing conclusions from rather slender premises.

The Romans, like the French, lived much in public: and yet the English, who lay such high claims to domesticity, do not cherish the domestic affections to the same degree as these very French. It is quite possible to enjoy baths, forums, public promenades, theatres, and circuses, and yet have no passion for celibacy, club-houses, and separate establishments. The Americans, who have less publicity than common in their pleasures, have scarcely any domestic privacy, on account of "the neighbours;" while the French have actually a species of family legislation, and a species of patriarchal government, that are both beautiful and salutary.

IX. *Roman Campagna* (1843) by Thomas Cole

x. *St. Peter's, Rome* (1857) by George Inness

XI. *St. Peter's at Rome*, drawn by Giovanni Battista Piranesi and engraved by D. Roberts

XII. *Cardinal Polignac Visiting St. Peter's, Rome,* by Giovanni Paolo Pannini.

Letter XX.

O UR time was up, and we reluctantly relinquished our hold of the "*pezzo di cielo caduto in terra.*" The weather had got to be wintry and wet, however,—a state of the seasons in which Naples appears to the least advantage; and then we had Rome before us,—a pleasure that few travellers who have been in Italy near fifteen months can anticipate. Although accident and the weather have in a great measure controlled our movements, I believe we have fallen on the pleasantest course, as we have kept the best for the last.

A gentleman of Rome having occasion to send his carriage back, we took that in addition to our own, and by the aid of two teams belonging to a Savoyard, were enabled to set every body, and, what has got to be almost as serious a matter, every *thing*, in motion. As the day was well advanced before the caravan could move, we had named Capua as the end of the first day's march, making a *détour*, however, in order to visit the palace and aqueduct of Caserta.

The latter was the place first seen; the road leading us directly across the plain which is so well termed the Campagna Felice. This plain is covered with habitations, like the great plain of Lombardy, and, although so desirable to the agriculturist, is a little tame to the traveller. However, as it rained most of the way, we lost little by its monotony.

We entered the Apennines by the valley of the aqueduct, amid very beautiful scenery. This aqueduct, or the portion of it that travellers come to see, is merely a bridge to span the valley; but it is on a scale so magnificent as to excite wonder. Apart from this, the structure is no great matter, being under ground; but the portion thrown across the valley is on a truly regal scale. The work is of bricks, beautifully laid, and is a succession of arches in rows, one standing on another, to the number of three. I cannot tell you the precise dimensions, for my guide-books say nothing of it; but I should think it near half a mile long, and two hundred feet high, a noble mass of masonry. It is easier to admire it, than to comprehend its necessity. The water is for the use of the palace of Caserta, and it is difficult to suppose a trunk of the necessary height might not be made sufficiently strong to contain a small column of water, or to see the necessity of crossing a hill which was easily turned.

I believe this is esteemed the second work of its kind now in existence; that at Lisbon alone ranking before it. I have rarely seen a structure that has so forcibly impressed me with the sense of its vastness. It is, in short, literally bridging a valley. We ascended to the road, after walking under and among the arches, and overlooked a fine view, in the direction of Naples. The weather had become pleasant, but the recent rain had set the mists in motion, and we got a glimpse of Italy in a new character. The valley was not large, but exceedingly pretty; and the road by which we had come wound through it, passing beneath the centre of the aqueduct. Our carriages had taken it, and were winding their way out of the valley, up to our own level, in order to rejoin us. The effect of the whole was both noble and soft; for the distant bay, Capri, Vesuvius, and the Campagna, were all bathed in the glories of a fine sun-light, relieved by fleecy mists. The road on the summit of the aqueduct is wide enough to receive the equipages of the King, who had passed over not long before we were there. The trunk for the water was by no means large.

The route from the aqueduct is very beautiful. It winds among the mountains and through valleys, and is constructed as a royal drive, leading merely to the aqueduct. Caserta, as a town, is not large; though the palace is one of the finest in Europe. The latter stands on a perfectly level plain, with no other view than can be got from the windows, and that of the Apennines, which are too near for effect, or indeed to be seen to advantage, the nearest heights concealing the more lofty ranges in the distance. This palace is said to owe its existence to the pride of Charles III, who, irritated at having been menaced by an English fleet which ran under the walls of his residence in Naples, and threatened to lay it in ruins unless the demands of its government were complied with, declared he would build a palace where no insolent foe could insult him. In this respect, Caserta has certainly the advantage of both Castel-a-mare and Portici; but this is all, unless the magnificence of the unfinished structure be included. The gardens, however, are extensive, and there is probably good shooting in the mountains.

The great staircase of the palace of Caserta is much the finest thing of its kind in Europe. It is noble, beautiful, sufficiently light, and admirably proportioned as well as ornamented. The state-rooms are good, though not more than half finished. But what palace in Europe *is* finished? There may be a few, but I suspect that most are not. The Louvre is half a waste, the Pitti has its uncovered arches mouldering with time, and this of Caserta has not more than half of the best rooms in a state fit to be used: still there are enough for so small a kingdom, and more than are furnished. The palace on the exterior is a parallelogram, of seven or eight hundred feet, by five or six hundred. Internally, it has a beautiful distribution of courts, clustered round a central nucleus, which nucleus contains the celebrated staircase. The staircase is on the plan of that in the City Hall, New York, or a single flight at the bottom, which is divided into two after the landing.

From Caserta we proceeded to Capua, where we passed the night. Some ruins of no great moment, that are immediately on the highway, are thought to point out the site of ancient Capua, the modern town being about a mile distant. The latter is a mean dirty town, and certainly was not the place that detained Hannibal so long.—By the way, this much-talked-of delay was probably no more than the common expedient of falling back from a wasted to a fertile country to recruit, and, in all probability, was quite as much owing to exhaustion, as to a demoralization of another kind. It is far more likely that his army corrupted Capua, than that Capua corrupted his army.

The only specimen we had of Capuan luxury was a guitar at supper. Finding we had lived in Florence, the musician gave us a song in honour of "*Firenze, bella città.*" The guide-books say this word, Firenze, means a red lily in the Etruscan dialect, and it is certain that there is a lily in its arms. The arms of the Medici are literally *pills*,—three *pills*, which were emblazoned all over the place. It is a pity these pills are not a little more active, activity being all that Tuscany wants.

We left Capua betimes next day, and, after driving some ten

or twelve miles, came to the termination of the Campagna Felice. This plain is certainly very beautiful; and its northern termination we thought the most beautiful of all, for it had much
the character of park scenery. We stopped to breakfast at a
place called St. Agata, which was scarcely more than a tavern. A
small town called Sessa, known to be the ancient Suessa Auruncorum, a Roman station, lies against the base of the Apennines,
about a mile distant. Between this town and St. Agata, is a broad
avenue-like road; and a noble bridge is thrown across a small
stream and a hollow on the way. When we had breakfasted, I
proposed to [Mrs. Cooper] to walk ahead of the carriages as far
as this town, which is said to contain some antiquities. We had
got into its principal street, when I perceived that the pavement
was up, and that there was no visible passage around the spot.
Surprised at finding a post-road in such a state, I inquired
of the workmen in what manner our carriages were to get
through. We were told that the road did not pass in this direction at all, but that it went *round* the corner of the inn, at right
angles to the broad avenue. Of course we had walked a mile at
right angles to the true road; and on looking back, we perceived
that the party had gone on, undoubtedly under the impression
that we were in advance of them. Nothing remained but to turn
and retrace our steps, in order to get on the proper road, as the
carriages would certainly return on finding that they did not
overtake us. Luckily a priest was passing, mounted on an ass,
and he overhead the dialogue with the paviours. Understanding our dilemma, he kindly offered to put us on a path which
led diagonally into the post-road, and by which we should save
a mile.

This road was little more than a bridle-path, leading among
bushes and through a thicket. At first I was too eager to get on,
to look about me; but, after walking a quarter of a mile along it,
I was struck with the magnitude of the stones with which the
path was still partly paved, though long intervals occurred in
which there was no pavement at all. Pointing to these stones, I
was about to ask an explanation, when the good father nodded
his head, with a smile, and said significantly, "*Via Appia.*" We
had thus blundered on near a mile of the Appian Way, the
greater part of which was still in tolerable condition, though in
part overgrown with bushes! I knew that the post-road between

Rome and Salerno, and indeed still farther south, ran, much of the way, over this old road; but the latter is buried, in a way not to be seen. Here it was above ground, and just as much the Appian Way as the bits that are seen at Pompeii and Pozzuoli. At the further end of this fragment of the celebrated road, is a bridge of some length; but, unfortunately, the priest had left us before we reached it, and I could not inquire as to its date. It certainly belongs to the Appian Way; but the architecture struck me as being that of the middle ages rather than that of Rome, for it has a strong resemblance to those ruins of which I saw so many on the shores of the gulf of Genoa, and which, I believe, are known to date from the latter period. It was long, narrow, and of irregular construction, but appeared as solid as the day it was built.

This bridge is within a few rods of the post-road, and travellers, by inquiring for the by-way to Sessa, when they get within a mile or a mile and a half of the post-house at St. Agata, can at any time see it by a delay of ten minutes,—and, with it, the first specimen of the Appian Way that remains paved and above ground, I believe, north of Capua. None of my guidebooks speak of it, and I presume we are among the first strangers who have seen it. The stones of the pavement are large and irregularly shaped, like those of Pompeii.

We had other interesting objects, and more ruins at a spot that is thought to have been the ancient Minturnum, after we found the carriages, which turned back to meet us. The Garigliano, which flows by this place, was the Liris, the stream that separated Magna Græcia from Latium.

We slept at Mola di Gaeta. The inn was beautifully placed on the gulf, and was reasonably good. The town of Gaeta is a short distance farther advanced, on a peninsula, which curves in a way to make a sort of port in front of Mola. Æneas has the credit of having founded Gaeta.

The next morning we passed a tomb, which vulgar report supposes to be erected on the spot where Cicero fell. He certainly was killed somewhere near this, and it is as likely to be here, as at another spot; although, if I remember the history of that event, he is said to have been attempting to escape in his litter *along the shore*, when overtaken and slain, and these remains do not stand literally on the shore, but at some distance from it. As *litus* means a coast, as well as the immediate beach, perhaps the difficulty may be got over.

The road now entered the mountains, which here buttress the Mediterranean, and we passed the spot occupied by the Neapolitan army in the late Austrian invasion. The position was strong, and most of the works remain; but no position can resist treachery. Fondi, a small crowded town in a valley, came next; and soon after, we reached a small tower by the roadside, which marks the boundaries between the kingdom of Naples and the States of the Church. The road, for several leagues, is very solitary; and, the Apennines with their glens and forests bounding it on all sides, this is the spot at which robbery is most apprehended. We passed unscathed, however, and without a sensation of uneasiness on my part, though there was among us so good a prize for the mountains.

Our halting-place for the night was Terracina, which is placed beautifully on the very margin of the sea, beneath the mountains. At this spot was the ancient Anxur, a city of the Volscians, and it is still rich in ruins of different kinds. Among other things are the remains of a port built by Antoninus Pius, which might still be used, did not the great essential, water, fail. The mole is of bricks, and the cement must have been as good as the material. Here our effects were examined, and were permitted to pass, though the books were regarded a little distrustfully. This caution is of little use; for several of the works known to be proscribed,—such as the "Prince" of Machiavelli, for instance,—were to be had even in Naples, without any difficulty.

We left Terracina *on empty stomachs*, notwithstanding the advice of the guide-books, and immediately afterwards entered among the formidable Pontine Marshes. The length of these marshes is more than twenty miles, and their breadth varies from six to twelve. The lowest side is near Terracina, where their waters find an outlet in the sea. Instead of being the waste I had expected to find them, the parts near the road were in meadows, covered with buffaloes. A canal runs near the highway, which is a capital road constructed on the Appian Way, Appius Claudius being the first person who attempted to drain the marshes. Perhaps it was unreasonable to suppose that people who had just enjoyed a night's rest should feel a propensity to sleep; but it is certain that the only thing drowsy we found about these marshes was the even monotony of the road. As the spot is favourable to robberies, a great extent of country being visible in either direction, the Papal government has placed military posts along the highway, and we scarcely passed a mile without seeing a patrole. These soldiers looked as well as other people; though it is probable they are often changed.

On the whole, the scenery was pleasant, particularly in the direction of the mountains, on the sides of which we could distinguish villages and other objects of interest. Towards the sea there was much wood, and nowhere any great appearance of impracticable bogs. The drainings, however, have probably altered the face of the country. The buffalo drivers, with long lances to goad their cattle with, and in a wild costume, were galloping about the meadows, which in particular places were also alive with wild geese feeding. I believe I speak within bounds when I say that we often saw thousands on two or three acres. They took no notice of us, though frequently quite near us, but continued to feed as leisurely as the domesticated birds. We saw many men on the road carrying muskets, but I did not observe one who appeared to be after the geese.

We breakfasted at a tavern near the upper end of the marshes, where several carriages arrived about the same time. Among others was that of a Dutch family, the ladies of which alighted from their coach in common caps, bringing with them their needlework, with an air of enviable comfort. I question if there is a civilized people on earth so much addicted to motion as our own, or another that travels with so little enjoyment or so few comforts. Railroads and steam-boats do something for us, it is true; but even they are reduced to the minimum of comfort, because all things are reduced to a medium standard of habits. The 'go-ahead' propensities and 'gregarious' tastes of the nation set anything above a very moderate mediocrity quite out of the question.

A league beyond the tavern, [Mrs. Cooper] had a good fright. I was reading, when she drew my attention to a group of three men in the road, who were evidently awaiting our arrival. I did not believe that three banditti would dare to attack five men,— and such, including the postilions, was our force,—and felt no uneasiness until I heard an exclamation of alarm from [Mrs.

Cooper]. These men had actually stopped the carriage, and one of them poked the end of a pistol (as she fancied) within a foot of her face. As the three men were all armed, I looked about me; but the pistol proved to be a wild duck, and the summons to "deliver," an invitation to buy. I believe the rogues saw the alarm they had created, for they withdrew laughing when I declined the duck. So endeth alarm the third.

Near Cisterna, a short distance further, we saw the skull of a robber, in an iron cage, placed at the gate as a warning to evildoers. This object, previously to the incident of the duck, might have helped to give greater interest to the adventure. This skull probably alarms the travellers much more than it alarms the rogues.

We slept at Velletri, a town that may fairly claim to be Roman, though more remotely a Volscian place. It is said Augustus came from this vicinity. We were much struck with the prettiness of the female costumes at this place, and quite as much so with the good looks of the wearers.

It was indeed a sensation to leave an inn in the morning with the reasonable hope of seeing Rome before night! We had felt this with respect to Paris; but how much more was it felt to-day on quitting Velletri! We were no laggards, as you may imagine, but entered the carriages betimes, and drove off to Albano to breakfast full of expectation. We were now in the classical region of *bona fide* Rome. Albano is said, by the ancient Roman traditions, to have been built by Ascanius (Iulus); and I have a faint recollection of having somewhere read that the Julian family, or that of the Cæsars, pretended to be derived from him. At all events, Iulus and Julius will make as good a pedigree as half of those the world puts faith in.

Albano, to quit blind tradition for better authenticated facts, is in the region so long contested in the early wars of Rome; and the celebrated battle of the Horatii is thought to have been fought here. A tomb is still standing, though a ruin, near the town, which, it is pretended, was erected in honour of them; but then the tomb of Ascanius is also shown! The site of ancient Alba is a disputed point, the town that now exists being quite modern, though surrounded by Roman remains. It is, however, time I should give you some more distinct notions of the localities.

Between Gaeta and Terracina the Apennines buttress the sea. At the latter place, the mountains retire inland, and the plain extends seaward, leaving between the coast and the crescent of the hills the Pontine Marshes. At Albano, the Apennines make another sweep north-easterly, as far as Tivoli, or even farther; when they again incline north-westerly, and encircle, on nearly three sides, a vast plain, which is the Campagna of Rome. Albano, therefore, stands at a point whence the eye overlooks a wide horizon towards the sea, and towards the mountains north of Rome. It is near a thousand feet above the level of the Mediterranean; though the Alban Mount, the summit of the range, is two thousand feet higher. On this mountain-top stood the temple of Jupiter, where all the Latin tribes offered annual sacrifices. The site of the ancient temple is now occupied by a Christian convent; the religious successors of those who died by thousands as martyrs under the decrees of the emperors!

From the town of Albano little is seen, on account of the surrounding buildings and the trees; the vicinity being much frequented by the nobles of Rome for country retreats. Even the popes have a palace near it. The Alban Lake, and that of Nemi too, are also on these heights, occupying the craters of extinct volcanoes. In the heats of summer, these elevated mountain sides are not only healthful, but delightful places to reside in. It was in this neighbourhood that the attempt was made by banditti, a few years since, to carry off Lucien Bonaparte to the mountains.

I was too impatient to await the slow movements of the *vetturino*, and hurried on alone, afoot, as soon as my breakfast was swallowed. Passing through a gateway, I soon found myself at a point whence I overlooked much of the surrounding scenery. Such a moment can occur but once in a whole life.

The road ran down a long declivity, in a straight line, until it reached the plain, when it proceeded more diagonally, winding towards its destination. But that plain! Far and near it was a waste, treeless, almost shrubless, and with few buildings besides ruins. Long broken lines of arches, the remains of aqueducts, were visible in the distance; and here and there a tower rendered the solitude more eloquent, by irresistibly provoking a comparison between the days when they were built and tenanted, and the present hour. At the foot of the mountain, though the road diverged, there was a lane of smaller ruins that followed the line of the descent for miles in an air line. This line of ruins was broken at intervals, but there were still miles of it to be distinctly traced, and to show the continuity that had once existed from Albano to the very walls of Rome. This was the Appian Way; and the ruins were those of the tombs that once lined its sides,—the "stop traveller" of antiquity. These tombs were on a scale proportioned to the grandeur of the seat of empire, and they altogether threw those of Pompeii into the shade; although the latter, as a matter of course, are in much the best preservation. There were several near Albano, circular crumbling towers, large enough to form small habitations for the living: a change of destiny, as I afterwards discovered, that has actually befallen several of them nearer the city.

Rome itself lay near the confines of the western view. The distance (fourteen or fifteen miles), and the even surface of the country, rendered the town indistinct, but it still appeared regal and like a capital. Domes rose up above the plane of roofs in all directions; and that of St. Peter's, though less imposing than fancy had portrayed it, was comparatively grand and towering. It looked like the Invalides seen from Neuilly, the distinctness of the details and the gilding apart. Although I could discern nothing at that distance that denoted ruins, the place had not altogether the air of other towns. The deserted appearance of the surrounding country, the broken arches of the aqueducts, and perhaps the recollections, threw around it a character of sublime solitude. The town had not, in itself, an appearance of being deserted, but the environs caused it to seem cut off from the rest of the world.

The carriages soon came rolling down the hill, and we proceeded in company, absolutely silent and contemplative from an indescribable rush of sensations. The distance across the waste appeared to be nothing, and objects rose fast on every side to heighten the feeling of awe. Here was a small temple, insignificant in size and material, but evidently Roman; there, another line of aqueducts; and yonder, a tomb worthy to be a palace. We passed beneath one line of aqueduct, and drew near the walls—the ancient unquestionable walls of Rome herself! How often had we stood with interest over the ruins of works that had belonged to the distant military stations of this great people! but here we were actually beneath the ramparts of the Eternal City, which may still stand another twenty centuries without material injury.

We were fortunate in entering Rome, for the first time, from the south, this being out of all comparison the finest approach. The modern city occupying the old Campus Martius, he who comes from the north is at once received into the bosom of a town of our own days; but he who comes in at the southern gate has the advantage of passing first among the glorious remains of the city of the Cæsars.

We entered Rome by the gate of St. John, and looked about us with reverential awe mingled with an intense curiosity. Little appeared at first besides a few churches, broken aqueducts, and gardens. On the left was a deserted-looking palace, with a large church attached, the buildings of St. John in the Lateran. An Egyptian obelisk, of great antiquity, pointed to the skies. These edifices were vast and princely, but they stood almost alone. Further in advance was a straggling sort of town, a mere suburb, and the line of houses was often broken by waste spots. Presently the carriage came under the walls of a huge oval structure of a reddish stone, in which arches rose above arches to the height of an ordinary church tower, a mountain of edifice; and, though not expecting to see it, I recognised the Coliseum at a glance. Objects now crowded on us, such as the arches of Constantine and of Titus, ruined temples, the Forum, and then the town itself. My head became confused, and I sat stupid as a countryman who first visits town, perplexed with the whirl of sensations and the multiplicity of the objects.

We drove to the Hôtel de Paris, entirely across the city, near the Porta del Popolo, and took lodgings. I ordered dinner; but, too impatient to restrain my curiosity, as there was still an hour of daylight, I called a *laquais de place*, and, holding little P[aul] by the hand, sallied forth. "Where will the signore go?" asked the laquais, as soon as we were in the street. "To St. Peter's."

In my eagerness to proceed, I looked neither to the right nor to the left. We went through crooked and narrow streets, until we came to a bridge lined with statues. The stream beneath was the Tiber. It was full, turbid, swift, sinuous, and it might be three hundred feet wide, or perhaps not quite so wide as the

Seine at Paris at the same season. The difference, however, is not material, and each is about half as wide as the Thames above London Bridge on a full tide, which is again three-fourths of the width of the Hudson at Albany. A large round castellated edifice, with flanking walls and military bastions, faced the bridge: this was the tomb of Adrian, converted into a citadel by the name of the Castle of St. Angelo, an angel in bronze surmounting the tower. Turning to the left, we followed the river, until a street led us from its windings, and presently I found myself standing at the foot of a vast square, with colonnades, on a gigantic scale, sweeping in half circles on each side of me, two of the most beautiful fountains I had ever seen throwing their waters in sheets down their sides between them, and the façade of St. Peter's forming the background. A noble Egyptian obelisk occupied the centre of the area.

Every one had told me I should be disappointed in the apparent magnitude of this church, but I was not. To me it seemed the thing it is, possibly because some pains had been taken to school the eye. Switzerland often misled me in both heights and distances, but a ship or an edifice rarely does so. Previously to seeing Switzerland, I had found nothing to compare with such a nature, and all regions previously known offered no rules to judge by; but I had now seen too many huge structures not to be at once satisfied that this was the largest of them all.

The laquais would have me stop to admire some of Michael Angelo's sublime conceptions, but I pressed forward. Ascending the steps, I threw out my arms to embrace one of the huge half columns of the façade, not in a fit of sentimentalism, but to ascertain its diameter, which was gigantic, and helped the previous impression. Pushing aside the door in common use, I found myself in the nave of the noblest temple in which any religious rites were ever celebrated.

I walked about a hundred feet up the nave, and stopped. From a habit of analyzing buildings, I counted the paces as I advanced, and knew how far I was within the pile. Still, men, at the farthest extremity, seemed dwindled into boys. One, whose size did not appear disproportioned, was cleaning a statue of St. Bruno, at the height of an ordinary church-steeple, stood on the shoulder of the figure, and could just rest his arm on the top of its head. Some marble cherubs, that looked like children, were in high relief against a pier near me, and laying my hand on the hand of one of them, I found it like that of an infant in comparison. All this aided the sense of vastness. The *baldacchino*, or canopy of bronze, which is raised over the great altar, filled the eye no more than a pulpit in a common church; and yet I knew its summit was as lofty as half the height of the spire of Trinity, New York, or about a hundred and thirty feet, and essentially higher than the tower. I looked for a marble throne that was placed at the remotest extremity of the building, also as high as a common church-tower, a sort of poetical chair for the popes; it seemed distant as a cavern on a mountain.

To me there was no disappointment. Everything appeared as vast as feet and inches could make it; and as I stood gazing at the glorious pile, the tears forced themselves from my eyes. Even little P[aul] was oppressed with the sense of the vastness of the place, for he clung close to my side, though he had passed half his life in looking at sights, and kept murmuring, "*Qu'est-ce que c'est? —qu'est-ce que c'est? —Est-ce une église?*"

It was getting dark, and perhaps the gloom magnified the effect. The atmosphere even,—for this stupendous pile has an atmosphere of its own, one different from that of the outer world,—was soothing and delicious; and I turned away impressed with the truth that if ever the hand of man had indeed raised a structure to the Deity in the least worthy of his majesty, it was this!

Letter XXI.

I shall not enter into the ordinary details of description at Rome, but treat it as I have treated places less celebrated, touching only on those points that it has struck me are not familiarly known, or, at least, were not known to me; and this, too, in my own desultory manner; for, as things have appeared to me differently from my expectations, so shall I communicate them to you. Let us then commence with an outline of the place, its general condition, and its *entourage*, before we proceed to more minute accounts.

Of the Campagna I have already communicated to you some general notions. It is not, however, literally a waste, for it bears grasses and even grain in parts, and has some kitchen-gardens near the walls. The portions nearest the mountains are sandy, but not bare; while you find marshes as you approach the sea. The Campagna di Roma, properly so termed, includes nearly the whole of ancient Latium, and is near three hundred miles in extent; but, by convention, the Campagna is now confined to the uncultivated district immediately around the city. Some annex the Pontine Marshes, which join it in the direction of the sea; but I think the Romans distinguish between the two. Much of the Campagna is grazed, though I think less of it near the town than on the parts more remote. I have seen spots of great fertility; but the portions of it over which I usually gallop in my rides, (and I am now in the saddle daily,)—rides that frequently extend eight or nine miles,—is a species of common that merely bears a tolerable grass. There are spots that are crowded with country-houses and gardens, particularly on the broken land north of Rome; but, in general, this waste is singularly naked of habitations, even up to the very ramparts of the town.

It is scarcely necessary to say, Rome has had various walls, which have been enlarged as the place has grown, for this is the history of every large walled town. It is, however, very necessary to know the positions of these walls, in order to establish the positions of many of the most interesting of the antiquities. Take, for instance, the Tarpeian Rock,—an object not only of interest in itself, but of importance in getting a clear idea of localities,—and we shall find that the heedless are commonly led astray, not only as respects this particular spot, but as respects others dependent on it. I mention this rock as its site is closely connected with the course of the ancient walls.

Most travellers give themselves up to the guidance of common *laquais de place*, who are dignified by the name of *ciceroni;* and even they who are sceptical, and smile at much of what they hear, are more or less imposed on by the ignorance and knavery of these men. We had one of these ciceroni for a week or ten days, simply with a view to get acquainted with the town, and he undertook to show us this Tarpeian Rock among his other curiosities. We were led into a common garden on the Capitol Hill, where a rock overlooked the site of the Forum, and were told it was the place in question. Even the maps of Roma Antica, and most of the guide-books, point out this spot as the Tarpeian Rock; though, I believe, there are very satisfactory reasons for showing, that while it must be near the celebrated place of punishment, this cannot be it in very fact. Conversing on this subject with one of the most industrious of the antiquaries here, he reasoned in this manner:—The punishment of the Tarpeian Rock was both a poetical and a literal punishment; the literal being death, and the poetical expulsion from the city. By throwing a criminal from the rock that is commonly exhibited, his body would be cast into the centre of the Forum, or into the heart of the place; and hence he infers that it is not the true Tarpeian Rock. There is, moreover, the narrative of a messenger of Camillus, I believe, who was sent to Rome at the time it was besieged by the Gauls, who says he landed at a particular point, and entered the town by climbing up the Tarpeian Rock. This account confirms the opinion that this rock must look outward as regards the walls.—The whole Capitol Hill is a rock, covered with a thin soil; and I believe it is generally admitted that the entire hill, or rock, bore the name of the unworthy Tarpeia, who is understood to have been buried on it. This may certainly account for the confusion in the names; though it would still seem that the precise place of punishment must be different from that which is usually shown as such. My antiquary pointed to a spot that is on the side of the hill nearly opposite to the Forum, along the margin of which the wall was known once to have run, and where the height, in addition to that of the wall, or perhaps of one of its towers, would be sufficient to ensure death, as would not be the case at the rock commonly seen, even after allowing for the manner in which the Forum has been filled by rubbish. Admitting his reasoning to be true, and it is certainly very plausible if no more, you see the importance of understanding the sites of the ancient walls.

Passing over the infancy of Rome, the two principal walls that succeeded are that of Servius Tullius, and that of Aurelian. The first was built about two centuries after the town had its origin. It included the Capitol, Viminal, Quirinal, Esquiline, Palatine, Celian, and Aventine, or the Seven Hills of Rome, with a small triangular piece of ground on the other side of the Tiber, which did not, however, include the present site of St. Peter's. The space within these limits would not exceed that which is now covered by New York, below Bleecker-street, and yet it was the Rome of the Augustan age. The hills are not large, though some are double the size of others. The Capitol and Palatine are both small, particularly the former, which, agreeably to our mode of constructing, could not hold a population to exceed two or three thousand, even with narrow streets and high houses. Admitting the lowest numbers that are given as the population of Rome at this period, it is difficult to imagine where they all lived. Pompeii proves that the Romans did not personally occupy much space, although the courts and gardens did. The slaves, who must have composed a large portion of the population of Rome, were probably crowded into a small space; and the great depth of the *débris* that now covers the ancient city proves that the materials were abundant: from all which it is fair to infer that the dwellings were of great height. The houses around Naples were low, probably on account of frequent earthquakes,—calamities that doubtless occurred oftener before the great eruption of the volcano than since. After making all these allowances, however, it will be necessary to people suburbs of great extent, or to diminish, by more than half, the popular accounts of the number of the inhabitants.

The Emperor Aurelian, fearful that the town might be taken by surprise, on account of the extent of the suburbs, about the year 276, caused new walls to be built. These walls in no place touched the wall of Servius Tullius, and may have a little more than doubled the size of the *enceinte*. These walls still exist, or, at least, walls exist that are attributed equally to Aurelian and Honorius, who lived more than a century later. Some of the antiquaries contend that the walls of Aurelian included a space more than twice, or even thrice as great as that contained within the present walls, and thus account for the mode of accommodating the population, which they complacently take at the highest number. A writer, who was a contemporary of Aurelian, affirms that the wall of this emperor was fifty miles in circuit; and Vasi appears to adopt his account of the matter, though he is obliged to admit that no traces exist of these prodigiously extensive works.

It strikes me, that there are several serious objections to this explanation. In the first place, it is impossible to believe that traces would not exist of these walls had they ever been built, when the walls constructed a little more than a century later are standing almost perfect. Allowing that *all* of the present wall is not as old as Honorius, which probably is the case, a part certainly is. There is a portion of the present wall that is called the *Muro Torto*, or the Crooked Wall, from the circumstance that it is so much out of the perpendicular as to excite apprehensions of its falling on the stranger who passes beneath it. Now there is a writer of the time of Belisarius, (530–40,) who says that this wall was exactly in such a condition in his day. It is difficult to believe that this should be the fact, and that all traces of the wall of Aurelian, which was built only two centuries and a half earlier, should have been lost. But it may be said this was a part of Aurelian's wall, for it is the foundation of Domitian's gardens, of unusual thickness and strength, and was made use of for the new city wall on that account, and that the wall of Aurelian still contained a circuit of fifty miles. If the *Muro Torto* be in truth a part of Aurelian's wall, then are not all traces of his wall lost; and it is very improbable that an emperor who was about to increase the walls of the city, which, exceedingly irregular, had a circuit of less than eight miles, to a circuit of more than forty-five of our miles, should choose to extend the town so short a distance towards the north, the quarter that was the most agreeable and the most healthy, and yet as far in the other directions as would be necessary to make up the required distance. In point of fact, the space between the wall of Servius and the present wall is much greater in this direction than in any other; the object having been, probably, to include the whole of the Campus Martius and the Pincian Hill.

The present wall is said to be sixteen Roman miles and a half in circuit, which would be not far from fifteen of our miles. I have often ridden round them on my morning's excursions, or nearly round them, and I take this to be near the distance; though the present *enceinte* of the Transtiberina, or the part of the town west of the Tiber, is much larger now, than when the wall of Honorius, or the present wall, existed in that quarter also. Paris, including soldiers and strangers, has often contained a million of souls, although the town has an unusual number of gardens, with many wide streets and public places, besides palaces and hotels without number; and yet Paris does not fill its walls, by perhaps a fifth of the entire surface. Were the *enceinte* of Paris compactly built up, two millions might comfortably dwell within the walls, and at need, by packing the people, as they were evidently packed at Pompeii and Herculaneum, three millions. The circuit of the walls of Paris is about eighteen miles. This would allow Rome to contain a million and a half or two millions within the present limits; and what good authority is there for supposing it ever had more people?

Rome was divided into fourteen quarters in the time of Augustus. These divisions have descended down to our own time and, although the names are changed, it is probable they are essentially the same. Aurelian lived near the end of the third century, and in the fourth century these fourteen quarters bore the following names, viz. Porta Capena, Cœlimontana, Isis et Serapis, Via Sacra, Esquilina, Alta Semita, Via Lata, Forum Romanum, Circus Flaminius, Palatium, Circus Maximus, Piscina Publica, Aventina, and Transtiberina. It is easy to trace the situation of all of these quarters within the present walls. Is it probable that Rome increased so much in the two centuries and a half that succeeded Augustus, as to require, that a space contained in a circuit of sixteen Roman miles and a half should be extended to a circuit of fifty, in order to receive the people? I do not believe it.

What then becomes of the statement of Vopiscus, the authority quoted by M. Vasi? I know nothing of him; but any man of observation must know that writers of a higher order of genius frequently betray great ignorance of positive things, and of nothing more than measurement. Sir Walter Scott, in his Life of Napoleon, says, "By the treaty of Presburgh, Austria is said to have lost *one million of square miles of territory, two millions and a half of subjects*, and a revenue to the amount of ten millions and a half of florins"! &c. &c.; and in speaking of another treaty, an error quite as gross appears. In the edition I read, letters were introduced, rendering the blunder still more serious.* Here the great poet, in a grave history, makes a fragment of the Austrian empire near four times as great as the whole empire, and almost a fifth as large as all Europe. Comparing population with surface, he makes the ratio about two souls and a half to the square mile, and that in a country where it probably exceeds three hundred.† Perhaps no men are less to be trusted in matters of this sort than purely literary men, and yet they usually produce the books. Let us suppose the art of printing unknown, and the only authority for the life of Napoleon, or rather for this one fact, to be, twenty centuries hence, a manuscript of a certain great author called Scotius, what marvels might not posterity believe of the extent of the Austrian empire!—such, probably, as M. Vasi would have us believe of the extent of Rome, on the authority of this Vopiscus. It is of no moment to the result, whether this error in the history of Napoleon was the consequence of ignorance or want of care in the author, or a blunder in the compositor. The circumstance, had it not been corrected, would have stood recorded; and in a manuscript, or an edition, might, in the lapse of centuries, pass for an established fact, on the authority of a great name.

*In the subsequent editions these errors of the author, or blunders of the press, whichever they may be, have been corrected.
†Mr. Washington Irving, in his Life of Columbus, vol. i. p. 83, has the following:—"Between them is placed the island of Cipango, or Japan, which, according to Marco Polo, lay fifteen hundred miles distant from the Asiatic coast. *In his computation, Columbus advanced this island about a thousand leagues too*

I have little doubt that we now see, essentially, the form and dimensions of the wall of Aurelian, if not the wall itself. Some alterations, we know, have been made, for the gates are changed, and it is probable the wall, in places, has also undergone repairs; but it is not much more difficult to believe that the walls which are now standing are sixteen hundred years old, than to believe they are fourteen, or of the time of Honorius.

I leave you to judge of the feelings with which I ride beneath these walls. The Muro Torto in particular gives me great satisfaction, as one can be reasonably certain that he sees the identical bricks in the identical places they have occupied since the time of Domitian, or near eighteen hundred years. You will be surprised to hear that these walls are nearly all of bricks,—as indeed are the aqueducts, temples, and most of the other ruins of Rome. Augustus boasted that he found the city of bricks and left it of marble; but time has left it of bricks again. This contradiction is explained by the fact that the marbles which cased most of the brickwork, in the baths, temples, palaces, and amphitheatres, have been removed for other works, and also by the fact that the saying of Augustus is not to be taken too literally.

You will be surprised, perhaps, at receiving these accounts so soon, and to find me speaking already of the environs of Rome with so much familiarity, on a month's acquaintance. Soon after reaching the Eternal City, I hired a saddle-horse, to accompany my old friend the —— of —— in his morning rides; and besides having the advantage of a learned cicerone, who has passed years in Rome, I have made the discovery, that one in the saddle can see more of this place in a week, than is seen in a month by those who use carriages, or who go on foot. You will better understand this by getting a clearer idea of the actual condition of the town and its environs.

The wall which, right or wrong, is called that of Aurelian, is said to be sixteen Roman miles and a half in circuit, being sep-

---

much to the east, supposing it to be about in the situation of Florida, and at this island he hoped first to arrive." The *centre* of Florida and the centre of the island of Japan lie about 130° asunder. A degree of longitude in those latitudes will average somewhere about fifty miles, (this is approximative, not calculated,) which will give *two* thousand leagues as the distance between them.

arated into two parts by the Tiber. Of the part east of the river, which contains Rome proper, about one-third, or perhaps a little less, is occupied by the modern town: the remainder is in common gardens, villas, and ruins, many of the latter being scattered over the whole surface. You are not to suppose, however, that any part of Rome to-day exhibits the appearance of a continued ruined town, like Pompeii, with its streets and squares. Though in the vicinity of the Forum there is an approach to such a character, it is not distinct and intelligible at a glance, as at Pompeii. So many objects are crowded together at this spot, as to render it the centre of interest, it is true; but it is far from preserving its outlines, as it existed of old. Even the site of the Forum has been disputed. The ruins, in general, are scattered, and, with comparatively few exceptions, are far from being well preserved. They are vast, particularly the baths, but not very distinct; and the *coup d'œil* gives an air of desolation to that part of the *enceinte*. They require study and investigation to excite a very deep interest,—or, at least, an interest beyond that which accompanies the general reflection that one sees the remains of Rome.

The modern town east of the river luckily covers little beside the Campus Martius; all in the region of the palace, the circuses, and the baths being virtually unoccupied. Houses there certainly are scattered over the space within the walls, and churches too; but, after all, they produce no very sensible effect on the general appearance of the place. Beyond the proper limits of the modern town, the prevailing character is that of antiquity and ruin, a little impaired perhaps by the presence of the gardens and garden-walls.

Much of the site of old Rome, or the region about the Seven Hills, is enclosed in these walls; but much also lies in common. One can enter many of the enclosures too, and a horse enables me to see whether there is anything within worthy of examination. As my object is less antiquarian research, than such pictures as may help to give you better ideas of things than are to be got from generalities, in my next letter I will take you with me in one of these morning rides, that you may see objects as they present themselves, as well as one can see who is obliged to use another's eyes.

Letter XXII.

In order to effect the purpose just mentioned, we will mount at the door of our lodgings, in the Via Ripetta, and quit the town by the nearest gate, which is that of "the People," or the Porta del Popolo. The obelisk in the centre of the area that we pass is Egyptian, as you may see by the hieroglyphics. It formerly stood before the Temple of the Sun, at Heliopolis, and was transported to Rome by order of Augustus, as an ornament to the Circus Maximus. It has now stood near three centuries, or longer than America has been settled, where it is.

The carriage-road that winds up the ascent on the right, by inclined planes, leads to the Pincian Hill, the site of Domitian's gardens, which are now used as a promenade for all classes, on foot, on horseback, or in carriages. I shall say nothing of the colossal statues, for they are modern. The three streets that, separated by twin churches, diverge from this square, penetrate the city, forming so many of its principal arteries; that in the centre, which was the ancient Flaminian Way, leads to the foot of the Capitol Hill, and is called the Corso.

When without the walls, we find a little suburb stretched along the road which leads to the Ponte Molle, the ancient Milvian Bridge. This is the road to Upper Italy, or Cis-Alpine Gaul, and follows, in the main, the course of the Flaminian Way. We will quit the suburb, by turning short under the walls.

The vineyard or garden on our left is that in which Raphael used to amuse himself, and the plain stone dwelling is both ornamented and defiled by the caprices of his pencil. He is anything but divine in that house. The grounds a little farther beyond, and which show factitious ruins, statues, walks, avenues, and plantations, are the celebrated Villa Borghese, which, by the liberality of the owner, are converted into a Hyde Park, or a Bois de Boulogne, for Rome and her visitors. It is said the public has used them so long, that it now claims them as its own;

the public in Rome being just as soulless, ungrateful, and rapacious as the public in America. God help the man (if honest) who depends on the public anywhere!

You will not be alarmed at the appearance of the walls, after what you have heard, for it is the celebrated Muro Torto that once propped the terraces of Domitian, and which, you already know, has seemed just as ready to fall these fourteen hundred years as it is to-day. This wall is said to be twenty-five feet thick, and it seems at least forty feet high. This height, however, rather exceeds that of the wall in general, which varies, perhaps, from twenty to thirty feet.

We are next passing by that part of the city wall where the Villa Ludovisi Buoncompagni lies, *within* the *enceinte* of the city; and the gate just passed, and which is not used, is the Pincian. There is a tradition that Belisarius asked alms at this gate; but it is more probable that he caused it to be rebuilt. The little Gothic-looking tower that appears on the wall is in the garden of the Villa Paolina, so called from Pauline, the sister of Napoleon. This garden and its very handsome pavilion are now the property of the Prince of Musignano, her nephew, the eldest son of Lucien, a gentleman well known in America for his work on its birds. The gate beyond is the Porta Salaria. Alaric entered the city at this point; and the Gauls, more remotely, penetrated by the Porta Collina, which was the counterpart of the present gate, in the wall of Servius, though necessarily less advanced than this. Hannibal is also said to have manifested an intention to attack the town on this side, whence it is inferred it was the weak quarter. It is not probable the walls were less strong here than elsewhere; but the military advantages of attacking the place on this side are sufficiently apparent to the eye.

The land both within and without the walls of Rome is higher here than anywhere else on this side of the Tiber. It is consequently drier and more healthy as an encampment, and, while equally easy to enter as any other quarter, offers great facilities to the assailant when gained. The gardens of Sallust lay just within this gate, and traces of the walls are still seen. The *agger* of Servius Tullius, beneath which the vestal virgins who violated their vows were interred, was also within this gate. Traces of the former are still seen. This additional wall would seem to imply the danger the city ran on this particular side. The Pretorian Camp lay outside of this agger, but within a wall of its own.

The country on our left is now getting to be more open, and is assuming the appearance of the Campagna; though gardens and a sort of meagre suburbs are still met with. After passing the Porta Pia, which is near the ancient Porta Nomentana, we come to a line of wall that is evidently different from the rest in construction, and even in elevation. It forms three sides of a square, or nearly so, projecting in that form beyond the regular walls of the town, of which, however, it forms a part. This is the enclosure of the Pretorian Camp, though now composing part of the defences of the town. All this part of Rome, within the walls, is in gardens or vineyards; though one can find his way among them on horseback, by means of paths, lanes and breaches.

We next approach the gate of San Lorenzo, which leads to Tivoli and the Sabine Hills. Here, half a mile from the walls, stands one of the basilicæ of Rome. It is an ancient church, and is remarkable for the variety and richness of its columns, many of which are of precious African marbles, or of porphyry, and all of which, I believe, are taken from the ruins of ancient Rome. One of the old writers, it is said, speaks of two columns that were made by certain artists, who marked them by a frog and a lizard, animals whose Latin or Greek appellations corresponded with their own, (at least this is the tradition,) and these columns still exist in this church. I can vouch for the columns, but not for the story, which may, nevertheless, be true.

The country now opens still more, and just before we reach the gate of Naples, and after passing under the arches of an aqueduct, we will turn upon the Campagna, and gallop across the swells, which are but little enclosed. After proceeding a mile or two, sometimes following roads, and at others coursing over fields that seem as deserted as the ruins with which they are dotted, we reach a small brick edifice, that is said to have been erected on the spot where Coriolanus was met by his mother. There are other accounts of this edifice, which is evidently ancient, though so diminutive and frail-looking; but the brick-work of Rome seems to have a power of endurance that the stone-work of other countries does not possess.

Seeing the line of ruined tombs which mark the course of the Appian Way on our right, we will now gallop in that direction.

The paths across the fields, the runs of water, and the wildness of scenery, harmonize well with the pictures of antiquity, and our spirits rise with the speed of the horses,—animals, by the way, of great powers of endurance, as well as foot and fire. These horses are derived from barbs. The breed of the Chigi, so called from the princes of that name, is of the best repute; and the horse I ride is noted for his courage, though he has seen near twenty years. This fine beast is as white as snow, and has long been a favourite with the strangers.

After crossing several low swells of land, we come to a place of more pastoral beauty than is common on the Campagna, in which the swales get to be almost diminutive valleys, through one of which trickles a run of water. Here we find another tiny brick temple, one not larger than the Catholic chapels that so frequently occur by the way-side, and which, at need, might contain thirty or forty devotees. It is called the temple of the God of Return,* a deity of whom you probably never heard before. It is said that this tiny temple, which is very prettily placed, was erected to celebrate the retreat of Hannibal from before the walls of Rome, and some go so far as to say that his determination was made in this precise spot; a conceit, by the way, not poetically fine, since there is scarcely a place in the vicinity so likely to tempt one to remain. The term *ridiculous*, which is universally applied to the building, would imply the idea of derision, and that the temple was erected in mockery. Allowing the history to be true, it may be considered a very extraordinary relic; but I believe the antiquaries ascribe it to a much later period, by the brick-work, which is a little peculiar, or to the reign of Nero. Admitting even this, it is near eighteen hundred years old.

Turning up the rivulet, we will ride on a knoll, about half a mile from this *Fanum Ridiculi*, where we find the ruins of another temple, though it is roofed and is even converted into a sort of chapel. This is called, and perhaps justly, a temple of Bacchus. It passed a long time for another edifice, but recent discoveries in a vault leave little doubt that it was erected in honour of Bacchus. It was of more pretension than either of

**Fanum Ridiculi.*

the other small brick edifices, though very little larger, and not of a very pure taste. It had a portico of four columns, evidently taken from some other edifice, and which are now built into the front wall, probably with a view to enlarge it as a church. This building has a *staggering* and *propped* look, which, while it may not be classically just, suggests the idea of drunkenness, very eloquently.

Taking into view the beauty of the spot, the distance from the walls (about two miles), and the neighbourhood, which, from remote antiquity, has been used for festivals, it is probable this temple was erected as a sort of religious memorial of merry-makings; a union of the profane and the sacred, that the ancients were addicted to, as well as the moderns. It may have been a drinking pavilion of some pious debauchee, who had the notion to sanctify his cups by the emblems, and even the services of the altar! Why not?—men are still found committing as flagrant acts of blasphemy, under the show of religion, every day—ay, and even every hour of the day.

Quitting this, and descending into the valley again—if valley it may be called, we find a sort of grotto, in the hill side, with a recumbent statue, a spring of pure water, the source of the rivulet, and the appearance of former decorations that are now wanting, particularly of statues. This place is popularly called the fountain of the nymph Egeria, so celebrated for the artifice of Numa. It is, however, pretty certain that this is not the true spot; and, considering the proximity of the temple of Bacchus, the grotto is probably the remains of some Roman expedient to cool wine, and to drink it luxuriously. Religion may have been mixed up of old with these debauches, as we know politics and dinners go together in our own times. The recumbent statue is clearly no statue of a nymph. The work is thought by even the sceptics to be as old as the time of Vespasian. This grotto and the temple of Bacchus, probably, had some allegorical connexion, the one being a place to carouse in, the other a temple to sanctify the rites; and if we add the other fane to the whole, as an emblem of the manner in which drunkards render themselves *ridiculous*, we may be quite as near the truth as the antiquaries.

We will quit these pleasant dales, and ride across the fields, a short mile, to the line of ruined tombs that marks the remains of the Appian Way. An extensive pile of ruins will naturally first attract our attention; and we will spur our horses up the sharp acclivity on which it stands, though by making a small *détour*, and getting into the rough road, that still leads out on the old route for a few miles, we might reach the summit more easily. On reaching this spot, we find the remains of a castle of the middle ages, with courts, walls, and towers, scattered about the fields, all built in the usual rude and inartificial manner of those structures, with a keep, however, that has the grace and finish of the Roman architecture. This keep is round, well preserved, much better, in short, than the rest of the edifice, which is crumbling around it. It is about eighty feet in diameter, and is constructed of vast hewn blocks of travertine; while the other parts of the work appear to be made of stones gathered in the fields, or taken from the foundations of the tombs. The latter was most probably the fact. The walls of this keep are thirty feet thick, the interior being little more than a small vaulted room. It formerly contained the sarcophagus that is still seen in the court of the Farnese Palace; for, in brief, this keep was merely one of the tombs of the Appian Way!

An inscription puts the name of the person in whose honour this extraordinary mausoleum was erected out of all doubt. It is the tomb of Cæcilia Metella, the wife of a mere triumvir, a *millionnaire* of his day. This tomb is, therefore, the Demidoff of the Via Appia. It is probably the noblest mausoleum now standing in Europe. There is no uncertainty about its history; and yet, while one looks at it with wonder as a specimen of Roman luxury and magnificence, it fails to excite one half the interest that is felt when we linger around a spot that is celebrated, by even questionable tradition, for any other sort of greatness. As I gaze at it, my mind compares this specimen of art with the civilization of Rome, endeavours to form a general picture from the particular object, and, certainly, it finds food for useful, as well as for agreeable reflection; but it scarcely turns to the wife of the triumvir at all: and when it does, it is rather to distrust her merits; for pure virtue is seldom so obtrusive or pretending as may be inferred from this tomb. Insignificance is ill advised in perpetuating itself in this manner. The rest of these ruins are said to be a fortress of the Popes, about five hundred years old; the tomb itself dating from the close of the republic.

We might follow the Appian Way with great interest; but, as our ride has already extended to nearly ten miles, it may be well to turn towards the city. The ruins of a temple, and some extensive remains of a very unusual and irregular character, attract our attention near the large tomb. A part of these ruins are thought to belong to a villa erected at the end of the third century; and it is probable that the remainder were incorporated in its ornaments, as we include ruins in the landscape gardening of our own time. There is clearly a temple which, it is conjectured, also, answered the purpose of a mausoleum. Attached to this temple, was a circus,—the only one, I believe, that still preserves enough of its ancient form to give us ocular proof of the real construction of these celebrated places of amusement.

By the popular account, the circus is ascribed to Caracalla, and the temple is called the *stables* of the circus; but, discoveries as recent as 1825 show that the latter is a temple, or mausoleum, and even in whose honour it was erected. Vasi disposes of the claims of Caracalla satisfactorily; and, to say the truth, they were not very great. He was fond of the amusements of the circus; a circus is seen on the reverse of his medals; and a statue of himself and his mother were found at no great distance from this particular circus, though not in it. On this authority, it was thought he had caused this particular circus to be built. The two first reasons amount to nothing, especially as the circus of the medals is clearly the Circus Maximus, which Caracalla caused to be repaired. The statues may have even belonged to this circus, and been placed there in honour of so great a patron of the sports; for we certainly should not deem it any great proof that Napoleon erected a military hospital because we found his statue in it, or that Nelson erected Greenwich if a picture of him should be discovered in its ruins. This reasoning is made all the stronger by the fact that this circus is of a workmanship much later than the time of Caracalla, who has left memorials enough of his age in his baths. But inscriptions have set the matter finally at rest; and it is now known that this circus was erected by Maxentius, about the year 311 of our era, who caused it to be consecrated to his son Romulus, who was *deified*. This *deification*, at so late a period, must mean something like the canonization of the Catholic saints in our own time. It was a declaration of peculiar sanctity. The lesser gods of antiquity were probably no more than the good men of modern days.

As the temple is but a temple, of which there are hundreds still standing, we will ride round through the fields, and enter the circus by the great gate, which has been recently opened. Within the area, we find a long narrow space, surrounded by low walls, with, here and there, a tower. It is divided into two parts by a sort of dwarf wall, which was called the *spina*. The sides are straight, but the two ends are circular. At that opposite to the gate, are the traces of the *carceres*, or the cells in which the chariots were stationed previously to starting; the circular form giving each a pretty nearly equal chance. In these cells or stalls the competitors were ranged, and at the signal, which it is thought was given from a particular tower about the centre of one of the walls, they dashed out towards the side of the circus that had the most room between it and the dwarf wall; for the greatest space was required at the commencement of the race, when the chariots were nearly abreast of each other. Space was also left to pass round the ends of this dwarf wall, on which statues and obelisks were commonly placed, and the chariots came in as they could. The side walls contained seats, like an amphitheatre, it is said, for 18,000 people.

The length of this circus is 1560 Roman feet, or rather more than a quarter of a mile; which, doubled, gives a course of more than half a mile long; but as many turns might be made as were desired. Judging from what I saw at Florence, the nicety of the sport must have very much depended on the skill of the charioteer in turning. The width is 240 feet. The dwarf wall is not quite 900 feet long, and it varies in height from two to five feet. The remains of pedestals show that there were many statues, besides those on the *spina*. There were thirteen stalls. The granite obelisk of the Piazza Navona was taken from this place, about two centuries since; an Egyptian obelisk appearing to be an ornament *d'usage*, for a Roman circus. The dwarf wall is not quite parallel to the side walls: an arrangement that was probably made with a view to facilitate the mode of starting. There is a tomb in this circus, that appears to be much older than the circus itself, and which was probably included in it, for want of space. The general direction is at right angles to the Appian Way, on which the circus stands. It was a place of amusement without the walls, and gives another blow to the theory of the extraordinary extent of the town.

It is fortunate that this circus, though an inferior specimen of its kind, did stand without the walls, for it would probably have shared the fate of the others had it been within them. As it is, it is very curious, for the reason just given, and because it is one of the best preserved ruins near Rome. The wall of Aurelian must have not only enclosed this circus, but it must have extended far beyond it, to have been fifty miles in circuit. I find sufficient evidence that, on whichever side of Rome I ride, the *enceinte* was probably never materially larger than it is at this moment.

We will now leave the circus and ride towards the city. As we pass along the narrow road, we see several rude dwellings constructed on the tops of ruined tombs, the living having dispossessed the dead. After passing through a species of suburb, leaving many ancient objects unvisited, we reach the walls again, and turn along beneath them towards the river. On reaching the last gate, having now made the entire circuit of the city proper, we enter, and find ourselves in an open space, or in one little intercepted by walls, and near the celebrated tomb of Caius Cestius. This tomb is a pyramid a hundred of our feet high, and sixty square at the base. Its walls are very thick, and it is faced with blocks of hewn marble. The summit is still a fine point, though it looks modern, which is probably the fact, as the tomb has been repaired. This pyramid is another proof that the Romans built for time, since it is of the date of Agrippa, and is astonishingly well preserved, the restorations having been little more than renewing the apex. It was also buried at the base a few feet, and the earth has been removed.

Near this monument is the cemetery of the Protestants. We can see on a modern stone, near the wall of the city, this inscription—"*Cor cordium.*" It marks the grave of Shelley; though I do not understand how his ashes came here, as his body was burned on the shore of Pisa. The inscription was written by his wife, the daughter of Godwin.

Across the open space, is a low isolated mount, perhaps a hundred and fifty feet high, and some four or five hundred feet in circumference, with vineyards clustering around its base, and with its summit and sides gay with the young grasses of March. Galloping to its foot, we follow a winding path, and ride to the top, where we are rewarded with a beautiful view, more particularly of the heights on the opposite side of the river. This little mountain is called Testaccio, from the circumstance of its having been entirely formed of broken pottery,* brought out of the town and deposited here. By kicking the grass, you still see the fragments beneath, the soil being scarcely two inches deep. Its history is not very well established; but that such is its origin, the eye sees for itself. An order of the police may have rendered this accumulation of broken pottery necessary.

Near this mount, the port is seen; vessels ascending the Tiber, from the sea, as far as this. But for the bridges, they might go even higher; though it would be without a sufficient object.

We will now descend, and pursue our way homeward, along the foot of the Aventine Hill. In the portico of the convent church which we pass, you may see the arms and name of the patron cardinal, or the dignitary under whose protection the establishment has placed itself. This is the old system of patron and client continued to the present day; a system which belongs to aristocracy, and must exist, in some shape or other, wherever the strong and the weak are found in contact. I have heard of countries in modern Europe in which the tribute of the clients forms no small portion of the revenue of the patrons. In England itself, we have seen Indian Rajahs returning members to parliament by means of their gold; in France, the king's mistresses, for a long time, had a monopoly of this species of power; and in several of the other great powers that have dependencies, I hear it whispered that the system still prevails to a great extent. In America, the clients are the nation; and the patrons the demagogues, under the name of patriots. If, however, our discontented, the salt of the earth in their own imagination, had a taste of the abuses of this hemisphere, they would gladly return to their own, bad as they are.

Testa.

When at Naples, I was told an anecdote of the good old King Ferdinando, which is in point. His generals were deliberating on a new uniform for the army, when the honest old prince, tired of the delay, and anxious to get at his game again, exclaimed—"Ah, Signori, dress them as you please, they will run away." I do not repeat this because I believe the Neapolitans are cowards, for I think them traduced in this respect, but because it is with politics as in war, "dress men as you will, they are still that godlike-devil man."

Objects crowd upon us in too great numbers now, and we will ride into the Via Ripetta and dismount, leaving the rest for another excursion.

Letter XXIII.

In my last, I took you round the walls,—an excursion I make weekly, for the road is excellent, and almost every foot of the way offers something of interest. We will now turn in another direction, which, if not so interesting as regards antiquities, may amuse you, by giving you better and more precise ideas of the region in which Rome stood nearly three thousand years since, and stands to-day.

We will quit the city by the same gate as before; but, instead of inclining to the right, let us take the opposite direction, which brings us, within a hundred yards, to the banks of the Tiber.

If you feel the same sensation that I did, on finding yourself riding along the shores of this classical stream, your seat in the saddle will be elastic, and you will feel a double enjoyment at galloping in a pure air and under a serene sky. You know the size of this river already, and I will merely add that, in the winter and spring, it is turbid, rapid, and apt to overflow its banks, particularly in the town,—for at the place where we now are, these banks are perhaps ten feet above the surface of the water. It is thought the bed of the river has been materially raised by *débris* within the walls, and projects have even been entertained for turning the water, with a view to discoveries.

As boats sometimes ascend, there is a towing-track, which, though little used, is a reasonably good bridle-path, the equestrians keeping this track beaten. As the stream is as meandering as our own Susquehanna, it presents many pretty glimpses; though the nakedness of the Campagna (which, north of Rome, while more waving and broken than farther south, is almost destitute of any other herbage than grass and a few bushes,) prevents the scenery from being absolutely beautiful. Still every turn of the river is pregnant with recollections, and one can hardly look amiss in quest of a historical site.

The eminence on the opposite side of the stream, that shows steep acclivities at its eastern and southern faces, and up which a road winds its way by the south-western ascent, is Monte Mario, a hill that overlooks Rome, very much as Montmartre overlooks Paris. The half-ruined country-house that stands against its eastern side is the Villa Madama, so termed from having been built by Margaret of Austria, a daughter of Charles V, from whom it has descended to the family of Naples. The house on the summit is the property of the Falconieri, the present owners of the mount. What a thing it is to own a Roman site! and what a cockneyism to convert it into a dandy residence,—a "half-horse, half-alligator" ruin!

After riding a little more than a mile, we reach the Milvian Bridge, a portion of which is ancient. We will not cross at this spot, so celebrated for the battle fought by Constantine near it, but pursue our way up the side of the stream, on which we still are. Crossing the highway, then, (the ancient Flaminian Way,) we continue our course up the river, which just here has been the scene of a melancholy event, of no distant occurrence. The horse of a young Englishwoman backed off the steep bank, and falling over her, she was drowned. What has rendered this calamity more striking, was the fate of her father, who is said to have left a post-house in the mountains, on foot, while travelling, and has never since been found.

Near the scene of this accident, or a hundred rods above the Milvian Bridge,* the river sweeps away towards the Sabine Hills, and our road leads us along the brow of a bluff, by a very pretty and picturesque path, which soon brings us to some mineral waters, that have a reputation as ancient as Rome itself. At this point, though distant only a mile or two from the city, nothing of it is to be seen, but, were it not for a few dwellings scattered near, one might almost fancy himself on a prairie of the Far West, such is the wasted aspect of the country, as well as the appearance of the rapid, turbid Tiber.

Diverging from the stream, which inclines north again, taking the direction to the mountains where it rises, we next enter

---

*This name is a proof of the manner in which words become changed by use. The bridge has been termed Milvius, Mulvius, Molvius, and Molle, the latter being its present Roman name.

some fields imperfectly fenced, among which a Tityrus or two are stretched under their *patulæ fagi*, not playing on the oaten reed, it is true, but mending their leather leggings. Rising some hills, we reach another great road, and crossing this, and the fields that succeed, we come to a spot where the Anio is spanned by another bridge, with a tower in its centre. The part of the environs between the last highway and this bridge has more of the character of a suburb than any other portion of the vicinity of Rome; and did the city ever extend far beyond the present course of its walls, it must have been principally in this direction, I think.

The bridge is the *Nomentanus*, and dates from the time of Narses, but was restored about the middle of the fifteenth century, and has much the character of a work of the latter period. Beyond this bridge is a naked hill, with the remains of some works or the ruins of villas on it. This is the Sacred Mount, so celebrated for those decided acts of the plebeians, who twice retired to it, in a body, on account of the oppression of the nobles, in the years of Rome 261 and 305. Here they resisted all persuasion to return, until Menenius Agrippa overcame their obstinacy by the famous apologue of the belly and the members of the human body. The tribunes owed their existence to this act of decision, which is probably the first trade's union that was ever established. These things, on the whole, work evil, because they are abused; but they are not without their uses, as well as tartar emetic. The Romans, however, found them unsuccessful, for they took a solemn oath never to revolt against their tribunes,—— the law, in other words,—and hence the mount, where the oath was taken, was called the Sacred Mount. No apologue ever contained more truth than that of Menenius; and yet the belly may disease all the limbs, as well as the limbs throw the belly into disorder, by sins of commission, as well as by sins of omission. One can write an apologue about anything, and, after all, a fact is a fact.

Proceeding another mile, some extensive ruins are seen between the road of Nomentum and that of Salaria, which are the remains of the country-house of Phaon, the freedman of Nero, where the last of the Cæsars committed suicide. Two hundred years intervened between the death of Nero and that of Aurelian, but they were hardly sufficient to bring all this space within

the walls, which must have been the case to give the latter a circuit of fifty miles. Besides, where are all the remains of this
huge town, without the present wall, if it ever existed there? We
see the remains of villas and camps and bridges all around us
even to-day, but none of a city. The Anio would not be spanned
by such rude arches, had Rome ever covered this spot.

Let us now enter the town by the Porta Salaria, and ride
through the vineyards and among the gardens of that quarter,
towards that of St. John in Laterano. Ruins are scattered about
on every side, and among them are aqueducts, from the arches
of some of which, water still trickles. The circular wall on our
left, as we approach the gate of St. John, is the remains of the
amphitheatre of the camp, in which the soldiers fought with
beasts. The exterior of this wall is better seen from without, for
it has also been incorporated with that of the town.

Of the vast palace and church of the Lateran I have nothing
to say at present, except that it strikes the traveller with an imposing grandeur as he enters the city. Some devotees before the
little church near it, however, will draw us in that direction, and
you will be surprised to see men and women ascending a long
plain flight of broad steps in it, on their knees. This is done because tradition hath it that these steps belonged to the palace of
Pilate, and that they were transferred from Jerusalem to this
spot because Christ descended them when he went from con-
demnation to the cross.

You probably know that this church of St. John in Laterano
is the first of the Christian world, and that the palace was long
celebrated for its bulls and councils. The present edifices are
about five centuries old, though the church is as fresh and rich
as if just finished. The obelisk came from Thebes, and was
brought to Rome in the fourth century, and placed in the great
circus. Sixtus V. had it disinterred and brought to this spot.

You will now follow the road to the Coliseum and the Forum.
All this quarter of the town, with the exception of some broken
fragments of suburbs (always within the walls,) is filled with
ruins, more or less conspicuous. Here, indeed, the objects and
recollections of the past crowd upon the senses oppressively,
and it requires time and use to visit the place with a sufficiency
of coolness and leisure to analyze the parts, and to separate the
works of different ages and reigns.

An intelligent Swiss who is now here, and who frequently accompanies me in these morning rides, exclaimed triumphantly the other day, "You will find, on examining Rome in detail, that all the works of luxury and of a ferocious barbarity belonged to the Empire, and those of use to the Republic. The latter, moreover, are the only works that seem to be imperishable." After allowing for the zeal of a republican, there is some truth in this; though the works of the republic, by their nature, being drains and aqueducts, &c., are more durable than those above ground. Still it is a good deal to have left an impression of lasting usefulness, to be contrasted with the memorials and barbarity of vain temples and bloody arenas.

Of the Coliseum it is unnecessary to speak, beyond the effect it will produce on us both. For me, unlike the effect of St. Peter's, some time was necessary to become fully conscious of its vastness. When one comes deliberately to contemplate this edifice, its beauty of detail and of material, the perfect preservation of its northern half, in the exterior at least,—it must be a dull imagination indeed that does not proceed to people its arches and passages, and to form some pictures of the scenes that, for near five hundred years, were enacted within its walls. This noble structure, noble in extent, in architecture, if not in its uses, was occupied in the eleventh, twelfth, and thirteenth centuries as a strong place, by the contending factions of Rome. This period, however, longer than that of the existence of our American community, is but a speck in the history of the building, as a short retrospect will show. Vespasian died in 79, Titus in 81, and Domitian in 96. The first commenced, the last is said to have finished this edifice. For three hundred years it was used for the exhibitions of the gladiators, and, down to the year 523, for battles of wild beasts. For five hundred years more there is little account of it; but it was probably too vast for the purposes of the people who then dwelt among the ruins of Rome. Then came the civil contentions, and near three centuries of military occupation. In 1381, it is said to have been much dilapidated, particularly on the southern side, when it was converted into a hospital. After this, the popes and their favourites began to pull it to pieces, for the stone. Several of the largest palaces of modern Rome have certainly been erected out of its materials; that of the Farnese, in particular. The quay of the

Ripetta, or the port, is also enriched from this classical quarry. It is only within a few years—less than thirty, I believe—that any serious attempts have been made to preserve what is left; and, to the credit of the papal government be it said, these attempts are likely to be successful. The walls require little but the "let us alone" policy, for they seem to defy time and the seasons. As there was a possibility of their crumbling, however, at the broken extremities of the outer circle, vast piers of brickwork have been erected, and in a style that in this species of construction is only equalled in Italy.

This edifice was 1641 feet in circumference, according to Vasi, who wrote in French; and if French feet are meant, this will exceed 1700 of our feet, which is near a third of a mile. The height is 157 feet, which is quite equal to an ordinary American church spire, even in the towns. From these facts you may obtain some ideas of the general vastness, for the summit was everywhere of the same elevation. The earth had accumulated to the height of several feet about the base; but it has been removed, a wall has been erected a short distance from the edifice, and, on that side, one may see the Coliseum very much as it existed under Nero. The arena, according to my former authority, was 285 feet long, by 182 wide. This arena is now encircled by fourteen little chapels, erected in honour of the Christians who are said to have perished here. The interior, however, is a wild and ruined place.

I know nothing, in its way, that gives one ideas of the magnificence and power of Rome so imposing as the Coliseum. It was erected in an incredibly short time, in a way to resist wars, earthquakes, time, and almost the art of man, and now offers one of the most imposing piles under which the earth groans; in some respects, the most imposing. The uncertainty that hangs about the Pyramids impairs their interest; but the Coliseum is almost as well known to us, through the lapse of eighteen centuries, as Drury Lane or the Théâtre Français.

As we are not making antiquarian examinations, let us proceed in the direction of the Forum, and look into its actual condition. The direction of the Via Sacra is well known. It commenced at the Coliseum, and passed near, if not beneath, the Arch of Titus, which is still standing; and, following a line of temples of which we still see many remains, it went beneath the

Arch of Septimius Severus, which is also standing, and, it is thought, ascended the Capitol Hill, by what are called the "Sacred Steps." The vacant space which vulgarly passes by the name of the Forum is in the shape of two parallelograms, united by a right angle. One of these open spaces lies between the Capitol and Palatine Hills, and the other stretches from the Arch of Titus to the base of the Capitol, the latter hill not lying directly in a line with the Palatine. Neither of these celebrated hills is large or very high, the Capitol having about two thirds of a mile in circumference at its base, and the latter a little less. As their sides are generally precipitous, the surfaces of the summits do not vary much from their dimensions. I should think the present elevation of the Capitol Hill may be about fifty feet above the level of the surrounding streets; though there is one point which is higher. These streets are, however, much higher than formerly, as is proved by discovering the bases of ancient structures some distance beneath their pavements. The other hill has about the same elevation, or is perhaps a little higher. Their bases are materially changed.

The Palatine, or the cradle of Rome, will first attract our attention. It lies on our left as we advance towards the Forum, and exhibits a confused surface of ruins, gardens, vines, and modern villas. Its prevailing appearance, however, is that of ruin. For several reigns, this mount sufficed not only to contain the residences of the kings of Rome, but all Rome itself. The antiquarians pretend, on what authority I do not know, but that of Livy, I believe, to point out the precise spots where several of the first princes lived. In time it did not suffice for the palace of a single monarch. The Palatine was probably much larger then than now, the eastern end having the appearance of being cut. Thus the house of Ancus Martius is said to have been on the summit of the Via Sacra, which would carry the hill near the present site of the Temple of Venus and Rome. On this hill, the Gracchi, Cicero, Catiline, Marc Antony, Catullus, and Octavius, with many others of note, are known to have lived; though, after the fall of the republic, it passed entirely into the hands of the emperors. In the time of Caligula, the imperial palace had a front on the Forum, with a rich colonnade, and a portico. A bridge, sustained by marble columns, crossed the Forum, to communicate with the Capitol Hill. One here sees the rapid progress of luxury in a monarchy. Augustus lived modestly in what might be termed a house; Tiberius, his successor, added to this house until it became a palace; Caligula, not satisfied with the Palatine, projected additions on the Capitol Hill; Claudius, it is true, abandoned this plan, and even destroyed the bridge, but Nero caused an enormous edifice to succeed.

The first palace of Nero must have occupied the whole of the Palatine Hill, with perhaps the exception of a temple or two, the ground around the Coliseum (the site of which was a pond), and all the land as far as the Esquiline, or even to the verge of the Quirinal,—a distance exceeding a mile. This was possessing, moreover, the heart of the town; although a portion of the space was occupied by gardens and other embellishments. When this building was burned, he returned to the Palatine, repaired the residence of Augustus, and rebuilt with so much magnificence, that the new palace was called the "Golden House." This building also extended to the Esquiline; though it was never finished. Vespasian and Titus, more moderate than the descendant of the Cæsars, demolished all the new parts of the palace, and caused the Coliseum and the baths that bear the name of the latter to be constructed on the spot. These emperors were elected, and they found it necessary to consult the public tastes and public good. Thus we find the remains of two of the largest structures of the world now standing within the ground once occupied by the palace of the Cæsars, on which they appear as little more than points. From this time the emperors confined themselves to the Palatine, the glory of which gradually departed. It is said that the palace, as it was subsequently reduced, remained standing, in a great measure, as recently as the eighth century, and that it was even inhabited in the seventh.

The ruins of the Palatine are now little more than the vaulted rooms of the foundation. One or two halls of the principal floor are thought to be still partially in existence; but as nearly everything but the bricks has disappeared, they offer little more than recollections to a visitor. Even their uses are conjectured rather than proved. It is possible, by industry and research, to get some ideas of the localities; but few things at Rome, compared with its original importance, offer less of interest directly to the senses than the Palatine Hill. The ruins are confused, and the study of them is greatly perplexing. Certainly, one is also op-pressed with sensations on visiting this spot; but, unless a true antiquary, I think the eye is more apt to turn towards the Coli-seum, and the other surrounding objects, than to the shapeless and confused masses of brickwork that are found here.

The site of the house of Augustus is now a villa, belonging to an Englishman, which is well kept up, and which may have its uses in a certain sense, but which struck me as being singularly ill placed as respects sentiment. One could wish every trace of a modern existence to be obliterated from such a spot; and, moreover, a man ought to have great confidence in the texture of his own skin, to stand constantly beneath the glare of a pow-erful sun.

You know that the Forum was originally established, in the time of Romulus and Tatius, when a hill was almost a country, as a market-place between the hostile people. Here the two *na-tions* met to traffic. Forums afterwards became common, and the remains and sites of several in the city are known; but this was *the* Forum, *par excellence*. This Forum remained in a state of preservation as lately as the seventh century, sufficient to re-ceive monuments; but since that time down to a period about the commencement of the present century, it was falling gradu-ally into a worse and worse condition; though its severest blow is attributed to Robert Guiscard, about the year 1000. He burned and laid waste all this part of Rome, much to the dam-age of modern travelling.

For several hundred years the Romans were in the practice of throwing rubbish in this spot, to which circumstance is ascribed the present elevation of its surface. To this cause, however, must be added the regular accumulation of materials from the crumbling ruins; for other parts of Rome prove that it is not the Forum alone which has been thus buried. You will be surprised to hear that, in disinterring many of the monuments that still remain, the pavement of the ancient Forum, and the bases of the works themselves, have been found at a depth varying from twenty to twenty-five feet below the actual surface.

The Forum is said to have been surrounded by a colonnade of two stories, which gave to the whole a form and arrangement something like those of the Palais Royal at Paris. The Curia, or senate chamber, was under the Palatine; and the Comitium, or the place for the popular meetings, was near it. As the emperors lived above, here was a shadowing forth of that sublime mystification which has so long blinded and amused the world, in the way of a political device, which it is the fashion to term the "three estates." I wonder if Nero said who should be his ministers, and the senate said who should not!

The Arch of Septimius Severus still remains, one may say, perfect. It stands at the foot of the Capitoline, and its base is cleared away, and the vacancy is protected, as usual, by a wall. The digging around it is not very deep. It dates from the commencement of the second century.

Not far from this arch, there stood, previously to the year 1813, a solitary column, with nearly half its shaft buried in the earth, the capital being perfect. This column, it was then believed, belonged to a temple, or, if not to a temple, at least to the bridge of Caligula; but, in 1813, the earth was removed from its base, and it was then found to stand on a pedestal, on which there is an inscription that proves the column was erected in honour of Phocas, and as lately as the year 608. I believe it is one of the last things of the sort ever placed in the Forum. The column itself, however, is supposed to be much older, and to have been taken from some ancient and ruined temple. It may have been truly one of those that supported the bridge. The name of Phocas, it would seem, had been partially erased, after his fall: a circumstance which shows that men have the same envious stone-defacing propensities under all circumstances.

There are many other remains in and about the Forum, some of which are of more interest than those mentioned; but I have taken these, as my object is to offer you a picture of Rome as it is, rather than to pretend to any great antiquarian knowledge. You know I am no antiquary. I do not think many of these constructions equal expectation, with the exception of the Coliseum, and perhaps I ought to add, the remains that give us notions of the vastness of the palaces.

By following a road up a sharp acclivity, we reach the summit of the Capitol Hill,—or rather its square, for the land is higher on both sides of it than in the area itself. The surface has undergone a good deal of change; though it is thought still easy to trace the sites of the ancient constructions. The Capitol of Rome and the Capitol of Washington were as different as the two countries to which they belonged. The former, originally, was a town; then a fortress, or a citadel; and, in the end, it became a collection of different objects of high interest, principally devoted to religious rites. If any particular *building* was called the Capitol, it was the Temple of Jupiter Capitolinus, which is described as not being very large, though very magnificent; not large as a *building*, though large as a *temple*; for few of the Roman temples appear to have been of any great size. The senate assembled in the Curia, which was on the Forum, as you know, and not in the Capitol at all.

The buildings that are now called the Capitol stand on the centre of the mount, facing the north. They consist of three detached edifices, that occupy as many sides of a square, with a noble flight of steps in their front. The central edifice contains prisons and offices, and the others are filled with works of art. The celebrated statue of Marcus Aurelius, the only equestrian bronze statue of ancient Rome in existence, stands in the centre of the area, and, although the horse is heavy and even clumsy, according to American notions, a noble thing it is. The ease and the motion of this statue are beyond description. It may, at once, be set down as the model of all we possess of merit in these two respects. The artist may have had a model for this in some other work of art; but, certain I am, this has been a model for all we now possess. The senatorial palace, or the centre building of the modern Capitol, from which we obtain the name and uses of *our* Capitols, is not very old, and it stands on the foundations of the ancient Tabularium, a structure that contained the table of the Roman laws, treaties, &c. The building was originally a sort of fortress, and probably obtained its name of the Capitol from its situation.

We call our legislative structures Capitols, under some mistaken notion, I think, about the uses of the Roman Capitol. Let this be as it may, the Romans gave this name to *their* hill from the circumstance of finding a head buried in it; and it might have been well had we waited until some signs of a head had appeared on our own, before we christened the edifices so ambitiously. But taste in names is not the strong point of American invention. After all, too, the American Capitol has proved the grave of divers sounding heads.

I cannot stop to speak of all the objects of interest that crowd

Rome, for descriptions of which you will search the more regular books; but we will descend from the Capitol Hill by the winding carriage road near the great stairs, and, riding round its base by narrow streets, for here the modern town commences in earnest, and crossing the end of the Corso, we find ourselves in a large open space, surrounded by houses, with a street around an area in the centre; which area lies several feet below the level of the streets, is paved, has a great many broken columns and other fragments scattered about it, and a noble column entire, standing at one end:—this is the Forum of Trajan.

Until the year 1812 this place was covered with houses. A beautiful column rose among them, half concealed by the buildings, and partly buried. The column is 132 feet high, was surmounted by a statue of the emperor, which has disappeared, and has been replaced by one of St. Peter. It is covered with *bas reliefs*, wrought in the marble, representing scenes from the Dacian wars. This column was the model of that of the Place Vendôme, at Paris. There is a staircase within, and, until the time named, those who chose to mount by the outside to examine it, descended as in a well.

The celebrity of this column is well established. The *bas reliefs* have a high reputation, and must have cost an immensity of labour, as there are more than two thousand figures, besides military insignia. The Forum was the richest of Rome; and its length is supposed to have been near 2000 Roman feet, and its breadth more than 600. This is more, however, than has been uncovered, and probably more than is certainly known to have ever existed. In 1812 the column was laid bare to the base, where a door affords entrance; and a good deal of the Forum has also been excavated, and walled, as usual. The diggings, however, are not so deep as those of the great Forum, the pavement of the place lying only about eight or ten feet below that of the town.

Returning to the Corso, we will next ride along that street, the principal avenue of Rome. It is probable, the Flaminian Way faced the Temple of Jupiter, or the Capitol; but the modern termination of this street is altogether unworthy of the street itself. Like the Rhine at Leyden, it is lost in a maze of narrow, crowded, and crooked passages.

Following this street between lines of palaces, we come to the Piazza Colonna, where we find the column that is usually called the Column of Antoninus. It is higher and larger, and a century later than that of Trajan, but by no means its equal in beauty. This column *appears* to stand, as it was erected, on a level with the surrounding earth: but we are told this is an error, as the pedestal now seen is a substitute in part, and the old one is still buried to the depth of eleven feet. Even the inscriptions, which are only about two centuries and a half old, (or about as old as ourselves, as a nation!) are thought to be incorrect; for it ascribes the column to Marcus Antoninus, in honour of his father-in-law Antoninus Pius, when, in fact, it was erected by the senate, in honour of Marcus Aurelius Antoninus, to commemorate his victories in Germany.

The palaces around this square belong to the great families of Piombino, Chigi, &c. and have thirteen or fifteen windows in a row, besides being built around courts. The square near, with an unequal little eminence and an obelisk, is called Citorio. The eminence is caused by the ruins of an amphitheatre. The obelisk, which Pliny attributes to Sesostris (!) was brought from Egypt by Augustus. It was placed in the Campus Martius, and found there as lately as in 1748.

We will now wend our way through narrow and crowded streets, for a short distance, until we come out in another square of a very different character. We find it filled with market people, dirty, and far from attractive; although there is an obelisk in its centre. On the side opposite to that by which we enter it, however, is an edifice, that, as a second look shows, possesses a strange mixture of beauty and deformity. Its form is round; though the adjoining buildings prevent this circumstance from being immediately seen. It has a noble portico, with a fine row of columns, but a tympanum which is altogether too heavy. Two little belfries peep out, like asses' ears, at each side of the portico, in a way to make a spectator laugh, while he wonders that the man who devised them did not stick them on his own head. An inscription on the cornice causes us to start; for we see in large letters, M. AGRIPPA. L. F. COS. TERTIVM. FECIT. This, then, is the Pantheon!

You will be disappointed with the *coup d'œil* of this celebrated structure, as well as I was myself. You will probably find the building too low, the appliances of the square unseemly, the manner in which the building is surrounded by houses oppressive, the *ears* too long, and, above all, the Roman heaviness of the pediment but a poor substitute for the grace and lightness of the Grecian architecture of the same form. It is thought that the body of the building and the portico are not of the same period. The inscription speaks for itself; and the last, at least, it is fair to infer, was erected about the year 727 of Rome, or a short time previously to the birth of Christ.

On entering the building, it is impossible not to be struck by its simple and beautiful grandeur. A vast vaulted rotunda, of solid stone, without a basement, and lighted by a graceful opening that permits a view of the firmament, are things so novel, so beautiful, not to say sublime, that one forgets the defects of the exterior. This idea is one of the most magnificent of its kind that exists in architecture. The opening, a circular hole in the top, admits sufficient light, and the eye, after scanning the noble vault, seeks this outlet, and penetrates the blue void of infinite space. Here is, at once, a suitable physical accompaniment to the mind, and the aid of one of the most far-reaching of our senses is enlisted on the side of omnipotence, infinite majesty, and perfect beauty. Illimitable space is the best prototype of eternity.

I believe the vulgar notion that the Pantheon was dedicated to *all* the gods is erroneous. It is a better opinion, it would seem, to suppose that it was dedicated to a few gods, in whom *all* or many of the divine *attributes* are assembled. This, after all, is begging the question, as the gods themselves, it is fair to presume, represented merely so many different attributes of infinite power and excellence. The niches are not sufficient to hold many statues, and there probably never were statues in the building to one half the deities of Rome.

One of the principal external faults of this edifice, as it is now seen, must not be ascribed to its architecture. Its majesty is impaired by its want of height; but it has been ascertained that eight steps anciently existed in front of the portico, in place of the two which are now seen. The diameter of the rotunda is 132 Roman feet; and this is the edifice, as you know, that Michael Angelo boasted he would raise into the air, as a cupola for St. Peter's. He has raised there something very like it.

Since the year 608 the Pantheon has virtually been a Christian church. There is a long period during which it is not mentioned; but it is fair to presume, it has always preserved its present character since the year just mentioned. At one time the palace of the popes adjoined this temple, and then it served as their private chapel.

We will not return to the Corso, but, winding our way out of this maze of streets, return home by the Via Ripetta. The huge palace we pass near the river, in the shape of a harpsichord, is that of the Borghese family, and it is at present occupied by the Prince Aldobrandini, the brother of Don Camillo, who married the sister of Napoleon. It is a huge edifice, with courts, and is worthy to be a royal abode. Still, it is by no means the best house in Rome; but he who has not seen this town, or rather Italy, can form no just idea of magnificence in this part of life.

Letter XXIV.

T H E close of the last letter reminds me of the propriety of saying something of the mode of living in Rome. Nothing has surprised me more than the accounts given in English books of the filth, nastiness, and other pretended abominations of the princely abodes here, as well as of the mode of life within them. The English, as a people, have been singularly unjust commentators on all foreign usages and foreign people; though they are fast losing their prejudices, and beginning to discriminate between customs. Neither the Italians, nor any other Continental nation, deem the English snuggeries indispensable to happiness. They admire a rich *parquet*, or a floor of imitation mosaic, more than a pine or an oaken floor carpeted. Their staircases are broad architectural flights, on which a stair-carpet and brass rods would be singularly misplaced; and the great size of their houses renders the minutiæ of our pigmy residences not only unnecessary, but would render them excessively troublesome and expensive. Certainly the English and the Americans are neater in their houses than the French or the Italians; but a large portion of what has been said against the higher classes of the two latter countries may, I think, be fairly explained in this way. As between the labouring classes of England and America on the one side, and those of the Continent of Europe in general on the other, there is no comparison, on the score of civilization and its comforts; the advantage being altogether with the former. The mass of no nation can have domestic comforts, or domestic cleanliness, when the women are subjected to field labour. Exactly in the proportion as the females can turn their attention within doors, does the home become comfortable and neat, other things being equal. But, beyond this, false notions exist. The Englishman of rank, through the perfection of the manufactures and the commerce of his country, has a detail of comforts of a certain class, and perhaps of a wider class than the

Continental nobility; but, on the other hand, there are other essential points in which he falls far behind them. What, for instance, are the chamber-comforts and elegancies of an English town-house, compared to those of an Italian town-house? Compare the baths, dressing-rooms, and ante-chambers of a French hotel, or an Italian palazzo, with the same things in a London residence! The baths, dressing-rooms, cabinets, and ante-chambers of our lodgings in Florence were as spacious, and much more elegant than our entire lodgings in London; and I think all our rooms in the latter town had not more space than one of the principal rooms in the former. I paid thirty-five dollars a week for the London house, and forty-two dollars a month for the Florence lodgings!

Travellers are too much in the practice of describing under the influence of their early and home-bred impressions. As a man sees the world, his prejudices diminish, his diffidence of his own decisions increases, and with both, his indisposition to write. Many a man has commenced travelling with a firm intention of faithfully describing all he saw, and of commenting, as he conceived, impartially, but who has gradually suffered this intention to escape him, until he gets to be too critical in his distinctions to satisfy even himself. Thus, the English cockney, who has never seen a house with more than two drawing-rooms, fancies it extraordinary that an Italian, with a palace larger than St. James's, should not always occupy its state apartments, although his own king is guilty of the same act of neglect. Instead of saying that the Princes Doria, Chigi, Borghese, Colonna, Corsini, &c. have vast palaces like George IV. and that their state apartments are liberally thrown open to the public, while, like King George and all other kings, they occupy, in every-day life, rooms of less pretension and of more comfort, they say, that these Roman nobles have huge palaces,—a fact that cannot be denied,—while they live in corners of them. This false account of the real state of the case arises simply from the circumstance that an English nobleman occupies *his* best rooms. The question whether the second-rate rooms of an Italian palace are not equal to the best apartments of an ordinary English dwelling, never suggests itself.

I visit in the Palazzo Borghese, which stands in our neighbourhood. The Prince himself resides altogether at Florence, where he has another noble house, and in which he receives magnificently; but, here, a large part of the building is filled with pictures, in order to be exhibited to strangers. It is true the *appartamento nobile*, or first floor, is not now opened, for the family of the Prince Aldobrandini is here merely on a visit: he is a younger brother, and his proper residence may be called Paris, the Princess being a French lady of the family De La Rochefoucauld. Accordingly, when admitted, I certainly do not enter the state apartments, but am shown into what we call the third story, where I find the family. A pretty picture might be made of this, but it would mislead you. Here is a princely family, with an enormous house, it might be said, that lives in a corner of it, even on the second floor, leaving all the principal rooms unoccupied. This is the ordinary English version of the custom, and, of necessity, the ordinary American. In point of fact, however, the ascent to this third story is far more imposing, and quite as easy, as the ascent to a common London drawing-room; and, with but very few exceptions, I have never seen an English nobleman so well lodged in London, in his best rooms, as the present occupants of the Palazzo Borghese are *in their corner*. The misconception has arisen from the difference in the habits of the two countries, and we have adopted the error, as we adopt all English mistakes that do not impair our good opinion of ourselves: in other words, we swallow them whole.

There are Italian nobles, out of doubt, who are not rich enough to keep up their vast palaces; and there are English nobles in the same predicament. In such cases, the Englishman retires to the Continent in order to live cheap; and the Italian retires to his attic, or *mezzanino*, which is frequently better than the first floor of an English town-house. The latter can live cheapest at home.

As to the filth on the staircases, which the English accounts had led me to expect, I have seen none of it, in any palace I have entered. It is possible that some deserted staircase, or that the corridor of one of these huge piles, may occasionally be defiled in that way, for it has happened in London to the best houses; but, as a distinctive usage, the accounts are altogether false, so far as eighteen months' experience of Italy can authorize me to decide. There are certain disadvantages belonging to magnificence, which is never so comfortable and so minutely nice as snugger modes of living; but if one cannot have snugness with magnificence and taste, neither can one have magnificence and taste with snugness. Homilies might be written on the moral part of the question; but to understand the physical merits, it is necessary to enter into all these distinctions.

I know too little of Italian society to say anything new about it, or even to speak very confidently on any of the old usages. The daughters of particular families, I believe, are getting to have more of a voice in the choice of husbands than formerly; though France is still much in advance of Italy in this respect. I take this one fact to be the touchstone of domestic manners; for the woman who has freely made her own selection will hesitate long before she consents to destroy the great pledge of connubial affection. Cicisbeism certainly exists, for I have seen proofs of it; but I incline to the opinion that foreigners do not exactly understand the custom. By what I can learn, too, it is gradually yielding to the opinions of the age. A foreigner married to an Italian of rank, and who has long been resident in Italy, tells me its social tone is greatly impaired by the habits of the women, who are so much disposed to devote themselves to their sentiment in favour of particular individuals, as to have no wish to mingle in general society. Whether these individuals were the husbands or not, the lady did not appear to think it necessary to say.

The females of Rome are among the most winning and beautiful of the Christian world. One who has been here a week can understand the *bocca Romana*, for no females speak their language more beautifully. The manner in which they pronounce that beautiful and gracious word "*grazie*," is music itself. A French woman's "*merci*" is pretty, but it is mincing, and not at all equal to the Roman "thanks." After all, as language is the medium of thought, and the link that connects all our sympathies, there is no more desirable accomplishment than a graceful utterance. Unfortunately, our civilization is not yet sufficiently advanced to see this truth,—or rather, the *summerset* habits of America cause us to forget it; for I can remember the time when a lady deemed an even, measured, and dignified mode of speaking, necessary to a lady's deportment. It is a little odd, in a country so ambitious of mere social distinctions as our own, distinctions that must exist in some shape or other, since social equality is incompatible with civilization, and in which girls can and do milk cows in silks and muslins, that so few think of setting up elegance, as a means of distinction! My life on it, those who succeeded would have it all their own way for a good many lustres.

Rome, just at this moment, contains a congress of all the people of Christendom. Its most obvious society, perhaps, is the English; but it is by no means the best, as it is necessarily much mixed. I was lately at a great ball given by the Prince of ——, and it certainly was faultless as to taste and style. I do not remember ever to have been in a society so uniformly elegant and high-toned. The exceptions were very few, and not very obtrusive. The apartments were vast and magnificent, and the supper equal to the rest. But the Italians of condition may be generally considered a polished and amiable people, whatever is thought of their energy and learning. In the latter there is no very apparent deficiency; though they attend less to this point, perhaps, than some other countries of Europe. In the studious classes, it strikes me there is much learning; not a knowledge of Greek and Latin quantities merely, but a knowledge of the sciences and of the arts, and a strong sympathy with the beauties of the classics.

In the lower classes I have been agreeably disappointed. Strangers certainly see the worst of them; for a kinder and quicker-witted, and a more civil people, than most of the country population, is not usually seen. Had we formed our notions by even the first nine months' observation, it would have misled us, for subsequent experience has made us acquainted with several dependants of the most excellent character and disposition.

Few foreigners, however, see much of Italian society; the great inroad of strangers causing them to be cautious of opening their doors, while the number of the strangers themselves is apt to make them satisfied with their own associations. It is said that there are some thousands of travellers in Rome at this moment; and you can judge of their effect on the modes of living of so small a town. The English, as a matter of course, predominate, at least in the public places and in the hotels. At the ball I attended, however, there were but three English present; though half the other nations of Christendom were fully represented. This fact was observed, and I ventured to inquire of a Roman the reason. The answer was, that the master of the house did not like the English; and although the entertainment was given to a prince of a royal family nearly connected with the royal family of England, but three of the latter country were invited. I was told that the disposition to force their own opinions and habits on the strangers they visited rendered the English unpleasant, and that there was a general feeling against receiving them. This may be just enough as respects a portion, perhaps the majority of those who come here; but it is singularly unjust as respects the better class of them, and it is the Romans who are the losers.

It is said the English bachelors here got up a ball lately, with a view to manifest a kind feeling towards their hosts, and that the invitations were sent out as "at homes;" a freedom that the Roman ladies resented by staying away. So much from not understanding a language; though delicacy and tact in conferring obligations and in paying compliments are not singularly English virtues.

We have had a dinner, too, in honour of Washington, at which I had the honour to preside. You will be surprised to hear that we sat down near seventy Yankees (in the European sense) in the Eternal City! We were very patriotic, but quite moderate in its expression.

I have ascertained that strong hopes exist here of advancing the religion of this government in America. If this can be done, let it, for I am for giving all sects fair play; but as such expectations certainly exist, it may be well for those who think differently to know it. One of the last things that an American would be likely to suspect, is the conversion of his countrymen to the Roman Catholic faith; and yet such a result is certainly here brought within the category of possibilities. I would advise you to take large doses of Calvinism, or you may awake, some fine morning, a believer in transubstantiation.

You will be surprised also to learn that there is less religious bigotry in Rome itself than in many of the distant provinces subject to her canonical sway. The government being in the hands of ecclesiastics, as a matter of course no open irreligion is tolerated; but beyond this, and the great number of the churches and of the ecclesiastics themselves, a stranger would scarcely suspect he was living purely under an ecclesiastical government. The popes are not the men they once were: nepotism, cupidity, and most of the abuses incident to excessive temporal influence, are done away with; and as the motive for ambition ceases, better men have been raised to the papal chair. Most of the last popes have been mild, religious men, and, so far as man can know,· suited to their high religious trusts; though the system is still obnoxious to the charge of more management, perhaps, than properly belongs to faith in God and his church. But all establishments are weak on this point, and the general assemblies, &c. of America are not always purely a convocation of saints.

Strangers are no longer expected to kneel at the appearance of the Host in the streets, or even in the churches. The people understand the prejudices of Protestants, and, unless offensively obtruded, seem disposed to let them enjoy them in peace. I saw a strong proof of this lately:—A friend of mine, walking with myself, stepped aside in a narrow street, for a purpose that often induces men to get into corners. He thought himself quite retired; but, as I stopped for him to rejoin me, a crowd collected around the spot he had just quitted. Without his knowing it, the image of a Madonna was placed in the wall, directly above the spot he had chosen, and of course it had been defiled! I saw all this myself; and it is a proof of the change that exists in this particular, that I dared to remain to watch the result, though my friend himself thought it prudent to retire. A priest appeared, and the wall was sprinkled with holy water, while the people stood looking on, some at the wall and some at me, in grave silence. Thirty years ago such a blunder might have cost us both our lives.

Indeed, liberality, in some respects, is carried to a fault. The singing of St. Peter's has a reputation far and near, and strangers are accustomed to go there to hear it. There is a particular chapel in which a service is sung, (vespers, I presume,) every Sunday afternoon, and where one can hear the finest vocal church music in the world,—music even finer than that of the Royal Chapel at Dresden. At the latter place, however, the music is chiefly instrumental; whereas here it is principally by voices. One who has never seen such a temple, or heard such a combination of science, skill, and natural—I may say *artificial* power, can form no just notion of the sensations that arise on walking among the wonders of the church and listening to the heavenly chants. Sometimes I withdraw to a distance, and the sounds reach me like the swells of airs in another world; and at times I go near the door of the chapel, and receive the full bursts of its harmony. Operas, concerts, and *conservatoires* sink into insignificance before this sublime union of the temple and its worship; for both may be considered as having reached the limits of human powers, so far as the senses are concerned.

Around the door of this chapel, which is, I believe, called the Chapel of the Choir, strangers assemble in crowds. Here, I regret to say, they laugh, chat, lounge, and amuse themselves, much as well-bred people amuse themselves in an evening party anywhere else. There is not much noise certainly, for well-bred people are not often noisy; but there is little or no reverence. After making all possible allowance for the difference between Catholic and Protestant worship, this want of respect for the altar and the temple is inexcusable. Happily, I have never yet seen an American indulging in this levity. The fact speaks volumes in reply to those who heap obloquy on the nation as wanting in religion. The larger American sects manifest a great disrespect for the mere house of God: they hold political meetings in their churches, even concerts and exhibitions, all of which I deem irreverent and unsuited to the place; but whenever anything like worship is commenced, silence and decency prevail. This feeling they have brought abroad with them; but other Protestants, especially the English, who are such observers of the decencies at home, do not appear to entertain the same feelings.

Still, it must be admitted that the Catholics themselves do not always set a good example. I was strolling lately through the vast temple, equally impressed with reverence and delight, when a cardinal entered by a side door. He was a young man, with a marked air of gentility; and I presume his early rise in the church was owing to his high birth. He was in his official dress, and carried the red hat pressed against his bosom. As he entered from the Vatican, I presume he had just been in the presence of the Pope. Four attendants followed, two of whom were in black, and were a species of clerical esquires, though their official appellation is unknown to me; and two were common livery servants. The cardinal advanced to the great altar, beneath the celebrated baldacchino, and, kneeling, he prayed. Nothing could be better than his whole manner, which was subdued, gentle, and devout. So far all was well. The two *esquires* kneeled behind the cardinal on the pavement, put their hats to their faces, and appeared also to pray. The two lacqueys kneeled behind the esquires, the distance between the respective parties being about twenty feet; and they too raised their hats before their faces,—but it was to laugh and make grimaces at each other! This buffoonery was so obvious as to amount to mockery, and one near them might see it.

You know my passion for the poetry of the Roman worship. The odour of the incense, the vaulted roofs, attenuated aisles and naves, the painted windows, and the grand harmonies of the chants, are untiring sources of delight to me. It is true, at Rome one sees no Gothic architecture; but its place is nobly supplied. The riches as well as the number of the churches are incredible, and one can only become reconciled to the apparent waste by remembering that the pretence is to honour God. A temple in the human heart is certainly better than one of stone; but I see no incompatibility between the two. These are distinctions into which I do not enter; or, if sometimes tempted to make them, I feel persuaded that it is quite as possible to strip the altar of its dignity and decencies, as it is to overload it with useless ceremonies and pageants.

No one who has not visited Rome can have a just appreciation of the powers of Domenichino and Guido, or perhaps of Raphael,—though the latter is to be seen to advantage elsewhere,—or any idea of the pass to which men have carried the magnificence of church architecture. I do not now allude solely to the unrivalled grandeur of St. Peter's, but to the splendour of the churches in general, and especially to that of the private chapels. These private chapels have been ornamented by different families for ages, and the result is, that they have literally become architectural gems, though less in the sense of a pure taste, perhaps, than in that of an elaborated magnificence. That of the Corsini, in St. John of the Lateran, is the richest I have seen; and I feel persuaded that I speak within bounds when I say, the money that would be necessary to build such a thing in America would cause ten or a dozen of our largest churches to be constructed. The great resources of Rome in antiques, columns, precious stones, and marbles, render these expenses less onerous than elsewhere; but their value even here is immense. The Prince of —— showed me a mosaic ornament in his vestibule, that had now been there some ages; and he told me that the precious stones it contained would sell for a very large sum.

Vasi has a list of one hundred and thirty-three churches; and as he describes them all, I presume the little chapels that have been made out of the ancient temples, of which there may be a dozen or two, are not included. The smallest of these churches, if the little temples are excluded, are as large as the largest of our own; and each of the basilicæ, of which there are now six, is nearly, if not quite as large, in cubic contents, as all the churches of New York united. St. Peter's, of course, is much larger; and, if the colonnade be included, I feel persuaded all the public buildings of New York might stand on its area,—to say nothing of the height.

We have lately ascended to the roof of this wonder of the world. It resembles a table-land on a mountain, and I was strongly impressed with the notion of having a horse to gallop about it. The two small domes rise from the plane like churches, and the great dome looks like a mountain. The sacristy of this church is of itself a great edifice, and it is rich beyond all American notions.

St. John *in Laterano* is said to get its name from Plautius Lateranus, whose house stood at the same place. The Lateran Palace joins the church, as the Vatican joins St. Peter's. The present palace was built by Sixtus V; but Constantine resided here. There is a very ancient baptistery in the group of buildings, in which it is pretended that emperor was baptised; though a man who had made up his mind to be a Christian, would hardly wait to build a church to perform the initiatory ceremony in, I think. The term "councils of the *Lateran*" came from their being held in this palace, as that of the "thunders of the Vatican" from the circumstance that the popes, who issue the bulls, usually live here.

St. Peter's of the Vaticano, as well as the palace, to which it is annexed, if such a term may be used, gets its name from the ancient Roman appellation of the spot. Nero had his circus and gardens here; and it is said that this is the place in which most of the Christians were martyred. The first church was relatively small, though subsequently much enlarged; but it was removed when the present building had got to be advanced. The palace is very ancient, though much changed, for Charlemagne lived in it while at Rome to be crowned, which was more than a thousand years ago. It fell into ruins, however, and was restored by Celestinus III. two centuries later. It has certainly been in its present form more than three centuries, as Raphael and Michael Angelo have left memorials on its walls not to be mistaken. The latter essentially roofed and raised St. Peter's, and it follows that the present palace is older than the present church. In truth, the latter was erected as an accessory to the former!

The Vatican is an immense structure, covering more ground than St. Peter's itself; though it is a succession of courts and palaces rather than a single edifice. Vasi gives its dimensions at about 1100 by near 800 feet. This includes the courts, but not the gardens. I have somewhere read, that if the buildings of the Vatican were placed in a line, they would reach a mile.

The palace and the church are incorporated in one edifice; but, owing to the noble colonnade by which one approaches St. Peter's, its unity and vastness, particularly its height, and the fact that the Vatican has no great visible façade, the latter is almost lost in the *coup d'œil* of the other, although it covers most ground of the two, unless the area of the vacancy between the colonnades be thrown in on the side of the church.

It is usual to say, the conclaves are held in the Vatican; but I understand here, that the last election of the Pope was held in the Quirinal, or rather in the building adjoining the Quirinal. The palace of the Quirinal is called the Pontifical Palace, and I believe most of the time of the Pope is passed in it. His apartments are very plain, so much so as to excite surprise: but here are the noble *bas reliefs* of Thorwaldsen.

The frescoes of Raphael in the Vatican, and those of the Sistine Chapel, in the same palace, by Michael Angelo, are deemed the respective *chefs d'œuvre* of these artists. The *loggie* of Raphael contain some extraordinary things. The paintings are on the ceilings of compartments, in what we should call piazzas, or open galleries. The subjects commence with the Creation. On one, God, in the form of a venerable old man, is throwing himself into the midst of chaos, in order to separate and reduce to order the materials of the universe. The sub-limest conception of this subject, the only one that will bear crit-ical examination, is that of a being whose will and knowledge, without an effort, can create a universe. The simple language of the Bible can never be surpassed. The representation of this majesty of a will might possibly be partially portrayed by the pencil; but few could enter even into the sublimest conceptions of the countenance of a being filled with so much power, admit-ting the success to be equal to the thought, in the application of the means. Failing this, we are driven to some such imagery as this of Raphael's. His idea is noble, and, considered in con-nexion with the usual means of his art, perhaps one of the best that could have been suggested. The idea of the Deity's throw-ing himself into chaos, to separate light from darkness, and to reduce the materials of the universe to order, is magnificent, and it might be made to tell in poetry. It never can equal the majesty of the exercise of the pure will; but, descending from this severe grandeur, it is one of the finest of the thoughts that follow. What a different thing it appears reduced to visible agencies! An old sprawling man, casting his body, with open palms and extended arms, into a chaotic confusion of gloomy colours, is not without the wild and indefinable feeling of po-etry, I admit; but how much is it inferior to mere thought, or even thought as it may be expressed in language! Had Raphael painted that sublime verse of the Bible—"And God said, Let there be light, and there was light," in this compartment of the gallery, he would have commenced his subject as well, perhaps, as by human means it can ever be presented to human senses.

It is wondered that one who could conceive of even the old man throwing his body into chaos, should have fallen so low as the idea of the next picture. In the compartment of the gallery that follows, the same old man is represented starting a planet in its orbit with each hand, and setting the moon, or some other heavenly body, in motion, with a kick of his foot! Criticism ap-plied to such a thought would be thrown away.

I am not going the rounds of the galleries and museums with you; but you will be curious to know what impression the great works of art have produced on me. Six or eight of the most cele-brated easel pictures of the world are in the Vatican. They are kept in a room by themselves, for the convenience of being copied. The Transfiguration is at their head; and the Communion of St. Jerome is placed at its side, as its great rival. Of these pictures I prefer the last; though the delineation of an old man certainly admits most of the trickery of the art. I think, were the choice mine, I would select many pictures before the Transfiguration. Still, it is a great picture, and in some respects, perhaps, unequalled. Its beauties, too, are of a high order, being principally intellectual, and its faults are more mechanical. I must think, however, that this picture owes a portion of its great reputation to the fact that it was the last the artist painted; and he died, as one may say, with its subject in his mind.

Most of the statuary is placed in long galleries, through which one walks for hours with absorbing interest. The precision and nature with which the ancients wrought brutes is surprising; more especially dogs in attitudes which, while they are both natural and beautiful, are seldom long maintained. This skill denotes a German minuteness that one hardly expects from the Romans. But the most precious of the statues are in a tribune, beautifully arranged as to light, and so placed as to permit the spectator, virtually, to see but one at a time. This is a great improvement on the ordinary gallery disposition; for the crowd of objects usually causes confusion rather than delight, on a first visit. A great number of grave-stones of martyred Christians have been collected, and are preserved here. They are recognised by the cross, which, it is known, was carved on them.

Certainly, it was a sensation when I first found myself in the gallery of this tribune,—perhaps it is better to call it a colonnade, or a portico. This place contains many minor attractions; but its principal works are the Apollo, the Laocoon, the Antinous, with the Perseus,—and the Boxers of Canova.

It is unfortunate that the Perseus should be so near the Apollo, for the points of resemblance are sufficiently obvious. This latter statue surpassed all my expectations, familiar as one becomes with it by copies; and yet it is now conjectured that it is itself merely a copy! I write with diffidence on so delicate a point; but such is the suspicion that it is whispered so loud that any one may hear it. It is said it has been ascertained that the marble is of Carrara,—a circumstance that at once destroys its Greek origin. If this be a copy, the original was probably of bronze, and is now corroding somewhere in the earth, if, indeed, it be not melted down. The polished roundness of this statue, which shows a pretty even surface for want of muscles, may account for a copy of so much beauty. The expression is principally in the attitude, which might be imitated with mathematical accuracy; and though the most pleasing, and, in some respects, the noblest statue known, I should think it one of those the most easily reproduced by skilful artists. For your comfort I will add, that the casts and copies of this statue that are usually seen in America bear some such resemblance to the original as a military uniform made in a country village bears to the regulation suit ordered by government and invented by a crack town-tailor. You get the colour, facings and buttons, with such a cut and fit as Providence may direct.—The Dying Gladiator and the Faun are in the collection of the Capitol. I think this distribution of the *chefs d'œuvre* unfortunate.

Whatever may be the truth as respects the Apollo, one would find it almost impossible to believe the Laocoon a copy; though I believe the profane have whispered even this calumny. There are one or two good copies of this work, but it struck me that no one could closely imitate the surface. It is true, we have no original to compare it with, and may fancy that perfect which, strictly, would prove to be otherwise; for men are often deceived in the details, when there is great merit in the principal features of a work. Certainly, I think the Laocoon the noblest piece of statuary that the world possesses.

Pliny mentions this statue, or at least one of the same nature, as the masterpiece of Grecian art that was then to be found in Rome. He ascribes it to *three statuaries!* If this fact were well authenticated, I should hesitate about believing it anything more than a copy from the bronze.—Is not Pliny's authority enough, you may be inclined to ask, to settle a question like this?—I think not. Pliny wrote about the year 90. Winckelmann refers this statue to the age of Alexander the Great, who died four centuries earlier. Now, you may judge how much more likely Pliny, in the condition of the world in his time, would be, than we ourselves, to get at the truth of a similar fact of as old date. Europe is filled with pictures that the imputed artists never saw. The celebrated "Belle Jardinière" of the Louvre is said to be a copy surreptitiously obtained by Mazarin; and I remember one day, when admiring the beautiful Marriage of St. Catharine, in the same gallery, to have been almost persuaded against my will that it was a copy, and yet Correggio has not been dead three centuries.

While writing this letter, I find proof of the doubtful character of authorities. The work of Mrs. Starke is well known, and it certainly has great merit in its way. This lady, however, like most of her sex, has no definite notions of distances, surfaces, &c. Few mere writers have; for they usually are not practical people. In speaking of the Vatican, Mrs. Starke, whom I had consulted with the hope of being able to give you something in feet and inches, says, "its present circumference is computed to be near *seventy thousand feet.*" To adopt this lady's own mode of expressing admiration, "!!!!" A mile contains five thousand two hundred and eighty feet; and this will make a circumference of rather more than thirteen miles, which is but little short of the circuit of the existing walls of Rome. Seven thousand feet may be true; though even that appears a large allowance to me.

As respects the comparison between manuscripts and books, the latter are more to be depended on for accuracy, since, although liable to errors of the press, the number of the editions leaves more opportunities for correction than the system of publishing by written copies. The last edition of a standard work is always chosen for its correctness, especially if printed during the author's life; but who can say when the few manuscripts of Pliny that we possess were written out? when, or by whom, or under what correction? To lay much stress, therefore, on a fact that must necessarily be traditional, or taken at second-hand, and which rests altogether on the testimony of a book, is far from safe. There are things of public notoriety in particular places, at the time of their publication, on which a writer may generally be trusted; but when we come to matters of second-hand intelligence, or which are less notorious, it is wiser to believe a circumstance, than to believe a sentence in a book, however well turned. If the Apollo be truly of Carrara marble, for instance, it is scarcely probable it can be a Grecian statue, and then it is at once reduced to the rank of a copy; for no Roman sculptor could have made it. The alternative is to suppose it the work of some Greek, in Italy. It is just possible, it is true, that a block of Carrara marble may have found its way to Greece; but, admitting this, it would scarcely have been used by the artist of *the* Apollo, on an original of so much merit and importance.

The fresco painting of the Last Judgement, by Michael Angelo, in the Sistine Chapel, is one of the most extraordinary blendings of the grand and the monstrous in art. You know the anecdote of this painter's coming into the Farnesina Palace here, when Raphael was employed on its celebrated frescoes, among which is the Galatea, and finding no one in the room, by way of contempt for the prettiness of the divine master, his sketching a gigantic head in a cornice with coal. This head still remains, Raphael having had the good-nature not to disturb it, and every one sees it as a proof of the rivalry of these celebrated men. Michael Angelo has painted the Last Judgement with the same ideas of the grand as he sketched the Farnesina head. It is not a pleasing picture, the subject scarcely admitting of this; but it is certainly an extraordinary one. I never see the works of these two men without thinking what an artist Buonarotti would have made had he possessed Raphael's gentleness and sensibility to beauty; as one is apt to fancy what Shakspeare might have done with Milton's subject, had he enjoyed the advantages of Milton's learning and taste. There would have been no stealing from Virgil, through Dante, in the latter case.

I refer you to the regular books for the detailed accounts of the treasures of art with which not only the Vatican, but all Rome abounds, my own gleanings being intended for little more than my own feelings and ruminations.

Letter XXV.

THE Princess V[olkonskaya], a Russian, now in Rome for her health, has lately given a pic-nic on Monte Mario,—if that can be called a pic-nic to which but few contributed.—A pic-nic on Monte Mario! This was not absolutely junketing *in* a ruin, but it was junketing *over* a ruin, and but for the amiable patroness I should have been very apt to decline the invitation. As it was, however, the* Chigi—not the *prince*, but the *horse* of the princely breed—was bestridden, and away I galloped, two or three hours before the time. By the way, I do not remember having anywhere spoken of the usages of Europe, as relates to the modes of ordinary address, except, as I have told you, that, in society, simplicity is a general rule of good taste; a law you know as well as the best here.

The Germans have a long-established reputation for the love of official titles. In this respect they resemble the people of New England, who are singularly tenacious of titles, while they are offensively forgetful of the ordinary appellations of polite intercourse. Thus, the very man who will punctiliously style a thief-taker "Officer Roe," will speak of a gentleman as "Doe," or "Old Doe," or "Jim Doe," or as one of his intimates. "Well-born," "nobly born," and such terms, are common enough among the Germans, used by the inferior; but woe betide the

---

*The Italians use this article very familiarly in speaking of persons. They say *the* Pasta, and even *the* Borghese and *the* Chigi, in speaking of the Princesses of those names. But this is not often done by people of breeding. The custom of speaking of female artists, such as Mademoiselle Mars, without using the prefix of Madame, or Signora, is deemed *mauvais ton*, I believe: certainly, it is not common among the better classes, though quite common among the cockney genteel, especially among those who have travelled just enough to be preeminently affected.

wight who forgets to give a man his official title! In France there is little of this; though, in business, titles are given freely. M. le Préfet, M. le Sous-Préfet, M. le Sergent, even, are common French styles of address; but, in society, one hears little of all this,—nothing, it might be said. Military titles, below that of general, are scarcely ever given. This arises from the fact that most officers are, or were, nobles, and their private appellations are thought the most honourable. The same rule exists, more or less, in England. There is at Rome, now, an Englishman of my acquaintance, who lately left a card with "Lt. Colonel" on it; and when I expressed to him my surprise that he should never have used this title before, he answered that until lately he was on half-pay, but that now he was attached, though his regiment was in another country, of course. In private, I never heard him called Colonel; and I presume half his acquaintances here, like myself, were ignorant, until lately, that he was in the army at all.

The common Italians are prodigal of titles. Almost every gentleman is styled "your excellency," and some of the addresses of letters that one gets are odd enough. Beyond this, the same simplicity exists as is found elsewhere.

To return to Monte Mario. It is a place to which I often go, and lately I was lucky enough to enjoy the spot all alone. There is an avenue lined by poplars, along the brow of the hill; and here I took my station, and sat an hour lost in musing. This hill does not impend over Rome absolutely as Montmartre overlooks Paris; but still it offers the best bird's-eye view of it that can be obtained from any height, though not better than can be had from St. Peter's, nor, in some respects, as good a one as is seen from the belfry of the Capitol. Still, it is a beautiful and impressive scene, and one takes it, pleasantly enough, in a morning ride.

On my mind, the comparison between Rome, as she now is, and one of our own large towns, has irresistibly forced itself on all such occasions. New York, for instance, and the Rome of today, are absolutely the moral opposites of each other; almost the physical opposites too. One is a town of recollections, and the other a town of hopes. With the people of one, the disposition is to ruminate on the past; with the people of the other, to speculate eagerly on the future. This sleeps over its ruins, while that boasts over its beginnings. The Roman glorifies himself on what his ancestors *have* been, the American on what his posterity *will* be.

These are the more obvious points of difference—such as lie on the surface; but there are others that enter more intimately into the composition of the two people. The traditions of twenty centuries have left a sentiment on the mind of the Roman, which a colonial and provincial history of two has never awakened in the Manhattanese. The people who now live within the walls of Rome are a fragment of the millions that once crowded her streets and Forums; whereas they who bustle through the avenues of New York would have to hunt among themselves to find the children of the burghers of the last generation. *Rome*, like Troy, *was;* but it does not seem that *New York*, though accumulating annually her thousands, is ever *to be*.

The learned, the polished, the cultivated of every people flock to Rome, and pay homage to her arts, past and present; while the inhabitant still regards *them* as the descendants of the barbarians. Money on one side, and necessity on the other, are gradually changing this contempt; but traces of the feeling are still easily discovered. An American, here, had occasion to prefer a request to this government lately, and the functionary addressed was told by a Roman that the applicant would be sustained by his countrymen. "What is America but a country of ships!" was the haughty answer. What is a ship to a cameo?

We are deemed barbarians by many here who have less pretensions than the Romans to be proud. They who crowd our marts appear there only for gain, and they bring with them little besides their money and the spirit of cupidity. A Roman, in his shop, will scarcely give himself the trouble to ascend a ladder to earn your *scudo;* but, let it be known in Gath that one has arrived having gold, and he becomes the idol of the hour. Nothing saves his skin but the fact that so many others come equally well garnished.

Rome is a city of palaces, monuments, and churches, that have already resisted centuries; New York, one of architectural expedients, that die off in their generations, like men. The Roman is proud of his birthplace, proud of the past, satisfied with the present, proud of being able to trace his blood up to some

consul perhaps. In New Yc rk, so little is ancestry, deeds, or anything but money esteemec., that nearly half of her inhabitants,
so far from valuing themselves on family, or historical recollections, or glorious acts, scarcely know to what nation they properly belong. While the descendants of those who first dwelt on
the Palatine cling to their histories and traditions with an affection as fresh as if the events were of yesterday, the earth probably does not contain a community in which the social relations,
so far as they are connected with anything beyond direct and
obvious interests, set so loosely as on that of New York.

"Which of these two people is the happiest," I said to myself,
as my eye roamed over the tale-fraught view; "they who dream
away existence in these recollections, or they who are so eager
for the present as to compress the past and the future into the
day, and live only to boast, at night, that they are richer than
when the sun rose on them in the morning?" The question is
not easily answered; though I would a thousand times rather
that my own lot had been cast in Rome, than in New York, or in
any other mere trading town that ever existed. As for the city of
New York, I would "rather be a dog and bay the moon, than
such a Roman."

The Roman despises the Yankee, and the Yankee despises
the Roman;—one, because the other is nothing but a man who
thinks only of the interests of the day; and this, because that
never seems to think of them at all. The people of the Eternal
City are a fragment of the descendants of those who, on this
precise spot, once ruled the world; of men surrounded by remains that prove the greatness of their forefathers; of those to
whom lofty feelings have descended in traditions, and who, if
they do not rise to the level of the past themselves, do not cease
to hold it in remembrance: while the great emporium of the
West is a congregation of adventurers, collected from the four
quarters of the earth, that have shaken loose every tie of birthplace, every sentiment of nationality or of historical connexion;
that know nothing of any traditions except those which speak of
the Whittingtons of the hour, and care less for any greatness
but that which is derived from the largeness of inventories. The
first are often absurd, by confounding the positive with the
ideal; while the last never rise far enough above the lowest of
human propensities to come within the influence of any feeling

above that which marks a life passed in the constant struggle for inordinate and grasping gain.—"Dollar, dollar, dollar, dollar; lots, lots, lots, lots!"

I repeat, that the earth does not contain two towns that, in their histories, habits, objects, avocations, origins, and general characters, are so completely the converse of each other, as Rome and New York. If the people of these two places could be made, reciprocally, to pass a year within each other's limits, the communion would be infinitely salutary to both; for while one party might partially awake from its dream of centuries, the other might discover that there is something valuable besides money.

How much longer Rome will stand, is a question of curious speculation. I do not remember to have seen a single edifice in the course of construction within its walls; those already in existence sufficing, in the main, for its wants. The long supremacy of the Papacy, succeeding so soon to that of the Empire, has been the means of bringing Rome down to our own times; else would the place have most probably been an utter ruin. The palaces of the great nobility, many of whom still possess large estates—the general advancement of Europe in taste, and in a love for art and antiquities, which induce crowds from other countries to resort hither—and the traffic in cameos, mosaics, statuary, and castings, which adds to the other receipts of the place, will probably suffice to keep Rome a town of interest for ages to come. Its greatest enemy is the *malaria*, which some people affirm is slowly increasing in malignity and extent annually, while others affirm it is stationary. As the descent towards the sea must, in the nature of things, be gradually lessening, it is quite within the limits of possibility that the fate of this illustrious place should be finally decided by the slow progress of those invisible and mysterious means that Providence is known to use in carrying out the great scheme of creation. After all its wars, and sieges, and conflagrations, Rome will, in all likelihood, finally fall "without hands." If you quicken your movements a little, however, it will probably be in your power to reach this memorable spot in time to anticipate the consummation. Like the often-predicted and much-desired dissolution of the American union, it will not arrive in your time or mine.

Our pic-nic on Monte Mario, all this time, is forgotten. It included Russians, Poles, French, Swiss, Germans, Italians, &c. but no English. I was the only one present who spoke the English as a mother tongue. We had a table placed beneath the trees, and ranged ourselves so as to overlook Rome, while we indulged in creature-comforts *ad libitum*. A thunder-cloud gathered among the Sabine Hills, forming a noble background to a panorama of desolation; but the sun continued to shine on Rome itself, as if to show that its light was never to be extinguished.

Among the guests was a clever Frenchman, who had written a witty work on a journey around his own bed-chamber. By way of a practical commentary on his own theoretical travels, he was now making the tour of Europe, in a gig!

Letter XXVI.

W<small>E</small> have had the Carnival, with its follies and fun, and are now in the Holy Week. During the former, the Papal Government relaxes much of its severity, admitting of balls, masquerades, ballets, and operas. Although Rome has several theatres, it is not allowed to open them unless in these seasons of licensed gaiety; the clerical character of the government imposing observances, that are not much attended to elsewhere.

The public masquerades take place in the theatres. One, in particular, in our immediate neighbourhood, is much frequented for such purposes, and the music alone repays one for the trouble of dressing and masking. The pit and stage are floored, so as to form an immense sala; and the boxes, which in Europe are almost always separated from each other by partitions, are privately hired by families and parties to sit in unmasked. I confess to the folly of preferring a mask, though my ambition has never yet tempted me to go beyond the domino. These places contain the usual proportions of warriors, Greeks, peasants, doctors, which are a favourite character at Rome, devils and buffoons. The Italians are a people of strong humour, and they act their parts, on the whole, better than most other nations; though a masquerade, at the best, is but a dull affair, it is so much easier to find money to cover the body with a rich dress, than brains to support the character!

A ludicrous occurrence to myself took place at one of the masquerades in the theatre mentioned. The families that occupy the lower tier of boxes are commonly of the middle classes, as the floor is so high as to destroy everything like retirement in them. The masks pass them, of course, and stop, at will, to converse with those who are not masked. Passing one of these boxes, I was struck with the singular beauty of a girl of about seventeen. Her costume was exceedingly pretty, and her face the very *beau idéal* of all that was classical and perfect. I was so much charmed with her appearance, that I went in quest of two or three friends, that they might not lose so rare a sight as a perfect beauty. The admiration was general, and the beauty received our homage with a coy consciousness that served to heighten her charms. At length the party to which she belonged left the box, and made its appearance in the sala. Two of us followed it with a view of getting a nearer sight of the beauty, in order to ascertain whether we could detect any blemish or not. As I was quite near her in the crowd, she spoke, and then, like Slender in the Merry Wives of Windsor, I discovered, by as croaking a voice as ever sang discordantly in the throat of fifteen, that "it was a great lubberly boy!" A classical outline, fine eyes, paint, and dress, had deceived us all. The effect of these masks is such, at times, as to render the legends of romance less improbable than sceptics fancy.

I have been amused at meeting several of our own people in these scenes who would hesitate about being seen in them in America. One may judge of the amount of freedom in private actions, in the land of steady habits, in particular, by watching the course of its children when out of it. A boyish freak came over W[illiam], an evening or two since, on observing a clergyman of New England standing in the midst of the dancers and masks, and he resolved to trot him. He went up and told the parson, in broken English, that there was a person there who was looking for him in every direction, and, if he was willing, he, W[illiam], would conduct him to the place where the other might be found. The parson consented, with a good face, and he was forthwith led up to and introduced to the most conspicuous devil of the evening. The priest took the thing goodnaturedly, and W[illiam] left him with his regular enemy, to battle the matter as best he might. I do not mention this circumstance with a view to censure this gentleman for being at a masquerade, but simply to contrast it with what is done at home. Cant never yet aided true religion, or protected morals, but, like the supervision of meddlers, it is certain to make hypocrites —the most odious of all sinners. This parson was a liberal at home; a fact that is infinitely to his credit.

I have been struck with the singular beauty of the women who appeared in the streets of Rome during the last week of the Carnival. Most of them are of the middling classes; but, as they appear in open daylight, there cannot be much deception about them. They have all the delicacy of American women, with better busts and shoulders, and are by no means wanting in colour. Their appearance is also singularly feminine and modest.

Certainly, in no place in which I have yet been are the gaieties of the Carnival conducted with so much spirit as here. The young strangers join in the fun with as much gusto as the natives, and it is impossible not to laugh at the follies that are committed. A usage that is peculiar to the Romans, consists in pelting each other with an imitation of sugar-plums. The gravest men may be seen passing in their carriages, and suddenly jumping up and casting a handful of these small shot into each other's faces. Not satisfied with this, a sort of artillery has been invented, by which they may be thrown with so much accuracy and force as to render a volley annoying. The young English here have appeared in cars made to resemble ships, with crews of ten or a dozen, dressed as sailors; and when two of these cruisers get yard-arm and yard-arm,—for the two lines of vehicles pass in different directions,—there are commonly exchanges of vigorous broadsides. Every one that can, engages a room that overlooks the Corso; and the windows and balconies are filled with ladies, who when they are not kissing their hands to their friends below, are busied in powdering them with sugar-plums. Altogether, one is singularly inclined to play the fool; and I feel satisfied that these *fêtes* contribute to the good-fellowship and kind feelings of a population. The police takes good heed that there shall be no serious horse-play; and some of the sugar-plum artillery even has been suppressed, as likely to lead to more serious contests. Any one who should resent a volley of sugar-plums, when fairly in the field himself, would be deemed a silly and ill-natured churl. It is rumoured here, that a challenge has passed in consequence of some shots; and, although the parties were delicately situated previously, the challenger is generally condemned as an ill-natured fellow who had no business in the streets.

The celebrated races, of which we had several in the last week, resembled those of Florence, though conducted with more spirit. The horses run about a mile, in the midst of a dense crowd, who excite them by shouts and gestures. You know, there are no riders, but leathern thongs are attached to a back-strap, that is secured by a crupper and a girth; and these thongs are loaded with balls of lead which contain short iron spikes, very sharp, that act as spurs, by being thrown about with the motion of the animal. This apparatus *seems* cruel; but, after all, it can be no worse than the armed heel of the jockey, or the lash. It is true, these balls are constantly in motion; but I do not think they inflict very grave wounds.

The race itself is a puerile thing; but there is something terrific in the mode of clearing the street previously to the start. Imagine a straight, narrow street, that is literally crammed with people. A platoon of horse gendarmes appear at one end, and commence clearing the way on a trot. Presently, this trot becomes a gallop; and then these ten or twelve men, riding knee to knee, and uncommonly well, dash through the crowd as fast as their horses can carry them. The people retire before them as water recedes from the bows of a ship in a gale; and, at times, it would seem that escape was impossible. Accidents occasionally happen, but they are rare. I have regarded this as much the finest part of the exhibition.

But the most *amusing* part of the street scenes of the Carnival is the last act. As the sun sets, every one appears with a light or two. These lights are usually tapers made for the occasion, but sometimes they are torches. Every one is privileged to extinguish his neighbour's light. Common street-masquers will clamber up on the carriage of a prince, and blow out his taper, which is immediately relighted, as if character depended on its burning. Some clamber up even to the balconies to effect their purpose, and others drop shades from them to extinguish a light. There is something extremely ludicrous in seeing a grave person carefully protecting his taper from an assailant in front, who merely amuses him while an extinguisher on a long stick advances from behind and cautiously descends on the flame. Every one laughs, and the defeated man joins the merriment and relights. This scene is called the *moccoletti*, and it is said to be a remnant of some of the Roman Saturnalia.

The calm of Lent succeeded to the fun and clamour of the Carnival. I ought to have said, however, that the people of quality terminate the festivities by meeting in *petits comités* and supping *gras*. The observances of the Lent have not struck me as being much more rigid than elsewhere, though the religious rites have been more general, and were conducted with greater pomp than is usual, even among the Catholics. When Passion Week arrived, however, we saw we were in the centre of Christendom. Palm Sunday was a great day, all the cardinals appearing in the Sistine Chapel, bearing palms. On this occasion, an Englishman, a Mr. Weld, appeared as a cardinal; the first of his nation, I believe, since the death of Cardinal York. This gentleman was a layman, has been married, and has descendants now in this place. He is a man of fortune, and of one of the old English Catholic families.

Several popular errors exist in relation to the rules of the Romish Church. The canonical orders are precisely the same as our own, being merely those of bishop, priest, and deacon. All above and below these are merely additions, which, it is admitted, have been devised by the Church, for its own convenience, in the way of government; just as the Church of England has created archbishops, archdeacons, deans, vicars, rectors, curates, &c. The Archbishop of Canterbury and the Pope, in a religious sense, are merely bishops. It is not necessary, I believe, that a cardinal should be even in holy orders at all. Most of them are, but I understand the rule is not absolute. I do not know that Mr. Weld has ever been ordained. The functions of a cardinal are properly of a civil nature, though they are intimately connected with the government of the church. They are ecclesiastics, and cannot marry; but it is said cardinals have retired, and then married. One or two of these have been named to me.

It is usually, almost invariably the case, that the Pope is taken from the Holy College; but it is not constitutionally necessary. You or I might be elected pope; but, previously to induction or installation, we should be required to enter the Romish Church by Romish baptism, and then pass through the several orders of deacon, priest, and bishop. The Pope is bishop of Rome in a canonical sense, and, in virtue of that office, head of the Roman Catholic Church. The cardinals are classed among themselves as cardinal bishops, cardinal priests, and cardinal deacons; but this is not their clerical rank. Thus, Cardinal Fesch, who is archbishop of Lyons, appears in the list as only a cardinal priest.

Cardinal Albani, the secretary of state, is a cardinal deacon, has no bishopric, and was once married. I presume he is not even in holy orders.

The notion that the Pope must be an Italian is false, of course, there being no constitutional restriction on the choice of the Holy College.

The ceremonies that succeeded those of Palm Sunday have been imposing and rich, and the music of the highest character. But these things have been too often told to find a place in these desultory gleanings. One thing, however, has astonished me: I mean the indecent and pertinacious pushing of strangers. There is a corps of halberdiers here, composed of Swiss. One of these men is of great strength and stature, and I saw the poor fellow in a premature purgatory, endeavouring to keep back the English women, who pressed for admittance into a room that was not ready to receive them. The perspiration rolled from him in streams, and finally he gave up the point in despair. It is necessary to have witnessed such a scene to believe it possible.

Towards the last, we had the Benedictions. There were two of these ceremonies, on one of which the Pope blesses Rome, and on the other, the earth. The latter was very imposing. The ambassadors went in state, as well as all the high nobility; and seats were prepared around the great altar in St. Peter's. Vast as this edifice is, it was well garnished with human faces; but it will scarcely do to say it was crowded. The Pope appeared among us, borne on men's shoulders, amid waving plumes, in a chair of gold—that is to say, famously gilt.

The benediction is given from a balcony in the front of the church, and the people are in the area between the colonnades. The space is sufficient for ten times the number that collected. The colonnades, too, are occupied, and in one of them I took my station. Observing a respectable-looking black man behind me, curious to know who he could be, I took an occasion to address him in French. He answered me imperfectly; and I tried Italian, but with little better success. Of English he knew nothing; but he threw me into the shade by commencing a conversation in Latin. I was too rusty to do much at this, but I understood enough to discover that he was a Romish priest from Africa—probably connected with the Propaganda. When I told him I was an American, he looked at me with interest, and I thought he was as much astonished at my colour as I could possibly be with his. What a missionary for America!

The ceremony of the benediction, though solemn and grand, is confined to mere gestures, so far as the people beneath are concerned. The voice of the Pope cannot be heard, but his gestures were graceful and pleasing. The Catholics kneeled, but the Protestants did not; to my surprise, for the blessing of no good man is to be despised. There is too much of the "D—n my eyes! change my religion? never," of the sailor, in us Protestants, who seem often to think there is a merit in intolerance and irreverence, provided the liberality and respect are to be paid to Catholics. He who comes voluntarily into a Catholic ceremony is bound to pay it suitable deference; and then, God is omnipresent. I never saw anything wrong in kneeling to the Host; for, while we may not believe in the real presence as to the wafer itself, we are certain that a homage to God himself can never be out of place or out of season. All men would be of the same way of thinking, had not politics become so much mixed up with religion.

If you ask for the general impressions left by these ceremonies, I answer, that these people appear to me to be the only people I know who are perfectly drilled in such things. The vastness of the edifices, the richness of the dresses, the works of art, the music, and the consciousness that one is in the heart of Christendom, serve to heighten the effect; and yet, after all, the soul of worship, it struck me, was sadly wanting. I have seen a decent solemnity in the congregation of our own little Christ's Church at C[ooperstow]n, that left a deeper impression than all the laboured pageantry of St. Peter's at Rome: and you know I am not of the class that has no sympathies with another parish. Want of reverence in the manner—the hurried and undignified mode in which the Romish offices are usually performed, and the obvious fact that the audience were assembled as curious observers, rather than as those who joined in the worship, were sad drawbacks on the more sublime sentiments that properly belong to such occasions.

The celebrated Illumination greatly surpassed my expectations. The vast dome is ribbed with lights, so disposed as to delineate all the grand outlines of the architecture, as are also the façade of the church itself and the colonnades. Knowing the magnitude of these edifices, you may fancy, in a degree, the effect. The lights are rich and full, suited to the scale of the buildings; and the rapidity with which they are set in a blaze, as it were in an instant, is truly astonishing. It is not literally true that *all* the lights appear at the same moment, for a great number of small lamps, which equally trace the lines of the architecture, are lighted while there is still day, and they appear gradually as the darkness advances, forming a very pretty spectacle of themselves. But a second set of lamps, or torches, of a different kind, blaze out at once at an appointed hour, when these fainter lamps form secondary lines to the tracery of the exhibition. No illumination that I have ever witnessed at all approaches this in magnificence; nor does any other show the same dramatic effect in lighting up. The word *instantly* is not to be taken literally either, for I dare say two or three minutes pass before the whole structure is illuminated; but this time is really so short, and the effect is so very great, that one does not stop to count moments amid the blaze of magnificence. The effect is like that of furling sails in a man-of-war. Time is taken, certainly; but so much is done in a minute, that it seems to the uninstructed as if all were done in a moment.

The fire-works of St. Angelo were also the richest I have ever seen. There was a volcano that surpassed all my previous notions of the powers of this branch of art. But the climate of Italy greatly favours this species of exhibition.

XIII. *The Capitol, Rome, and the Church of the Ara Coeli*, engraved by William Bernard Cooke

xiv. *Interior of an Upper Corridor of the Coliseum*, drawn by Colonel James Patrick Cockburn and engraved by W. B. Cooke

XV. *Interior of the Pantheon, Rome*, drawn by David Roberts, A.R.A., and engraved by Frederick Smith

xvi. *Venice*, drawn by James Baker Pyne and engraved by S. Bradshaw

Letter XXVII.

$\mathbf{A}$FTER five delightful months passed at Rome, the moment for departure arrived. Every one waited to the end of the Holy Week, and then every one seemed impatient to fly. We delayed a few days, in order to visit Tivoli, and a few other places that had been neglected; and then we reluctantly drove through the Porta del Popolo, with the rest of them. Our own carriage, drawn by four active white horses, and a carriage of the vetturino, drawn by four sturdy brown ones, made the cortège. I took the vetturino carriage on account of its conveniences; for it was roomy, and rendered a *fourgon* unnecessary.

The first stage was altogether on the Campagna, and it brought us to an insignificant village where we breakfasted. The road was lined with carriages, but some knowledge of horse-flesh had given us cattle that passed everything but the post-horses. Now, you are to know that the throngs on the highway, just at this moment, are so great as to render it a matter of some importance who reaches the end of a stage first. At the house where we breakfasted was an English post-chariot, drawn by three horses, and containing three people besides servants; the master wearing a particularly expressive countenance, that induced my children to name him the *Grognon*. He scolded a little about his breakfast, which was certainly anything but excellent, and preceded us on the road. The man appeared to have screwed himself up to a week of grumbling.

The country for the rest of the day was volcanic, and, although it was still a plain, it was more cultivated and habitable than the Campagna had been. Soracte appeared on our right, and we were gradually working our way into its rear. The stopping-place for the night was Cività Castellana. This town, like Sorrento, has a natural ditch formed by the crevices of the volcanic rock. When we entered its principal square, I thought all the vetturini carriages in Italy had got there before us. My man, however, drove boldly up to the best inn, where only a carriage or two were visible, and, winking, he told me to be prompt.

I sought the landlord, whom I found in hot discourse with the *Grognon*, concerning certain rooms, the best he had. These rooms, he swore volubly, were already bespoke by a gentleman who had sent a courier from Rome for that express purpose. This much I overheard as I approached, and thought it augured ill. In the mean time, the rogue looked out of the window, and perceiving that, including postilions and servants, we were a party of eleven, with eight horses, he drew in his head, and exclaimed, "Ah! this is the very gentleman. Here, Signore, this is the apartment that you can have. I am very sorry for this other Signore, but he must be satisfied with those rooms opposite. You know *you* have bespoken these."

Though ready to laugh in the fellow's face, I did not deem it necessary to enter into explanations with the Englishman, but, asking pointedly of the innkeeper, if I could have these rooms, and receiving a satisfactory answer, I took possession of them with a determination not to be easily ejected. The *Grognon*, who now began to merit his title, was obliged to succumb, though I believe he suspected the truth. I went on the principle of doing as I *should have been* done by.

Every one was off with the dawn, the carriages streaming out of the gate of Cività Castellana in a line like that of the baggage of a regiment. We took the lead, and soon had the road to ourselves. A bridge carried us over the Tiber, and we began to ascend the Apennines. We breakfasted on their side at a hamlet, and, leaving the horses to bait, I walked ahead. It was a solitary wild mountain road, though perfectly good; and I soon fell in company with a party of pilgrims on their return from Rome. These men carried the staves and scrips, and wore a species of light cloak, with the capes covered with scallops. They were conversable, and anything but solemn or way-worn. They had been employed in some of the recent ceremonies of the Church.

When the carriages came up, we had a wild picturesque country, especially about Narni, where were also some Roman remains. Here we descended into a beautiful valley; and in the bottom are the remains of a fine bridge of the time of Augustus. Passing through vineyards, olive-trees and fruit-trees, we reached the little city of Terni, a place of six or seven thousand

souls, and which is prettily placed on the river Nera, in the centre of a very fertile region. This is the country of Tacitus.

Although still early, we drove to an inn, and secured good
lodgings; after which we proceeded to the falls. The latter lie
more than a league from the town, as we found to our cost, for
we made the mistake of undertaking to walk to them. We luckily got a few asses on the road; though W[illiam] and myself
walked the entire distance there and back.

These celebrated falls are artificial, having been made by the
Romans some centuries before Christ, by turning the course of
a pretty little stream. They are reputed the finest waterfalls in
Europe; a quarter of the world that, while it has many cascades,
has few fine cataracts. These of Terni are between the two, being insignificant for the last, and large for the first. Those of
our party who have seen the Falls of Trenton think them much
finer than these of Terni; but I have never seen the first myself.
There is a "method in the madness" of these falls that I think
slightly impairs their beauty, though very beautiful they are.
The thing at Tivoli will not compare with them; but I am told
the falls of Tivoli have been much injured by some public
works. This, you know, is the case with the Cohoes.

Between Terni and Spoleto, next day, we had another reach
of mountains, and of mountain scenery. There are Roman remains at the latter place, which is prettily placed on a rocky and
irregular hill that is thought to be an extinct crater. An aqueduct, that is called Roman, has arches of the Gothic school, and
is probably a work of the middle ages. There is also a high
bridge across a valley, that communicates with a hermitage; a
proof of what religious feeling can effect even when ill directed.
There is a poetry, notwithstanding, about these hermitages that
makes them pleasing objects to the traveller. I may have seen,
first and last, a hundred of them in Europe, though many are
now untenanted: these of Italy are generally the finest.

At Spoleto there was another rush of coaches, and the *Grognon*, looking war and famine, made his appearance at the same
inn as ourselves. The scuffling for breakfast and rooms was
sufficiently disagreeable, though, preceding all the others, we
escaped the *mêlée*.

The valley beyond Spoleto was very beautiful. On one side
there is a *côte*, as the French term it, and houses and churches

were clinging to its side, almost buried in fruit-trees. While trotting along pleasantly, beneath this teeming hill-side, we came up to a small brick edifice that stood near the highway, and between it and the meadows, which had spread themselves on our left, more like a country north, than one south of the Alps. This little building was about the size of the small temples of the Campagna so often mentioned, and, like them, it is, beyond question, of Roman origin. It is called the Temple of Clitumnus, from the circumstance of its standing at the sources of that classical stream; but is now a Christian chapel. You would be surprised to find these temples so small, for this makes the twentieth I have seen, all of which are still standing, that has not been much larger than a large corn-crib. The workmanship of this is neat but plain; though it is probable that its marbles have shared the fate of those of so many amphitheatres, theatres, forums, and temples that are found all over Italy. It is with these ruins as with our departed friends: we never truly prize them until they are irretrievably lost.

We reached Foligno in good season, and, by a little manœuvring, managed to get nearly the whole of a retired but very respectable inn to ourselves. As we intended to diverge from the beaten path at this point, we now flattered ourselves with being so far out of the current, that we should no longer be compelled to scuffle for our food, or to wrangle for a room or a bed.

Letter XXVIII.

THE day was just dawning as we drove through the gate of Foligno. Until now we had merely skirmished with the outposts of the Apennines; but here we were compelled to cross the great ridges, as had been done in the year 1828, between Bologna and Florence. All eyes looked curiously ahead, as, having passed some distance into a gorge by the side of a stream, we began to ascend a winding road where the nakedness of the hills permitted us to see a mile or two in advance; for everybody was anxious to know whether any of the great flight were likely to take the same direction as ourselves. Nothing was seen, and we went our way rejoicing.

This passage of the Apennines is called the Col Fiorito, and although the road is good and the mountains are not Alpine, the ascent is long and sharp. We alighted and walked two or three miles before we gained the summit of the pass. Before we reached the top, however, I gave a look behind us, and was half amused and more vexed at seeing the eternal yellow chariot and three horses of the *Grognon* toiling its way up after us, perhaps a league in our rear! It appeared as if the man had come this way expressly to bring matters *à outrance*.

This sight quickened our movements, for it was understood that breakfast, which everybody was in a good humour to enjoy, must be had in a poor mountain hamlet, or delayed until afternoon. Luckily, when we took this alarm, we had little more climbing to do, and our road was nearly all descent to the village; whereas our pursuers would be obliged still to walk an hour before they could break into a trot. This made the betting in our favour, "Lombard-street to a china orange."

In an hour we were at the inn door. A boy was put on a horse and despatched for milk, for you may have wine in Italy when you cannot get milk. Lucie was sent into the kitchen with a biggin, (not the cup, but the coffee-pot,) and in twenty minutes everybody was at table, and, literally, every eatable in the house, bread excepted, was devoured. I had been informed that two roasted fowls might be had at a sort of eating-house in the village, and these were also secured, and eaten, by way of precaution against a rescue.

Breakfast over, we left the inn and were about to walk ahead of the carriages, as the chariot and three came rolling down the declivity into the village. Seeing us apparently in possession, the *Grognon* thrust out his head, gave a growl and an order, and the equipage moved proudly on, as if it disdained stopping. We followed, telling the servants they would find us on the road below. To our surprise, at the bottom of the hamlet we met the *Grognon* and his party on foot, walking sulkily back towards the inn, with the manner of people humbled by misfortune, and yet not totally above indignation. The last house was the eating-house in question, and stopping to inquire, we discovered that he had heard of the two roasted fowls, in Foligno probably, and finding us at the inn, had pushed on to seize these devoted birds, which, alas! were already eaten. Necessity has no law, and this gallant man was compelled to subdue his stomach, lest his stomach should subdue him. We sympathized with his situation, precisely as the well-fed and contented are apt to sympathize with the unlucky and hungry; or, in other words, we determined that, in an extremity, one might breakfast even on bread. W[illiam] affirmed that the man was rightly served;— "Let him take a fourth horse, instead of compelling three to drag that heavy chariot up these mountains, if he wish to eat chickens."

The road was beautiful the remainder of the day. It had at first a sort of camera-lucida wildness about it; a boldness that was quite pleasing, though in miniature, after the grandeur of the Alps; and as the day drew towards a close, we rolled, by a gradual and almost imperceptible descent, into a lovely region, affluent in towns, villas, hamlets, and all the other appliances of civilized life. This was in the March of Ancona, and our day's work terminated at Tolentino, a place celebrated for one of Napoleon's early negotiations.

Tolentino stands on an insulated hill, in the midst of a beautiful but broken country, and it struck us as a place more important as lying near this pass, than from any other cause. The

Serra valle, a gorge in the road above, has a reputation, but it is not of Swiss frightfulness. Earlier in the spring and in winter, however, the passage of the Col Fiorito is a matter of more gravity. Starvation was the only danger on this occasion. We watched impatiently the arrival of the *Grognon*, but he disdained entering within the walls of Tolentino that night.

The fine country continued next day, the road being principally a descent until we rose another eminence, and stopped at Macerata. This was once the capital of the March, and the Adriatic became visible from the inn, a silvery belt in the horizon, distant some eight or ten leagues. All the towns in this district appear to be built on isolated hills, that once admitted of being strongly fortified. As other hills are all around them, however, the circumstance is of little use as against modern warfare. Of these towns, we passed two after breakfast, one of which, Recanati, stands on a ridge, the ascent to and descent from which were like *Montagne des Russes*.

About three in the afternoon we came to the foot of another ridge, that runs at right angles to the coast of the Adriatic, from which it might be distant a league. The ascent was longer and easier than that of Recanati; and having overcome it, we found ourselves in a village of a single long street, that was terminated by a pretty good square and a large church, with other ecclesiastical edifices, of pretty good architecture, and which were tolerably spacious even for the States of the Church. These were the village and the celebrated shrine of Loretto, a spot that formerly filled a place in the Christian world second only to Jerusalem.

The books say Loretto contains five thousand souls: my eyes would reduce this number one half, but it may be true nevertheless. It is simply, not to say meanly, built, the ecclesiastical edifices excepted; and, as at Einsiedeln, in Schwytz, most of the small houses are either inns, or shops for the sale of rosaries and other similar accessories of Catholic worship. We took rooms—no *Grognon* near—ordered dinner, and went forth to see sights.

The Church of Loretto is of better architecture than that of Einsiedeln, but scarcely so large. Its riches and construction are Italian, which it would be hardly fair to the latter to put in competition with those of the Cantons. It stands at the head of the square, and on its left stretches a large pile, which I believe is the palace of a bishop, and a library; and partly facing the church are other buildings connected with the establishment, for many ecclesiastics are kept here to do the service of the shrine. There are many chapels within the church, and some of them are curious by their associations.

The *Santa Casa* itself, or the shrine, as you most probably know, is affirmed to be the house of Joseph. It stands near the centre of the church, which has been erected around it, of course, as an honourable canopy. The house is also cased externally with Carrara marble, wrought beautifully, after designs of Bramante. It is ornamented with sculpture, that represents scenes from the history of the Mother of Christ. The original wall, which is exposed in the interior, where little is concealed, is of brick, pieces of stone being intermixed, as was much practised formerly in Europe, whatever may have been the case in Palestine. It is fair to presume it was a general usage. The image of the Virgin, which is separated from those within the house by a grating, is said to be made of the cedar of Lebanon, and it wears a triple crown. It is gorgeously attired, bears a figure of the Child in one arm, and has the bronzed, mysterious countenance that it is common to find about all the more renowned altars of Mary. There is a small fireplace and a solitary window. By the latter the angel is said to have entered at the Annunciation. The dimensions of the house of Joseph are about thirty feet long, fourteen wide, and near twenty high. If there ever was an upper room, no traces of it remain.

The history of this shrine, as it is given in a little book sold on the spot, is virtually as follows:—The house, of course, was originally built in Nazareth, where Jesus was reared. In 1291, angels raised it from its foundations and transported it to Dalmatia. Here it remained between four and five years, when it was transferred to Italy by the same means. It was first placed in a wood near Recanati, on the land of a lady named Laureta; whence the present name of Loretto. The road to it being much infested by robbers, the angels again removed it a short distance, leaving it on the property of two brothers. These brothers quarrelled and fought about the profits of the pilgrims, who began to frequent the shrine in throngs, and both were killed; whereupon the house was finally removed to its present site.

Various physical proofs are alleged in support of this history.

The house in Nazareth is said to have disappeared, and the foundation to have remained. This foundation and the house, it is affirmed, correspond as to fractures, materials, and dimensions; and, I believe, some geological proof is also adduced, in connexion with the materials.

What is one to think of such a history? Do they who promulgate it believe it themselves; or is it a mere fiction invented to deceive?—*Can* it be true? Certainly it might, as well as that this earth could be created, and continue to roll on in its orbit.—*Is* it true? That is certainly a great deal more than I shall presume to affirm, or even to believe, accompanied with circumstances of so little dignity, and facts so little worthy of such a display of Divine power.—Do the people themselves, they who frequent the shrine, believe it? Of that I should think there is little doubt, as respects the great majority.—I cannot express to you the feelings with which I saw my fellow-creatures kneeling at this shrine, and manifesting every sign of a devout reliance on the truth of this extraordinary legend. One woman, a well-dressed and respectable female to all appearances, was buried in the recess of the fireplace, where she remained kneeling, nearly an hour, without motion!

Loretto is no longer much frequented by pilgrims from a distance. Formerly, the treasury had the reputation of being immensely rich, and a garrison was maintained in the place to guard it. There are, even now, the remains of military defences around the church, which stands at a point where the rock falls away rapidly towards the Adriatic. It has been said, the popes availed themselves of these riches at different times; and it is pretty certain most of them have disappeared since the period of the French invasion. The French bear the opprobrium of having despoiled the shrine; but it is quite as probable that they were anticipated; for who that knew their career in Upper Italy would have waited, on such an occasion, until the enemy was at the gate? Little remains; though we saw some things of price in the treasury, several of which were quite recent gifts from royal personages.

There is an infirmary for the pilgrims annexed to the establishment, and I went into it to see some designs of Raphael's that were painted on the jars and other vessels which held the medicines. They are extraordinary things in their way, and prove that the divinity of the school of Raphael is not the divinity of an anchorite. These gallipots, and the house near the *Porta del Popolo* at Rome, exhibit the author of the Transfiguration, very much as Ovid betrays his taste in the Metamorphoses, and Juvenal his in his Satires.

We passed the night at Loretto, where we purchased sundry rosaries made of shells from the adjoining coast, candles, *agnus dei*, and other memorials of the place, all of which were properly authenticated by a certificate.

I cannot discover how far the Church of Rome at this day attaches importance to belief in the history of the Santa Casa. It is not now, and probably never was, a matter essential to communion with the Catholic Church, though it certainly did receive support from the head of the Church at one time. So far as I can discover, intelligent Catholics, especially those out of Italy, wish to overlook this shrine, which, they say, may be believed in, or not, as one credits or discredits any other legend of ancient date. Its history is not sacred, and it is not obligatory to put faith in it. Certainly, I should say, that the more enlightened Catholics, even here, regard the whole account with distrust: for he who really believed that God had made such a manifestation of his will, would scarcely hesitate about worshiping at the shrine, if he worshiped at all, since the building would not have been transferred by a miracle without a motive. It is fair, then, to suppose that few among the intelligent now put any faith in the tradition; for it is certain few of that class continue to make pilgrimages to the spot. The time will probably come when shrine and legend will be abandoned together.

The next day's work was short, carrying us only to Ancona. The road was through a pleasing country, and some of the views, especially towards the mountains, were exceedingly beautiful. The eastern faces of the Apennines, like the southern faces of the Alps, appear to be more precipitous than those of the reverse side. The summit of the range was now white with snow, while the entire foreground offered an exquisite picture of verdure and sunny fertility, imparting to the view, notwithstanding the principal elements were the same, peculiarities that were not often observable among the Swiss peaks. There was a warmth in the tints—a softness that, though it left the

brilliancy, destroyed the chill of the summits,—and, all together, a gentleness of atmosphere and a calm about this landscape,
that I do not remember to have ever witnessed in Switzerland,
except on the Italian side of the mountains.

Ancona is only some sixteen or eighteen miles from Loretto.
We got in, therefore, early, and had an opportunity to examine
the place. The port is formed, in part, by the bluff against the
side of which the town is principally built, aided by a mole of
considerable extent. A part of this mole is very ancient, for
there is an arch on it, which was raised in honour of Trajan,
though it is vulgarly called the Arch of Augustus. Another arch,
farther advanced, shows that the popes have greatly added to
the work. The harbour is pretty and safe, but it appears to want
water. Here we first stood on the shores of the Adriatic. The
colour of this sea is less beautiful than that of the Mediterranean; its waters having a stronger resemblance to those of our
own coast than to those of the neighbouring sea.

The view was fine from the promontory above the town; but
I looked in vain for the opposite coast of Dalmatia. There is a
cathedral on this height, and in it a picture of great merit by
Guercino, an artist little appreciated by those who have not visited the States of the Church. This town is pretty well fortified,
and seems intended for a military post of some importance.

On leaving Ancona next morning, we commenced a journey
of some twenty or thirty leagues, nearly every part of which was
within a mile or two of the Adriatic, and much of it so near
as to give us constant views of that sea. The first stage was to
Sinigaglia, a pretty little town with a sort of a port; for all the
places along the shore have some pretension to be considered
sea-ports, although the coast is a low sandy beach, almost without points, or bays, or headlands: a small creek has usually
sufficed to commence a harbour, and by means of excavations,
and perhaps of a small mole at the outlet, to prevent the accumulation of sands by the south winds, the thing has usually
been effected. Some of the connexions of the family of Bonaparte reside in or near Sinigaglia, which has many good houses
in its vicinity.

We passed the night at Fano, a town of several thousand
souls, in which there are some respectable Roman remains,

though of the later periods of the empire. The next morning we went to La Cattolica, a small and insignificant place, to breakfast; passing Pesaro, a place of more importance, without stopping.

We saw the remains of a considerable castle near La Cattolica, which had once belonged to the Dukes of Urbino, and is even now, I believe, kept up as a sort of fortress of the pope's. It was rather a striking structure of the sort for Italy; this country not being at all remarkable for buildings of this nature. One reads of moated castles among the Apennines in Mrs. Radcliffe's novels; but I have not yet seen an edifice in all Italy that would at all justify her descriptions. Such things may be, but none of them have lain in my path. With the exception of the Castel Guelfo, near Modena, and the regular forts and citadels, I do not remember to have seen a moated building in the whole country. Some of the castles on the heights are gloriously picturesque, it is true, of which that of Ischia is a striking example; but, on the whole, I should say few parts of Europe have so little embellishment in this way as Italy. The Romans do not appear to have built in the castellated form at all, it being a fashion of the middle ages; and during the latter period, most of the fastnesses of this part of the world were made out of the ruins of Roman works. At all events, after passing near two years in Italy, and traversing it from Nice to Naples, and from Naples to this point, I have not seen the castles of the romances at all.

The English novels in general, more particularly those written a few years since, give very false notions of the state of the Continental society; as, indeed, do those of the Continent give false notions of that of the English. Nothing, for instance, can be more outrageously absurd than Richardson's story of Clementina, in Sir Charles Grandison, which betrays an entire ignorance of Italian usages. But Richardson evidently knew very little of the better classes of his own country; for though lords and ladies in his time may have worn wigs and hoops, they were not the arrant coxcombs and formalists he has made them.

This morning, walking ahead of the carriages, we amused ourselves for several hours on the beach. I felt what wanderers we had truly become, when I beheld the children I had seen gathering shells on the coast of America, on the shores of the Mediterranean, and those of the North Sea, now amusing themselves in the same way on the beach of the Adriatic. We quitted the duchy of Urbino and entered the Romagna, as it is called, near La Cattolica.

The scenery improved as we advanced, the mountains drawing nearer to the coast, and the foreground becoming undulating and verdant. We had the sea always on our right, and seized every good occasion to stroll on its beach. Our day's works were easy, the towns lying at convenient distances asunder, and, what rendered this part of the journey more pleasant, not a travelling vehicle of any sort was met on the road: even the *Grognon* had vanished, a defeated man.

The second night from Ancona we slept at Rimini. At this town the Emilian and Flaminian Ways joined each other; for we had followed, most of the distance from Rome, the great route of the ancients between the capital of the world and Cis-Alpine Gaul. Here is still a triumphal arch in honour of Augustus, and a bridge as old, or nearly as old, as his age. They show a tribune, also, from which it is said Cæsar harangued the people the morning after he had passed the Rubicon! There was, at least, something manly in the audacity of this tradition.

At Rimini we witnessed a ceremony that a two years' residence in Italy had never before given us an opportunity of seeing. There had been a long drought; and a procession, in which hundreds of the peasants from the adjoining country appeared, was made to implore rain at different shrines. A Madonna of repute was borne in front, and great devoutness and faith were manifested by those who followed. There is probably no essential difference between these prayers and those of our own Church for a similar favour; though the formalities observed on this occasion were singularly addressed to the senses. I was amused by observing that the clouds looked dark and menacing over the Apennines, and that these ceremonies were commenced under good omens. And yet it did not rain! I do not know, after all, that we are to consider these ceremonies as possessing more virtue in the eyes of the Catholics than our Church prayers possess in our own: it is but another form of petition.

Not far from Rimini is a high mountain that stands insulated from the great range of the Apennines. It is irregular in form, and a small town is seen near its summit, while, all together, it appears rather more cultivated and peopled than is common for the hills. This is San Marino, the oldest republic of Christendom. It had been my intention to visit the place, but indisposition prevented me. The territory includes the mountain and a small hilly district at its base, with a population of about five thousand souls. I was told at Rome by one who had ruled the Romagna, that this little community betrayed a good deal of jealousy of its independence, and that its government was believed to be very justly administered. Of course, such a State exists only by sufferance: the pope can, at any moment, imprison the whole community, by forbidding them to trespass on his States. At this point the Grand Duchy of Tuscany extends to the summits of the Apennines, coming within a very few leagues of the Adriatic.

It is a matter of dispute where the Rubicon really is. The inhabitants of Rimini say it is the Marecchia, the small river that is spanned by the ancient bridge I have mentioned; while those of Savignano claim the honour for the Pisatello, a still smaller stream that runs near their place. I believe the prevalent opinion is in favour of the latter; and there is certainly a monument near the road to say as much. The first, notwithstanding, is the most plausible-*looking* stream for a boundary, as it runs nearly in a direct line across the narrow neck of land that lies between the mountains and the sea. These things are often arbitrary; but, were any one to reason coolly on probabilities, I think he would select the Marecchia for the Rubicon. As the great roads commenced and terminated at this point, it renders it still more likely that this was the Rubicon. Emilius or Flaminius would be more likely to commence such works at a frontier, than at a few miles distant. *Au reste*, I am too ignorant of the learned part of the question to give an opinion.

The stream that commonly passes for the Rubicon (the Pisatello) is a mere rivulet that certainly offered to Cæsar no other obstacle than that of the prohibition, as it might be forded with dry knees. We breakfasted, the day we left Rimini, at Cesena. This is the country of the Malatesta family; and the place contains some works of the middle ages, that are still in tolerable condition. We had now diverged from the sea, and were fairly on the great plain of Lombardy, though still in the Romagna. The road ran nearly parallel with the mountains, which here quitted the Adriatic to cross to the other sea, leaving the whole of the wide country between their bases and those of the Alps, in the vast plain of which I have already spoken. We slept at Forli, a town of some size, and which we found neat and convenient. At all these places we amused ourselves with looking at pictures, cathedrals, and ruins; but none are of sufficient note to call for an especial mention of them. Our stages were short, and the road from Ancona to Bologna was almost without hills. Forli was the Forum Livii of the ancients, and, of course, was on the Emilian Way, which pursued nearly, if not precisely, the route of the modern road. All these great highways are kept in excellent repair; and it is not easy to find any country in Europe that has better post-routes than Italy. Indeed, most of Europe is well off in this particular; France, perhaps, ranking among the least favoured countries in this respect, notwithstanding all the praises that have been lavished on Napoleon because he caused an inlet to be made, here and there, into his conquered provinces. It is true, Italy owes the Emperor much in this respect; but the motive is too apparent to render his benefactions fit themes for eulogium. A man who left the roads between his own capital and its nearest towns in a condition to break half the carriage-wheels that pass over them, is to be distrusted when he constructs a garden-path across the Alps. This conduct reminds one of those zealots who are for converting the heathen, and who neglect their own neighbourhoods. In the one case, it is the love of excitement and a morbid zeal; while in the other, however, it was a cool and selfish calculation.

We passed Faenza next day without stopping, having become wearied with seeing towns of ten and twenty thousand souls. This place is known for its pottery wares; whence the French word *faïence*. At Imola we breakfasted. This was another of the Forums (that of Cornelius); and the town is said to lie on the verge of the plain of Lombardy, though in truth this plain ought to commence at Rimini, if not at Ancona. Here the poplars began to show themselves; though this tree is much more abundant in France than in the country from which it has derived its American name. Indeed, I am not sure one did not see more poplars in America twenty years ago than are now seen here; though everybody seems as anxious to be rid of the tree to-day, as our fathers were to procure them. It is said at home, that the dead naked tops which are so common in the poplar, are owing to there not being a sufficient intermingling of the sexes; but the same peculiarities are observed in Europe.— From Imola we drove to Bologna, which we reached in good season.

The distance between Ancona and Bologna is one hundred and thirty-five miles, which we had passed in four easy days' work, with scarcely a hillock on the whole road, with the exception of a little broken ground between Sinigaglia and Pesaro. Most of the country was beautiful; and the Apennines the whole time relieved the monotony of a plain. In its way, it has proved to be one of the pleasantest journeys we have yet made in all Europe.

Letter XXIX.

OUR stay at Bologna was short, for we were fearful of being too late in the season for Venice. The first day's work was to Ferrara, which place we reached early, having left Bologna with the appearance of the sun. The country was low, and had in places a *reedy* look, bordering on the low marshy lands that environ Ravenna. The whole of the eastern margin of the plain of Lombardy is of this character, the descent from the base of the mountains being constant, as is proved by the rivers, though so gradual as to be imperceptible.

Ferrara has the most deserted air of any considerable town I remember to have seen. It lies on a dead flat, in a grassy, not to say *reedy*, region also. In the centre of the place is a massive gloomy castle surrounded by a ditch, in which the Dukes of the family of Este once dwelt; but we could not enter it. We did visit a cell that has the reputation of having been the prison of Tasso, where we found the name of Byron written on the walls. Such a homage as this may be tolerated; but one dislikes the cockney-isms of writing names on walls. Being no poet, I did not presume to leave mine in the crowd.

The streets of Ferrara are straight and wide; circumstances that render its desolation more apparent. The grass literally grew in them, and I can best compare the town with the portion of Schenectady, that lies off the canal; though allowance must be made for the ancient magnificence of this place. We saw many curious books and manuscripts here, and many memorials of Tasso and Ariosto. A small stream runs through the town; but the whole country, like Holland, while there is no sea visible, appears to be nearly "a wash." It is said to be unhealthy in the autumn, and one can readily believe it.

We were now touching once more on the Austrian dominions. Although Ferrara belongs to the Church, it has an Austrian garrison, for the place is fortified. We reached the Po a short distance from the gates of the town, next morning, and crossed on what is called a flying bridge, or a *ponte volante*. These bridges are common enough in Europe; though, properly speaking, they are ferries. They consist of a large floating stage, or a boat, that can receive several carriages. This is anchored by a long hawser to some ground-fastening, one or two hundred fathoms up-stream; the length of the hawser being, of course, proportioned to the width of the river. To keep the rope above water, it is sustained by more or less small boats, which sheer with the motion of the ferry-boat, or stage. All that is necessary is to let the current take the bows of the latter obliquely, when it sheers across the river, as a matter of course. We crossed, with our two carriages and eight horses, in a very few minutes, and without getting out of our seats.

On the Austrian bank is a custom-house; but we were not detained longer than was necessary to examine the passport. Notwithstanding all that is said against this government, it certainly is not obnoxious to the charge of giving unnecessary trouble, except in cases that have probably excited its suspicion. Despotic governments, moreover, have a power to do polite and kind acts that free governments do not possess. In a government of equal rights, the administration of the laws must be equal, although a thousand cases occur in which this rule works injuriously to those who, it is known, might with safety be exempted from the operation of the rule; but in a government like this, instructions emanating from the power that frames the laws may temper their administration. It is true, this faculty leads often to gross abuses; but, in an age like this, it oftener leads to an exemption from onerous, and, in the particular cases named, useless regulations. It is on this principle that men of known character and pursuits obtain passports that entitle them to proceed without the delays and trouble of the custom-house examinations.

You are not to understand, however, that I had any such privil*_*ge; what I have told you of the *bonhomie* of the authorities in ref*_*rence to my own baggage, is to be taken as general, and in no manner as particular towards an individual. You well know that I am no advocate for any government but that which is founded on popular rights, protected from popular abuses; but I am thoroughly convinced that the every-day strictures on these points that are made by a large portion of our travellers, are conceived in ignorance and prejudice, and are just as worthless as are the common strictures of Europeans on our own institutions. The disposition in every government is to do justice in all ordinary cases, and we are no more peculiar in this wish than the Emperors of Austria and of Russia. The faults of these systems lie much deeper than the surface.

We found Rovigo, where we breakfasted, much smaller certainly, and every way less important than, but with the same air of desertion as, Ferrara. In front of us, after quitting Rovigo, appeared an island of hills in the midst of the plain, and our route lay towards it. At their foot was Monselice, where we passed another night. These hills form an oasis of mountain in the desert of monotony around them. A party of Venetians were at the inn, and the women had brilliant complexions and fair hair; one had hair that was nearly red;—this was a proof that we were drawing near the scene of Titian's works. The Signora Guiccioli, so well known to the admirers of Byron, is of the same style of beauty. It is odd that Raphael, and indeed most of the Italian masters, painted their females as *blondes*, when the prevalent style of the beauty of the women is that of brunettes. Of the eight Americans of our party, I am the only one that has not light hair and a fair complexion; a circumstance that has excited much surprise in this part of the world, where we are deemed to be, *ex officio*, black.

From Monselice we made one stage to Padua, a place that we entered with a good deal of interest. It is a large and, for Europe, a straggling town. As this was the country of Palladio, we here met his architecture. I cannot say I like it so much as I had anticipated. It has more pretension than beauty or simplicity; though it strikes me there is an effort at both. Still, this style is not without the noble. Boston is the only place I know of in America that has anything resembling it in general outline; though Boston has nothing, within my knowledge, that can be truly termed Palladian.

The great hall of Padua pleased us extremely. It is near three hundred feet long, and near one hundred feet wide, though not very lofty. It is the largest room I have seen, with the exception of the galleries. The style is a mixed Gothic, the roof being of open rafters, and the effect is quaint and striking. I prefer it, on the whole, to Westminster-hall: though it is scarcely so noble.

A miracle had just been performed in one of the churches of Padua, a Madonna giving some signs of animation. I went to see it, but found that the visit was ill-timed; the image remaining as immovable as any other image, during the presence of a heretic. I believe these things are much less frequent than formerly, the French occupation not only destroying most of the marvels of religion, but, in a great measure, religion itself. It is a grand commentary on human wisdom and on human consistency, that one may now see a king and his courtiers carrying candles in those streets where rulers appeared in their shirtsleeves attending a trull in the assumed character of the Goddess of Reason! Infidelity no longer comes to us naked; but it wears a mask of philosophy and logic, in the pretended character of a *mitigated Christianity*. The citadel that cannot be stormed, must be sapped.

We took the road to Mestre on quitting Padua. I cannot say that the villas on the Brenta, or the canal, at all equalled my expectation. The houses themselves were well enough; but the monotony of a country as level as Holland, and the landscape gardening that is confined to flowers and allées and exotics, compare ill with the broader beauties of the Hudson, or the finish of the lawns on the Thames. The road and river showed signs of a crowded population, and we were amused in that way, but were scarcely in raptures with a sylvan scene. A part of our road, however, was athwart a sort of common. At this point, looking across the bay on our right, a town appeared rising above the water, singularly resembling the view of New York as seen from the low lands near Powles Hook. The presence of domes and the absence of ships marked the difference between the places; but the likeness was sufficiently strong to strike us all at the same moment. I need scarcely add, that the town was Venice, and that the water was, the Lagoons.

The carriage was housed at Mestre, and the luggage was put into a large gondola. We took our places in the same boat, and in less than ten minutes after reaching the shore, we were all afloat. There was a short river, or creek, to descend,—I know not which it is,—and then we fairly entered the bay. The Lagoon is formed by the deposit of several streams, and the action of the waves of the Adriatic, which have piled long low banks of sand across the broad mouth of a bay, where they have been gradually accumulating from time immemorial. A number of islands formed within this chain of banks, and channels necessarily made their own way for the passage of the waters of the rivers. On these islands the fishermen erected their huts. From this beginning, by the aid of piles, quays, and the accumulations of a seaport, Venice grew to be the Queen of the Adriatic, literally seated in the mud.

We stopped a moment at a small island, about half-way across the Lagoon, to have our passports examined, but met with no delay. The place was barely large enough to hold a building or two, though the effect of this aquatic post-house was odd. Not far from this, the boat passed a line of posts with painted tops, that encircles the whole town, perhaps a mile and a half from the islands. The posts stand a few hundred feet asunder. These are to mark the limits of the place, Venice having just been declared a free port. Of course, the gondola that is caught with unentered goods within these posts would be seized.

After a pull of an hour or more, the boat entered a broad canal that was lined by palaces and noble houses. Passing through this, which proved to be short, it came out in another passage, that seemed to be a main artery of the town, smaller lateral canals communicating with it at short distances. Across the latter we could see, among the dark ravines of houses, numberless bridges trodden constantly by foot-passengers; but across the larger channel, which was the grand canal, there was only one. This was of stone, and it was covered with low buildings. Of course, its length was much greater than that of the others; and its single arch was high and pointed, though not strictly Gothic. As we glided beneath it, vessels that might contend with the Adriatic appeared beyond, the water gradually widening. The bridge was the Rialto; the water, the continuation of the canal, and the commencement of the Giudecca, which is, in fact, the port.

A gondola was lying on its oars as we approached the grand

canal, recognising a boat from Mestre; and as we came up to it, Mr. C[ruger], of Carolina, who had preceded us a day or two, jumped on board, having taken lodgings in expectation of our arrival. Under his guidance we stopped at some stone steps, and disembarked at the *Leone Bianco*.

Letter XXX.

I appeared as if we were in the centre of a civilization entirely novel. On entering the inn, we found ourselves in a large paved hall, but a step or two above the water, in the corner of which lay a gondola. Ascending a flight of steps, we were received in a suite of good apartments, and I ran to a window. Boats were gliding about in all directions, but no noise was heard beyond the plash of the oar; not a wheel nor a hoof rattling on a pavement. Even the fall of a rope in the water might be heard at a considerable distance. Everything was strange; for, though a sailor and accustomed to aquatic scenes, I have never before seen a city afloat.

It was necessary to eat, and I restrained my impatience until after dinner. By this time it was evening; but a fine moon was shedding its light on the scene, rendering it fairy-like. C[ruger] and myself quitted the inn, for he told me he had something that he was desirous I should see before I slept. Instead of taking a boat, we passed into the rear of the inn, and found ourselves in a street. I had heard of the canals, but, until then, believed that Venice had no streets. On the contrary, the whole town is intersected in this way; the bridges of the smaller canals serving as communications between these streets, which, however, are usually only eight or ten feet wide. That we took was lined with shops, and it seemed a great thoroughfare. Its width varied from ten to twenty feet.

Following this passage, in itself a novelty, we inclined a little to the right, passed beneath an arch, and issued into the great Square of St. Mark. No other scene in a town ever struck me with so much surprise and pleasure. Three sides of this large area were surrounded by palaces, with arcades; and on the fourth stood a low ancient church, of an architecture so quaint, having oriental domes, and external ornaments so peculiar, that I felt as if transported to a scene in the Arabian Nights.

The moon, with its mild delusive light, too, aided the deception; the forms rising beneath it still more fanciful and quaint. You will know at once, this was the church of St. Mark.

Another area communicated with the first, extending from it, at right angles, to the bay. Two sides only of this square, which is called the Piazzetta, were built on; the side next the Piazza, or Great Square, and that next the sea, being open. On one of the other sides of this area the line of palaces was continued, and on the other rose the celebrated Ducal residence. This was, if possible, still more quaint and oriental than the church, transferring the mind at once to the events of the East, and to the days of Venetian greatness and power.

On every side were objects of interest. The two large columns near the sea were trophies of one conquest; the ranges of little columns on the side of the church were trophies of a hundred more; the great staircase at which we looked through an arch of the palace were the Giant's Stairs, and the holes in the walls above them the Lions' Mouths! This huge tower is the Campanile, which has stood there a thousand years rooted in mud; and those spars let into the pavement in front of the church are the very same on which the conquered standards of Cyprus and Candia, and the Morea, were wont to flap. The noble group of horses in bronze above the great door, is *the* group, restored at last to its resting-place of centuries.

Passing by the side of the palace of the Doges which fronts the sea, by an arcade walk that lines its whole exterior, which is the celebrated Broglio, where none but the noble once could walk, and where intrigues were formerly so rife, we came to the bridge which spans the canal that bounds the rears of the church and palaces. The covered gallery that is thrown across this canal, connecting, at the height of a story or two above the ground, the palace with the prisons on the other side, was the Bridge of Sighs! By the side of the water-gate beneath were the submarine dungeons, and I had only to look towards the roof to imagine the position of the *Piombi*.

Then there was the port, lighted by a soft moon, and dotted with vessels of quaint rigs, with the cool air fanning the face,—the distant Lido,—and the dark hearse-like gondolas gliding in every direction. Certainly, no other place ever struck my imagination so forcibly; and never before did I experience so much pleasure, from novel objects, in so short a time. A noble military band played in the square; but though the music was, what German instrumental music commonly is, admirable, it served rather to destroy the illusion of magic, and to bring me down to a sense of ordinary things. After passing an hour in this manner, I returned to the *Leone Bianco*, and excited every one's curiosity to see the same things. Poor W[illiam] issued forth immediately; but, after an unsuccessful search in the maze of lanes, he returned disappointed.

The travellers' book was brought me to write my name in; and I find that an American or two who had preceded me have been lampooned, as usual, *in English!* One would think pride, in the absence of good taste, would correct this practice.

Letter XXXI.

W E have left the *Leone Bianco* for lodgings near the Piazza San Marco, where we control our own *ménage*, avoiding the expense and confusion of an inn. I have set up my gondola, and we have been regularly at work looking at sights for the last week. I shall continue, in my own way, to speak only of those things that have struck me as peculiar, and which, previously to my own visit here, I should myself have been glad to have had explained.

In the first place, Titian, and Tintoretto, and Paul Veronese, are only seen at Venice. Good pictures of the first are certainly found elsewhere; but here you find him in a blaze of glory. I shall not weary you with minute descriptions of things of this sort, but one story connected with a picture of Titian's is too good not to be told. You know, the French carried away every work of art they could. They even attempted to remove fresco paintings; a desecration that merited the overthrow of their power. One great picture in Venice, however, escaped them. It stood in a dark chapel, and was so completely covered with dust and smoke that no one attended to it. Even the servitors of the church itself fancied it a work of no merit.

Within a few years, however, some artist or connoisseur had the curiosity to examine into the subject of this unknown altarpiece. His curiosity became excited; the picture was taken down, and being thoroughly cleaned, it proved to be one of the most gorgeous Titians extant. Some think it his *chef-d'œuvre*. Without going so far as this, it is a picture of great beauty, and every way worthy of the master. The subject is the Assumption, which he has treated in a manner very different from that of Murillo, all of whose Virgins are in white, while this of Titian's is red. The picture is now kept in the Academy, and imitations of it are seen on half the ornamented manufactures of Venice.

The Martyrdom of St. Peter, (not the Evangelist,) Sir Joshua Reynolds pronounced a wonder, in its way; but it stands in a bad light, and it did not strike me as a pleasant subject. All Martyrdoms are nuisances on canvass. Like the statues of men without skins, they may do artists good, but an amateur can scarcely like them. The better they are done, the more revolting they become.

We have visited half the churches, picture-hunting: and a queer thing it is to drive up to a noble portico in your gondola, to land and find yourself in one of the noblest edifices of Europe. Then the sea-breezes fan the shrines; and sometimes the spray and surf are leaping about them, as if they were rocks on a strand. This applies only to those that stand a little removed from the bulk of the town, and exposed to the sweep of the port. But St. Mark's is as quaint internally as on its exterior. It is an odd jumble of magnificence, and of tastes that are almost barbarous. The imitation mosaics, in particular, are something like what one might expect to see at the court of the Incas. The pavement of this church is undulating, like low waves—a sort of sleeping ground-swell. C[ruger] thinks it is intentional, by way of marine poetry, to denote the habits of the people; but I fancy it is more probably poetic justice, a reward for not driving home the piles. The effect is odd, for you almost fancy you are afloat as you walk over the undulating surface. St. Mark's, if not the very oldest, is *one* of the oldest Christian churches now standing. There were older, of course, in Asia Minor; but they stand no longer,—or if they do stand, they have ceased to be Christian churches.

Lady Mary Wortley Montagu says, if it were the fashion to go naked, the beauties of the human *form* are so much superior to that of the *face*, that no one would regard the latter. Clothes have produced a different effect on the art of painting. All the painters who create or revive their art commence with the countenance, which they paint well long before they can draw the form at all. You may see this in America, where the art is still in its infancy, in one sense; many drawing good heads, who make sad work with the body and the hands. The works of the old masters exhibit heavenly countenances on spider's limbs, as any one knows who has ever seen a picture by Giotto. A picture here, by the master of Titian, has much of this about it; but it is a gem, after all. John of Bellino was the painter, and I liked it better than anything I saw, one fresco painting excepted.

Some of the carvings of the churches, that are in *high relief*, surpass anything of the sort I have ever seen; and, in general, there is an affluence of ornaments, and of works of merit, that renders these edifices second to few besides those of Rome. A monument by Canova, that was designed for Titian, but which has received a new distinction by being erected in honour of the sculptor himself, is an extraordinary thing, and quite unique. Besides the main group, there are detached figures, that stand several feet aloof; and the effect of this work, which is beautifully chiselled out of spotless marble, beneath the gloomy arches of a church, is singularly dramatic and startling. One is afraid to commend the conceit, and yet it is impossible not to admire the result. Still, I think, the admirable thought of Nahl renders his humble Swiss tomb the sublimest thing in Europe.

What shall I tell you of the famous palaces? They are more laboured externally, and have less simplicity and grandeur than I had expected to see; but many of them are magnificent houses. All stand on a canal, very many on the principal one; but they all extend far back towards the streets, and can be entered as well by land as by water. There is a large vestibule or hall below, into which one first enters on quitting the gondola; and it is very usual to see one or more gondolas in it, as one sees carriages in a court. The rooms above are often as rich as those of royal residences, and many capital pictures are still found in them. The floors are, almost invariably, of the composition which I have already mentioned as resembling variegated marble. A much smaller proportion of them than of those at Rome appear to be regularly occupied by their owners.

You may suppose that I have had the curiosity to visit the renowned Arsenal. It stands at one end of the town, and of course commands the best water. The walls enclose a good deal of room, and ships of size can enter within them. An Austrian corvette was on the stocks, but there was no great activity in the building-yard. A frigate or two, however, are here.

There is a museum of curious objects attached to the Arsenal, that is well worth seeing. Among other things, we saw plans and even some of the ornaments of the Bucintoro, which is broken up, the sea being a widow. One does not know which is the most to be pitied, *la Veuve de la grande armée*, or the bereaved Adriatic.

I have told you nothing of the gondolas. The boats have a canopied apartment in the centre, which will contain several people. Some will hold a large party, but the common gondola may seat six in tolerable comfort. With the front curtain drawn, one is as much concealed as in a coach. The gondolier stands on a little deck at the stern, which is ridged like a roof, and he *pushes* his oar, which has no rullock, but is borne against a sort of jaw in a crooked knee, and may be raised from one resting-place to another at will. It requires practice to keep the oar in its place, as I know by experience, having tried to row myself with very little success. By his elevated position, the gondolier sees over the roof of the little pavilion, and steers as he rows. If there are two gondoliers, as is frequently the case, one stands forward of the pavilion, always rowing like the other, though his feet are on the bottom of the boat. The prow has a classical look, having a serrated beak of iron, that acts as an offensive defence.

The boats themselves are light, and rather pretty; the mould, a little resembling that of a bark canoe. The colour is almost invariably black; and as the canopy is lined with black cloth, fringed, or with black leather, they have a solemn and hearse-like look, that is not unsuited to their silence and to the well-known mystery of a Venetian. There is something to cause one to fancy he is truly in a new state of society, as his own gondola glides by those of others with the silence of the grave, the gentle plashing of the water being all that is usually audible. My gondolier has a most melodious voice, and the manner in which he gives the usual warning as the boat turns a corner is music itself.

The private gondolas are often larger, and on great occasions, I am told, they are very rich. The livery of a private gondolier used to be a flowered jacket and cap; and a few such are still to be seen on the canals.

Of course we have visited the cells, the halls of the Ducal Palace, and the *piombi*. There are several Lions' mouths, all let into the wall of the palace, near the Giant's Stairs; and the name is obtained from the circumstance that the head of a lion is

wrought in stone and built into the building, the orifice to receive the paper being the mouth of the animal.

The Square of St. Mark is a delightful place of resort at this
season; I pass every evening in it, enjoying the music and the
sports. Here you can also see that you are on the eastern confines of Europe, Asiatics and Greeks and European Turks fre-
quenting the place in some numbers. There is one coffee-house,
in particular, that appears to be much in request with the Mus-
sulmans, for I seldom pass it without finding several grave tur-
baned gentlemen seated before it. These men affect Christian
usages so far as to sit on chairs; though I have remarked that
they have a predilection for raising a leg on one knee, or some
other grotesque attitude. They have the physical qualifications,
in this respect, of an American country buck, or of a member of
Parliament, to say nothing of Congress.

The attempt to revive the importance of Venice, by making it
a free port, is not likely to result in much benefit. It requires
some peculiar political combinations, and a state of the world
very different from that which exists to-day, to create a commercial supremacy for such places as Venice or Florence. Venice does not possess a single facility that is not equally enjoyed
by Trieste, while the latter has the all-important advantage of
being on the main. The cargo brought into Venice, unless consumed there, must be re-shipped to reach the consumer; or,
vice versâ, it must be shipped once more on its way from the
producer to the foreign port, than if sent directly from Trieste.
A small district in its immediate vicinity may depend on Venice
as its mart, but no extended trade can ever be revived here until
another period shall arrive when its insular situation may make
its security from assault a consideration. A general and pro-
tracted war might do something for the place, but the prosper-
ity that is founded on violence contains the principle of its own
destruction.

I have been so much struck by the beauty of the composition
floors that are seen here in nearly every house, as to go to the
mechanics, and to employ them to let me see the process of
making them. Enclosed you have the written directions they
have given me. In addition to this I can add, that the great point
appears to be beating the mortar, and to put it on in separate
layers. The time required to make a thoroughly good floor of

this kind is about two years, though one may suffice; and this, I well know, will be a serious objection in a country like our own. Their great beauty, however, their peculiar fitness for a warm climate, and the protection they afford against fire, are strong inducements for trying them. As they can be carpeted in winter, there is no objection to them on account of the cold: indeed, if properly carpeted, they must be warmer than planks, insomuch as they admit no air when thoroughly constructed.

I have now been in Europe four years, and I have *seen* but *two* fires, although most of my time has been passed in London, Paris, Rome, Florence, Naples, &c. &c. It is true, some portion of this exemption from alarms is to be ascribed to the system of having regular corps of firemen, who are constantly on duty, and who go noiselessly to work: but, after making every allowance for this difference, and excluding New York, which is even worse than Constantinople for fires, I am persuaded there are ten fires in an ordinary American town, for one in a European. The fact may be explained in several ways, though I incline to believe in a union of causes. The poor of America are so much better off than the poor of Europe, that they indulge in fires and lights when their class in this part of the world cannot. The climate, too, requires artificial heat, and stoves have not been adopted as in the North of Europe, and where they are used, they are dangerous iron stoves, instead of the brick furnaces of the North, most of which receive the fire from the exterior of the room. But, after all, I think a deficient construction lies at the bottom of the evil with us. Throughout most of Europe, the poor, in particular, do not know the luxury of wooden floors. They stand either on the beaten earth, coarse compositions, stones, or tiles. In Italy, it is commonly the composition; and you may form some idea of the consistency to which the material is brought, by the fact that good roofs are made of it.

It is the misfortune of men to push their experiments, when disposed at all to quit the beaten track, into impracticable extremes, and to overlook a thousand intermediate benefits that might really be attainable. Every one, of any penetration or common sense, must have seen, at a glance, that the social scheme of Mr. Owen was chimerical, inasmuch as it was destructive of that principle of individuality by which men can be induced to bestow the labour and energy that alone can raise a community to the level of a high civilization,—or when raised, can keep it there. Still his details suggest many exceedingly useful hints, which, by being carried out, would add immeasurably to the comfort and security of the poor in towns. What a charity, for instance, would a plan something like the following become!—Let there be a company formed to erect buildings of great size, to lodge the labouring mechanics and manufacturers. Such an edifice might be raised on arches, if necessary, with composition floors. It might enjoy every facility of water and heat, and even of cooking and washing, on a large scale, and, of course, economically. The price of rooms could be graduated according to means, and space obtained for the exercise of children in the greater area of so many united lots. Even entire streets might be constructed on this community-plan, the whole being subject to a company-police. Here, however, the community principle should cease, and each individual be left to his own efforts. America may not need such a provision for the poor; but Europe would greatly benefit by taking the practicable and rejecting the impracticable features of the Owen System. Among other benefits, there would be fewer fires.

Letter XXXII.

ALTHOUGH Venice was so attractive at first, in the absence of acquaintances it soon became monotonous and wearying. A town in which the sounds of hoof and wheel are never known, in which the stillness of the narrow ravine-like canals is seldom broken, unless by the fall of an oar or the call of the gondolier,—fatigues by its unceasing calm; and although the large canals, the square, and the port offer livelier scenes, one soon gets to feel a longing for further varieties. If I do not remember to have been so much struck with any other place on entering it, I do not recollect ever to have been so soon tired of a residence in a capital. It is true, we knew no one, nor did any one know us; and an exclamation of pleasure escaped me on suddenly meeting the *Grognon*, in the Piazzetta; a pleasure which, I regret to say, did not seem reciprocal. But he had just arrived.

We took boat daily for the last week of our residence, living on the water, and among the palaces and churches. I was surprised to find that the Adriatic has a tide; for banks over which we have rowed at one hour, were bare a few hours later. In all this place, there are but two or three areas in which the population can seek the air, except by resorting to the canals and the port. Napoleon caused a garden to be planted, however, near the northern extremity of the town, which will eventually be a charming spot. It is larger than one might suppose from the circumstances; and here only can a Venetian enjoy the pleasures of verdure and shade.

You will be surprised to hear, that, by the Rialto of Shakspeare, one is not to understand the *bridge* of that name. This bridge is divided into three passages, by two rows of low shops, which are occupied by butchers and jewellers (a droll conjunction), and the height has rendered broad steps necessary to make the ascents and descents easy. Some travellers describe a small platform on the summit of the bridge as the Exchange, or the place where Shylock extorted gold. I believe this is altogether a misconception. The Rialto is the name of the island at one end of the bridge, and on this island the merchants resorted for the purposes of business; and "meeting me *on* the Rialto," did not mean, on the *bridge*, but on the *island*, after which island the bridge, in fact, is named. Mr. Carter, among others, seems to have fallen into this error.

> "I stood in Venice on the Bridge of Sighs,"
> &c.   &c.   &c.

is pure poetry. This bridge is thrown across the narrow dark canal that separates the Ducal Palace from the Prison, and is, in fact, a covered gallery. The description of

> "A palace and a prison on each hand,"

though bad grammar, is sufficiently literal. It is bad grammar, because there are *not* a palace and a prison on *each* hand, but a palace on one side and a prison on the other. As poetry, the verse is well enough; but you are not to trust too implicitly to either Shakspeare or Byron, if you desire accuracy. The remainder of the description is not to be taken as at all faithful, though so very beautiful. It is morally, but not physically true. The Bridge of Sighs, if open, would be one of the worst places in all Venice to obtain the view described. I mention this, not as criticism, for as such it would be hypercriticism, but simply that you may understand the truth.

> "Her palaces are crumbling to the shore,"

is also exaggerated. One or two buildings have been destroyed for the materials, I am told; and one palace remains half demolished, the government having interfered to save it. At least, such is the account of my gondolier. But, beyond this, there is little apparent decay in Venice, except that which is visible in the general inactivity of the business of the port and town.

The accounts that there are passages for foot-passengers along the margin of the canals is also untrue. Such may be the fact in particular spots, but it is by no means true as the common mode of communication by land. I have seen places on the Grand Canal where one may walk some distance in this manner; but it is on planks raised against and secured to the houses for the purpose, and not by any permanent footways. The intercourse by land is in the centre of the different islands, access being had to all the principal buildings both by land and by water, as I have told you before. On the side of the canals, the boats touch the door-steps, while in the rear narrow alleys serve as outlets. Most of these alleys are only four or five feet in width. These, again, communicate with the streets, which are usually very narrow. Perhaps half the buildings do not touch a canal at all, especially the smaller shops and dwellings.

You may imagine the effect of the celebrated regattas of Venice by considering the situation of the Grand Canal. This is a small river in appearance, a little winding to relieve the monotony; and it is literally lined with the large buildings that in Italy are called palaces. Every window has its balcony. The terms 'canals' and 'lagoons' are, however, misapplied as respects the bay and channels of Venice. You know, of course, there are no gates, which we are apt to associate with the idea of a canal, though improperly; but it is the land that is artificial here, and not the water. The Grand Canal is not unlike the letter S in its direction, and it widens sensibly near the port, which is a broad estuary between the islands of the town and the Lido.

This Lido is the bank that protects the Lagoon from the Adriatic. It is long, low, and narrow, and is not entirely without vegetation. There are a few houses on it, and in one or two places something like villages. Most of the islands, of which there are many that do not properly belong to the town, are occupied; one containing a convent with its accessories, another a church, and a third a hamlet of the fishermen. The effect of all this is as pleasing as it is novel; and one rows about this·place, catching new views of its beauties, as one rows round and through a noble fleet, examining ships. Still, Venice must be left, the warm weather admonishing us to retire; and I am now actually occupied in the preparations necessary to a departure.

Letter XXXIII.

A novel mode of travelling was suggested to me, and I determined to try it, merely to compare it with the others. In most of the countries of the Continent, the governments control the diligences, or public coaches, which are drawn by post-horses. In the Austrian States one can travel in the diligences at his own hours, provided a certain number of places are paid for. The size of my family admitting of this, I have come up from Venice to Innspruck in that mode; the advantages being those of paying once for all at Venice, of travelling entirely under the authority of the government, and of not being under the necessity of wrangling with the postilions. The disadvantage, as I have since discovered, was that of paying considerably more than I should have done, after quitting Italy, had we come post in the old way. In Lombardy we had no difficulty, postmasters and postilions conducting themselves admirably; but in the Tyrol it was a constant scene of wrangling about hours and horses. I shall not repeat the experiment, after we have fairly crossed the Alps.

We left Venice quite early, in a public boat, being now fairly in the hands of government. At Mestre we found our own carriage, and, entering it, we were soon furnished with four horses and two postilions. The latter cut a strange figure, in yellow coats and cocked hats. They were perfectly civil, however, and we soon found ourselves in Padua.

Changing horses, we now diverged from our old route, taking the road to Vicenza, where we dined. The country was not so tame as Lombardy is in general, and we were rapidly approaching the advanced hills of the Alps. Still, the road, a good one in every sense, ran along a very even surface.

Vicenza is the city of Palladio, and a house he built for himself, a small but tasteful edifice, and a theatre of his own on a new plan, were shown us. This theatre, instead of the ordinary painted scenery, had a real perspective, and houses and streets, *en petit*, as one sees them in a town. This invention was founded in hypercriticism. A play is, at the best, but a conventional and poetical representation of life, like a romance, a statue, or a picture; and while it is properly subject to laws that are founded in nature, this nature may, in all, be respected to absurdities. Who but a bungler would put eyes in a statue, give a real perspective to a picture, rigid nature instead of its *beau idéal* to a romance, or real streets to a theatre? The common scenery is sufficient to the illusion we require; for, like the unities, after all, a theatrical street, which of necessity must be contained in a single house, is but a conventional street. The thing, as a matter of course, was a failure.

After quitting Vicenza, the country became even prettier, and we passed a few small towns. It was still early when we came in sight of a town lying in part against the side of a hill, with ancient walls and other objects of a picturesque appearance. The environs were particularly verdant, and altogether the place had a more lively and flourishing air than any city we had seen since quitting Bologna. This was Verona, the end of our journey for the day. We had done near a hundred miles since morning, with great ease to ourselves, having almost crossed the whole of the ancient Venetian-Italian States.

Although this town stands on the great plain of Lombardy, it is at its commencement, and at the point where the Adige issues from among the Alps, to incline eastward before it throws its waters into the Adriatic. We found a genteel and good inn, as well as neatness and perfect civility. After giving our orders, we sallied forth to see the only two things of which our 'time would allow,—the amphitheatre, and the tomb or sarcophagus of Juliet, for you will remember we were now in the country of the Montagues and the Capulets.

The amphitheatre stands on an area in a corner of the town, where it is seen to great advantage. Unlike the Coliseum, it is perfect, or nearly so, on the exterior, so that one can get an accurate notion of its general effect. The interior, also, is almost as perfect as that at Pompeii; and as the building is much larger, it may be included among the greatest of the works of the kind that have descended to our own times. There is a portion of it set apart for theatrical representations, by the erection of a stage and enclosing a few of the seats; and, truly, the difference between the scale of a Roman arena and that of one of our own modern edifices is here made sufficiently manifest. I do not wish to be understood that this temporary little theatre is of extraordinary dimensions; but still it is large enough to contain an ordinary audience. It struck me as being more intended for *spectacles* than for the regular drama. It had no roof, though I was told the climate admits of representations at night in it. We see the same thing in New York during the summer months.

Perhaps the dimensions of the amphitheatre of Verona are not much more than half of those of the Coliseum, (in cubic contents, I mean,) and yet it is a stupendous edifice. It is relatively low,—or, it might be safer to say, it struck me so after dwelling five months so near the Coliseum; but, standing on its summit, it is a fearful fall to look at. It is said that the amphitheatres of Rome, Verona, and Nismes contain among them all that is wanting to give us the most accurate notions of the details of this sort of structure. Certainly, as a whole, this is the most perfect of any I have seen. There is no visible reason why this immense building should not still stand, until destroyed by some natural convulsion.

The sarcophagus is no great matter. It stands in a garden, and is merely a plain marble chest, without its lid. Shakspeare is known to have taken the story of Romeo and Juliet from a tale of the misfortunes of two young lovers of this place; and it is certainly possible that this may have been the very tomb of the lady. The names are anglicised in the play, but not materially varied. The guide showed us a house which, he affirmed, belonged to one of the warring families—the Montagues, I believe; but there are so many English travellers, just now, that the temptation to embellish is exceedingly strong. One looks at these things with an easy credulity, for it is the wisest way, when there is no serious historical or antiquarian question dependant on the truth. What matters it now, whether a young lady named Giulietta died of love, and was buried in this tomb? The name of Montague came from the Continent, and is still met with in France: among the connexions of General Lafayette is a Marquis de Montaigu, whom I have seen in his company, and who is his neighbour, at La Grange. I dare say there were Capuletti also in scores. These people must have had houses, and they

must have had tombs; and it is as well for us travellers to believe
we see them here at Verona, as to believe anything else. For the
laquais de place and the keeper of the garden, it is even much
better.

We breakfasted at Verona, which struck us as a bustling and
pleasing town, with a singular air of *bon ton* about it; and then
we went our way. The *enceinte* of this city, like that of Genoa,
embraces a large side-hill that is mostly in villas and gardens;
but the defences are of no great account.

Shortly after quitting the walls, we turned into the valley of
the Adige, and reached a point where one may be said to take
his last look at Italy. [Mrs. Cooper] laughed at me, for this was
the only country, as she affirmed, that she had ever known me
to quit looking over a shoulder. Certainly, the tendency in common is to look ahead, and I confess to the truth of the charge
of having looked behind me on this occasion. I have never yet
quitted any country with one half the regret that I quitted Italy.
Its nature, its climate, its recollections, its people even, had been
gradually gaining on my affections for near two years, and I felt
that reluctance to separate, that one is apt to experience on
quitting his own house.

I have told you little in these letters of the Italians themselves,
and nothing of what may be called their society. I have seen
much of the former, of necessity, and a little, though not much,
of the latter. A diffidence of my own knowledge lies at the bottom of this forbearance; for I am fully sensible that he who
would describe beyond the surface, must have had better
means of information than mine have been. Still, I will not quit
this charming region without giving you, in a very few words,
a summary of my opinions, such as they are.

I came to Italy with too many of the prejudices that had got
abroad concerning the Italian character. The whole country is
virtually a conquered country—and men are seldom wronged
without being abused. In the first place, the marvels about banditti and assassins are enormously exaggerated. Banditti there
have been, and robbers there still are. The country is peculiarly
adapted to invite their presence. With unfrequented mountains
nearly always in sight, roads crowded with travellers, great poverty, and police of no great energy, it could hardly be otherwise; and yet, a man of ordinary prudence may go from one

extremity of the country to the other with very little risk. Assassinations I believe to be no more frequent than murders in France or England. If the *quasi* duels or irregular combats of the south-west be enumerated, I believe, in proportion to population, that three men lose their lives by violence in that portion of the republic, to one in Italy.

The lower classes of Italy, with the exception of those who live on travellers, appear to me to be unsophisticated, kind, and well-principled. There is a native activity of mind about them that renders their rogues great rogues; but I question if the mass here be not quite as honest as the mass in any country under the same social pressure. An American should always remember the exemption from temptation that exists in his own country. Common crimes are certainly not so general with us as in most of Europe, and precisely for the reason named; but *uncommon meannesses* abound in a large circle of our population. The vices of an American origin are necessarily influenced by the condition of American society; and, as a principle, the same is true here. It may be questioned if examination, taking into view all the circumstances, would give a result so much in our favour as some pretend. Once removed from the towns and the other haunts of travellers, I have found the Italians of the lower classes endued with quite as many good qualities as most of their neighbours, and with more than some of them. They are more gracious than the English, and more sincere than the French, and infinitely more refined than the Germans; or, it might be better to say, less obtuse and coarse. Certainly, they are quick-witted; and, physically, they are altogether a finer race, though short, than I had expected to see.

Shades of difference exist in Italian character, as between the different States, the preference being usually given to the inhabitants of Upper Italy. I have not found this difference so manifestly clear against the South; though I do believe that the Piedmontese, in a physical sense, are the finest race of the entire country.

Foreigners would better appreciate the Italian character if they better understood the usages of the country. A nation divided like this, conquered as this has been, and lying, as it now does, notoriously at the mercy of any powerful invader, loses the estimation that is due to numbers. The stranger regards the people as unworthy of possessing distinctive traits, and obtrudes his own habits on them, coarsely and, too often, insolently. This, in part, is submitted to, from necessity; but mutual ill-will and distrust are the consequences. The vulgar-minded Englishman talks of the "damned Italians," and the vulgar-minded American, quite in rule, imitates his great model, though neither has, probably, any knowledge of the people beyond that which he has obtained in inns, and in the carriages of the *vetturini*.

In grace of mind, in a love, and even in a knowledge of the arts, a large portion of the common Italians are as much superior to the Anglo-Saxon race as civilization is superior to barbarism. We deride their religious superstitions; but we overlook the exaggerations, uncharitableness, and ferocity of our own fanaticism. Of the two, I firmly believe a Divine Omniscience finds less to condemn in the former. I do not know any peasantry in which there is more ingenuousness, with less of rusticity and vulgarity, than that of Tuscany.

The society of Italy, which is but another word for the nobles of the country, so far as I have seen it, has the general European character, modified a little by position. They have a general acquaintance with literature, without being often learned; and there is a grace about their minds, derived from the constant practice of contemplating the miracles of art, that is rather peculiar to them. An Italian gentleman is more gracious than an Englishman, and less artificial than a Frenchman. Indeed, I have often thought that in these particulars he is the nearest a true standard, of any gentleman of Europe. There is a sincerity in this class, also, that took me by surprise; a simplicity of mind rather than of manner, that is not common on the other side of the Alps. Notwithstanding what has been said and written about *les esprits fins*, I question if the trait can be properly imputed to the general Italian character. After all this, however, I freely admit the limited nature of my own observation, and you will not attach to these opinions more value than they deserve; still, they merit more attention than the loose notions on the same subject that have been thrown before the world, unreflectingly and ignorantly, by most of our travellers.

Nature appears to have intended Italy for a single country. With a people speaking the same language—a territory almost surrounded by water, or separated from the rest of Europe by a barrier of grand mountains—its extent, ancient history, relative position, and interests, would all seem to have a direct tendency towards bringing about this great end. The —— of —— assured me that such was the intention of Napoleon, who looked forward to the time when he might convert the whole of the peninsula into a single state. Had he continued to reign, and had he been the father of two or more sons, it is quite probable that he would have distributed his kingdoms among them at his death; but, while he lived, no man would have got anything back from Napoleon Bonaparte with his own consent.

Italy, instead of being the consolidated country that one could wish it were, is now divided into ten states, excluding little Monaco. These countries are, Piedmont or Sardinia, Lombardy, Modena, Parma, Massa, Lucca, Tuscany, the Papal territories, San Marino, and the Two Sicilies. This is an approach towards consolidation; the Venetian States, the duchy of Genoa, and a great many smaller countries being swallowed up by their more important neighbours, as has been the case in Germany. Massa will soon be joined to Modena,* and Lucca to Tuscany, which will reduce the number of independent governments to eight—or, deducting San Marino, a community of no account, to seven. The entire population is thought to be from eighteen to nineteen millions.

The study of Italy is profitable to an American. One of the greatest, indeed the only serious obstacle, to consolidation of all the Italian States, arises from the hereditary hatreds and distrusts of the people of one country to those of another. Such is it to separate the family tie, and such would soon be our own condition were the bond of union that now unites us severed. By playing off one portion of the country against the others, the common enemy would plunder all.

The Italians, while they are sensible that Napoleon did them good by introducing the vigour and improvements of France, do not extol his reign. They justly deem him a selfish conqueror, and, I make no doubt, joyfully threw off his yoke. The conscription appears to have been the most oppressive of his measures; and well it might be, for, even admitting that his ulti-

---

*This junction has since been made.

mate ends were to be beneficial, the means were next to intolerable. He improved the roads, invigorated the police, reformed many abuses, and gave new impulses to society, it is true; but, in the place of the old grievances, he substituted King Stork for King Log.

The laws and customs of the Italian countries have so many minute points of difference, that the wishes of some of the patriots of this region point towards a Confederated Republic, something like that of Switzerland. Sooner or later, Italy will inevitably become a single State: this is a result that I hold to be inevitable, though the means by which it is to be effected are still hidden. Italy as one nation, would command the Mediterranean and the Adriatic, and the jealousies of France and England are likely to oppose more obstacles to the consolidation than the power of Austria. The Confederation would be played on by both these powers; and it appears to me that it is just the worst mode of attempting a change that could be adopted. In the absence of great political events, to weaken the authority of the present governments, education is the surest process, though a slow one. In no case, should the people of a country confide in foreigners for the attainment of their political ends. All history has shown that communities are not to be trusted in such matters; and if I were an Italian bent on consolidation, I would not turn my eyes beyond the Alps for relief. After all, there is so much room for meliorations more immediately serviceable, that perhaps the wisest way is, to direct the present energies to reforms, rather than to revolutions; though many here will tell you the former are to be obtained only through the latter.

Our road soon led us into a great valley, the Alps gradually closing on us as we advanced, until we again found ourselves in their gigantic embraces. The Adige, a swift but brawling stream, flowed on our left, and the country gradually lost the breadth and softness of Italy in the peculiarities of a mountain district. About two o'clock, we passed a village called Avio, where we changed horses. Here we got but one postilion, short traces for the leaders, a long whip, and a new livery,—the certain signs that we were in Germany: in fact, we had crossed the line of the Tyrol, about a league to the southward. Rovereto was a town of some importance, and here we began to see some

of the independence of the Tyrolese, who paid very little attention to the printed regulations of the road. I had been furnished with a *carte de route*, with instructions to enter any com-
plaints about speed, delays, or other failure to comply with the
law; and this I did at one post-house in the presence of the post-
master, who had not only made a false entry as to the time of
our arrival and departure, but who was impudent and dilatory.
This complaint he endeavoured to defeat by correcting his own
entry. To effect this, he had asked me for the way-bill; and
when I found out the object, he refused to give it back again.
Thereupon, I seized him by the collar, and wrested the paper
out of his hands. For a moment there were symptoms of blows;
but, distrusting the result, the rogue yielded. He menaced me
loudly, notwithstanding; and when I carried off the prize to the
carriage, we were surrounded by the rascal with a dozen other
blackguards to back him. He refused to give us horses, and I
noted the time on the way-bill again before his face. This frightened him, and I believe he was glad to get rid of us.

It would seem I had adopted a mode of travelling peculiarly
disagreeable to the post-masters; for, while it cost me more than
the ordinary posting, they were paid less, the government
pocketing the difference. This I did not know, or certainly I
would have saved my money; but being in the scrape, as a *pis
aller*, I was determined to fight my way out of it. I do think there
is enough of Jack in me yet to have threshed the fellow, had we
got to facers,—a termination of the affair that the short struggle
gave the rascal reason to anticipate.

It was dark before we drove into a small city that stands between lofty mountains, one of which rose like a dark wall above
it, quite *à la Suisse*. The Adige flowed through this town, which
was Trent, só celebrated for its religious council.

The inn here was semi-Swiss, semi-German. When I put the
usual question as to the price of the rooms, the landlord, a
hearty Boniface-sort of a person, laughed, and said, "You are
now in Germany; give yourself no trouble on that score." I took
him at his word, and found him honest. There was a sort of
great *sala* in the centre of the house, that communicated with
the different apartments. Something like a dozen escutcheons
ornamented its walls; and, on examining them, I found inscriptions to show that they had been placed there to commemorate

the visits of sundry kings and princes to the larder of mine host. Among others, the Emperor, the late and the present Grand Dukes of Tuscany, and the King of Bavaria, were of the number. The latter sovereign is a great traveller, running down into Italy every year or two. The Marquis of Hertford was also honoured with a blazonry,—probably on account of his expenses. I have seen this usage, once or twice, in other parts of Europe.

The next day, our road, an even, good carriage-way, led up the valley of the Adige, along a valley that might have passed for one of Switzerland, a little softened in features. There were ruined towers on the spurs of the mountains, and here and there was a hold that was still kept up. One in particular, near Botzen, struck us as singularly picturesque, for it was not easy to see how its inhabitants reached it. The costumes, too, were singular; prettier, I thought, than any of Switzerland. The men wore cock's feathers, stuck obliquely with a smart air in their high conical hats: some carried guns, and all had a freedom of manner about them that denoted the habits of mountaineers. At Botzen we left the Adige, following a branch, however, that was not smaller than the stream which retains the name. The country now became more romantic and more wild. The châteaux were of a simpler kind, though always picturesque. The road continued good, and the horses were excellent: they reminded us strongly of American horses. We did not arrive at Brixen until after dark; but we found German neatness, German civility, German honesty, and German family portraits. Every man has ancestors of some sort or other, but one sees no necessity for lampooning them with a pencil after they are dead.

Brixen stands in a mountain-basin, a town of a German-Swiss character. Soon after quitting it, next morning, we began to ascend the celebrated Pass of the Brenner, which offered nothing more than a long and winding road among forests and common mountain scenery. We had been too recently in Switzerland to be in ecstasies, and yet we were pleased. It began to be stormy; and by the time we reached the post-house, the road had several inches of snow in it. Two days before, we had been eating cherries and strawberries at Verona!

One gets to be sophisticated in time. On landing in England, I refused a beggar a sixpence *because he asked for it,* my American habits revolting at the meanness of begging. To-day [Mrs. Cooper] had a good laugh at me for a change of character. By the arrangement at Venice, I was not obliged to give anything to the postilions; but I usually added a franc to their regular receipts from the government. On this occasion the postilion very properly abstained from asking for that which he knew he could not properly claim. The money, however, was in my hand; but seeing that he kept aloof, I put it up, unconsciously saying, "Hang the fellow! if he will not ask for it, let him go without it." This is the way we get to be the creatures of habit, judging of nations and men by standards that depend on accidents. Four years earlier, I should certainly have refused the postilion, *had* he asked for the money; and now I denied him because he did *not!* I hope to reach the philosophical and just medium in due time, in this as well as in some other matters.

We went a post on the mountain, a wild without being absolutely a savage district, before we turned the summit. This point was discovered by the runs of water at the road-side, one of which was a tributary of the Adige, sending its contributions to the Adriatic, while the other flows into the Inn, which communicates with the Danube. The descent, however, soon spoke for itself, and we went down a mountain on a scale commensurate with that by which we had ascended.

At a turn in the road, a beautiful fairy-like scene suddenly presented itself. There was a wide and fertile plain, through which meandered a respectable river. Our own mountain melted away to its margin on one side, and a noble wall of rock, some two or three thousand feet high, bounded it on the other. Directly before us lay a town, with the usual peculiarities of a mountain-city, though it had a cathedral and even a palace. This was Innspruck, the capital of the Tyrol, and the immediate object of our journey. We drove into it at an early hour, and in time to enjoy the play of mists, and the brilliancy of the snows that still rendered the adjacent cliffs hoary.

We had glimpses of glaciers to-day, and saw an abbey or two in poetical situations. Innspruck reminded us a good deal of Berne. The palace is respectable though not large, and the cathedral is quaint and venerable. In the latter there is a row of knights in their ancient armour, or rather a row of armour which is so placed as to resemble knights ranged in order. I believe the armour is that of the former sovereigns of the Tyrol.

There is also a little castle, a mile or two from the town, that now belongs to the Emperor, and was once the hold, or palace, of the Counts of the Tyrol. We had the curiosity to visit it. Certes, a small prince a few centuries since lived in a very simple style. There were the knights' hall, a picture-gallery, and other sounding names; but a more unsophisticated abode can hardly be imagined for a gentleman. To compare any of these mountain-castles to a modern country-house even in America, is out of the question, for nothing can be plainer than most of their accommodations. This was a little better than a common Yankee palace, I allow, for that is the *ne plus ultra* of discomfort and pretension; but, after all, you might fancy yourself in a barn that had been converted into a dwelling.

The gallery was awful—almost as bad as that one occasionally meets in an American tavern, or that we actually enjoyed last night at Brixen. Still, the place was quaint, and of great interest from its associations. It even had its armour.

We are now at a stand. Vienna is on our right, Switzerland on our left, and the last pass of the Alps is before us. Examining the map, I see the "Isar rolling rapidly," Munich, and a wide field of Germany in the latter direction, and it has just been decided to push forward as far as Saxony and Dresden before we make another serious halt.

Explanatory Notes

3.3 Doveiria: the river which flows through the Gondo Gorge on the Italian side of the Simplon Pass.

3.13 Old Caspar: Cooper's postilion on the drive from Bern to Florence.

3.15 15th of October: Cooper noted in his journal that the family "Quit Milan at 6" on the following morning, 16 October 1828 (*Letters and Journals*, I, 351).

6.34–35 reminded . . . Spain: At the age of seventeen, Cooper had shipped before the mast on the merchant ship *Stirling*, visiting London and Àguilas, Spain.

6.36–7.8 intermarriage . . . Etruria: Elizabeth Farnese married Philip V of Spain in 1714. In 1731, the Duchy of Parma passed to their son, Charles de Bourbon, later Charles III of Naples. From 1735–1748, Parma was under Austrian rule; but in 1748, at the Peace of Aix-la-Chapelle, it was returned to the Spanish Bourbons by Emperor Francis I, and Philip, the younger brother of Charles III, was recognized as Duke of Parma and Piacenza. He was succeeded by his son Ferdinand and his grandson Louis, whom Napoleon made King of Etruria (the ancient name for Tuscany) in 1801. Napoleon's wife, Marie Louise, held Parma from 1814 to 1847.

7.38 Castel Guelfo . . . Ghibellines: Cooper's presumption is correct. The castle, originally called Torre d'Orlando for the Ghibelline Orlando Pallavicino, had been captured and re-named during the conflict between the Guelphs and the Ghibellines.

8.29 one . . . by Correggio: In his journal for 17 October 1828, Cooper identified this painting as "the St- Jerome," that is, the *Madonna of St. Jerome* (*Letters and Journals*, I, 352).

8.40–9.1 bas reliefs . . . Capitol: In *Notions of the Americans* (1828), Cooper defended the subjects of the four bas-reliefs (the landing of the Pilgrims, Penn's treaty with the Indians, the story of Pocahontas and Captain Smith, and a meeting of Boone with the Indians) against a criticism in the *Personal Narrative of Lieutenant the Honourable Frederic de Roos* (1827); but, understandably, confessed an unwillingness to criticize their "execution" (*Notions of the Americans* [London, 1828], II, 35–36).

10.10 church: La Madonna di S. Luca, a church recommended for

a special visit by John Chetwode Eustace in *A Classical Tour
Through Italy* (London, 1821, I, 263), a work Cooper owned
and used (hereafter referred to as Eustace).

10.18 wax-work preparations: Eustace described the hall of
anatomy and midwifery in the Academy of Sciences at
Bologna as "celebrated for a remarkable collection of wax
figures, representing the female form in all the stages, and in
all the incidents of parturition" (I, 267).

10.22 two ugly motiveless brick towers: the Asinella and the
Garisenda, both twelfth-century. Eustace called these towers
"deformed monuments of a barbarous age" (I, 264). Like
dozens of towers built in Bologna between the twelfth and the
fifteenth centuries, they were designed to display the wealth
and prestige of their owners.

14.35 Lord Lansdowne: Henry Petty Fitzmaurice, third Marquess
of Lansdowne, fourth Earl of Kerry (1780–1863). According
to Cooper, one of only four Englishmen of high rank who
"knew how to be civil," Lord Lansdowne had entertained the
novelist in London in 1828. Cooper's partiality to Lansdowne
was based partly on his youthful refusal of a financially
advantageous match and his marriage instead to Lady Louisa
Emma Fox-Strangways, a daughter of the Earl of Ilchester,
whom Cooper thought "one of the most natural sweet
tempered women in the world" (*Letters and Journals*, I, 354
and 357).

18.5 Lucie: the family's Swiss cook.

19.27 apartment: The ten-room apartment in the Palazzo Ricasoli
occupied by the Coopers overlooked the Via del Cocomero,
now the Via Ricasoli, which runs north-northeast from the
Piazza del Duomo.

21.14–15 "the rising . . . same": Psalms 113:3.

23.24 Count di V[idua]: a Piedmontese traveller (1785–1830) who
met Cooper, Aaron Burr, Presidents Adams, Jefferson and
Madison, and many other well-known Americans during a
ten-month visit to the United States beginning in April 1825.
His experiences are described in *Lettere del Conte Carlo Vidua*,
3 vols., ed. Cesare Balbo (Torino, Pompa, 1834).

23.33 Baron P[oerio]: Giuseppe Poerio (1775–1843), an eloquent
republican lawyer, appointed *procureur général* (attorney
general) of Naples by Murat in 1808.

24.20–24 Prince Borghese: Camillo Borghese (1775–1832),
widower of Pauline Bonaparte. Of his receptions, Cooper had
written: "Prince Borghese used, on great occasions, to open
twenty [rooms], if I remember right, at Florence, one of
which was as large as six or eight of our ordinary drawing-
rooms" (*Sketches of Switzerland*, Pt. II, Vol. I, Letter VII). Both
he and his brother, Francesco Borghese-Aldobrandini, were

generous hosts to the Coopers during their stay in Florence. Cooper was especially grateful for extraordinary attentions by the latter's wife, the Princess Aldobrandini.

24.27 Lord B[urghersh]: John Fane, envoy extraordinary and minister plenipotentiary to Tuscany from 1814 to 1830. He was not a favorite of Cooper, who had been offended by an affirmative but curt reply to a request of the United States consul, James Ombrosi, to bring the Coopers to Lord Burghersh's soirées. Cooper was again affronted when Lady Burghersh did not respond to calling cards, sent at her husband's suggestion (*Letters and Journals*, I, 354, 360).

24.27–28 Lord N[ormanby]: Constantine Henry Phipps (1797–1863), second Earl of Mulgrave, first Marquess of Normanby, author, diplomatist, politician, later minister to the court of Tuscany at Florence. One of Cooper's four favorite English lords, he wrote romantic tales, sketches, and novels, among them, *Matilda* (1825), *Yes and No* (1828), and *Clarinda* (1829).

26.29–36 Count St. Leu . . . daughter or two: Cooper's glance at the tiara section of the opera house revealed his friends Louis Bonaparte, Jerome Bonaparte, and Elizabeth Patterson of Baltimore, whose marriage to Jerome, Napoleon had refused to recognize. Others included the brother of Frederick William III, and Marie-Louise Christophe, the widow of Henry I of Haiti, with her daughters Améthyste and Anne-Athénaïre.

28.1 G[ouverneur] W[ilkins]: Gouverneur Morris Wilkins (1799–1871), nephew and adopted son of Gouverneur Morris. During the reign of Louis Philippe, he served briefly as an attaché of the United States Legation in Paris.

31.37–32.1 *Santa Maria della Spina* . . . town-house of Louvain: Earlier Cooper had written of this town-house: "on the whole, it is one of the most extraordinary edifices I know. It is a sort of condensation of quaintness, that is quite without a rival even in this land of laboured and curious architecture" (*Sketches of Switzerland*, Pt. II, Vol. I, Letter X).

32.13 "redolent . . . youth": Thomas Gray, "Ode on a Distant Prospect of Eton College," l.19.

32.32–33 Algerine Rais: Muslim ship's captain.

33.36 American graves . . . Captain Gamble: At Leghorn on 6 December 1828, Cooper unexpectedly came upon the grave of Thomas Gamble (d. 1818), his messmate at Oswego, New York, during the winter of 1808–1809. He wrote the following verses in tribute:

Sleep on in peace within thy foreign grave,
Companion of my young and laughing hour—

Thought bears me hence to wild Ontario's wave—
To other scenes, to time when hope had power.

Then life to us was like yon glittering main
Viewed in the calm, beneath its sunny skies,
Then impulse bound the mind in pleasure's chain,
And colors rose in gold before the eyes.

We based our rocks of fame on moving seas,
To us their trackless paths were beaten ways—
The spirit stirring gale, the milder breeze,
The battle's carnage teemed with laurel'd praize—

But twice ten wiser years have drawn a ray
Of austere truth athwart this treacherous sphere,
To me life stands exposed, yet I obey
Its luring smile—Thou—sleepest ever here—

—James Fenimore Cooper [the novelist's grandson], *The Legends and Traditions of a Northern County* (New York and London, 1921), pp. 221–222.

35.5 grand duke: Leopold II (1797–1870), Grand Duke of Tuscany from 1824 to 1859, a cultivated, relatively liberal ruler who favored freedom of the press and was hospitable to political exiles.

37.17 Count Fossombrone: Vittorio Fossombrone (1754–1844), Prime Minister from 1814 until his death.

40.8 M. Eynard: Jean Gabriel Eynard (1775–1863), an influential advocate of the Greek cause at the Congress of Vienna (1814).

41.19 Osages: David Delauney, an enterprising Frenchman, had assisted six Indians—Kihegashugah (Little Chief), aged 38; Washingsahba (Black Spirit), aged 32; Marcharkitahtoonhah (Big Soldier), aged 45; Minkchatahook (Young Soldier), aged 22; and the eighteen-year-old wives of two of the men, Gretomih and Myhanghah—with their interpreter, Paul Loise—to sail to Havre in the summer of 1827 in order to exhibit them for profit. In their native costume, they were at first the center of attention—at the theatre and opera in Rouen and Paris, at their hotel in the rue de Rivoli, and at the court of Charles X—but by the fall, interest was waning. When Delauney was arrested for debts, the fortunes of the group declined. The French, however, everywhere befriended them, General Lafayette finally raising money for the return of some to America in the spring of 1830.

42.4–17 Not long before . . . personal discontent: Cooper refers here to his purpose in writing *Notions of the Americans* (1828) and to the hostile reception of the book. He had written

Notions of the Americans at the urging of General Lafayette to correct erroneous opinions about America perpetrated in condescending accounts by English travelers. British and American critics vigorously attacked *Notions* and its author.

45.6 M. de Vitrolles: Eugène François-Auguste d'Arnaud, Baron de Vitrolles (1774–1854), Secretary of State and minister plenipotentiary during the Restoration.

48.33–34 Prince Napoleon Bonaparte: Napoleon Louis Bonaparte, brother of Napoleon III, and his wife, Princess Charlotte, daughter of Joseph Bonaparte, became friends of Cooper. He renewed his friendship with her in 1833 in London, where she was living as a widow.

50.1 A sudden call: Cooper had set out for France, expecting to print *The Wept of Wish-ton-Wish* in Paris. *En route*, however, he found a printer, Richard Heaviside, who could set type in English and returned with him to Florence to print the novel at the "Dante's Head" Press—with the help of the Grand Duke's librarian. At his farewell audience, Cooper presented a copy to the Grand Duke. (See p. 79.)

60.17 expedition of 1815: On 1 March Napoleon had landed at Cannes, marching upon and entering Paris on 20 March, to begin the rule of the Hundred Days.

62.25 Lazaretto: quarantine station.

62.29 Navarino: a battle (20 October 1827) in the Greek War of Independence in which the Turkish and Egyptian fleet of Mohammed Ali (1769–1849) had been destroyed.

63.2 expedition to Greece: a French expeditionary force, sent to Greece during the winter of 1828–1829 to evacuate Egyptians.

67.12 St. Illario: Via di S. Illario a Colombaia, off Via Senese, outside Porta Romana. The building survives with a commemorative plaque dedicated to Cooper.

73.40–74.1 *la Reine Julie*: The wife of Joseph Bonaparte, Marie Julie Clary of Marseilles, was the well-dowered daughter of a wealthy Marseilles soap-boiler.

74.1–3 Prince Napoleon . . . Princess of Musignano: Prince Napoleon (brother of Napoleon III) was Napoleon Louis, son of Louis Bonaparte and Hortense de Beauharnais, who married Charlotte, daughter of Joseph Bonaparte and Julie Clary. The Prince and Princess of Musignano were Charles Lucien Jules Laurent, son of Lucien Bonaparte and Christine Boyer, and his wife Zenaïde, the other daughter of Joseph Bonaparte and Julie Clary. Cooper had known Charles Lucien while he lived at Joseph Bonaparte's estate in Bordentown, New Jersey, between 1822 and 1828, where he began his study of American birds, leading to the publication of his four-volume *American Ornithology; or, The Natural History of Birds Inhabiting the United States* (1825–33), a continuation of the work of Alexander Wilson.

74.32 His wife: Hortense Eugenie de Beauharnais, daughter of Empress Josephine and stepchild of Napoleon I, lived in Rome apart from her husband. Cooper thought her "an affable good hearted woman of fifty, with no remains of beauty whatever, and with manners that are not in the least dignified. She seems frank and easy by nature, but she is too much of a fidget for manner" (*Letters and Journals*, I, 427).

74.35–36 Jerome . . . his brother-in-law, the King of Bavaria: At the time of which Cooper wrote, Jerome's brother-in-law, Wilhelm I, was King of Wurtemberg, not of Bavaria. Jerome's title had been bestowed by his father-in-law, Frederick I, in 1816.

74.39–40 Princess Hercolani: Anna Hippolyte Alexandrine (b. 1799), wife of Prince Alphonse Hercolani, was actually the daughter of Lucien's second wife and M. de Jouberthon.

75.29 Princess of Wurtemberg: Friedrique Catharine, Joseph Bonaparte's second wife. Cooper wrote that she was "a good natured, fat personage, who has much merit for her domestic virtues, but who is a little absurd on account of her airs of Royalty. I was at her parties, when I believe there was scarce another man in the rooms who did not write Prince before his name" (*Letters and Journals*, I, 427).

75.30 *Madame Mère*: So that his mother would outrank her daughters, Napoleon revived the title *Madame*, which, under the Bourbons, had been reserved for the king's eldest daughter and the wife of his eldest brother. To maintain the distinction should he have a daughter, Napoleon added the designation "*Mère de Sa Majesté l'Empereur.*" Hence: *Madame Mère*.

76.32 Park Theatre: This popular New York theatre at 13–17 Park Row was used for civic, operatic, and dramatic presentations.

77.3–4 doubly their time: Cooper's meaning is not entirely clear. On being sued by his servants for a full month's pay or $18 for three days' work, he had settled the claim with a lawyer for one dollar, the actual amount owed, and $18 in costs. He was threatened subsequently with another suit for $18 for the same claim. This time he refused payment (see *Letters and Journals*, I, 413).

84.16 W[illiam]: Cooper's nephew and secretary-copyist, William Yeardley Cooper, who died of consumption in Paris, October 1831, at the age of twenty-two.

87.18–19 Mr. Carter . . . horrors: In his *Letters from Europe* (New York, 1827), II, 400–02, Nathaniel Hazletine Carter describes the scorpion as "a black odious looking animal, several inches in length, with feelers like a lobster" and refers to scorpions as "venomous reptiles."

99.26–28 Pliny . . . stone pine: According to Pliny the Younger, the ascending cloud from the eruption of Vesuvius resembled "a pine tree," shooting up "to a great height in the form of a very tall trunk, which spread itself out at the top into a sort of branches." Pliny's two eyewitness accounts of the event are contained in letters to Tacitus, the historian (*Epist.* 6.16, 20).

106.3 statues . . . Balbi: Cooper saw these sculptures of the most distinguished family of Herculaneum in the Royal Museum at Naples.

107.22 royal proclamation: Cooper is reporting his refusal to submit to arbitrary authority—like William Tell who, in refusing to doff his hat according to Gessler's orders, inspired the famous episode of the shooting of the apple.

109.25–110.11 below the citadel stands a convent . . . its "incense-breathing" chapels: Cooper here describes the Carthusian monastery of San Martino, with its Baroque art and architecture and the magnificent view from its Belvedere. The memorable painting by Spagnoletto or José Ribera (1590–1652), a Spanish painter of the Neapolitan school, was presumably "The Descent from the Cross." The phrase "incense-breathing" is from Thomas Gray's "Elegy Written in a Country Churchyard," l.17.

111.30 Chapman: John Gadsby Chapman (1808–1889), a young American painter trained at the Pennsylvania Academy of the Fine Arts, who became one of Cooper's protégés. See the "Historical Introduction." The Chapman painting reproduced following page 78 is presumably the painting to which Cooper refers.

112.35 The house we took: The Coopers rented an apartment at Sorrento in the Villa del Tasso, now a part of the Hotel Tramontano, called the Hotel du Tasso, which, according to Mariana Starke's *Travels in Europe between the years 1824 and 1828* (London, 1828), I, 317, belonged "to the Duca di Laurito, who descends, in the female line, from Tasso's family." Its chief attraction was its elevation high on a tufa cliff above the Bay of Naples, which provided a magnificent view, described by Seadrift in *The Water-Witch*, the romance Cooper wrote at Sorrento. According to Mrs. Starke, "the chamber in which Torquato Tasso was born is fallen into the sea": but the Villa displayed "on an outside Wall, a mutilated Bust, in *terracotta*, of the immortal Bard; and in the Saloon upstairs . . . a marble Bust, called Bernardo Tasso . . . ; a Medallion of Alexander, finely executed; another of Julius Caesar when young; another of Agrippina; and another of Marcus Aurelius: they are ancient, and were all found at Sorrento" (see *Italy*, 145.25ff.).

114.27 "unhonoured dead": "Elegy Written in a Country Church- yard," l. 93.

116.25 Contoit: John H. Contoit was a well-known early nineteenth- century confectioner. His "New York Garden" at 355 Broad- way was popular for the flavors of its ice creams and other delicacies.

119.39 "Hundred Chambers": the so-called *Cento Camerelle*, the re- mains of a large water reservoir.

124.25 the men in buckram: an allusion to Falstaff's "rogues in buckram," *I Henry IV*, II.iv.196–220.

127.5–12 She was called . . . Puteoli: Acts 28 : 11–13.

127.21 the well-known allusion of Josephus: *Antiquities of the Jews*, bk. 8, ch. 3.

127.39–40 "Myra . . . Lycia": Acts 27 : 5.

128.5–16 "the south wind . . . sixteen souls": Acts 27 : 13–37.

129.13 Mr. Hammett: Alexander Hammett, United States consul at Naples, 1809–47 and 1848–61.

132.19 Claude: Claude Lorrain (Claude Gelée or Gellée, 1600– 1682), so-called as a native of Lorraine, was a Baroque land- scape painter who lived and worked in Rome. His Arcadian scenes, the hallmark of his revolutionary compositional in- sights, were cherished by all lovers of the picturesque. See the "Historical Introduction."

133.17 Gelsomina: According to Susan Fenimore Cooper, this young Sorrentine peasant girl, "half nurse, half play-fellow" to the Cooper children, was the probable prototype for Gelsomina, the jailer's daughter of the same name in Cooper's *The Bravo* (see *Pages and Pictures* [New York: W. A. Townsend, 1861], 251–52).

138.6 West-Farms: a nineteenth-century village in Westchester County, now assimilated into the Bronx, New York City.

139.35 "catch crabs": a derisive nautical term for false strokes (to miss time in rowing by pulling an oar too lightly or deeply), probably derived from the Italian *chiappar un gragno*.

145.18–35 our own house . . . Tasso: Compare note for 112.35.

152.4 "*facilis descensus Averni*": Lake Avernus, near Naples, was in classical times a deep, gloomy crater, surrounded by hills and forests, appropriately considered the entrance to the infernal regions. Just before Virgil's Aeneas begins his tour of the lower world where he finally meets the shade of his father Anchises, the prophetess or sybil cautions him that "the de- scent to Avernus is easy; the door of gloomy Dis stands open night and day; but to return and issue into upper air, this is the task, this the burden!" (*Aeneid* 6.126–29). The copy-text reading "Averni" has some manuscript authority, though "Averno" is the more common reading.

157.14–15 lost Pandects of Justinian . . . Amalfi: Cooper here referred to a popular but apocryphal story that a manuscript copy of the Pandects or Digesta of Justinian I fell into the hands of the Pisons during a war with Amalfi and was acquired by the Laurentian Library at Florence, becoming one of its principal treasures.

160.13–14 the fabulous adventurers of the Bohan upas: A fabrication in *The London Magazine*, 52 (December 1783), 512–17, aroused much popular interest in this mythical Javanese tree whose venomous exhalations were supposed to extinguish all life in their vicinity. Its image intrigued the Romantic imagination. Cooper's allusion may derive from a play, *The Law of Java*, produced by Colman the Younger on the London stage in the 1820s. In it, the Sultan permitted condemned criminals to choose between being executed outright and becoming "adventurers" commissioned to bring back the poison gum of the bohan (or bohon) upas. Few such "adventurers" returned to be pardoned and rewarded.

160.20 Silaro: an unusual name for the river Sele, the ancient Silarus, also used by Mariano Vasi in *A New Picture of Naples* (London: Samuel Leigh, 1820), p. 326.

164.25–26 a particular and a remarkable comet: Halley's.

167.5 Royal Museum: The Museo Nazionale at Naples has housed the treasures discovered at Pompeii and Herculaneum since the eighteenth century.

167.20 *Sans Souci*: literally, "Without Care," a palace in Potsdam, designed by Frederick the Great (Frederick II), begun in 1745 and completed in 1749.

170.22–31 A President . . . outrage!: On 4 July 1831, President Andrew Jackson negotiated a treaty by which France agreed to pay $5,000,000 to satisfy American spoliation claims. When France later suspended payment, Jackson recommended the seizure of French property to bring her to terms. Cooper applauded his successful tactics.

173.4 her uncle: The Princess Christina was actually a second cousin of Ferdinand VII, her grandfather's brother's son.

183.6–7 Suessa Auruncorum: This is the name used in Vasi's *Naples* (1820), p. 44. Other sources give the ancient name of Sessa as Suessa Aurunca.

192.8 Trinity: Cooper referred to the third Trinity Church, completed in 1788 and pulled down in 1839.

195.13 Servius Tullius: According to legend, Servius, the sixth king of Rome (578–534 B.C.), extended the city's limits and surrounded it with the so-called Servian Wall.

196.12–13 A writer . . . a contemporary of Aurelian: Flavius Vospiscus (c. 300–320 A.D.), a Latin historian, accounted one of the ablest writers of the *Historia Augusta*, to which he contributed the life of Aurelian, Tacitus, and others. His account of Aurelian is mentioned in Mariano Vasi's *Rome* (1829), I, p. X.

196.27 writer of the time of Belisarius: Procopius, a sixth-century Byzantine historian.

197.33–36 Porta Capena . . . Transtiberina: Vasi's *Rome* (1829), I, p. XII, lists these fourteen sections of the city in the same order.

198.14 blunder still more serious: Cooper seems to attribute these errors to Scott rather than Scott's compositors, because compositors would be more likely to misread Arabic numerals than numbers spelled out as words.

198.40–199.36 "*In his computation . . . arrive*": Italics Cooper's.

201.31–202.2 It is said . . . America: an allusion to the public controversy in 1837 over Three Mile Point, a piece of land owned by descendants of Judge Cooper, three miles north of Cooperstown on the western shore of Otsego Lake, which the townspeople had used freely for picnics during the family's seventeen-year absence and come to regard as public property. Cooper's assertion of private ownership of the Point led to a bitter controversy and a series of libel suits brought by the novelist against certain New York State newspapers.

202.13 Buoncompagni: The name of this noble Roman family is "Boncompagni." Cooper's addition of the "u," but not his breaking the name into two words, may have been justified by contemporaneous usage.

203.17 one of the basilicæ of Rome: San Lorenzo Fuori le Mura.

206.24 Cæcilia Metella: daughter of Metellus Creticus and wife of Crassus, one of Caesar's generals in Gaul.

209.24 Caius Cestius: a praetor, tribune of the people, and member of the college of Septemviri Epulones (priests who superintended sacrificial feasts).

209.35–38 *Cor cordium* . . . daughter of Godwin: Edward Trelawney supervised the cremation of Shelley's remains on the beach at Viareggio and arranged to have his ashes buried at Rome. Leigh Hunt, not Mary Shelley, wrote the poet's epitaph.

211.1 old King: Ferdinand I (1751–1825), as Ferdinand IV, King of Naples (1759–1806) and (1815–1816), and King of the Two Sicilies (1816–1825). His reign had been interrupted during the Napoleonic era.

214.1–2 Tityrus . . . *fagi*: Virgil, *Bucolica, Ecloga* I.1: a reference to "Tityre, tu patulae recubans sub tegmine fagi" ("Oh Tityrus, reclining beneath the cover of a spreading beech-tree").

214.17 those decided acts of the plebeians: 494 B.C. is the date generally given for the plebeian move to the Sacred Mount.

216.1 Swiss: Jean Etienne Duby (1798–1885), a Protestant minister at Chancy, Switzerland, Cooper's riding companion in Rome and later in Geneva in 1832.

224.11–12 father-in-law Antoninus Pius: Antoninus Pius was actually the uncle of Marcus Antoninus.

224.37 M. AGRIPPA . . . FECIT: An abbreviation on the Pantheon for "Marcus Agrippa Lucii filius consul tertium fecit" ("Marcus Agrippa, son of Lucius, consul for the third time, made this").

230.15 Cicisbeism: the eighteenth-century convention by which a married woman might have a *cicisbeo* or *cavalier servente*, a recognized gallant.

236.26 whose house stood: Nero had put Plautius Lateranus, the last owner, to death and appropriated the palace.

237.32 *bas reliefs* of Thorwaldsen: the Alexander frieze of 1812, completed in three months in preparation for a visit by Napoleon.

239.1 Transfiguration: Raphael's painting, commissioned in 1517 by Julius, Cardinal de Medici and finished by two of the master's pupils. See "Historical Introduction," p. xxiv.

239.1–2 Communion of St. Jerome: a painting by Domenichino (1581–1641).

240.26–28 Pliny . . . *statuaries*: Pliny (*Nat. Hist.* 36.37) refers to Agesander, Polydorus, and Athenodorus as "authors" of the famous group of the Laocoön.

240.32 Winckelmann: Johann Joachim Winckelmann (1717–1768), companion and librarian for Alexander, Cardinal Albani in Rome and later Superintendent of Antiquities in and about Rome. His monumental *History of Ancient Art* was first published in 1764.

240.38 "Belle Jardinière": a painting by Raphael.

241.6 the work of Mrs. Starke: Mariana Starke, *Travels in Europe between the years 1824 and 1828* (London: John Murray, 1828).

243.1 Princess V[olkonskaya]: Zinaida Aleksandrovna Volkonskaya (1792–1862), author of French and Russian works and friend of such writers as Pushkin and Gogol.

243.26 Mademoiselle Mars: Anne Françoise Hippolyte Mars-Boutet (1779–1847), a celebrated French actress in the Comédie Française.

246.20–21 "rather . . . Roman": *Julius Caesar*, IV.iii.27–28.

248.10–11 Among . . . bed-chamber: Comte de Xavier de Maistre (1763–1852), *Voyage Autour de ma Chambre* (Paris, 1828).

250.12 "it was a great lubberly boy!": *The Merry Wives of Windsor*, V.v.184.

253.7 Mr. Weld: Thomas Weld (1773–1837), husband of Lucy

Bridget Clifford, a grand-daughter of the third Lord
Clifford. When Weld's wife died in 1815, he took holy orders
and, in 1830, became a cardinal.

253.8 Cardinal York: Henry Benedict Maria Clement, Cardinal
York (1725–1807), the last of the family of James II, was
made cardinal in 1747.

253.38 Cardinal Fesch: Joseph, Cardinal Fesch (1763–1839), half
brother of Napoleon Bonaparte's mother, appointed archbishop of Lyons in 1802 and created cardinal in 1803.

254.1 Cardinal Albani: Giuseppe, Cardinal Albani (1750–1834), a
nobleman who became cardinal in 1801.

254.40 Propaganda: the *Congregatio de propaganda fide*, established
in 1622 by Pope Gregory XV.

257.21 the *Grognon*: the grumbler.

259.17 "method . . . madness": *Hamlet*, II.ii.205–06.

259.21 Cohoes: Cohoes Falls, New York, a cataract of the Mohawk
River.

261.28 "Lombard-street to a china orange": Sir Edward Bulwer-
Lytton's *The Caxtons*, Pt. 4, Ch. 3.

263.17 *Montagne des Russes*: French town in the department of Jura.

264.27–28 little book sold on the spot: *Relazione Istorica delle Pro-
digiose Translazione della Santa Casa di Nazarette* by Vincenzo
Murri, the curato of Loreto. The book was issued several
times, beginning as early as 1809. Cooper's succinct summary
parallels Murri's narrative, which is a shorter version of his
1791 work.

273.14 Este: one of the ancient princely houses of Italy. Its members were leaders of the Guelphs in the thirteenth and four-
teenth centuries.

273.15 cell . . . prison of Tasso: Tasso had been confined for in-
sanity by order of Alphonso d'Este in the Hospital of St.
Anne.

276.32 Powles Hook: Jersey City, New Jersey.

278.2 C[ruger]: Henry Nicholas Cruger (1800–1867), a South Car-
olinian whom Cooper apparently met in Venice, became a
life-long friend of the novelist. A brother-in-law of James
Hamilton, Governor of South Carolina who was a leading
nullifier, Cruger married the celebrated and eccentric heiress
Harriet Douglas.

279.27–32 Square of St. Mark . . . Arabian Nights: Cooper used
this setting in his novel *The Bravo* (1831).

280.22–24 The noble group of horses . . . centuries: At the fall of
the French Empire, the four bronze horses Napoleon had
taken to Paris in 1797 were restored to the position they had
occupied since the early thirteenth century, when Doge Dan-
dolo brought them from Constantinople.

283.1–2 The Martyrdom . . . way: Sir Joshua Reynolds comments
that one of the finest of Titian's background landscapes is to
be found in this painting (*The Works of Sir Joshua Reynolds*, II
[London: T. Cadell, 1798], pp. 59–60).

283.29–31 Lady Mary Wortley Montagu says . . . the latter: The
statement does not appear in Lord Wharncliffe's *The Letters
and Works of Lady Mary Wortley Montagu* (London: Richard
Bentley, 1837), the edition to which Cooper evidently refers.
He may have been recalling obliquely a spurious letter (II,
344–45), in which the overpowering effect of the Florentine
statues of the naked Antinous and "the famous Venus de
Medicis" is contrasted to the lesser impact of clothed human
figures or sculptures. This letter is rejected as spurious by
Robert Halsband, ed., *The Complete Letters of Lady Mary Wortley
Montagu* (London: Oxford, 1966), II, 202.

284.2 John of Bellino: Giovanni Bellini (1430–1516).

289.32–290.8 Some travellers . . . this error: According to the notes
furnished by Horace H. Furness to *The Merchant of Venice* in *A
New Variorum Edition of Shakespeare* (Philadelphia, 1888), p. 34:
"There were in ancient Venice three distinct places properly
called *Rialto*: namely, the island at the farther side of the
Grand Canal; the Exchange erected on that island; and the
Ponte di Rialto, which connected the island with St. Mark's
Quarter." Cooper's information apparently derived from
Count Pierre Antoine Daru's *Histoire de la république de Venise*
(1829), a work the novelist had studied before writing *The
Bravo* (1831). Cooper's friend, N. H. Carter, in his *Letters from
Europe*, II, 440, applied the name "Rialto" to the "far-famed
bridge, immortalized by the allusions of Shakespeare."

290.9–27 "I stood in Venice . . . is also exaggerated: The lines
Cooper quotes are all from Canto IV of *Childe Harold's Pil-
grimage*: 1:1, 1:2, 3:3. The descriptions of Venice to which
the novelist refers are contained in the first nineteen stanzas
of Canto IV.

294.37–38 connexions of General Lafayette . . . Montaigu:
Lafayette and the Marquis de Montaigu married sisters,
Adrienne and Pauline, two of the five daughters of the Duke
d'Ayen.

299.4–5 King Stork for King Log: When the frogs asked Jove for a
King, according to the fable, Jove tossed a log into their
pond, but they soon discovered that the log was not a king
and again went to Jove. This time he gave them an eel, but it
was stupid. The third time Jove became angry and sent King
Stork, who caught them one by one and ate them.

Appendix A
Bentley's Analytical Table of Contents

sovereignty of Tuscany.—The author presented to the
Grand Duke and to the Princesses.—His Conversation
with the Grand Duke.—Political Reflections.

Appendix B
Guide to Parallel Passages in the Italian Journal, 1828 – 29, and the Cooper Edition

Entry Date in the Italian Journal, 1828–29	Journal Text in *Letters and Journals*, vol. I	Expanded Text in Cooper Edition
Wednesday, 15 October 1828	p. 351	p. 3
Thursday, 16 October	351–352	3–6
Friday, 17 October	352	6–8
Friday, 31 July 1829	373	81
Saturday, 1 August	374–375	29–32, 81
Sunday, 2 August	375	82–83
Monday, 3 August	375	33–34, 83–84
Tuesday, 4 August	376	84–85
Wednesday, 5 August	376–377	85–88
Thursday, 6 August	377–378	88–90
Friday, 7 August	378	41, 90–92
Saturday, 8 August	378	92–93
Sunday, 9 August	378–380	93–96
Monday, 10 August	380	114–116
Tuesday, 11 August– Saturday, 15 August	380	106–107, 108–113
Sunday, 16 August	381	98–106
Monday, 17 August–Tuesday, 18 August	381	174–178
Wednesday, 19 August	381	113–114
Thursday, 20 August	381–382	118–120
[Thursday, 20 August–Sunday, 27 September]	382–384	118, 121, 136–137, 141–142
Sunday, 27 September	392	144
Monday, 28 September	392	137
Tuesday, 29 September	392–393	137–140
Wednesday, 30 September– Wednesday, 7 October	393	121, 144–145

TEXTUAL APPARATUS

Textual Commentary

In sending the manuscript of *Gleanings in Europe: Italy* to London for its first printing,[1] Cooper was breaking a firmly established precedent. Always before, even when travelling in Europe, he had made it his invariable rule to have his works set in sufficient geographical proximity to permit him to read and correct first proofs. When forwarding the manuscript to London on 8 July 1837, he knew that *Italy* would be published in England without his corrections. His compelling reason for violating this hitherto inviolable rule was economic.

When Cooper offered the book to Carey, Lea, and Blanchard on the usual terms in June 1837, Carey declined, partly because of the severity of the general economic depression and partly because the four earlier travel books had been financial failures. Cooper found it necessary, in this instance, to devise a new publishing procedure. Carey had set the American editions of the earlier travels from manuscript; and his proof sheets, which incorporated the author's corrections in proof, had been sent to Richard Bentley in London as printer's copy. Now, however, as Cooper informed his wife in a letter written in New York on 29 June 1837, "I shall not print but send my manuscript, and draw against that. By this arrang[e]ment, I shall get on for a month or six weeks, and receive back the sheets from England." He was optimistic that Carey would "take the book when it returns,"[2] and, in a reversal of the usual practice, print the American edition from corrected Bentley sheets.

On 6 July 1837, Cooper notified Bentley that *Italy* would leave New York two days later on the ship *Pennsylvania*. He explained: "I am compelled to be absent from town, and I have sent you the manuscript of this work, instead of printed sheets. It is pretty carefully corrected, but will require a vigilant proof-reader . . . I might have sent a more fairly written copy, but I thought it might be some little compensation for the extra trouble, if I gave you the original, in my own hand." In the same letter, he wrote: "I beg you will send me back the sheets of this book, as soon as it is printed—This would be a favor, as I might still reprint from it, here, for such is the state of things, the Messrs Carey dare not publish just yet." "Let me again request a careful reader," Cooper reiterated in closing, "and that you will remember the sheets."[3]

On 5 August 1837, Bentley acknowledged Cooper's letter and receipt of the manuscript of *Italy*. "I shall cause every attention to be paid in passing the work through the press, and feel obliged by the compliment you pay me in sending the original MS. The printed sheets, as they pass through the press, shall be forwarded as you desire."[4]

On 8 September 1837, in a letter from Cooperstown, Cooper resumed negotiations with his American publisher: "I found things so bad in New-York," he wrote to Carey, Lea, and Blanchard, "that I did not print Italy, but sent the manuscript to Bentley, who is to return me the sheets, as the book goes through the press. A letter received this morning, informs me that he is going on, and that I may soon expect the sheets. . . . I have directed the sheets to be sent to John Wiley, who will forward them to you, as received."[5] Cooper was apparently so confident that Bentley would have followed his instructions in employing "a vigilant proof-reader, one like him who corrected the Headsman,"[6] that his own proofreading would not be required. His confidence in the superiority of Bentley's shop lasted at least until 6 December 1837, when Cooper requested Bentley to send the sheets of *Homeward Bound* (also set from manuscript) as they were struck off so that he would be released "from the trouble of reading proof" for the American edition.[7]

This excessive confidence was short-lived. Cooper must not have inspected Bentley's sheets carefully when the first 168 pages of *Italy* were forwarded to Carey in mid-November 1837.[8] When he did examine the sheets thoroughly, evidently on his visit to New York and Philadelphia in December, he discovered that *Italy* was, in fact, "infamously printed."[9] Writing to Bentley on 21 January 1838, he complained, "Italy is de *pis en pis*. It is to say the truth full of misprints—I shall send you an American Copy to compare."[10] The implication of Cooper's remark is that he had abandoned his assumption that Bentley's sheets could be reprinted without correction. He had now "received the sheets of Italy down to 215 or 20 pp. Vol. II[d]" in the Bentley edition.[11] Collation of the Carey and Bentley editions suggests that he recalled any Bentley sheets in Carey's hands and treated them as uncorrected proof for the Carey edition. "The most extraordinary errors exist in Italy," he remarked to Carey on 1 April 1838; "'North' is printed for 'South,' and 'right' for 'left.'" "I liken the top of St. Peters to a 'table-land on a mountain,'" he exclaimed to Horatio Greenough in a letter of 31 June 1838, "and it is printed in the English edition, 'a table *laid* on a mountain.'"[12] In the letter to Carey of 1 April, "I corrected, and sent to you, about ten days since, the remainder of Italy."[13]

Three editions of *Italy* were published in 1838. The English edition, set from Cooper's manuscript, and published in two volumes by Richard Bentley on 12 February 1838, was entitled *Excursions in Italy*.[14] Neither this manuscript nor any pre-publication material other than Cooper's original Journal has been located. The size of this impression was 1,000 copies.[15]

Carey, Lea, and Blanchard published the American edition entitled

Gleanings in Europe. Italy on 28 May 1838 in two volumes, with Griggs as printer.[16] This edition of 1,000 was set from sheets of the Bentley edition corrected by Cooper.[17]

A French edition in English, *Excursions in Italy*, a reprint of the Bentley, was announced on 12 May 1838.[18] It was published in Paris in one volume under the separate imprints of Baudry's European Library and A. and W. Galignani.[19] Collation shows the London and Paris editions to be exactly parallel except for compositorial corrections and corruptions: at six places the French compositor has corrected errors in Cooper's French,[20] at five other places corrected obvious errors in the Bentley,[21] and in ninety-nine instances initiated errors and corruptions in the English text. Since the French edition derives directly from the Bentley, whose title it duplicates, and since Cooper, who was in the United States at the time of its preparation, could not have exerted any authority over its publication, the Baudry/Galignani edition is not considered authorial and does not appear in the Textual Apparatus.

The copy-text of the Cooper Edition of *Italy* is the Bentley edition, which was set from the author's unlocated manuscript. The copy used for the present edition is that deposited for copyright in the National Library of Scotland. Hinman collation discloses broken type (at 87.39, some copies read "protestations of" while others read "protestations # # f") and loose type ("have its" at 220.7 becomes "haveits"). Since these differences are apparently not the result of intervention in the press run, the copy-text exists in one state. The title page of the Bentley edition, however, exists in four states. The original title page of the two-volume format (A-F₁a) erroneously attributes authorship to C. Fenimore Cooper. Other copies of this format contain a tipped-in, two-leaf gathering correcting the authorship to J. Fenimore Cooper (A-F₁b). A second format (A-F₂), with the title page undated and reading *Excursions in Italy*, by C. Fenimore Cooper, was published as "two volumes in one"; a third format (A-F₃), with the title page reading *Travel and Excursions in Various Parts of the World: Italy*, by C. Fenimore Cooper—volumes eight and nine of an eleven-volume collection of Cooper's travel works—is also undated. The multiple states of the title page are evidently, in the first instance, Bentley's correction of an initial error, and, in the other two instances, Bentley's effort to use a variety of formats to dispose of the original printing. The variant title pages do not seem to indicate new impressions.[22]

The Carey, Lea, and Blanchard edition, set by Griggs and Co. in Philadelphia between November 1837 and April 1838, exists in two states. At 296.3–4, "combats of the south-west," the correct form, appears in some copies as "combats if the south-west." Hinman collation shows that the texts with the "of" reading are identical in all other respects to those with the "if" reading. Though this is the only variant in the copies of the Carey edition, it does demonstrate (unlike the broken and loose type of the British edition) intervention in the press run. The Textual Apparatus, therefore, cites the incorrect "if" reading as State 1 (B$_1$) and the correct "of" reading as State 2 (B$_2$).[23]

Of the 333 substantive changes appearing in the Carey edition, many are obviously authorial. As one would expect from Cooper's letter to Carey, at 92.26, "north" becomes "south"; at 98.11, "north-east" becomes "south-east"; at 269.6 and 303.20, "left" becomes "right"; and at 303.21, "right" becomes "left." And, as Cooper's letter to Greenough predicts, "table laid on a mountain" becomes "table-land on a mountain," at 236.19. These and corrections like them indicate Cooper's efforts to correct his text; and, numbering about 235, they demonstrate his characteristic concern to improve it. Some correct errors, like those cited above; others accomplish a more precise expression, show movement towards concision, or clarify diction and usage. These improvements are accepted as authorial, since they are likely to have resulted from Cooper's revision of Bentley's "infamous printing." Samples of these readings appear in the footnotes.[24] However, ninety-seven substantive variants introduce obvious errors. Because they violate his intention to correct the text, they have been rejected in the Cooper Edition and appear in Rejected Readings.[25]

Included among the accepted Carey variants are some which, under different circumstances, might not be considered authorial. Since Cooper took particular care with his correction of the Bentley sheets for Carey, the Cooper Edition accepts variants which make marginal but definite improvements of the text and rejects those which do not. Instructive examples are the changes from singular to plural at 19.2 ("lodging" to "lodgings") and at 60.39 ("frontier" to "frontiers"). Though they appear to be exactly the same kind of variant, the former is accepted, while the latter is not. The plural form "lodgings," used a dozen times throughout *Italy*, seems more idiomatic in the context of the passage than the singular; the plural "frontiers," however, is not required by the context. Editorial discrimination between the two variants, if it is to be made at all, has to be made on that basis. Twenty-one other substantive variants which are not obvious errors but which, like "frontiers," do not improve the text, are rejected.[26]

The Carey edition of *Italy* is not error-free. Even with Cooper's careful revision of the Bentley sheets, some errors escaped his attention, and there is no evidence of his having read Carey's proofs. The present edition makes sixteen additional substantive corrections in the text: at 89.15, for example, the word "preferring" or some equivalent is needed to clarify the syntax.[27] The Cooper Edition also corrects three errors in accidentals, deleting commas at 112.5 (twice) and 124.27–28. Other necessary emendations of accidentals follow precedents in the Carey edition although they are made on the authority of the Cooper Edition.[28] The Cooper Edition does not presume that Cooper necessarily made them.

Since Cooper often followed the nineteenth-century penchant

for privacy by printing names of persons and places with a three- or four-em dash, the Cooper Edition has supplied the appropriate name, where possible, within square brackets. For example, at 84.16, "W———" becomes "W[illiam]" and at 255.29, "C———n" becomes "C[ooperstow]n." All such instances of expansion of names are recorded in the Emendations list.

The spelling of the copy-text has not been silently corrected or regularized. In two instances, apparent errors in spelling have been emended on the authority of Noah Webster's *An American Dictionary of the English Language* (New York, 1828).[29] Since Cooper was inconsistent in spelling—he often interchanged British and American preferences like "enquire" and "inquire" or "defence" and "defense"—variant but acceptable spellings have been retained.

In twenty-eight instances, erroneous spellings of foreign words (French, Italian and Latin) have been emended.[30] In forty-nine instances where Cooper's usage has not been corroborated in a contemporaneous text, unusual spellings of proper and geographical names have been emended.[31] Any unusual spelling of a word (as "Pausilippo" for Posillipo) that has been corroborated in at least one other nineteenth-century source has been left unchanged. Two misspelled words Cooper probably derived from other sources ("Winkelman" for "Winckelmann" and "*Rediculi*" for "*Ridiculi*") have been corrected in the text, entered in the Emendations list and explained in Textual Notes. Certain idiosyncratic spellings (such as "Schwytz") have been retained, along with eccentric divisions of proper names (such as "Serra valle"). Erroneous diacritical marks have been corrected, but the use of the circumflex instead of a macron over the Latin long "a" ("*bonâ fide*"; "*pro formâ*"; "*vice versâ*"), a general nineteenth-century printing practice, has been preserved. Erroneous dates and measurements which Cooper probably derived from another source have not been corrected in the text, but each is discussed elsewhere.

The Cooper Edition, then, reprints the copy-text of *Gleanings in Europe: Italy*, set from Cooper's manuscript, and retains all its accidentals, if they are not determined to violate early nineteenth-century practice. Substantive emendation of the "infamously printed" Bentley edition occurs when the variants in the Carey edition (which used Cooper's corrected Bentley sheets as printer's copy) seem clearly authorial or accomplish common proofreading objectives. On its own authority, the Cooper Edition corrects obvious errors and supplies missing names in square brackets, when possible. Though the analytical table of contents might appear to be part of the Bentley copy-text, it was not retained in the Carey reprinting, the precedents of the four previous travel works corroborating that it originated in the Bentley shop. The Cooper Edition, despite the non-authorial nature of the table of contents, reproduces it for the reader's convenience in Appendix A, pp. 319–25.[32] The Cooper Edition also retains the title of the American edition, *Gleanings in Europe. Italy*, which presumably had Cooper's approval and follows the precedent of two earlier travel volumes. It does not reproduce the visual appurtenances of the copy-text.

Notes

1. *The Letters and Journals of James Fenimore Cooper*, ed. James Franklin Beard. 6 vols. (Cambridge: Harvard University Press, Belknap Press, 1960–1968), III, 268 (hereafter cited as *Letters and Journals*).
2. *Letters and Journals*, III, 266.
3. Ibid., 269.
4. Ibid., 269, n. 2; MS: Collection of American Literature, Beinecke Rare Book and Manuscript Library, Yale University (hereafter cited as YCAL).
5. Ibid., 289.
6. Ibid., 269.
7. Ibid., 302.
8. Carey, Lea, and Blanchard to Cooper, 17 November 1837; MS: YCAL.
9. *Letters and Journals*, VI, 326.
10. Ibid., III, 306.
11. Ibid.
12. Ibid., 329.
13. Ibid., VI, 325.
14. Bentley Papers, Vol. LXXVIII, British Museum, Add Mss 46, 637. See also *A List of the Principal Publications Issued from New Burlington Street During the Year 1838* (London: Richard Bentley and Son, 1894), entry for 12 February 1838. An erroneous publication date, 28 February 1838, is given in Robert E. Spiller and Phillip C. Blackburn, *A Descriptive Bibliography of the Writings of James Fenimore Cooper* (New York: R. R. Bowker Company, 1934), p. 93, and in *Letters and Journals*, III, 307.
15. BM Add Mss 46, 637.
16. David Kaser, *The Cost Book of Carey and Lea: 1825–1838* (Philadelphia: The University of Pennsylvania Press, 1963), p. 269. *The National Union Catalog Pre-1956 Imprints* erroneously notes that *Gleanings in Europe. Italy* was published in one volume; see v. 121, p. 609. The two volumes were sometimes bound as one.
17. Photostat of a page from the cost book of Carey, Lea, and Blanchard for 1838. David Kaser, ed., *The Cost Book of Carey and Lea: 1825–1838*, does not include this information.
18. *Bibliographie de la France* (Paris, 1838), 2391–2392.

19. BAL, II, 3882. *The National Union Catalog Pre-1956 Imprints*, v. 121, p. 609, incorrectly asserts that this volume was first published in London under the title *Gleanings in Europe: Italy*.
20. At 17.7 (*des* becomes *de*), 22.37 (*agrémens* becomes *agréments*), 26.31 (Monfort becomes Montfort), 30.38 (*en profile* becomes *en profil*), 46.30 (*fol* becomes *fou*), and 76.8 (Salmes becomes Salm).
21. These changes include the addition of a lost letter (87.39: "f" becomes "of"); the correction of a preposition (131.32: "or" becomes "of"); the addition of an article (223.19: "staircase" becomes "a staircase"); the excision of a preposition (237.7: "in in" becomes "in"); and the addition of a pronoun (239.36: "that is" becomes "that it is").
22. See also BAL, II, 3879. Blanck cites only the variant title-pages of the two-volume format, A-F₁a and A-F₁b, makes no distinction between the copy-text and title-pages, and, therefore, describes *Italy* as existing in two states. He suggests: "[T]here is a possibility that . . . these states were printed simultaneously from a multiple setting and published at the same time": a most unlikely procedure for such an unpopular book. *The National Union Catalog Pre-1956 Imprints* does not record an *Excursions in Italy* by J. Fenimore Cooper. Examination of nine available copies of A-F₁b has revealed five with tipped-in title-pages. These copies are located at the American Antiquarian Society, and at the libraries of Columbia University, the University of Connecticut, the University of Pennsylvania, and the University of Washington. Rebinding of the other four (at the Boston Public Library, The New York Public Library, the Cornell University Library, and the Fales Library at New York University) makes a definitive conclusion impossible. The present edition is based on two complete sight collations by two independent readers of the Bentley and Carey editions and of the Bentley and Baudry editions. All three volumes are in the collection of The New York Public Library: Bentley (BWX), Baudry (D-18.4282), and Carey (*KL). In addition, copies of the English edition in the following libraries were fully compared on the Hinman Collator: A-F₁a, the National Library of Scotland (Advocates' Library, Edinburgh; unnumbered); A-F₁b, the American Antiquarian Society (unnumbered), The New York Public Library (BWX), and the University of Pennsylvania Library (*AC8 C7862. 838e); A-F₂, the Duke University Library (813.24 C777E); A-F₃, the University of Rochester Library (DG 426 C77e). These six copies included three attributed to C. Fenimore Cooper and three to J. Fenimore Cooper. The New York Public Library copy was the standard of collation in all five collations. Additional copies examined are located at the following libraries: A-F₁a, the

American Antiquarian Society, the British Library, Buffalo and Erie County Public, Indiana University, the University of Michigan, Tulane University, the University of Wisconsin, and YCAL; A-F$_3$, YCAL. Copies of the American edition examined by Hinman Collator are located in: B$_1$, University of Wisconsin (G36 .C78), and Yale University (Edh 830); B$_2$, the collection of James F. Beard (copy 1), Enoch Pratt Free Library (914.5 C777), Indiana State (914.5 C777), University of Minnesota (Z81 C78 Ogl), New York Public Library (*KL), University of North Carolina (PS 1421 .G54), and Wayne State University (813.24 C786xg 1c 0.52). The New York Public Library copy was the standard of collation in three of the six collations. An additional copy of B$_1$ examined is located in the Fales Library at New York University; additional copies of B$_2$ examined are located at the American Antiquarian Society, the British Library, the Cleveland Public Library, the Library of Congress, the University of British Columbia, University of California at Berkeley, University of Pennsylvania, University of South Carolina, and Williams College. Copies of the French edition examined against the variants found as a result of the Bentley/Baudry sight collation are located in: the American Antiquarian Society (unnumbered), the collection of James F. Beard, the British Library (10130. bbb. 33), Harvard University (Ital. 2148 38.5), Louisiana State University (DG 426 C77 1838b), and the Fales Library at New York University. The seven copies of the French edition include three (at the British Library, Louisiana State University, and the Fales Library at New York University) with the imprint of A. and W. Galignani.

23. Blanck, BAL, II, 3882, asserts that Volume I of this impression occurs in two states, arguing that in state A the imprint and the copyright notice appear on page ii, whereas in state B, the copyright notice alone appears on that page. While Blanck is correct in adducing two states to the Carey impression, the textually significant variant, which he does not mention, occurs in Volume II. Further, there is no consistency between Blanck's two states with the variant Volume I pages and the two states created by the substantive variant in Volume II, for variant Volume II readings were paired indiscriminately with the variant Volume I title-pages either in the printing house, the bindery, or the booksellers.

24. The variant readings here and in footnote 25 are set off by double bars.

Correction of obvious substantive errors:

	BENTLEY EDITION	CAREY EDITION
3.27–28	We saw //people with	We saw //many people with

	Bentley	Carey
	many *goîtres*// in the streets	*goîtres*// in the streets
20.38–39	our wine commands fully a cent a flask, or about four //nills// a bottle	our wine commands fully a cent a flask, or about four //mills// a bottle

Precision:

27.1–3	The winter has come upon us sharply, ice forming freely in the ditches around the town, and skates //coming// into requisition.	The winter has come upon us sharply, ice forming freely in the ditches around the town, and skates //being brought// into requisition.
31.27–30	It is contained within cloisters, the monuments being under cover, and the space //to contain// the bodies is not larger than a considerable court in a palace.	It is contained within cloisters, the monuments being under cover, and the space // occupied by// the bodies is not larger than a considerable court in a palace.

Concision:

1.1–2	If the author were required to give a reason why he has written // these volumes// on a country so well known as Italy	If the author were required to give a reason why he has written on a country so well known as Italy
16.18–19	the spot was on the brow of the southern margin // of the range//	the spot was on the brow of the southern margin

Diction and Usage:

9.11–12	pieces of marble are stuck in it, so as to variegate the //effect//	pieces of marble are stuck in it, so as to variegate the //surface//
15.3–4	but I was not //disposed// to humour roguery	but I was not //inclined// to humour roguery

25. Substantive errors by Carey:

	BENTLEY EDITION	CAREY EDITION
9.1	But //all// nations have	But //the// nations have

their Gothic ages	their Gothic ages

16.35   //caste// of *voituriers*   //cast// of *voituriers*

26. Readings that do not follow Cooper's pattern of correction:

BENTLEY EDITION	CAREY EDITION
51.27 A jog from the //con- ducteur// awoke me	A jog from the //conductor// awoke me
70.30–31 we soon reached the door that communicates with the //cloisters//	we soon reached the door that communicates with the //cloister//

27. The other corrections are located in Emendations at 33.18,
40.20, 52.2, 97.15, 104.29, 109.36, 131.32, 223.19, 244.2,
244.3 (twice), 261.20, 263.17, 283.12, and 295.39.
28. Spelling: 20.2–3, 84.5, 86.21, 94.15, 131.14, 146.17, 167.19,
172.1 and 195.20; punctuation: 10.23 and 122.33.
29. See 91.5 and 153.38–39.
30. French: 17.7, 22.37, 30.38, 40.20, 46.13–14, 46.30, 61.21, 63.34,
90.2, 104.35, 133.7, 234.6, and 261.20; Italian: 20.1, 32.25,
61.5, 72.8, 73.5, 87.8, 109.2, 129.25, 171.4, 171.31, 229.4,
229.30, 235.2, and 252.34; and Latin: 185.1.
31. American: 259.21; French: 26.31, 61.13, 61.21, 61.21 [*bis*],
61.24, 76.8, 116.25, and 263.17; German: 153.38, 240.32 and
303.22; Italian: 8.35, 52.18, 52.27, 84.28, 89.1, 89.36, 89.37,
93.17, 95.23, 107.6, 120.9, 140.40, 158.30, 161.5, 172.33,
210.6, 213.9, 214.36, 235.27, 263.15–16, 263.21, 264.33,
268.2, 268.5, 269.3, 270.15, 270.25, 284.40 and 299.39; and
Latin: 80.37, 119.37, 131.10, 131.14, 134.13, 134.25, 202.22,
204.38, and 214.36.
32. The headnotes of the copy-text, reproductions of the appropriate sections of the table of contents preceding each letter, are
retained in the Carey reprinting, but are, due to their non-
authorial origin, omitted in the Cooper Edition. Other evidence confirms their non-authorial nature. Although Cooper
had the opportunity to revise them for the Carey reprinting,
he did not, for the Carey headnotes retain the substantive
errors originating in their Bentley printer's copy:

	Table of Contents	Bentley Headnotes	Carey Headnotes
Letter XXI	not well	well	well
Letter XXII	of the town	the town	the town
Letter XXIX	no unnecessary	unnecessary	unnecessary

Textual Notes

The following notes explain emendations and rejected readings requiring more specific information than the Textual Commentary could provide.

7.35 Since in *Italy* Cooper generally describes details as they are at the time of his observation, the strategy of the book requires the present tense here. His journal entry for 17 October 1828, which describes this bridge as having been "just finished by Marie Louise" (*Letters and Journals*, I, 352), verifies the copy-text reading.

9.1 The Carey change to "But the nations" makes no sense in the context. Cooper is not referring to specific nations but rather making a general remark about all nations.

10.23 The change from a colon to a comma in the Carey has been accepted on the authority of the Cooper Edition because of its appropriateness to the substantive change.

12.16 Cooper obviously means to suggest a contrast between the road and the rest of the scene, making the Bentley reading more appropriate.

19.2 This change has been accepted because of the use of "lodgings" at 19.7.

24.7 The deletion of the adjective "mere" in the Carey is consistent with Cooper's practice of rendering the text more concise, but the deletion of the article "a" renders the phrase exceedingly awkward. The Cooper Edition, therefore, reinstates the article.

36.7 At the time of Cooper's visit, there was only one great staircase leading to the reception rooms, and he would have had to ascend it, not descend.

38.5 The present edition retains the paragraphing of the copy-text. Here and at the following points the Carey edition begins a new paragraph where the copy-text does not: 54.23, 204.18, and 259.29–30.

40.20 Without "*sens*" the expression is non-idiomatic.

42.13 Cooper appears to be careful during his revision (see 112.6, for example) to attain parallelism, which this Carey variant violates. The Cooper Edition therefore rejects it.

51.27 This substantive change obviates the necessity for italics here yet the italics remain. Moreover, *conducteur* is used throughout, making this unique occurrence of English spelling of the word a probable compositorial error.

52.2 Without this emendation, the sentence at 51.37–52.3 is unintelligible.

54.23 See Textual Note for 38.5.

86.22 While a substantive change has been accepted here, the punctuation and spelling of the copy-text have been retained. See also 113.35 and 244.38.

89.14–15 The addition of "preferring" renders the sentence intelligible and is consistent with Cooper's style. See 21.5–6.

101.20 Cooper is discussing several homes. See 101.8–10.

109.36 The addition of "not" is essential to the sense of the sentence.

112.5 The presence of the comma after "that" renders the verb "blended" an erroneous past participle.

112.5 Cooper's substantive change requires the deletion of the comma after "way."

113.32–33 Without the addition of "not" provided by the Carey edition, the sentence is illogical in its context.

113.35 See Textual Note for 86.22.

124.27–28 Cooper's revision requires the deletion of the comma after "modestly."

140.18 The deletion of "not" in the Carey destroys the sense of the sentence.

185.12 Since Cooper is referring to robbery in general, the addition of "the" in the Carey renders the sentence less idiomatic and has been rejected.

204.17–18 See Textual Note for 38.5.

204.38 *Fanum Ridiculi*: Cooper's original spelling, *Rediculi*, appears in Vasi's *Rome* (1829), II, 410, an apparent blending of the Latin *Ridiculi* and the French *de Rédicule*.

214.36 Cooper is mistranslating two Roman road names. The *Via Nomentana* is "the road to Nomentum" (literally, of Nomentum). The *Salaria Via* (or *Via Salaria*) means "the Salt Road," so called because the Sabines used it to fetch salt from the sea. (Salaria is not a place, simply an adjective meaning "of, or belonging to, salt.")

240.32 Winckelmann: Cooper's original spelling of this name (Winkelman) appears in Eustace's *A Classical Tour of Italy*, II, 66.

244.38 Parallelism requires that the punctuation of the copy-text be retained.

259.29–30. See Textual Note for 38.5.

295.39 In the context, "police" is preferred to "policies," the only other possible emendation.

298.20 The fact that Massa was joined to Modena in 1830 and Lucca to Tuscany in 1847, at the death of Marie Louise, necessitates the shift of the asterisk indicated in the Carey.

298.20–21 See Textual Note for 298.20.

Emendations

The following list records all changes in substantives and accidentals introduced into the copy-text. The reading of the Cooper Edition appears to the left of the square bracket; the authority for that reading, followed by a semicolon, the copy-text reading and the copy-text symbol appear to the right of the bracket. The abbreviation CE indicates emendation made for the first time in the Cooper Edition and not found in any of the authoritative editions examined in the preparation of this text. Within an entry, the curved dash ~ represents the same word that appears before the bracket and is used in recording punctuation variants; a caret_A to the right of the square bracket signifies the absence of punctuation found to the left of the square bracket. An asterisk before an entry indicates that the entry is discussed in Textual Notes. A dagger † indicates that the entry is discussed in Explanatory Notes. Where there are more than two occurrences of an identical emendation, the initial entry includes a blanket note listing each recurrence.

The following texts are referred to:

A   *Excursions in Italy*. London: Bentley, 1838.
B₁   *Gleanings in Europe. Italy*. Philadelphia: Carey, Lea and
     Blanchard, 1838. [First State]
B₂   *Gleanings in Europe. Italy*. Philadelphia: Carey, Lea and
     Blanchard, 1838. [Second State]

1.2	written] B₁; written these volumes A
†3.3	Doveiria] CE; Doverie A; Doveria B₁–B₂
3.20	railway] CE; railways A
3.27	many people with *goîtres*] B₁; people with many *goîtres* A
5.30	precise thing] B₁; thing A
8.35	*Battistero*] CE; *Battisteria* A
8.39	all] B₁; the A
9.7	itself,] B₁; itself, again, A
9.12	surface] B₁; effect A
*10.23	low, that lean] B₁; low: one leans A
13.7	an air] B₁; the air A
14.21	[Mrs. Cooper]] CE; A————A (*Also emended at* 77.15, 77.22, 77.24, 77.33, 88.29, 183.11, 186.35,

186.40–187.1, 295.12, *and* 302.1–2.)

15.3	inclined] B₁; disposed A
15.22	wants,] B₁; few wants, all A
16.19	margin] B₁; margin of the range A
16.29	savoured] B₁; savoured more A
17.7	*de*] CE; *des* A
*19.2	lodgings] B₁; lodging A
19.13	become] B₁; became A
19.24	pacific,] B₁; pacific, however, A
20.1	*mezzanino*] CE; *mezzinino* A
20.2–3	ceilings] B₁; cielings A
20.39	mills] B₁; nills A
21.38	approaching the] B₁; approaching a A
22.37	*agréments*] CE; *agrémens* A
23.4	all] B₁; all of A
23.24	V[idua]] CE; V———A (*Also emended at* 23.36 *and* 24.15.)
23.33	P[oerio]] CE; P———A
*24.7	a run] CE; a mere run A; run B₁–B₂
†24.27	B[urghersh]] CE; B———A
†24.27–28	N[ormanby]] CE; N———A
26.31	Montfort] CE; Monfort A
27.2	being brought] B₁; coming A
†28.1	G[ouverneur] W[ilkins]] CE; G——— W——— A
28.8	W[ilkins]'s] CE; W———'s A
30.38	*profil*] CE; *profile* A
31.29	occupied by] B₁; to contain A
32.23	rigs] B₁; brigs A
32.25	speronara] CE; sparranara A
33.18	residence] CE; residences A
33.34	religion] B₁; religious A
34.30	on this] B₁; in this A
36.14	[Ricasoli]] CE; ——— A
*40.20	*sens dessus-dessous*] CE; *dessus-dessous* A
46.13–14	polonaise] CE; polonnaise A
46.30	*fou*] CE; *fol* A
50.7	receive] B₁; receive the A
*52.2	matters] CE; on matters A
52.18	Serra] CE; Sava A
52.27	Serra] CE; Sava A
53.30	villages] CE; village A
61.5	*e*] CE; *et* A
61.13	Draguignan] CE; Draguinan A (*Also corrected at* 61.21 *and* 61.24.)
61.21	*maniéré*] CE; *maniérée* A
61.32	about] B₁; but about A
63.34	*mistral*] CE; *mistrail* A

70.10	Signor [Cooper]] CE; Signor ——— A
72.8	*corse*] CE; *corsi* A
73.5	*corsa*] CE; *corso* A
76.8	Salm] CE; Salmes A
80.38	Vespucius] CE; Vesputius A
82.7	former] B₁; latter A
82.27	town, notwithstanding] B₁; town, A
82.28	is peculiarly] B₁; is A
82.38	for] B₁; but A
84.5	Nero] B₁; Nera A
†84.16	W[illiam]] CE; W——— A (*Also emended at* 89.7, 107.18, 114.9, 119.4, 121.23–24, 121.40, 137.23, 141.8, 148.17, 150.24, 152.7, 152.33, 153.24, 155.20, 157.27, 250.21, 250.26, 250.30, 259.7, 262.25, *and* 281.7.)
84.28	*Genovese*] CE; *Genovesa* A
85.2	a] B₁; the A
86.21	*Quattro*] B₁; *Quattri* A
*86.22	dinner; furthermore] CE; dinner; and furthermore A; dinner farthermore B₁–B₂
87.8	*tarantola*] CE; *tarantula* A
89.1	Troia] CE; Troas A
*89.14–15	formidable, preferring] CE; formidable, A
89.36	Genovese] CE; Genovesa A
89.37	Cristo] CE; Christo A
90.2	mistral] CE; mistrail A
91.5	galleys] CE; gallies A
92.26	south] B₁; north A
93.17	Genovese] CE; Genovesa A
93.18	smooth] B₁; a smooth A
93.20	a shore] B₁; shore A
93.25	thousands] B₁; its thousands A
94.15	Palisadoes] B₁; Plaisadoes A
95.22	the hotel *delle*] B₁; the *delle* A
95.23	Chiaja] CE; Caiga A; Caija B₁–B₂
97.15	stand] CE; stands A
97.36–37	in the crater] B₁; in A
97.37	mountain] B₁; water A
98.11	south-east] B₁; north-east A
99.7	prior] B₁; antecedently A
99.7	eruption] B₁; eruptions A
99.9	tolerably deep] B₁; deep A
99.16	a cone] B₁; cone A
99.37–38	death, it is to be presumed, was] B₁; death was probably A
101.15	detract] B₁; detracts A
101.16	our] B₁; an A

104.5	buried / B₁; burned A
104.13	enlarged / B₁; cut A
104.15	that particular / B₁; the A
104.29	63 / CE; 69 A
104.35	*débris* / CE; *debris* A; *dèbris* B₁–B₂
105.15	the soil / B₁; soil A
105.36	it / B₁; this theatre A
106.16	Many villas / B₁; Villas A
106.17	discovered, and / B₁; discovered, however, and A
106.19	truth, / B₁; truth, however, A
106.37	hind / B₁; *back* A
107.4	hind / B₁; back A
107.6	Conte / CE; Conde A
107.22	proclamation / B₁; proclamations A
107.37–38	conversation / B₁; conversations A
108.6	us / B₁; me A
108.18	carved / B₁; caned A
109.2	*villeggiatura* / CE; *villagiatura* A
*109.36	not even / CE; even A
110.36	soundings / B₁; sounding A
111.22	These / B₁; But these A
111.24	but / B₁; for A
112.4	threw / B₁; throw A
*112.5	that / CE; ~, A
*112.5	reality in a way / CE; reality, A; reality in a way, B₁–B₂
112.6	nor ever / B₁; or never A
112.22	at / B₁; in A
112.38	greater part / B₁; great point A
113.3	so as to / B₁; as they A
113.24–25	expense and this is the spot to which we will now go. / B₁; expense. A
113.28	use / B₁; uses A
*113.32–33	has not / B₁; have A
*113.35	ring, / CE; ring in the centre, A; ring∧ B₁–B₂
113.36	all of which are / B₁; and all A
114.31	are / B₁; is A
115.3	imaginable, and / B₁; imaginable, A
115.29	convert / CE; converts A
115.32	fellows / B₁; fellow A
115.33	look / B₁; looks A
115.33	their / B₁; his A
115.34	have / B₁; has A
115.34	they exist / B₁; he exists A
†116.25	Contoit / CE; Curtois A; Contois B₁–B₂
117.16	bits / B₁; bit A
117.26	rather to those / B₁; rather A

118.9	which cliffs,] B₁; which A
118.9	spot,] CE; ~ₐ A
118.13	heed] B₁; care A
118.13	to] B₁; for A
118.21	standing] B₁; stands A
118.23	on] B₁; in A
118.24	only] B₁; alone A
119.14–15	court, on the street, and on the sea. A] B₁; court; a A
119.24	P[aul]] CE; P——— A (*Also emended at* 136.22, 190.33, *and* 192.16.)
119.29	doors,] B₁; doors, directly A
119.32	as] B₁; so A
119.37	Misenum] CE; Mycenum A (*Also corrected at* 131.10, 134.13, *and* 134.25.)
120.2	Avernus, and] B₁; Avernus, A
120.9	Felice] CE; Felicia A
120.20	follows] B₁; follow A
120.23–24	most of] B₁; all A
121.21	Midway] B₁; About midway A
121.25	and perfectly] B₁; perfectly A
121.40	manage] B₁; pull A
122.33	them.] B₁; ~ₐ A
123.1	never] B₁; and never A
123.23	make] B₁; make of themselves A
*124.28	modestly aside, permitting] CE; aside, modestly, permitting A; modestly, aside, permitting B₁–B₂
124.37	now daily review] B₁; daily reviewed A
127.1	projection that runs] B₁; projection A
128.39	Baian] B₁; Baiae A
129.18	occasions, a source of happiness] B₁; occasions, A
129.19	a *laquais*] B₁; *laquais* A
129.25	speronara] CE; sparranara A
130.18	thought] B₁; said A
130.21	man-of-war] B₁; men-of-war A
131.14	Stabia] B₁; Statia A
131.32	sort of] CE; sort or A
132.23	impulses] B₁; interests A
132.35	south] B₁; north A
133.7	*couchée*] CE; *coucher* A
135.24	travellers] B₁; *passagères* A
136.3	at] B₁; from A
137.7	as is the case with] B₁; like A
137.29	town] B₁; towns A
138.4	when] B₁; where A
139.21	running to] B₁; running A
139.34	before] B₁; to A

140.40	*Genovese*] CE; *Genovesa* A
141.17	have] B_1; had A
141.24–25	*Camaldoli*] B_1; *Camaldole* A
141.33	feeling on such places was] B_1; feeling was A
141.33	fly,] B_1; fly from such places A
142.2–3	that distinguishes] B_1; of A
146.17	Wall] B_1; Well A
147.4	opinion] B_1; opinions A
148.10	crater] B_1; water A
148.12	in the] B_1; in a A
150.1	spot] B_1; latter A
152.3	of] B_1; for A
153.38	Lowerz] CE; Lowertcz A
153.38–39	Morganatic] CE; Morganic A
154.1	but] B_1; though A
155.20	Pennsylvanian] B_1; Pennsylvanic A
155.28	of] B_1; for A
156.5	have been] B_1; be A
157.35	in that direction] B_1; there A
158.30	Angri] CE; Angra A
159.6	spacious] B_1; large A
159.8	brazier] B_1; brazier that was A
159.11	and with] B_1; and A
159.24–25	such a town as] B_1; a town like A
161.5	Angri] CE; Angra A
161.16	horse's head] B_1; horses' heads A
162.28	history] B_1; history to be sought for A
164.4	each to] B_1; to each A
166.26–27	to comprehend which] B_1; that to comprehend A
167.19	*sana*] B_1; *sane* A
168.33	complain] B_1; complains A
170.26	enough] B_1; enough so A
171.4	*tramontana*] CE; *tramontane* A
171.31	speronara] CE; sparanaro A
172.1	wallowed] B_1; wellowed A
172.33	Pulcinello] CE; Polichinello A
175.6–7	a little resembles] B_1; resembles, a little, A
175.15	proper] B_1; paper A
177.9	another class] B_1; another A
179.6	are] B_1; is A
180.3	state of the seasons] B_1; season A
184.24–26	ruins at a spot that is thought to have been the ancient Minturnum, after we found the carriages, which turned back to meet us] B_1; ruins, after we found the carriages, which turned back to meet us at a spot that is thought to have been the ancient Minturnum A

185.1	*litus*] CE; *littus* A
188.25–26	that the attempt was made by banditti, a few years since,] B₁; that, a few years since, the attempt was made by banditti A
191.13	them] B₁; these A
191.34	walked] B₁; walked unconsciously A
191.36–37	Still, men, at the farthest extremity, seemed dwindled into boys] CE; Still, men seemed dwindled into boys, seen at the farther extremity A; Still men, at the farthest extremity, seemed dwindled into boys B₁–B₂
191.37–40	One, whose size did not appear disproportioned, was cleaning a statue of St. Bruno, at the height of an ordinary church-steeple, stood on the shoulder of the figure, and] B₁; One who was cleaning a statue of St. Bruno, at the height of an ordinary church-steeple, stood on the shoulder of the figure, whose size did not appear disproportioned, and A
192.12	it seemed distant as a cavern on a mountain] B₁; and it seemed as distant as a cavern or mountain A
193.32	town] B₁; place A
194.39	on] B₁; in A
195.4	have run] B₁; run A
195.8	filled] B₁; filled up A
195.20	Bleecker] B₁; Bleecher A
196.25	apprehensions] B₁; apprehension A
197.11	them on] B₁; these in A
198.6	higher] B₁; high A
198.8	measurement] B₁; of measurement A
198.31	the compositor] B₁; a compositor A
199.27	cicerone,] B₁; cicerone, one A
199.35–36	*and at this island he hoped first to arrive*] B₁; and at this island he hoped first to arrive A
200.38	present themselves] B₁; arise A
201.12	which are] B₁; and which is A
†202.13	Buoncompagni] CE; Buon Compagni A
202.22	Salaria] CE; Salara A
204.12	swales] B₁; swells A
*204.38	*Ridiculi*] CE; *Rediculi* A
205.10	remote antiquity] B₁; time immemorial A
205.18	day.] B₁; day. The heathen mythology, moreover, was a *rum* thing, throughout. A
205.24	artifice] B₁; expedient A
206.3	attention] B₁; attention to itself A
207.20	satisfactorily] B₁; very satisfactorily A
208.29	sport] B₁; sports A
210.6	Tectaccio] CE; Testaceo A

212.18	for at] B₁; for above it, or at A
213.9	Falconieri] CE; Falonieri A
213.29	have] B₁; have had A
213.32	himself] B₁; oneself A
214.17	those decided acts] B₁; the decided act A
214.28	the law] B₁; which was the law A
214.31–32	limbs, as well as the] B₁; limbs, and the A
*214.36	Nomentum] CE; Nomentanum A
214.38	the last] B₁; this last A
215.6	rude] B₁; rude and ancient A
217.37	direction] B₁; course A
219.15	rebuilt] B₁; rebuilt his residence A
222.13	as many] B₁; three A
223.19	a staircase] CE; staircase A
228.17	indisposition] B₁; disposition A
229.4	*appartamento*] CE; *appartamente* A
229.7–8	De La Rochefoucauld] CE; De Larochefoucauld A
229.30	*mezzanino*] CE; *mezzinino* A
†230.15	Cicisbeism] CE; Cecisbeism A
230.27	One who has been here a week] B₁; One A
230.28	*Romana*] B₁; *Romana* who has been here a week A
231.28	observation] B₁; experience A
231.29	subsequent] B₁; the subsequent A
231.31	society;] B₁; society; for A
231.32	causing] B₁; causes A
231.33	while] B₁; and A
231.34	associations] B₁; association A
234.6	*conservatoires*] CE; *conservatoirs* A
235.2	baldacchino] CE; baldachino A
235.15	untiring] B₁; uniting A
235.27	Domenichino] CE; Dominichino A
236.19	table-land] B₁; table‿ laid A
237.7	in] B₁; in in A
238.5	The] B₁; A A
238.29	wondered] B₁; wonderful A
239.27	perhaps] B₁; or perhaps A
239.30	with] B₁; and A
239.35	itself merely] B₁; merely A
239.36	that it is] B₁; that is A
239.37	hear it.] B₁; hear. A
239.40–240.1	if, indeed,] B₁; indeed, if A
240.22	men are] B₁; the world is A
†*240.32	Winckelmann] CE; Winkelman A
†243.1	V[olkonskaya]] CE; V—— A
243.26	artists] B₁; artistes A
244.2–3	M. le Préfet, M. le Sous-Préfet, M. le Sergent] CE; M. Préfet, M. Sous-Préfet, M. Sergeant A

*244.38	the other, to / CE; its converse, to A; the other ⌃ to B₁–B₂
252.34	*moccoletti* / CE; *mocheletti* A
254.34–35	address / B₁; render an apology necessary for one of my nation, when I spoke to A
255.29	C[ooperstow]n / CE; C———n A
257.8	vetturino / B₁; vetturini A
259.21	Cohoes / CE; Choes A; Cohoos B₁–B₂
261.20	*à outrance* / CE; *à l'outrance* A
263.15–16	Recanati / CE; Reconati A (*Also corrected at* 263.21 *and* 264.33.)
†263.17	*Montagne des Russes* / CE; *Montagnes Russes* A
268.2	Cattolica / CE; Catolica A (*Also corrected at* 268.5 *and* 269.3.)
269.6	right / B₁; left A
270.15	Marecchia / CE; Marcochia A
270.25	Marecchia / CE; Marcochia A
273.22	portion / B₁; position A
273.23	that / B₁; which A
†278.2	C[ruger] / CE; C——— A (*Also emended at* 279.14 *and* 283.20.)
283.12	are / CE; is A
283.15	on / B₁; in A
284.40	Bucintoro / CE; Buccentauro A
289.9	other place / B₁; place A
289.14	regret to say / B₁; regret A
289.14	But / B₁; But then A
292.3–4	governments control / B₁; government controls A
292.31	his own / B₁; his A
295.23	called their / B₁; called its A
*295.39	police / CE; polices A
*298.20	Modena, * and / B₁; Modena, and A
*298.20–21	Tuscany, which / B₁; Tuscany, * which A
298.26	consolidation / B₁; a consolidation A
299.20	no / B₁; every A
299.20	should the people / CE; the people A
299.20	a country] B₁; no country A
299.20	country / CE; country should A
299.39	Rovereto / CE; Roveredo A
300.15	we were / B₁; it was A
300.16	us / B₁; me A
300.18	him / B₁; him at last, A
303.20	right / B₁; left A
303.21	left / B₁; right A
303.21	is before / B₁; before A
303.22	Isar / CE; Iser A

Rejected Readings

The following list records all substantive variants from the two Carey, Lea and Blanchard impressions which were rejected in the Cooper Edition. The reading of the Cooper Edition appears to the left of the square bracket; the authority for that reading, followed by a semicolon, each variant reading and its source appear to the right of the bracket. The curved dash ~ represents the same word that appears before the bracket and is used in recording paragraphing variants. An asterisk indicates that the reading is discussed in Textual Notes. Where there is more than one occurrence of an identical rejected reading, the initial entry includes a blanket note listing each recurrence.

The following texts are referred to:

A   *Excursions in Italy*. London: Bentley, 1838.
B₁   *Gleanings in Europe. Italy*. Philadelphia: Carey, Lea and
       Blanchard, 1838. [First State]
B₂   *Gleanings in Europe. Italy*. Philadelphia: Carey, Lea and
       Blanchard, 1838. [Second State]

1.11–13	company. Cooper's Town, 1838.] A; company. B₁–B₂
5.17–18	the few] A; a few B₁–B₂
*7.35	has] A; had B₁–B₂
*9.1	all] A; the B₁–B₂
*12.16	otherwise] A; other B₁–B₂
16.35	caste] A; cast B₁–B₂
23.27	with an] A; with a B₁–B₂
24.23	style] A; stile B₁–B₂
*36.7	ascending] A; descending B₁–B₂
37.2	further] A; farther B₁–B₂ (*Also rejected at* 184.5, 187.8, *and* 190.19.)
37.22	know] A; known B₁–B₂
*38.5	Rhine. The] A; ~.¶~ B₁–B₂
40.11	yeomanry] A; yeomany B₁–B₂
41.9	a] A; a a B₁–B₂
*42.13	nor] A; or B₁–B₂
43.30	despotisms] A; despotism B₁–B₂
48.19	the] A; he B₁–B₂
*51.27	*conducteur*] A; *conductor* B₁–B₂

52.5	were] A; where B₁–B₂
53.33	were] A; was B₁–B₂
*54.23	court. The] A; ~.¶~ B₁–B₂
55.1	as much] A; as much as B₁–B₂
60.39	frontier] A; frontiers B₁–B₂
63.12	to *terra*] A; *terra* B₁–B₂
65.27	berth] A; birth B₁–B₂
66.14	witnessed] A; witnessed a B₁–B₂
66.24	fancy] A; fancy that B₁–B₂
69.18	believe] A; believed B₁–B₂
69.39	overhearing] A; everhearing B₁–B₂
69.40	them] A; hem B₁–B₂
70.3	*patois*] A; *patios* B₁–B₂
70.31	cloisters.] A; cloister, B₁–B₂
72	Letter X] A; Chapter X B₁–B₂
72.20	invention] A; nvention B₁–B₂
73.37–38	overlook] A; overlooked B₁–B₂
75.17	pedestals] A; pedestale B₁–B₂
75.30	little] A; the little B₁–B₂
78.12	afterwards] A; have afterwards B₁–B₂
83.5–6	marble. ¶The] A; marble ^The B₁–B₂
92.6	intense, and] A; intense, B₁–B₂
94.11	coasts] A; coast B₁–B₂
97.1	expectation|] A; expectations B₁–B₂
*101.20	dwellings] A; dwelling B₁–B₂
103.23	idea] A; ideas B₁–B₂
105.11	has] A; have B₁–B₂
106.10	arts] A; art B₁–B₂
106.21	but] A; and B₁–B₂
107.10	remonstrance] A; remonstrances B₁–B₂
107.36	hear] A; here B₁–B₂
108.15	overlook] A; overlooked B₁–B₂
111.4	sea,] A; sea, and B₁–B₂
112.34	opposite to] A; opposite B₁–B₂
113.33	the same] A; thes ame B₁–B₂
115.15	Castel] A; Castle B₁–B₂
116.17	the musk] A; musk B₁–B₂
118.24	I] A; I I B₁–B₂
122.17	where] A; were B₁–B₂
125.3	Sta.] A; St. B₁–B₂
125.7	signore] A; signor B₁–B₂
128.3	sea] A; see B₁–B₂
131.32	of] A; or B₁–B₂
132.3	themselves] A; th emselves B₁–B₂
133.7	miles] A; mile s B₁–B₂
137.25	art] A; arts B₁–B₂

138.21	than *]* A; then B$_1$–B$_2$
139.3	lugs *]* A; luggs B$_1$–B$_2$
*140.17–18	did not pass *]* A; did pass B$_1$–B$_2$
150.36	that *]* A; at that B$_1$–B$_2$
152.37	Pliny *]* A; Pliney B$_1$–B$_2$
164.19	America *]* A; Ame-ca B$_1$–B$_2$
181.5–6	sufficiently strong *]* A; sufficient-strong B$_1$–B$_2$
*185.12	robbery *]* A; the robbery B$_1$–B$_2$
190.20	houses was often *]* A; houses often B$_1$–B$_2$
190.31	Porta *]* A; Porto B$_1$–B$_2$
192.3	hand of *]* A; hand B$_1$–B$_2$
193.12	kitchen-gardens *]* A; kitching-gardens B$_1$–B$_2$
194.35	rock *]* A; work B$_1$–B$_2$
195.25	and *]* A; with B$_1$–B$_2$
195.33–34	all which *]* A; all of which B$_1$–B$_2$
197.37	these *]* A; those B$_1$–B$_2$
198.2	fifty *]* A; fif y B$_1$–B$_2$
*204.17–18	before. It *]* A; ~.¶~ B$_1$–B$_2$
212.32	a *]* A; an B$_1$–B$_2$
214.3	leather *]* A; leathern B$_1$–B$_2$
215.2	where are *]* A; where B$_1$–B$_2$
224.3	Antoninus *]* A; Antonnius B$_1$–B$_2$ (*Also rejected at* 224.11, 224.12, *and* 224.13.)
224.35	that *]* A; at B$_1$–B$_2$
241.29	rests *]* A; rest B$_1$–B$_2$
243.22	woe *]* A; wo B$_1$–B$_2$
247.10	the *]* A; the the B$_1$–B$_2$
258.7–8	augured *]* A; argued B$_1$–B$_2$
*259.29–30	directed. There *]* A; ~.¶~ B$_1$–B$_2$
271.27	passed *]* A; had passed B$_1$–B$_2$
284.9	distinction *]* A; destination B$_1$–B$_2$
296.3	of *]* A; if B$_1$
296.20	in *]* A; on B$_1$–B$_2$
299.17	adopted *]* A; adapted B$_1$–B$_2$

Word-Division

List A records compounds or possible compounds hyphenated at the end of the line in the copy-text and resolved as hyphenated or one word as listed below. If the words or constructions (such as "-looking") occur elsewhere in the copy-text or if Cooper's manuscripts of this period fairly consistently follow one practice respecting the particular compound or possible compound or construction, the resolution is made on that basis. First editions of works of this period are also used as guides. In the absence of any definitive evidence, the Carey edition of *Italy* is used as a guide to contemporary practice. List B is a guide to transcription of compounds hyphenated at the end of the line in the Cooper Edition: compounds recorded here should be transcribed as given; words divided at the end of the line and not listed should be transcribed as one word.

List A

3.21	carriage-wheels	66.13	maintopsail
4.24	frog-eaters	66.19	bower-anchor
4.37	sand-banks	68.18	chestnut-covered
6.7	gate-way	69.26	greencoated
6.22	outworks	75.11	well-disposed
14.37	innkeeper	87.1	carriage-road
21.5	shopkeepers	89.3	watch-tower
23.7	gaming-table	90.35	roadstead
28.11	backbone	97.19	-north-east
28.18	half-an-	99.30	umbrella-shaped
28.30	semi-modern	102.28	twelvemonth
32.1	town-house	107.39	purse-proud
40.30	drawing-room	113.13	Castel-a-
47.26	sisterhood	117.17	noseband
56.39	country-house	123.17	fore-ground
57.24	afternoon	124.21	fellow-creature
58.33	table-land	126.25	headland
58.34	bird's-eye	126.27	land-breeze
59.3	ship-shape	127.33	old-school
60.5	olive-trees	128.1	seventy-six
61.24	night-work	140.20	warehouses
64.16–17	companion-way	141.4	noon-day
64.34	go-by-	141.8	pack-saddle
65.29	topsails	143.28	to-day

146.35	twenty-four	243.2	pic-nic
151.11	haystack-looking	243.3	pic-nic
154.19	flag-ship	243.20	Well-born
157.35	-and-twenty	244.34	to-day
159.5	hunting-seat	246.12	tale-fraught
159.26	hunting-seats	246.33	birthplace
171.9	fireplaces	247.38	much-desired
173.24	sunset	251.40	back-strap
181.22	sun-light	258.39	vineyards
182.26	-talked-of	260.13	corn-crib
182.34	guide-books	260.15	amphitheatres
184.15	post-road	261.23	afternoon
190.28	countryman	261.28	Lombard-street
192.11	church-tower	270.21	plausible-*looking*
193.12	kitchen-gardens	277.29	foot-passengers
195.20	Bleecker-street	280.33	water-gate
212.23	towing-track	283.8	picture-hunting
214.7	highway	286.19	to-day
220.16	market-place	293.23	Venetian-Italian
228.5	dressing-rooms	300.5	post-master
228.7	dressing-rooms	300.20	post-masters
228.12	forty-two	300.34	Boniface-sort
229.17	drawing-room	301.40	sixpence
236.7	thirty-three	302.18	road-side

LIST B

12.30	picturesque-looking	96.27	sea-beach
13.27	ex-dragoon	97.19	east-north-
26.37	ex-ambassadors	121.32	wheel-track
28.8	bachelor-like	131.29	country-houses
29.38	half-depopulated	157.35	five-and-
33.29	country-houses	158.22	drinking-house
42.1	stumbling-block	169.14	right-feeling
51.24	carriage-wheels	175.13	fiddle-strings
60.4	orange-groves	180.32	guide-books
65.12	lord-lieutenant	184.20	guide-books
66.6	mole-head	187.9	evil-doers
67.17	olive-trees	191.3	three-fourths
74.23	well-informed	196.39	forty-five
75.11	well-disposed	203.36	brick-work
85.2	south-easterly	205.11	merry-makings
85.12	back-ground	228.7	ante-chambers
87.9	nine-tenths	234.14	well-bred
92.35	south-east	243.20	Well-born

244.34	to-day	285.11	resting-place
250.29	good-naturedly	285.24	hearse-like
251.40	back-strap	285.25	well-known
262.15	eating-house	292.4	post-horses
269.15	Cis-Alpine	297.4	vulgar-minded
276.14	shirt-sleeves	300.5	post-master
282.22	altar-piece		

INDEX

Index

This index includes persons, places, things, and topics of concern mentioned or alluded to in Cooper's text, including his own footnotes. Subjects glossed in the Explanatory Notes of this edition are indicated by an asterisk (*) placed before the appropriate page number. The abbreviation m. is employed for items of brief or unspecified mention.